Context

Cornelsen

Context

Im Aufrag des Verlages herausgegeben von
Dr. Annette Leithner-Brauns, Dresden

Erarbeitet von
Martina Baasner, Berlin; Irene Bartscherer, Bonn; Lisa Braun, Meppen; Sabine Buchholz, Hürth; Wiebke Dietrich, Göttingen; Sylvia Loh, Esslingen; Benjamin Lorenz, Bensheim; Dr. Paul Maloney, Hildesheim; Dr. Pascal Ohlmann, Tholey; Birgit Ohmsieder, Berlin; Andreas Sedlatschek, Esslingen; Veronika Walther, Rudolstadt

In Zusammenarbeit mit der Englischredaktion
Dr. Marion Kiffe (Koordinierende Redakteurin), Dr. Christiane Kallenbach (Projektleitung), Aryane Beaudoin, Dr. Jan Dreßler, Hartmut Tschepe, Dr. Christian von Raumer, Freya Wurm *unter Mitwirkung von* Janan Barksdale, Irja Fröhling, Katrin Gütermann, Anne Müller, Neil Porter, Evelyn Sternad, Mai Weber

Beratende Mitwirkung
Sabine Otto, Halle (Saale); Heiko Benzin, Neustrelitz

Layoutkonzept
Klein & Halm, Berlin

Layout und technische Umsetzung
Straive
designcollective, Berlin

Umschlaggestaltung
Rosendahl, Berlin

Lizenzmanagement
Britta Bensmann

www.cornelsen.de

1. Auflage, 1. Druck 2022

Druck: Firmengruppe APPL, aprinta Druck, Wemding

ISBN: 9783060345045

PEFC
PEFC/04-32-0928

PEFC zertifiziert
Dieses Produkt stammt aus nachhaltig bewirtschafteten Wäldern und kontrollierten Quellen.
www.pefc.de

Contents

Contents

Contents

Abbreviations and labels used in *Context*

AE/BE American English / British English
ca. *(Latin* circa = about, approximately
cf. confer (compare), see
derog derogatory *(abfällig, geringschätzig)*
e.g. *(Latin)* exempli gratia = for example
esp. especially
et al. *(Latin)* et alii = and other people/things
etc. *(Latin)* et cetera = and so on
f./ff. and the following page(s)/line(s)
fml formal English
i.e. *(Latin)* id est = that is, in other words
infml informal English
jdm./jdn. *jemandem/jemanden*
l./ll. line/lines
n noun
pt(s) point(s)
p./pp. page/pages
pl plural
sb./sth. somebody/something
sin singular
sl slang
usu. usually
v verb
vs. *(Latin)* versus *(gegen, im Gegensatz zu)*

(map icon)	marks tasks that refer you back to the chapter's guiding question
Challenge	marks a more difficult task
► Support	refers you to the Support and Partner B pages (p. 00) where you can find more help to do the assignment
You choose	lets yo decide which of the two given assignments you'd like to do
*metaphor	indicates that a word or expression (here: *metaphor*) is explained in the Glossary (p. 00)
► SF 9	directs you to the Skills File (here: Skill 9)
(sound icon)	indicates that the sound file can be found in the Cornelsen Lernen App (9783060345649), eBook and UMA
(video icon)	indicates that the video can be found in the Cornelsen Lernen App (9783060345649), eBook and UMA
► More info	indicates that additional information can be found in the Cornelsen Lernen App (9783060345649)
► More language	indicates that tips or further information regarding language can be found in the Cornelsen Lernen App (9783060345649)
► Check	indicates that solutions to tasks can be found in the Cornelsen Lernen App (9783060345649)
► Getting started	indicates that tips or ideas to get started on tasks can be found in the Cornelsen Lernen App (9783060345649)

Chapter 1

Finding One's Place – the Individual in Society

Imagine John Lennon

Imagine there's no heaven
It's easy if you try
No hell below us
Above us only sky
Imagine all the people
Living for today... Aha-ah...

Imagine there's no countries
It isn't hard to do
Nothing to kill or die for
And no religion, too
Imagine all the people
Living life in peace... You...
You may say I'm a dreamer
But I'm not the only one
I hope someday you'll join us
And the world will be as one
Imagine no possessions
I wonder if you can
No need for greed or hunger
A brotherhood of man
Imagine all the people
Sharing all the world ... You ...

You may say I'm a dreamer
But I'm not the only one
I hope someday you'll join us
And the world will live as one

From: Imagine, *1971*

▸ More info

1 In his song 'Imagine' John Lennon describes his vision of an ideal society.

- **a** In one sentence describe the world that John Lennon imagines.
- **b** Which aspects in the song do you find still relevant?
- **c** What would you mention in a version of the song for the 21st century?
- **d** Write a verse for your own song called 'Imagine'.

2 Take a look at the Chapter map on the right-hand page.

- **a** Make notes about each of the terms in the boxes and what they mean to you.
- **b** Speculate about the content of this chapter.
- **c** Look at the guiding question on p. 13. Write one short paragraph in which you answer the question. Keep your paragraph for later.

Chapter map

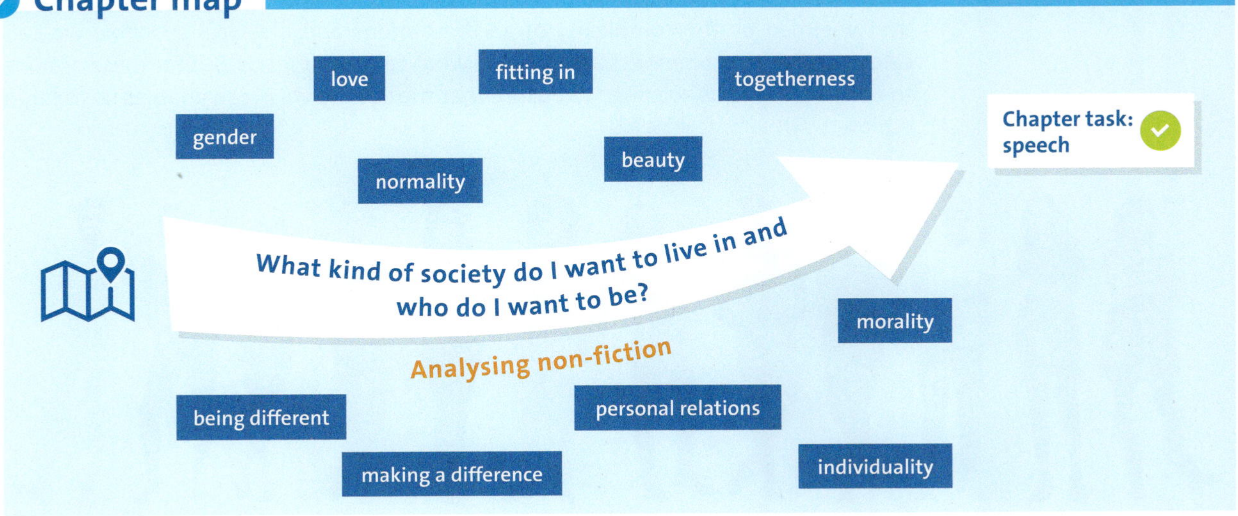

love
fitting in
togetherness
gender
beauty
normality
Chapter task: speech
What kind of society do I want to live in and who do I want to be?
morality
Analysing non-fiction
being different
personal relations
making a difference
individuality

▸ More language

Finding my own path

Today's world offers more choices than ever before. Living in a free democratic society, we can make our own choices about our friends, our lifestyles, our jobs, our political affiliations. We take these rights for granted even though they are actually a privilege. If we wish to develop our characters so that we become the person we are supposed to be, then we need to protect these rights. There are many opportunities for participating in activism concerning issues that affect our lives.

Our sense of self is defined by the people we surround ourselves with and by how they perceive us as well as by our own aspirations about the person we want to be. As individuals we strive to be unique and to stand out, while trying to find our place in society. Learning about our differences and needs is as much a part of this process of developing a sense of identity as focusing on our dreams. Throughout life we will be faced with the question as to whether we want to conform to social norms or whether we want to stand out from the crowd.

Whereas in the past, a person's background, the family he or she came from, his or her economic status and social class seemed to be the most important factors that predetermined a person's future, nowadays increased social mobility means that people are able to shape their own destiny.

Nevertheless, equality of opportunity still does not exist. Opposing the discrimination of certain groups and addressing social inequalities while upholding the values of tolerance and equality is essential to ensure that everyone can fulfil their dreams.

Awareness of the risks inherent in prejudice and stereotyping can help society to become more diverse and open and accepting of people who do not fit into the mainstream society. While in recent decades people campaigned for gender equality, now the campaign has become much broader, so that we are becoming aware of new gender roles. Many people unable to adhere to the binary roles of male and female have urged society to accept the idea of gender fluidity and to accept that ideas about beauty should not be tied to one particular form of body or face. From the way we dress to the people we love we are spoilt for choice. Rather than being confused and overwhelmed by the complexity of all the options and lifestyles available we can celebrate this new openness and find out what feels right for us. But for these options to be available to us, we need to ensure that the society we live in enables us to forge our own path.

1 Words words words

a Pick five phrases from the highlighted phrases in the text that you consider essential to the topic and write them in a list.
b Explain them by using definitions or by giving examples of them in your own life.
c Present your list and explanations to a partner and together agree on a list of the three most essential aspects.

► SF 8: Working with dictionaries

2 Organizing words

a Go through the text and collect nouns (and chunks with nouns) and verbs (and chunks with verbs) under the headings: society, individual, gender. You can use the table below as an example.

Concept	Nouns and noun phrases	Verbs and verbal phrases
society	political affiliation ...	participate in sth. ...
individuality	sense of self ...	make our own choices ...
gender	equality of opportunity ...	campaign for sth. ...

b Now choose ten words from the phrases you have listed that you think are important and fill in a table showing the *word families. You can use the table below as an example.

Noun	Verb	Adjective
politics	*politicize*	political
affiliation	*affiliate*	*affiliated*

3 Chunk it!

Replace the gaps in the following *chunks with verbs. You can check the text for help if you are not sure.

► Check

1 ... your rights
2 ... a sense of identity
3 ... with the question
4 ... your own path

► SF 27: Writing a blog post

4 Text production

Write a short blog post about issues that you think are important in today's society. Try to use at least ten words and chunks from tasks **1** and **2** and mark them.

► More language

A beautiful portrait

Oscar Wilde

Think In your view, what makes a photograph of a person perfect? Collect ideas.
Pair Compare the criteria with a partner and rank them according to their importance.
Share Present your rankings in a group and discuss whether a person's photograph can also reveal something about the person who took it.

Oscar Wilde was one of the greatest writers in Britain at the turn of the 19th century. This is the beginning of his novel The Picture of Dorian Gray.

The studio was filled with the rich odour of roses, and when the light summer wind stirred amidst the trees of the garden, there came through the open door the heavy scent of the lilac, or the more delicate perfume of the pink-flowering thorn.

From the corner of the divan of Persian saddle-bags on which he was lying, smoking, as was his custom, innumerable cigarettes, Lord Henry Wotton could just catch the gleam of the honey-sweet and honey-coloured blossoms of laburnum, whose tremulous branches seemed hardly able to bear the burden of a beauty so flame-like as theirs; and now and then the fantastic shadows of birds in flight flitted across the long tussore-silk curtains that were stretched in front of the huge window, producing a kind of momentary Japanese effect, and making him think of those pallid jade-faced painters of Tokyo who, through the medium of an art that is necessarily immobile, seek to convey the sense of swiftness and motion. The sullen murmur of the bees shouldering their way through the long unmown grass, or circling with monotonous insistence round the dusty gilt horns of the straggling woodbine, seemed to make the stillness more oppressive. The dim roar of London was like the bourdon note of a distant organ.

In the centre of the room, clamped to an upright easel, stood the full-length portrait of a young man of extraordinary personal beauty, and in front of it, some little distance away, was sitting the artist himself, Basil Hallward, whose sudden disappearance some years ago caused, at the time, such public excitement, and gave rise to so many strange conjectures.

As the painter looked at the gracious and comely form he had so skillfully mirrored in his art, a smile of pleasure passed across his face, and seemed about to linger there. But he suddenly started up, and, closing his eyes, placed his fingers up on the lids, as though he sought to imprison within his brain some curious dream from which he feared he might awake.

'It is your best work, Basil, the best thing you have ever done,' said Lord Henry, languidly. 'You must certainly send it next year to the Grosvenor. The Academy is too large and too vulgar. Whenever I have gone there, there have been either so many people that I have not been able to see the pictures, which was dreadful, or so many pictures that I have not been able to see the people, which was worse. The Grosvenor is really the only place.'

'I don't think I shall send it anywhere,' he answered, tossing his head back in that odd way that used to make his friends laugh at him at Oxford. 'No: I won't send it anywhere.'

Annotations

1 **odour** smell
4 **divan** a long soft seat
5 **custom** *(fml)* the way a person constantly behaves
6 **gleam** *(n)* pale light reflected off sth.
6 **laburnum** *Goldregen*
9 **tussore silk** an expensive kind of silk, usu. rich in texture and gold in colour
11 **pallid** pale
15 **woodbine** *Geißblatt*
16 **bourdon note** (here) very low note
17 **easel** *Staffelei*
21 **conjecture** an idea that is not based on definite knowledge
22 **gracious** elegant
22 **comely** attractive
23 **linger** stay for a moment
28 **languidly** moving slowly and elegantly without much effort
28 **the Grosvenor** (here) an art gallery
28 **the Academy** the Royal Academy of Arts

Lord Henry elevated his eyebrows, and looked at him in amazement through the thin blue wreaths of smoke that curled up in such fanciful whorls from his heavy opium-tainted cigarette. 'Not send it anywhere? My dear fellow, why? Have you any reason? What odd chaps you painters are! You do anything in the world to gain a reputation. As soon as you have one, you seem to want to throw it away. It is silly of you, for there is only one thing in the world worse than being talked about, and that is not being talked about. A portrait like this would set you far above all the young men in England, and make the old men quite jealous, if old men are ever capable of any emotion.'

'I know you will laugh at me,' he replied, 'but I really can't exhibit it. I have put too much of myself into it.'

Lord Henry stretched himself out on the divan and laughed.

'Yes, I knew you would; but it is quite true, all the same.'

'Too much of yourself in it! Upon my word, Basil, I didn't know you were so vain; and I really can't see any resemblance between you, with your rugged strong face and your coal-black hair, and this young Adonis, who looks as if he was made out of ivory and rose-leaves. Why, my dear Basil, he is a Narcissus, and you – well, of course you have an intellectual expression, and all that. But beauty, real beauty, ends where an intellectual expression begins. Intellect is in itself a mode of exaggeration, and destroys the harmony of any face. The moment one sits down to think, one becomes all nose, or all forehead, or something horrid. Look at the successful men in any of the learned professions. How perfectly hideous they are! Except, of course, in the Church. But then in the Church they don't think. A bishop keeps on saying at the age of eighty what he was told to say when he was a boy of eighteen, and as a natural consequence he always looks absolutely delightful. Your mysterious young friend, whose name you have never told me, but whose picture really fascinates me, never thinks. I feel quite sure of that. He is some brainless, beautiful creature, who should be always here in winter when we have no flowers to look at, and always here in summer when we want something to chill our intelligence. Don't flatter yourself, Basil: you are not in the least like him.'

'You don't understand me, Harry,' answered the artist. 'Of course I am not like him. I know that perfectly well. Indeed, I should be sorry to look like him. You shrug your shoulders? I am telling you the truth. There is a fatality about all physical and intellectual distinction, the sort of fatality that seems to dog through history the faltering steps of kings. It is better not to be different from one's fellows. The ugly and the stupid have the best of it in this world. They can sit at their ease and gape at the play. If they know nothing of victory, they are at least spared the knowledge of defeat. They live as we all should live, undisturbed, indifferent, and without disquiet. They neither bring ruin upon others, not ever receive it from alien hands. Your rank and wealth, Harry; my brains, such as they are – my art, whatever it may be worth; Dorian Gray's good looks – we shall all suffer for what the gods have given us, suffer terribly.'

From: Oscar Wilde, The Picture of Dorian Gray, *1891*

Annotations

36 **elevate sth.** lift sth.
37 **whorl** *Windung, Kringel*
39 **chap** *(old-fashioned)* man
40 **reputation** (here) fame
50 **rugged** (usu. about the face of a man) having strong and attractive features
51 **Adonis** (in Greek mythology) an extremely attractive young man
52 **Narcissus** (in Greek mythology) man who fell in love with his own reflection
68 **fatality** belief that you have no control over sth.
69 **dog sth.** follow sth. closely
70 **faltering** hesitant or less effective
72 **gape** *(v)* stare with an open mouth
72 **be spared** *verschont bleiben*
75 **rank** position in society

Oscar Wilde (1845–1900)

▸ More info

Comprehension

1 Outline the *setting and the situation presented in this excerpt: Who is present, what are the men talking about and what do they disagree about?

Analysis

2 Analyse the *atmosphere created in the first three paragraphs of the *novel.

▸ SF 18: Reading and understanding narrative texts

3 Analyse the means Lord Henry employs to convince Basil that he and the picture have nothing in common.

Language help

use imagery/exclamations • flatter sb. • address sb. directly • admit/concede sth. • use/employ long/elliptical/incomplete/complex sentences/syntax

Language awareness

4 In the first two paragraphs, Oscar Wilde paints a picture of the studio with words. Examine how he achieves this effect by looking at his choice of words.

5 You choose Work on either **a** or **b**.

a Rewrite the first two paragraphs in a less *formal register.

b Challenge Rewrite the first two paragraphs in a less formal register. Explain the difference between your version and the original.

Beyond the text

6 'It is better not to be different from one's fellows.' (l. 70)
Discuss if you agree with Basil Hallward's opinion.

▸ SF 22: Analysing visuals
▸ SF 41: Giving a presentation

7 You choose Speaking Work on either **a** or **b**.

a Find a photo or painting that in your opinion reveals a lot about the character of the person portrayed. Give a three-minute speech about the picture, also explaining how the artist achieved this effect.

b Research the stories of Adonis and Narcissus from Greek mythology (cf. ll. 51–52) and give a short presentation about them. Speculate what their relevance for the novel could be.

Going to university

Think How can you determine if someone is successful at university? Collect ideas.
Pair Exchange your ideas with a partner, and write down three factors that you agree on.
Share Present your ideas in class. Agree on a list of three factors.

Viewing *Watch this video about a young student who has just started university.*

Annotations
Classics study of ancient Roman and Greek civilizations and their language and history
Humanities *Geisteswissenschaften*
alumna (*male* **alumnus**) female student who has graduated from a university

Comprehension

1 Go back to your results from your exchange in the pre-viewing task and point out how they might apply to Zaynab.

► SF 39: Analysing films and videos

Analysis

2 You choose Work on task **a** or **b**.
a Analyse the way in which the video was filmed. Take into consideration the settings that were chosen.
b Explain why the college may have chosen Zaynab to be in its video.

Info
The University of Cambridge (founded in 1209) is made up of 31 colleges, where the students live and where a lot of their teaching is also based. Newnham College (founded in 1871) is a women's college.

Beyond the text

3 Intercultural communication Assess whether this video would be helpful to prepare you for a university in Germany.

Not being normal Sally Rooney

- *Quick write: What is *normal*?
- Would you describe your life as normal? Why or why not?

Language help
My definition of *normal* would include ...
Being normal means that a person ...
By and large, I would say that I ...

You are going to read an excerpt from Sally Rooney's novel Normal People. *Marianne and Connell are two Irish teenagers who are classmates but who come from very different backgrounds. Connell's mother works as a cleaner for Marianne's mother.*

Marianne's classmates all seem to like school so much and find it normal. To dress in the same uniform every day, to comply at all times with arbitrary rules, to be scrutinised and monitored for misbehaviour, this is normal to them. They have no sense of the school as an oppressive environment. Marianne had a row with the History teacher, Mr Kerrigan, last year because he caught her looking out a window

Annotations
2 **arbitrary** seeming unfair and not based on reason
3 **scrutinised** looked at very closely

Annotations
14 **jurisdiction** authority
18 **delude sb.** deceive sb.
33 **superior** better than everyone else
41 **confined** restricted, kept inside
46 **taciturn** not saying very much
46 **inscrutable** *undurchschaubar*
47 **drained** very tired, without energy

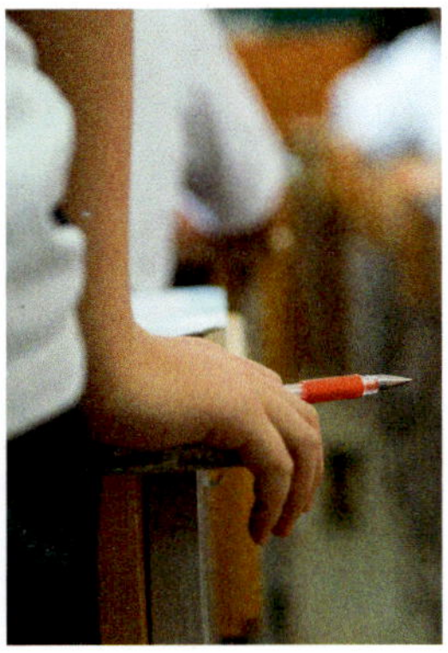

during class, and no one in the class took her side. It seemed so obviously insane to her then that she should have to dress up in a costume every morning and be herded around a huge building all day, and that she wasn't even allowed to move her eyes where she wanted, even her eye movements fell under the jurisdiction of school rules. You're not learning if you're staring out the window daydreaming, Mr Kerrigan said. Marianne, who had lost her temper by then, snapped back: Don't delude yourself, I have nothing to learn from you.

Connell said recently that he remembered that incident, and that at the time he'd felt she was being harsh on Mr Kerrigan, who was actually one of the more reasonable teachers. But I see what you're saying, Connell added. About feeling a bit imprisoned in the school, I do see that. He should have let you look out the window, I would agree there. You weren't doing any harm.

After the conversation in the kitchen, when she told him she liked him, Connell started coming over to her house more often. He would arrive early to pick his mother up from work and hang around in the living room not saying much, or stand by the fireplace with his hands in his pockets. Marianne never asked why he came over. They talked a little bit, or she talked and he nodded. He told her she should try reading *The Communist Manifesto*, he thought she would like it, and he offered to write down the title for her so she wouldn't forget. I know what *The Communist Manifesto* is called, she said. He shrugged, okay. After a moment he added, smiling: You're trying to act superior, but like, you haven't even read it. She had to laugh then, and he laughed because she did. They couldn't look at each other when they were laughing, they had to look into corners of the room, or at their feet.

Connell seemed to understand how she felt about school; he said he liked hearing her opinions. You hear enough of them in class, she said. Matter-of-factly he replied: You act different in class, you're not really like that. He seemed to think Marianne had access to a range of different identities, between which she slipped effortlessly. This surprised her, because she usually felt confined inside one single personality, which was always the same regardless of what she did or said. She had tried to be different in the past, as a kind of experiment, but it had never worked. If she was different with Connell, the difference was not happening inside herself, in her personhood, but in between them, in the dynamic. Sometimes she made him laugh, but other days he was taciturn, inscrutable, and after he left, she would feel high, nervous, at once energetic and terribly drained.

He followed her into the study last week while she was looking for a copy of *The Fire Next Time* to lend him. He stood there inspecting the bookshelves, with his top shirt button undone and school tie loosened. She found the book and handed it to him, and he sat down on the window seat looking at the back cover. She sat beside him and asked him if his friends Eric and Rob knew that he read so much outside school.

They wouldn't be interested in that stuff, he said.

You mean they're not interested in the world around them.

Connell made the face he always made when she criticised his friends, an inexpressive frown. Not in the same way, he said. They have their own interests. I don't think they'd be reading books about racism and all that.

Right, they're too busy bragging about who they're having sex with, she said.

He paused for a second, like his ears had pricked up at this remark but he didn't know exactly how to respond. Yeah, they do a bit of that, he said. I'm not defending it, I know they can be annoying.

Doesn't it bother you?

He paused again. Most of it wouldn't, he said. They do some stuff that goes a bit over the line and that would annoy me obviously. But at the end of the day they're my friends, you know. It's different for you.

From: Sally Rooney, Normal People, *2018*

Annotations
59 **brag about sth.** boast about sth.

► More info

Comprehension

1 Outline Marianne's criticism of school rules.

2 State why Connell does not talk to his friends in the same way he talks to Marianne.

Analysis

3 Analyse how the two teenagers are depicted in the excerpt.

► Support p. 244

Language awareness

4 Examine how Marianne's language is different from Connell's and how that contributes to the depiction of the *characters. Give examples.

Beyond the text

5 You choose | Writing | Work on task **a** or **b**.

a Write a diary entry for either Connell or Marianne reflecting on their conversation and the idea of being 'different'.

b After her conflict with Mr Kerrigan, Marianne is asked to the headmaster's office. In pairs write her conversation with the headmaster about the incident. If you like, you can act it out.

► SF 36: Creative writing

Focus on tests formats

In tests at school and in your school-leaving exam you will encounter the task of analysing non-fiction, for example newspaper articles, excerpts of non-fiction books, etc. This skill will also be helpful in your life beyond school and support your critical reading and understanding of texts.

Read the following task:

> *Analyse how the author tries to persuade the reader of her position.*

► SF 25: Essentials: the stages of writing
► SF 4: Writing a text analysis

Work it out

1 Step by step

When doing an analysis of a text, you should approach it step by step. Together with a partner decide which of the strategies below you would use to do a successful analysis.

1 Read the text first and then the task.
2 Read the task first and then the text.
3 Read the task and say in your own words what you need to focus on.
4 Mark the verbs for tasks ('Operatoren') in the task.
5 Read the text at least twice and mark important passages.
6 Make sure you understand the content of the text before starting the analysis, e.g. by writing down keywords next to each paragraph.
7 Look up unknown words in a dictionary.
8 Make a list of stylistic devices and literary terms and see if they can be found in the text.
9 Underline elements in the text that you think are interesting for the analysis.
10 Quote as many passages from the text as possible.
11 Write a summary of the text and then start the analysis.

Add and discuss other strategies that you have used before. You may want to collect them on a *method card.

2 Reading the task

Without having read the text, what can you deduce from the task? Answer the following questions with yes or no and discuss your answers with a partner.

Do you have to ...
1 give a short summary of the text?
2 provide information about the author?
3 identify the author's attitude and position?
4 identify and understand a line of argument(s)?
5 identify the narrative perspective?
6 find stylistic devices such as rhetorical questions, enumerations?
7 explain why the stylistic devices that are used are effective?

3 Possible answers

a Read the excerpts from two analyses and discuss with a partner whether or not they are good.

b Rewrite them to improve them.

1 The author uses a lot of rhetorical questions. She also uses enumerations of things. She uses these things to persuade the reader. She is very convincing. The text contains a lot of humour. Her arguments are good ...

2 In line 5 the author uses an alliteration. In line 6 and 7 she uses a metaphor. There is also an anaphora in lines 10 and 11. The effect is ...

Do it

4 Getting started

Now read and analyse the text below using strategies that you assessed as being successful. Remember, the task is:

Analyse how the author tries to persuade the reader of her position.

Professor Mary Beard

Women and power Mary Beard

Dame Mary Beard is a professor of Classics at the University of Cambridge.

It is happily the case that there are now more women in what we would all probably agree are 'powerful' positions than there were ten, let alone fifty years ago. Whether that is as politicians, councillors, police commissioners, managers, CEOs, judges or whatever, it is still a clear minority – but there are *more.* (To give just one figure, around 4 per cent of UK MPs were women in the 1970s; around 30 per cent are now.) But my basic premise is that our mental, cultural template for a powerful person remains resolutely male. If we close our eyes and try to conjure up the image of a president or – move into the knowledge economy – professor, what most of us see is not a woman. And that is just as true even if you *are* a woman professor: the cultural stereotype is so strong that, at the level of those close-your-eyes fantasies, it is still hard for *me* to imagine *me*, or someone like me, in my role. I put the phrase 'cartoon professor' into Google UK Images: 'cartoon professor' to make sure that I was targeting the imaginary ones, the cultural template, not the real ones; and 'UK' to exclude the slightly different definition of professor in the USA. Out of the first 100 that came up, only one, professor Holly from Pokémon Farm, was female.

Annotations

3 **councillor** *Stadtratsmitglied*

5 **MP** (in the UK) Member of Parliament

6 **premise** *Voraussetzung, Prämisse*

6 **template** model

Annotations
- **20 Hillary Clinton** former senator, U.S. Secretary of State and Democratic candidate in the 2016 presidential election
- **21 clothes horse** *Kleiderständer*
- **22 timbre** tone
- **26 Melissa McCarthy** U.S. comedian and actor
- **30 decode sth.** *etwas entschlüsseln*
- **34 interloper** intruder
- **35 loo** *(BE infml)* toilet
- **38 citadel** castle
- **41 entitled** feeling that you have a right to sth.

Put this the other way round, we have no template for what a powerful woman looks like, except that she looks rather like a man. The regulation trouser suits, or at least the trousers, worn by so many western female political leaders, from Angela Merkel to Hillary Clinton, may be convenient and practical; they may be a signal of the refusal to become a clothes horse, which is the fate of so many political wives; but they are also a simple tactic – like lowering the timbre of the voice – to make the female appear more male, to fit the part of power. Elizabeth I (or whoever invented her famous speech) knew exactly what the game was when she said she had 'the heart and stomach of a king'. And it was that idea of the divorce between women and power that made Melissa McCarthy's parodies of the one-time White House press secretary Sean Spicer on *Saturday Night Live* so effective. It was said that these annoyed President Trump more than most satires on his regime, because, according to one of the 'sources close to him', 'he doesn't like his people to appear weak'. Decode that, and what it actually means is that he doesn't like his men to be parodied by and as women. Weakness comes with a female gender.

It follows from this that women are still perceived as belonging outside power. We may sincerely want them to get to the inside of it or we may, by various often unconscious means, cast women as interlopers when they make it. (I still remember a Cambridge where, in most colleges, the women's loos were tucked away across two courts, through the passage and down the stairs in the basement: is there a message here, I wondered.) But, every way, the shared metaphors we use of female access to power – 'knocking on the door', 'storming the citadel', 'smashing the glass ceiling', or just giving them a 'leg up' – underline female exteriority. Women in power are seen as breaking down barriers, or alternatively as taking something to which they are not quite entitled.

From: Mary Beard, Women & Power. A Manifesto, *2017*

Language help

The author uses/employs ...
This enhances/underlines/stresses/shows ...
The author explains/examines/compares/expresses ...

▶ Getting started

Don't forget:
1. You can start your analysis with a TATT-sentence: title, author, text type, topic.
2. Use your notes to write a clearly structured main part. Use *linking words and a new paragraph for each new idea.
3. Write a conclusion that sums up your most important findings.
4. Then check your spelling and punctuation.

▶ Check

Feedback

5 Peer assessment

a Exchange your first draft of the text with a partner. Read your partner's text and make suggestions for improvement if necessary.

b Taking into account your partner's feedback, start a *method card in which you make a note of areas you need to improve.

We are in this together

Vicky Bristow

- In 2020 the world experienced the start of a global pandemic, which led to several lockdowns. Name three aspects of your life that changed during the lockdowns. Then write two sentences on your feelings about those changes.

The following poem was written during the first lockdown in the spring of 2020 by a student at the University of East Anglia.

We are in this together, is often said
So here are my thoughts, spun out like a thread
And here is my very first suggestion
Who is the 'we' – an important question
Some groups of 'we' more likely to thrive
Other 'we' more likely to die
And if you think this is purely fable
The truth is on the mortality tables
Can your 'we' work from the inside
Or are you a 'we' on the front-line?
Higher survival if you are white
Poverty, diabetes, and also to mention
Racism, stress and hypertension
Factors not evenly shared
To the dark of skin not fair
Are you the 'we' who's missing your mates?
Or one of the 'we' with an empty plate?
For the 'we' we are is broadly diverse
Experience and outcome, for better or worse
So the 'we' can be good or grim,
Now let's move on and explore the 'in'
Because the notion of 'in' is bogus
If you are the 'we' who is homeless
The 'in' for the lonely who live in silence
Or those in fear of domestic violence
Is your 'in' feeling fed up and bored
Or praying for the safety of being ignored
Is your 'in' comfortable and safe
Or do you dream of such a space
Children with no Wi-Fi or computer
No digital learning and brighter future
This situation is not clever
Now for the final word 'together'
A funny thing to say for a start
When we are all far apart
But for some this is not a game
For 'together' for some is not the same
For some have plenty, some do not
For some the fear just does not stop
This poem could be one of despair
So I will not leave it there

Annotations

2 **spin sth.** (spun – spun) *etwas spinnen*
5 **thrive** do well
13 **hypertension** high blood pressure
16 **mate** *(infml)* friend
22 **bogus** nonsense

Info

In Britain the mortality rates among people from BAME (Black, Asian and minority ethnic) communities were especially high during the first wave of the pandemic. There was also a notable rise in domestic violence

Annotations
43 **compassion** empathy
45 **forgot** *(usu. AE)* forgotten

I pray so hard for a new world fashion
That we discover a genuine compassion
That valuing wealth and what you've got
Will be a memory soon forgot
That education, food and healthcare
Will be all right, for all to share
And the 'we' will be an all inclusive
And human rights not elusive
The 'in' a safe place in-side
Where friendship and family thrive
To shelter us from life's great storms
No matter to whom or where we are born
And this tragedy will have no sequel
Because we will be more equal
And when the world becomes more fair
Then we can proudly declare
This will happen again never,
Because now – we are in it together

From: R. Barratt, ed., Lockdown 2020. Poetry and prose from around the world on living in isolation and surviving the coronavirus, *2020*

Comprehension

1 Name the groups of people mentioned in the poem that suffered disproportionately during the pandemic, and say why they suffered more.

2 Describe the impact the pandemic has had on social relationships, according to the poem.

Analysis

► SF 19: Reading and understanding poetry

3 Analyse the structure of the poem and the effect this has.

Language awareness

4 Analyse the language used in the poem (e.g. *register, *stylistic devices) and speculate on what this tells us about the intended audience of the poem.

► Getting started
► SF 36: Creative writing

5 Rewrite the poem as a newspaper column.

Beyond the text

► SF 33: Writing a formal letter or email

6 Writing Write a letter to your local MP based on the criticism raised in the poem and make two suggestions for improvements. Include your results from the pre-reading task if applicable.

► SF 36: Creative writing

7 You choose Writing Work on task **a** or **b**.

a Discuss whether there are aspects in the poem that would have been written differently today.

b Challenge Write a more up-to-date version of the poem.

Voluntary work

Für das „Wohl und Wehe' der Engagementlandschaft sind die gesellschaftlichen Rahmenbedingungen von großer Bedeutung. Kein unerheblicher Faktor ist der demografische Wandel, der Sachsen schon jetzt und auch in Zukunft stark verändern wird. Das Berlin Institut für Bevölkerung und Entwicklung rechnet bis 2035 mit einem Rückgang der Bevölkerung in Sachsen um etwa 9 %. Nur die Großstädte Leipzig und Dresden werden wachsen, alle anderen Landkreise und die Stadt Chemnitz voraussichtlich schrumpfen. In vielen ländlichen Regionen ist schon jetzt zu beobachten, was eine abnehmende und alternde Bevölkerung bedeutet.

Vereine und zivilgesellschaftliche Organisationen sorgen besonders auf dem Land für Angebote in Freizeit, Kultur, Gemeinwesenarbeit, Kirchen, Sport oder Bildung. Typische Probleme des Ehrenamts zeigen sich dort aber noch stärker als in den Städten: Fehlender Nachwuchs etwa für Leitungs- und Führungspositionen, die kulturellen Grenzen in der Zusammenarbeit zwischen den Generationen, mangelnde Infrastruktur oder digitale Ausstattung. Wie hoch Menschen die Lebensqualität und damit die Attraktivität einer Region wahrnehmen, orientiert sich zunächst an harten Faktoren wie Infrastruktur, Daseinsvorsorge, Ausbildungsmöglichkeiten und Arbeitsplätzen. Nicht unterschätzt werden dürfen aber auch die sogenannten weichen Faktoren: Ein aktives Vereinsleben, die Verwurzelung in gesellschaftlichen Gruppen oder Möglichkeiten der sozialen und politischen Beteiligung sind ebenfalls wichtige Standort und Bleibefaktoren. Gilt also: Je lebendiger die Zivilgesellschaft, desto mehr Zuzug oder zumindest weniger Abwanderung?

An das freiwillige Engagement wird in „politischen Sonntagsreden' oft der Anspruch erhoben, wieder für mehr gesellschaftlichen Zusammenhalt zu sorgen. Diese Erwartungshaltung muss angesichts der gesellschaftlichen Polarisierung in Sachsen überprüft werden. Landes- und auch bundesweit sind eine Reihe von Organisationen verunsichert, inwieweit klare politische Aussagen und Handlungen ihren Gemeinnützigkeitsstatus in Frage stellen. In Sachsen gibt es seit den letzten Kommunalwahlen an manchen Orten Spannungen, wenn allzu kritische oder politisch möglicherweise etwas einseitige Vereine kommunale Fördermittel unter dem Stichwort der mangelnden „politischen Neutralität' gestrichen bekommen. Abgesehen von der Frage, ob von Vereinen in einer vielfältigen, freiheitlichen Gesellschaft überhaupt – anders als bei einer Landeszentrale – dezidiert „Überparteilichkeit' oder gar „Neutralität' erwartet werden kann, zeigen diese Einzelfälle: Gesellschaftliche Spannungen kommen auch in sächsischen Vereinen und Organisationen an und beschäftigen sie. Wie stark sich die bisher insgesamt eher politisch zurückhaltende sächsische Zivilgesellschaft in gesellschaftliche Debatten einmischen will, werden die Diskussionen der kommenden Jahre zeigen. Veränderungen sind jedoch absehbar, weil sich in den letzten Jahren viele junge Initiativen gebildet haben: von „Fridays for Future' über Jugendclubs mit gesellschaftlichen Anliegen bis zu Gruppen, die sich für Geflüchtete einsetzen. Ihnen ist gemeinsam, dass sie selbstbewusst politische Mitsprache einfordern. Sie werden die sächsische Zivilgesellschaft in den kommenden Jahren verändern.

Gänzlich diesen Fragen ausweichen werden aber auch Feuerwehren und Katastrophenschutz, Kirchgemeinden, der organisierte Sport, Gewerkschaften und Genossenschaften, Bildungsvereine und Sozialverbände nicht. Schon heute zeigen viele dieser Organisationen einen Bedarf an politischer Bildung und Beratung an. Blickt man auf die gesellschaftlichen Entwicklungen insgesamt, so zeigt etwa der Sachsen-Monitor 2018 eine nervöse und gespaltene Mitte der Gesellschaft. Diese besaß vor Ausbruch der Corona-Pandemie durchaus positive Zukunftserwartungen im Hinblick auf die wirtschaftliche Entwicklung und Stabilität der Demokratie. Dem standen aber auch große Zukunftssorgen gegenüber: So befürchteten große Teile der Bevölkerung, dass die Gegensätze zwischen Arm und Reich zunähmen und der gesellschaftliche Zusammenhalt schwände, dass die Rente nicht zum Leben ausreichte und die deutsche Kultur durch Zuwanderung verloren ginge. Hohe diskriminierende und rassistische Einstellungen arbeitete der Sachsen-Monitor ebenfalls 2018 heraus, wobei fremdenfeindliche Einstellungen in Sachsen häufiger als im Bundesgebiet ausgeprägt sind, Antisemitismus, Muslimfeindlichkeit oder Antiziganismus dagegen unter dem Bundesdurchschnitt liegen. Die öffentliche Debatte über diese Umfrageergebnisse ist deshalb nicht nur mit Ursachenforschung beschäftigt gewesen, sondern dreht sich auch um die Frage, welchen Beitrag Ehrenamt und Engagement, die sächsische Zivilgesellschaft und die politische Bildung zur Veränderung des gesellschaftlichen Klimas leisten können. Es gehört aber auch zu den ernüchternden Erkenntnissen des Sachsen-Monitors 2018, dass sich in ihnen nur ein begrenzter Willen der Bürgerinnen und Bürger zur politischen Verantwortungsübernahme niederschlägt, viele dagegen nach dem Staat rufen, ihm aber zugleich misstrauen. Diesen Ambivalenzen gilt es auch auf der Grundlage dieser Studie weiter nachzugehen, schließlich gehört politisches Engagement in Parteien, Verbänden und Kommunen – neben der gesamten Breite der Vereinslandschaft – zu den tragenden Säulen unseres Gemeinwesens. Zugleich verweisen die besagten Befunde aber auch auf das Potenzial und die Bedeutung des freiwilligen Engagements im vorparlamentarischen, gemeinnützigen Raum: Wer sich für eine Sache einsetzt, übernimmt bereits gesellschaftliche Verantwortung. Wenn sich dieses Engagement verbreitern und vervielfältigen ließe, entstünden viele Gelegenheiten für Bürgerinnen und Bürger, Selbstwirksamkeitserfahrungen zu machen, also um zu erleben: Meine Ideen lassen sich gemeinsam mit anderen umsetzen und tragen Früchte. Das sind entscheidende Schritte zu einer gesellschaftlichen Veränderung. Verantwortung wird eingeübt, der Blick von Problemen auf Lösungen gerichtet, eine „Brücke zu den Nächsten“ wird geschlagen – ganz gleich, ob sie bereits über Generationen hierzulande leben oder sich gerade erst niedergelassen haben. Eine dynamische Gesellschaft wie die des Freistaates braucht immer zugleich Stabilität, soziale Absicherung und Öffnung. Gegen Nervosität helfen nicht nur Zuhören und Dialoge, sondern auch gemeinsame Ziele, das tatkräftige Anpacken, ein Mehr an gesellschaftlicher Kooperation zwischen Politik, Wirtschaft, Wissenschaft und Zivilgesellschaft. Zukunftsfragen, die nur aus der Mitte der Gesellschaft heraus bearbeitet und gelöst werden können, gibt es in Sachsen genug.

From: Engagement in Sachsen, *2021*

▸ SF 47: Mediating from German into English

1 Mediating You are preparing an international youth conference on the future of modern society, at which your group is giving a presentation on opportunities for young people to participate in political processes. In your research you have come across an official publication on the situation in the Federal State of Saxony. Based on your findings, write an email to your project group explaining the role of voluntary work now and in the future.

We can do something really cool to this world

Marina Keegan

- In class, collect the criteria that will determine your choice of career. Rank them in order of importance, and explain what this shows about your needs.

Shortly before graduating from Yale University Marina Keegan wrote an essay reflecting on the plans of her fellow students for their future careers.

If this year is anything like the last ten, around 25 percent of employed Yale graduates will enter the consulting or finance industry. This is a big deal. This is a huge deal. This is so many people! This is one-fourth of our people! Regardless of what you think or with whom you're interviewing we ought to be pausing for a second to ask why.

I don't pretend to know any more about this world than the rest of us. In fact, I probably know less. (According to the Internet, a consultant is 'someone who consults someone or something.') But I do know that this statistic is utterly and entirely shocking to me. In a place as diverse and disparate as Yale, it's remarkable that such a large percentage of people are doing anything the same – not to mention something as significant as their postgraduate plans.

I want to understand. [...]

Are consulting firms inherently evil? Probably not. Are banks inherently evil? Probably not. Frankly, I don't know enough about *everything* to make a statement like that one way or another. So is there anything intrinsically wrong with the fact that 25 percent of employed Yale graduates end up in this industry?
Yeah. I think so.

Of course, this is my own opinion, but to me there is something sad about so many of us entering a line of work in which we are not (for the most part) producing something, or helping someone, or engaging in something that we are explicitly passionate about. Even if it's just for two or three years. That's a lot of years! And these aren't just years. This is twenty-three and twenty-four and twenty-five if it were a smaller percentage of people, perhaps it wouldn't bother me so much. But it's not.

What it boils down to is that we could be doing other things. Sure, working at Bain or McKinsey or J.P. Morgan might be one way to gain skills to help us get hired elsewhere, but it's obviously not the only option. There's a lot of cool shit we could all be doing – and I don't need to enumerate the clichés.

Obviously, some people need to make money. They have school loans to pay off and families to support. For those of us with an actual need to make money quickly, these industries might make a lot of sense. In fact, I think that working hard to earn a decent amount of money can be quite noble. I'm still struggling with the fact that due to my own (selfish) desire to be a writer, my children probably won't have the same opportunities I had growing up. For most students, however, I genuinely don't think it's about the money. It's a factor, sure. But it just feels like a factor.

Annotations
1 **Yale** famous elite U.S. university
2 **consulting** *Unternehmensberatung*
13 **inherently** in itself
15 **intrinsically** in itself
25 **Bain, McKinsey, J.P. Morgan** leading consulting firms

Annotations
37 **validation** approval

What bothers me is this idea of validation, of rationalization. The notion that some of us (regardless of what we tell ourselves) are doing this because we're not sure what else to do and it's easy to apply to and it will pay us decently it will make us feel like we are still successful. I just haven't met that many people who sound genuinely excited about these jobs. That's super depressing! I don't understand why no one is talking about it.

Oftentimes at Yale, I'll be sitting around studying or drinking or hanging out when I'll hear one of my friends talk about the project they're doing for a class or rally they're organizing or a play they're putting on. And I'll just think, really, honestly, how remarkably privileged we are to hang around with such a talented group of people around here. I am constantly reminded of the immense passion and creativity of those with whom I get to spend time every day.

Maybe I'm overreacting. Maybe it really is a fantastic way to gain valuable, real world skills. And maybe everyone will quit these jobs in a few years and do something else.

But it worries me.

I want to watch Shloe's movies and I want to see Mark's musicals and I want to volunteer with Joe's non-profit and eat at Annie's restaurant and send my kids to schools Jeff has reformed and I'm *just scared* about this industry that's taking all my friends and telling them this is the best way for them to be spending their time. Any of their time. Maybe I'm ignorant and idealistic but I just feel like that can't possibly be true. I feel like we know that. I feel like we can do something really cool to this world. And I fear – at twenty-three, twenty-four, twenty-five – we might forget.

From: Marina Keegan, 'Even Artichokes Have Doubts', The Opposite of Loneliness, *2014*

Comprehension

1 Complete the following sentences with information from the text.

1. Keegan criticizes the fact that a quarter of Yale graduates …
2. Keegan believes that the banking and consulting industries are …
3. Keegan understands that people who need money …
4. Many people decide to work in the world of finance because …
5. Keegan believes that a lot of talent …

Analysis

2 Keegan makes use of *contrast in her text. Explain its purpose.

Language awareness

► SF 17: Reading and understanding non-fictional texts

3 Examine how the author uses *register to underline her line of argument.

Beyond the text

4 You choose Work on task **a** or **b**.

a Discuss whether you agree with the last line of the text.

b Evaluate the choice the writer made (ll. 32–34).

Words revisited

Some of the terms you noted in Words in Context (cf. p. 15) in the category of gender are only used in certain contexts. People might even feel offended if you use them in the wrong way.

► SF 6: Essentials: language and study skills

1 Gender forms

Look at the list below and think of situations in which the terms might be considered appropriate or inappropriate.

gender • sexual orientation • sexual preference • LGBTQ+ • gay • homosexual • woman/man • feminine/masculine • male/female • binary/non-binary • queer • trans

Language awareness

When you read argumentative texts, you will notice ways in which writers try to influence their readers and convince them of their point of view.

2 Matching

► Check

Match the following definitions to the explanations.

1	bias	A	the way in which a subject is treated, which shows the writer's attitude to a particular topic
2	register	B	the writer's subjective view; a strong feeling in favour of or against sth.
3	tone	C	the way in which a text is written
4	style	D	the language used in a particular situation, e.g. formal, neutral or informal

3 Collecting ideas

Name three stylistic devices which you think are especially useful to influence the readers in an argumentative text, and describe the effect they can have.

4 Register

The register of any text has to be appropriate for the audience and the situation. Broadly speaking a text can have a formal, neutral or informal register.

a Sort these elements according to register: formal, neutral or informal.

► Check

colloquial words • hard words (often of Latin origin) and grammar • long and complex sentences • short forms (e.g. wasn't) • simple often incomplete sentences • slang words • straightforward sentences • taboo words

b Decide which register is used in each of the situations below. Think of one more situation for each register.
   1 telephone conversation between friends
   2 academic writing
   3 feature story

5 Influencing the reader

The phrases below are intended to influence the reader.

a Explain how these phrases can be used effectively to convince readers.
b Try to group them into more neutral ones and ones expressing strong bias.

As you are all well aware, ...
None of you can say that ...
Nobody will disagree with me when I say that ...
Statistically speaking, ...
However, ...
Obviously, ...
Only a fool would argue that ...

Practice

► Check

6 Convincing people of an absurd idea

Work with a partner.

a Pick one idea from the box below and brainstorm three (fictional) arguments to support it.
b Write a short speech convincing your partner of the truth of this idea.

Partner A: Try to write your speech in a neutral register.
Partner B: Try to write your speech in an informal register.

Robots will take away our jobs and homes.

Dogs add to the greenhouse effect.

Tall people are better mathematicians.

Carrots are bad for your health.

c Compare your speeches and talk about the differences. Which speech do you find more convincing and why? Share your most interesting findings with the class.

The privilege backpack

- A privilege is defined as 'a special right or advantage for a person or a group of people'. Which of the following would you consider a privilege, which would you consider a basic right? Discuss with a partner.

  1 going on holiday once a year
  2 being in contact with influential people
  3 having access to free education
  4 the freedom to marry the person you love
  5 the ability to afford anything you like
  6 no need to be afraid of being attacked on your way home

Comprehension

1 Look at the illustration and text about 'straight privilege' on the following page. Point out what privilege means according to the 'privilege backpack', and for whom.

2 Outline what we learn about the lives of people who do not have such a 'privilege backpack'. Consider both the contents of the backpack and the four items in the 'straight privilege checklist'.

Analysis

3 Examine how the idea of straight white male privilege is presented on the page. Consider both the contents of the backpack and the layout of the page.

► SF 22: Analysing visuals

4 Analyse how effective the format is in raising awareness for the situation of people who are not part of the straight-white-male group.

Language awareness

5 **a** In the text a privilege is defined as a 'blank cheque to' or a 'safety net' for something. Find similar expressions in the text and think of others you could use.

b Describe the privileges you have or don't have using some of these expressions.

Beyond the text

6 Make privilege checklists of at least three items for groups of people who are discriminated against because of belonging to this group, e.g. women, (ethnic) minorities, homosexuals, handicapped people. Try to devise authentic situations which describe how the privilege would work.

7 Speaking The concept of a 'privilege backpack' was developed by the U.S. scholar and speaker Peggy McIntosh (cf. her portrait in the lower right on p. 34). Do some research about her and give a presentation in class.

► SF 41: Giving a presentation

8 Think back to the guiding question of the chapter and consider whether society allows everyone to fit in.

STRAIGHT PRIVILEGE

Straight privilege builds on the work of feminist and anti-racism activist Peggy McIntosh on *male privilege* and *white privilege*. McIntosh looks at how these privileges interlock to give straight white men advantages in life.

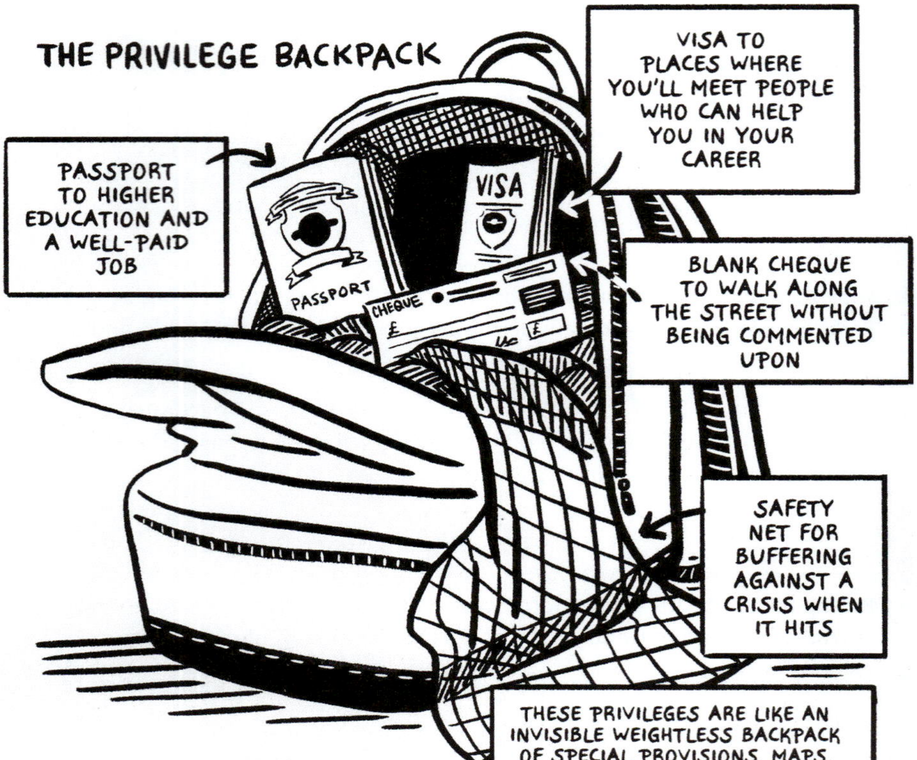

Many people have written *straight privilege checklists* containing items like:

- If I watch a movie or TV programme I can be sure that my sexuality will be represented.
- I didn't grow up surrounded by everyday phrases that attack my sexuality (e.g. "That's so gay").
- I'm never asked to speak for everybody who is straight.
- I don't have to tell anybody about my sexuality; it's assumed.

From: Meg-John Barker, Julia Scheele, Queer: A Graphic History, *2016*

Annotations
straight heterosexual
interlock connect
blank cheque (here) freedom to do sth.
buffer sth. lessen the harmful effect of sth.

A prank Dashka Slater

Think Define the term *hate crime* in your own words.
Pair Compare your definition with a partner's. Decide which is better or agree on a new one, based on both your definitions.
Share Share your definition in class. Agree on one definition.

You are going to read an extract from a novel based on true events.

Sasha liked the back of the bus. A platform seat they could spread out on, tuck their legs under. There they could read, do homework, nap. They had trained themself to wake as the bus rounded the sharp S-curve just before their stop. On 4 November they were unusually tired, having stayed up late the night before writing an essay for their Russian Lit class. Less than twenty-four hours earlier, they'd shared their exhaustion on Tumblr:

Do u ever just get rly tired when u have a lot of shit
to do and u just start crying for no reason

Now, as the 57 bus rattled up MacArthur Boulevard, Sasha's eyes drifted close.

4:52 P.M.

In Oakland, every AC transit bus is equipped with cameras that continuously record sound and video from multiple vantage points. The 57 bus was no exception. The cameras recorded Lloyd and Richard climbing on at the front a little before five p.m. and walking down the aisle towards the back – Lloyd chubby in a zipped-up black hoodie, Richard lean in a black hoodie over a white T-shirt and an orange-billed New York Knicks hat. [...]
Richard recognised a boy named Jamal sitting at the back of the bus and greeted him with a dap. [...]
As the bus started up again, the two cousins gripped the silver pole in front of Jamal. Behind them, Sasha slept. A paperback copy of *Anna Karenina* lay closed in their lap. Their skirt, gauzy and white, dangled over the edge of the seat.
It couldn't have been easy to sleep with Lloyd nearby. He bounced up and down trying to make the bus shake, rapped a snippet of the song *Started from the Bottom* by Drake, screeched random words like 'Chinchilla!' and 'Obituary!' He shouted down the aisle to a girl he'd noticed when they climbed on board, 'Hey! Girl! Excuse me!'
A girl in blue basketball shorts turned to look at him.
'No, your friend, the light-skinned one.'
Jamal pointed at Sasha, whispered, 'Look at this dude.'
Lloyd turned and looked over his shoulder. He cackled.
On the video, you can't hear what Jamal says as he hands Richard the lighter. But you can see him take out his iPhone and point it towards Sasha as if planning to record. Later Richard would say that it was supposed to be funny, like that prank show on MTV with Ashton Kutcher, *Punk'd*. He thought the fabric would smoulder for a minute and then Sasha would wake up and slap it out, startled.
'I *need* a good laugh,' he'd said just after getting on the bus. Now he showed the lighter to Lloyd and then swung to the opposite side of the silver pole, closer to Sasha. He flicked the lighter by the hem off Sasha's skirt. Nothing happened.
Lloyd was still shouting up to the front of the bus.
'Hey! Light-skinned girl!'

Annotations
2 **nap** *(v)* sleep
5 **Lit** Literature
14 **chubby** slightly overweight
15 **lean** slim
16 **New York Knicks** basketball team
18 **dap** form of greeting originally popular among young African-Americans
20 ***Anna Karenina*** novel (1873) by Russian author Leo Tolstoy
21 **gauzy** [ˈgɔːzi] made of thin, translucent fabric
24 **Drake** Canadian rapper
29 **cackle** *(v)* make an unpleasant laugh
30 **lighter** *Feuerzeug*
33 **Ashton Kutcher** U.S. actor
33 ***Punk'd*** TV series in which practical jokes were played
33 **smoulder** burn slowly without a real flame
34 **startled** surprised
37 **hem** *Saum*

Annotations
46 rebuffed rejected
53 brandish sth. *mit etwas herumwedeln*
58 poised in position
59 slink (slunk – slunk) move very quietly and slowly, esp. because you are ashamed
64 transfixed unable to move, fascinated
73 careen move very quickly
83 in unison together
83 shove sb. push sb.
84 smother sth. stop the air reaching sth.
86 kerb *Kantstein*

'Light-skinned girl.' Jamal kept repeating what Lloyd said, his deep voice like an echo from the bottom of a well.
Lloyd bounced up the aisle to where the girls were sitting, perching on the edge of a nearby seat.
'Go ahead, you do it,' Jamal said to Richard. Richard flicked the lighter again. Nothing.
Rebuffed by the girls, Lloyd returned to his companions, stopping in front of Sasha's sleeping form to shout an abrupt, parrotlike 'Hey!'
Sasha stirred, but didn't wake.
'Whoa, nigga. You said, "'Hey!'" Jamal echoed. 'Screamin' and shit.'
Lloyd leaned close and screeched in Jamal's ear. Richard laughed and slapped Lloyd's head.
'Aw, nigga, you just broke my neck,' Lloyd yelled. 'Damn, pussy, bitch, fuck!'
Richard brandished the lighter, pretending to light Lloyd's sleeve. He looked at Jamal.
'Do it,' Jamal urged.
Lloyd danced between them, landing half on Jamal's lap.
'Move, nigga! Get off me,' Jamal grumbled. He kept his eyes on Richard, his phone poised. 'You might as well do it,' he said again.
Richard slunk back to Sasha, flicked the lighter. Nothing. He glanced at Jamal, grinned, and flicked the lighter a fourth time.
'Back door! Back door!' Lloyd called to the driver, ready for them to make their escape.
The doors opened. Richard leaped off the bus. Lloyd started to follow. Then he looked back and stopped, transfixed, as Sasha's skirt erupted into a sheet of flame. When the doors closed again, he hadn't moved.

*

The next few seconds of the surveillance video are hard to watch.
Sasha leaps up, slapping the flaming skirt. 'Oh, fuck! Oh, fuck!' The skirt looks unearthly, impossible, a ball of white fire.
'Ow! *Ow!*' Sasha screams, voice high and terrified. '*I'm on fire. I'm on fire!*' Their hands snatch at the skirt, shaking it, waving it. Specks of flaming fabric swirl through the air. Sasha runs for the door and finds it closed. They turn, dance in place, screaming.
Jamal howls with laughter. Then, as Sasha careens toward him, he cringes and climbs on to his seat. 'He's on fire!' he yells. 'Put him out!'
Passengers sprint for the exits, shrieking and coughing. 'It's a fire! It's a fire!' Some of the other kids on the bus are giggling. The bus still moving, the driver just starting to register that something is going on way back at the far end of his vehicle.
'I ain't got time to be playin' with y'all, man,' he calls over his shoulder.
Near the middle of the bus, two men leap from their seats and elbow through the press of people trying to escape. One man is short and balding; the other is taller, with a walrusy moustache and sad basset-hound eyes.
'Get down!' the moustached one yells. 'Get on the ground!' The two men don't know each other, but they work in unison, shoving Sasha to the floor. The moustached man smothers Sasha's flaming skirt with his coat while the balding man stamps out the burning tatters that flame around them.
It's over in seconds. The driver pulls the bus to the kerb. Sasha scrambles to a standing position, dazed and in shock. 'Oh, Lord. Fuck.'

'That boy was on *fire*, wasn't he?' a man remarks as Sasha pushes through the back doors to the pavement. Behind him, Sasha's moustached rescuer paces the aisle. 'Call an ambulance,' he croaks. He goes to the door of the bus and calls to Sasha, who roams the pavement with a mobile phone, charred legs. 'You need to call an ambulance, man.'

The girl in the blue basketball shorts calls to Sasha through the doors of the bus. Are you OK?'

Sasha doesn't answer.

The bus empties out. Passengers climb off, shaking their heads.

From: Dashka Slater, The 57 Bus, *2018*

Annotations
91 charred burned

Comprehension

1 Choose the correct option.

▶ Check

1 Sasha likes the back of the bus because ...
   a it gives them plenty of space to do what they want.
   b they can feel the bus make a sharp turn before their stop.
   c they are separated from the other passengers.

2 When the boys dance around them, Sasha ...
   a pretends to sleep through the noise and movement.
   b is too tired to wake up.
   c hopes to be left alone by the boys.

3 The boys set fire to Sasha's skirt in order to ...
   a impress the girls on the bus.
   b do something funny.
   c harm someone who seems different.

4 The girls react to Lloyd's attempt to get their attention by ...
   a moving to the front of the bus.
   b asking him to go back to his friends.
   c ignoring him completely.

5 When the bus doors opened, Lloyd ...
   a follows Richard out onto the street.
   b wants to jump out but is transfixed.
   c stays with Jamal to film the event.

6 How exactly are the flames extinguished from Sasha's skirt?
   a Two men cover Sasha with clothes.
   b The balding man smothers the fire on the skirt with his boots.
   c The man with the moustache uses his coat to cover Sasha.

7 At the end of the episode Sasha ...
   a is by and large ok when walking around.
   b is dazed and confused but not badly injured.
   c has been burned on the legs and needs an ambulance.

2 Draw a diagram depicting the relationship of the characters in this scene.

Analysis

3 Explain how the author uses things such as clothes and accessories to characterize the teenagers.

4 Analyse the different *narrative perspectives the author employs in the excerpt.

Language awareness

5 Analyse the use of the pronoun *they* in the extract.

Beyond the text

6 Examine whether what happened can be called a 'hate crime'. Refer to your ideas from the pre-reading task.

► SF 36: Creative writing

7 You choose Writing Work on task **a** or **b**.
Richard is arrested and sent to court.

a In order to make him understand the harm he has caused and take responsibility for his actions, Richard has been ordered by the court to meet up with Sasha to talk about the event. Sasha is not sure if they want to take part in this scheme and so they discuss the idea with a friend. Write their dialogue.

b As part of the process to rehabilitate Richard, Richard has been ordered by the court to attend a meeting with Sasha. They talk about what happened and the effect it has had on both their lives. Write their dialogue.

► SF 21: Analysing diagrams

8 Work with a partner. **Partner B:** Go to p. 244. **Partner A:** look below.
Study your chart and tell your partner what information it gives.

Registered hate crimes by bias motivation, USA 2018

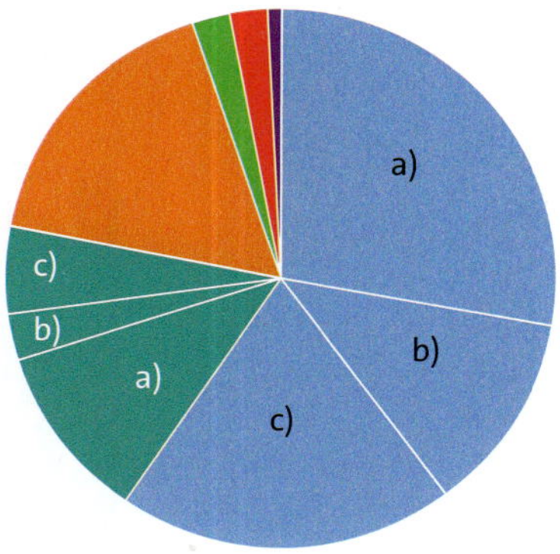

Total	**8496**
Race/Ethnicity:	**4954**
a) anti-Black or African American	2325
b) anti-White	1001
c) other	1628
Religion:	**1550**
a) anti-Jewish	896
b) anti-Muslim	225
c) other	429
Sexual orientation	**1.404**
Gender identity	**184**
Disability	**177**
Gender	**58**

From: www.fbi.gov

My journey into the world of men's beauty

- Discuss in class what you understand by male beauty.

▶ Getting started

Listening *You are going to listen to a radio report on male beauty.*

▶ SF 38: Listening/Viewing for gist and detail

Comprehension

1 *Quick write: Describe the changes in the make-up industry.

2 Choose the correct option.

▶ Check

1 The reporter hopes that the result of the makeover ...
  a will make him look younger.
  b will persuade more men to wear make-up
  c won't be noticed by his colleagues in the office.
  d will impress his colleagues.

2 A survey found that more than half of U.S. men...
  a can imagine wearing make-up.
  b have worn make-up.
  c would refuse to wear make-up.
  d think make-up is unmanly.

3 Some men use make-up to ...
  a cover up marks in business meetings.
  b look better for a woman.
  c look exciting and interesting.
  d improve their looks in photos.

4 Beauty companies have started to ...
  a sell female beauty products to men.
  b offer products and advertising that is more gender-fluid.
  c separate male and female make-up lines more clearly.
  d advertise male products in the same way as female products.

5 Social media offers an opportunity for ...
  a make-up to be targeted more towards men.
  b men to watch tutorials at home without being noticed.
  c people to show that beauty can be defined in different ways.
  d everyone to discover new make-up trends.

6 Zamora welcomes these new trends because ...
  a they question beauty norms.
  b anyone can do what they like.
  c because high-school boys all wear make-up now.
  d they promote the make-up industry.

Beyond the text

3 In groups, conduct a survey in class on attitudes towards make-up for men.

▶ More language

4 Design an advert for a gender-neutral beauty product. Discuss what it should look like and how it should be different from other beauty ads.

Sonnet 130 William Shakespeare

▶ Getting started

- Discuss what you think are today's beauty ideals for women. Write down five aspects.
- Discuss what you think were the beauty ideals for women during Shakespeare's lifetime. Write down five aspects.

My mistress' eyes are nothing like the sun;
Coral is far more red than her lips' red;
If snow be white, why then her breasts are dun;
If hairs be wires, black wires grow on her head.
I have seen roses damask'd, red and white,
But no such roses see I in her cheeks;
And in some perfumes is there more delight
Than in the breath that from my mistress reeks.
I love to hear her speak, yet well I know
That music hath a far more pleasing sound;
I grant I never saw a goddess go;
My mistress, when she walks, treads on the ground:
    And yet, by heaven, I think my love as rare
    As any she belied with false compare.

From: William Shakespeare, Sonnets, *1609*

Annotations
1 **mistress** lover
2 **coral** *Edelkoralle*
3 **dun** grey-brown
5 **rose damask'd** type of rose
8 **reek** stink, smell
12 **tread** walk

Info

The sonnet originated in Italy in the 13th century and was adapted to many languages. A classic sonnet follows a very strict structure of fourteen lines (three quatrains ending with a rhymed couplet: *abab cdcd efef gg*) and a typical rhyme scheme (in English, the iambic pentameter). The sonnet was a very popular form of love poetry.

Comprehension

1 Sum up in one sentence how the speaker of Sonnet 130 views their lover.

2 Compare the idealized beauty and the lover of the speaker, by making a table like the one below.

Conventional beauty	Their lover
bright, sparkly eyes (eyes like the sun) ...	Her eyes are probably normal (nothing like the sun) ...

Analysis

▶ SF 19: Reading and understanding poetry

3 List all the *images Shakespeare uses in his *sonnet and explain their use.

4 Explain what point Shakespeare is making in his poem.

Beyond the text

5 **a** Write two lines of poetry which start 'Beauty is ...'.
b In groups compare your lines and together make a poem that uses the lines that each person wrote.

Scars to your beautiful

Alessia Cara

► More info

Annotations
- scar *Narbe*
- 3 **crave sth.** long for sth.
- 9 **woe** unhappiness

She just wants to be beautiful
She goes unnoticed, she knows no limits
She craves attention, she praises an image
She prays to be sculpted by the sculptor

Oh, she don't see the light that's shining
Deeper than the eyes can find it
Maybe we have made her blind
So she tries to cover up her pain
And cut her woes away
'Cause covergirls don't cry
After their face is made

But there's a hope that's waiting for you in the dark
You should know you're beautiful just the way you are
And you don't have to change a thing
The world could change its heart
No scars to your beautiful
We're stars and we're beautiful

Oh-oh-oh-oh
Oh-oh-oh-oh

And you don't have to change a thing
The world could change its heart
No scars to your beautiful
We're stars and we're beautiful

She has dreams to be an envy, so she's starving
You know, covergirls eat nothing
She says, beauty is pain and there's beauty in everything
What's a little bit of hunger?
I could go a little while longer, she fades away

She don't see her perfect
She don't understand she's worth it
Or that beauty goes deeper than the surface
Oh-oh, oh-oh
So to all the girls that's hurting
Let me be your mirror
Help you see a little bit clearer
The light that shines within

There's a hope that's waiting for you in the dark
You should know you're beautiful just the way you are
And you don't have to change a thing
The world could change its heart
No scars to your beautiful
We're stars and we're beautiful

Oh-oh-oh-oh, oh-oh
Oh-oh-oh-oh-oh

And you don't have to change a thing
The world could change its heart
No scars to your beautiful
We're stars and we're beautiful

No better you than the you that you are
(No better you than the you that you are)
No better life than the life we're living
(No better life than the life we're living)
No better time for your shine, you're a star
(No better time for your shine, you're a star)

From: Know-It-All, *2016*

Comprehension

1 Describe the situation of the unnamed girl in the song in two to three sentences.

2 Pick one adjective from the box below or choose one of your own to describe the girl. Discuss your choice with a partner.

> aggressive • ashamed • tender • gentle • miserable • angry • troubled • devastated • pessimistic • helpless • at a loss • fearful • desperate • strong • weak • independent • self-confident

Analysis

3 Describe the attitude of the singer to the situation expressed in the song.

► SF 19: Reading and analysing poetry

4 Examine the *imagery used in the song.

Language awareness

5 The songwriter plays with words by making nouns out of adjectives and pronouns. Find three examples and say how they could be written in standard English.

► SF 36: Creative writing

Alessia Cara

Beyond the text

6 You choose Work on task **a** or **b**.

a Speaking Imagine the girl is one of your friends and you are worried about her. What advice would you try to give her? In pairs, act out the conversation.

b Writing You are a specialist taking part in a project for teenagers and their mental health. Write down some notes on the pressure that beauty ideals can put on young people. Then write a short statement for a leaflet aimed at teenagers.

Art in Context – 'We can do it!'

The poster on the right was created during the Second World War.

J. Howard Miller, 'We Can Do It', 1942

Comprehension

1 Describe the poster.

Analysis

2 Explain the message of the poster.

3 The poster was not well known during World War II, but has since become very popular. Assess why it might be so popular.

Language help

inspirational image • iconic figure • uplifting attitude • self-empowerment • strong female • war production worker • promote feminism • inspire women workers • female empowerment • fight against gender inequality

Beyond the text

4 Research how the image has been used in contemporary campaigns or by people today.

5 In small groups, create a contemporary poster with a similar message encouraging people to become involved in a social project today.

Chapter task

Change for the better!

You are a member of a social movement that wants to give voice to younger voters. You have been invited to write a speech about the relationship between individuals and society.

Your speech should refer to one or more of the following aspects:

- individuals between conformity and rebellion
- the contribution of the individual to society
- identity and diversity
- changing gender roles.

▸ Getting started

Chapter 2: **Science and Technology – Transforming Life?**

1 Art in Context

- a **Think** Work on your own. Examine the picture of Ai-Da above and take notes on the following questions: What do you think is happening in the photo? What associations does the image evoke in you?
- b **Pair** Work in pairs. Compare your ideas. Agree on a statement regarding the picture and provide a caption for it.
- c Find out the story behind the picture. Who or what is Ai-Da?
- d **Share** Discuss in class how the picture might be related to the title of this chapter: Science and technology: transforming life?

► Getting started

2
- a Look at the Chapter map opposite and speculate about the topics and the guiding question in this chapter. Choose one item from the map and brainstorm ideas. Then exchange your ideas with different partners.
- b Discuss in what ways science and technology might transform YOUR lives in the future for the better or the worse.

Robot artist Ai-Da in front of one of her self-portraits, 2018

▶ More info

Chapter map

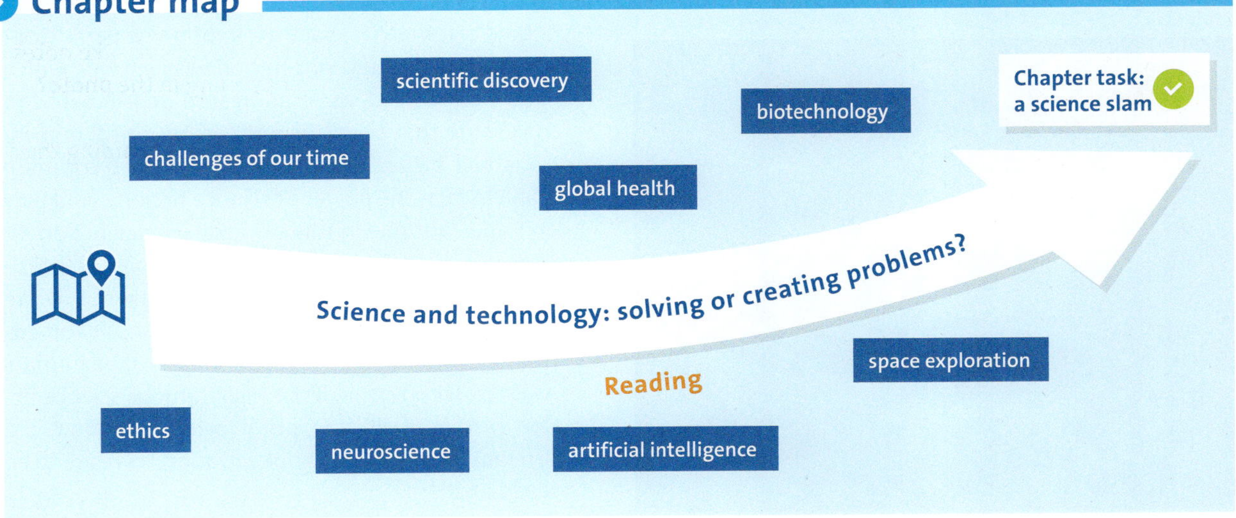

▸ More language

Science and technology today and tomorrow

The role of science and technology in the 21st century

Science can be broadly defined as the way human beings figure out how the world works. The 21st century has seen numerous breakthrough discoveries in science and technology which have increased our knowledge of the world and improved the way we live. Researchers have, for example, produced scientific evidence for liquid water on Mars, developed effective therapies for diseases like HIV or cancer and created robotic body parts that can be controlled by patients' minds. Scientific and technological progress will continue to play a decisive role in the coming decades if humankind is to overcome the economic, social and environmental challenges we face today. Devising innovative technologies based on scientific research will be vital for combatting future pandemics, mitigating the dangers of climate change and solving many other global problems.

Science: an unfinished book

Science will never be 'finished'. As our knowledge of science advances, new fields of research emerge. Biotechnology, which uses biology to create new products such as vaccines, drugs or genetically modified crops, is a rapidly changing field with huge potential for innovation, for example in gene editing, which, if applied carefully, could cure chronic diseases such as Alzheimer's by repairing an organism's DNA. Similarly, advances in neuroscience, a discipline that investigates the workings of the human brain, could lead to a better understanding of how human thoughts, feelings and actions are determined. This could help patients who suffer from health issues affecting the brain. Moreover, while progress in artificial intelligence might soon make it possible for machines to accomplish increasingly specialized tasks such as driving a vehicle or performing surgery, advances in space science could provide us with more sophisticated answers to fundamental questions about the history of the universe and our place in it. Science is indeed an unfinished book.

Ethical challenges

Humankind has reached a level of scientific and technological development that raises a host of ethical questions and dilemmas. For example, should scientists be allowed to edit an unborn child's genome? Should animals and humans be used in clinical trials? Should robots replace humans as doctors, teachers and drivers? And should commercial space exploration be permitted? None of these questions has an easy answer, which is why they need to be addressed and debated to make sure that scientific and technological innovations will be applied responsibly for the common good. In fact, the power of science fiction could play an important role in this context. Science fiction invites us to look to the future and explore the possibilities of science and technology. It makes us aware of the ethical dilemmas these might entail and encourages discussion on what it means to be human. As Isaac Asimov, one of the most famous science fiction writers of all time, put it, science fiction could turn out to be 'crucial to our salvation, if we are to be saved at all.'

1 Words words words

a Read the text and finish the sentences in as many ways as possible.
1 Science and technology have transformed the 21st century by ...
2 Future advances in science and technology may pose risks because ...
3 The future of humankind depends on science and technology to ...

b Copy the table and add as many words as possible using the appropriate forms of the *word families. You may use a monolingual dictionary.

► Check
► SF 8: Working with dictionaries

Verb	Noun (thing/idea)	Noun (person)	Adjective
?	?	?	scientific
?	technology	?	?
?	?	?	ethical
advance	?	?	?
?	discovery	?	?

c Find synonyms and antonyms for the verbs and adjectives in **b**, then work with a partner and quiz each other.

► Check

Language help

What's the verb/noun/adjective of ...? • Make a sentence with ... • Can you give me a synonym/antonym for ...?

2 Clustering and brainstorming

a Read the text again and create a *cluster about science and technology and their contribution to the progress of humankind.
b Choose one aspect in your cluster in **a** and, for one minute, *brainstorm more ideas you could use to talk about it. Add the ideas to your cluster.
c Work with a partner. Using your clusters, take turns talking for one minute about 'your' aspects.

3 Chunk it!

► More language

Find as many suitable words as possible that *collocate with each group of nouns below. Use a collocations dictionary to check your answers.
1 ... *(adj)* + dilemmas | concerns | implications
2 ... *(v)* + tasks | experiments | tests
3 ... *(adj)* + advances | discoveries | progress
4 ... *(v)* + cooperation | dialogue | participation | use
5 ... *(adj)* + behaviour | brain | nature

4 Writing a speech

Write a short speech to be given at a science youth conference. Your topic is: 'Future innovations in science and technology I'm looking forward to.' Use as many *chunks from the text and the exercises above as possible and mark them.

► SF 42: Preparing and giving a speech

▶ SF 17: Reading and understanding non-fictional texts

Info

Stephen Hawking (1942–2018) was a British theoretical physicist and cosmologist working and teaching at the University of Cambridge. His work focused on studying black holes and on extending Albert Einstein's general theory of relativity. Hawking also published several popular science books which became bestsellers and made him famous among a wider public. After losing the ability to speak because of a motor neuron disease, Hawking used a speech generator to communicate with the rest of the world.

Annotations

2 **bother with sth.** take the time to deal with sth.
5 **advocate** speak out in favour
7 **literate** having knowledge of sth.
17 **threshold** point at which sth. starts to happen
22 **extra-terrestrial** from outside the earth
24 **habitat** natural environment
26 **endeavour** *(n)* attempt to achieve a goal
27 **strive to do sth.** make great efforts to achieve sth.
28 **viable** (here) capable of surviving
29 **transcend sth.** go beyond sth.

The thrill of scientific discovery

Stephen Hawking

- Do you like science? Discuss what gets you excited about it and what makes science difficult for you.

Language help

take satisfaction from sth. • deepen one's knowledge of sth. • be able to make connections to reality • deal with abstract/complex ideas • solve/understand difficult problems • use scientific language / numbers / formulas • lack knowledge of sth.

The excerpt below is from Brief Answers to the Big Questions, *the last book by Stephen Hawking, which was published posthumously.*

When I was growing up it was still acceptable – not to me but in social terms – to say that one was not interested in science and did not see the point in bothering with it. This is no longer the case. Let me be clear. I am not promoting the idea that all young people should grow up to be scientists. I do not see that as an ideal situation, as the world needs people with a wide variety of skills. But I am advocating that all young people should be familiar with and confident around scientific subjects, whatever they choose to do. They need to be scientifically literate, and inspired to engage with developments in science and technology in order to learn more.

A world where only a tiny super-elite are capable of understanding advanced science and technology and its applications would be, to my mind, a dangerous and limited one. I seriously doubt whether long-range beneficial projects such as cleaning up the oceans or curing diseases in the developing world would be given priority. Worse, we could find that technology is used against us and that we might have no power to stop it.

I don't believe in boundaries, either for what we can do in our personal lives or for what life and intelligence can accomplish in our universe. We stand at a threshold of important discoveries in all areas of science. Without doubt, our world will change enormously in the next fifty years. We will find out what happened at the Big Bang. We will come to understand how life began on Earth. We may even discover whether life exists elsewhere in the universe. While the chances of communicating with an intelligent extra-terrestrial species may be slim, the importance of such a discovery means we must not give up trying. We will continue to explore our cosmic habitat, sending robots and humans into space. We cannot continue to look inwards at ourselves on a small and increasingly polluted and overcrowded planet. Through scientific endeavour and technological innovation, we must look outwards to the wider universe, while also striving to fix the problems on Earth. And I am optimistic that we will ultimately create viable habitats for the human race on other planets. We will transcend the Earth and learn to exist in space.

This is not the end of the story, but just the beginning of what I hope will be billions of years of life flourishing in the cosmos.

And one final point – we never really know where the next great scientific discovery will come from, nor who will make it. Opening up the thrill and wonder of scientific discovery, creating innovative and accessible ways to reach out to the widest young audience possible, greatly increases the chances of finding and inspiring the new Einstein. Wherever she might be.

So remember to look up at the stars and not down at your feet. Try to make sense of what you see and wonder about what makes the universe exist. Be curious. And however difficult life may seem, there is always something you can do and succeed at. It matters that you don't give up. Unleash your imagination. Shape the future.

From: Brief Answers to the Big Questions, *2018*

Annotations
44 unleash sth. release sth., allow sth. to have an effect

Comprehension

1 Complete the following sentences with information from the text.
1. To be 'scientifically literate' means ...
2. Acquiring scientific literacy is important because ...
3. In the next few decades, Stephen Hawking expects science to ...
4. Exploring the cosmos will be essential if humanity ...
5. Science is thrilling because ...

Analysis

2 Stephen Hawking was famous for his ability to write popular science books in which he communicated complex scientific ideas in clear, non-technical language. Take another close look at the text and analyse how Stephen Hawking tries to make his ideas appealing and intelligible to his readers.

► SF 4: Writing a text analysis

Language awareness

3 a Explain what Stephen Hawking wishes to imply by using:
- the pronoun *we* repeatedly throughout the text;
- the pronoun *she* in l. 36;
- the pronoun *you* in the last paragraph.

b Using the pronouns above, write three sentences which could be added to Stephen Hawking's text.

► SF 13: Doing research
► SF 26: Argumentative writing

Beyond the text

4 You choose | Writing | Work on task **a** or **b**.

a Research more information about Stephen Hawking's life and write a personal comment in which you point out what you find most fascinating about the scientist and his work.

b Pick a scientific discovery you find exciting (by Stephen Hawking or another scientist) and write a personal comment in which you point out why this discovery fascinates you so much.

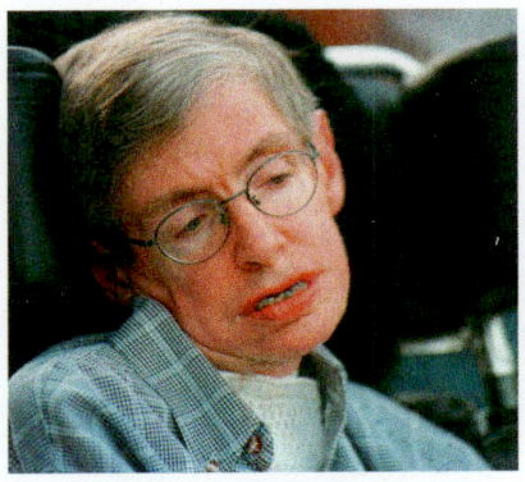

Stephen Hawking

▶ More info

Info

Richard Feynman (1918–1988) was an American theoretical physicist who made major contributions to the field of quantum electrodynamics, for which he was awarded the Nobel Prize in Physics in 1965. In a talk given in 1959, Feynman is thought to have planted the seeds for what would later become known as nanotechnology.

▶ SF 18: Reading and understanding narrative texts

Scientists at work

Lawrence Wright

- *Taking the quote by Richard Feynman as a starting point, explain the way scientists work.*

> The only way to have real success in science, the field I'm familiar with, is to describe the evidence very carefully without regard to the way you feel it should be. If you have a theory, you must try to explain what's good and what's bad about it equally.
>
> *Richard Feynman,* The Quotable Feynman, *2015*

Below is the opening chapter of the novel The End of October *by Lawrence Wright. During a meeting at the WHO headquarters in Geneva, Henry Parsons, an American epidemiologist, learns about a mysterious new disease whose sudden appearance in Indonesia is stirring a heated debate among scientists.*

In a large auditorium in Geneva, a parliament of health officials gathered for the final afternoon session on emergency infectious diseases. The audience was restless, worn out by the day-long meetings and worried about catching their flights. The terrorist attack in Rome had everyone on edge.

'An unusual cluster of adolescent fatalities in a refugee camp in Indonesia,' the next-to-last speaker of the conference was saying. Hans Somebody. Dutch. Tall, arrogant, well fed. An untrimmed fringe of gray-blond hair spilled over his collar, the lint on his shoulders sparkling in the projected light of the PowerPoint.

A map of Indonesia flashed on the screen. 'Forty-seven death certificates were issued in the first week of March at the Kongoli Number Two Camp in West Java.' Hans indicated the spot with his laser pointer, followed by slides of destitute refugees in horrible squalor. The world was awash in displaced people, millions pressed into hastily assembled camps and fenced off like prisoners, with inadequate rations and scarce medical facilities. Nothing surprising about an epidemic spilling out of such places. Cholera, diphtheria, dengue – the tropics were always cooking up something.

'High fever, bloody discharges, rapid transmission, extreme lethality. But what really distinguishes this cluster,' Hans said, as he posted a graph, 'is the median age of the victims. Usually, infections randomly span the generations, but here the fatalities spike in the age group expected to be the most vigorous portion of the population.'

In the large auditorium in Geneva, the parliament of health officials leaned forward to study the curious slide. Most mortal diseases kill off the very young and the very old, but instead of the usual U-shaped graph, this one resembled a crude W,

Annotations
- 6 **on edge** nervously excited about sth.
- 7 **fatality** death caused by illness or violence
- 12 **West Java** province in Indonesia
- 13 **destitute** very poor
- 14 **squalor** state of being extremely dirty
- 16 **scarce** [skeəs] *(adj)* insufficient
- 19 **discharge** *(n)* (here) fluid from body parts
- 19 **lethality** capacity to cause harm or death
- 22 **spike** rise quickly

with an average age of death of twenty-nine. 'Based on sketchy reports from the initial outbreak, we estimate the overall lethality at 70 percent,' Hans said.

'Pediatric or natal ...?' Maria Savona, director of epidemiology at the World Health Organization, interrupted the puzzled silence.

'Largely accounted for in the reported cohort,' Hans replied.

'Possible sexual transmission?' a Japanese doctor asked. 'Unlikely,' said Hans. He was enjoying himself. Now his face drifted into the projection, casting a bulky shadow over the next slide. 'Reportable deaths stay consistent for the following weeks, but the overall total drops significantly.'

'A one-time event, in that case,' the Japanese woman concluded.

'With forty-seven bodies?' Hans said. 'Quite an orgy!'

The Japanese doctor blushed and covered her mouth as she giggled.

'Okay, Hans, you've kept us guessing long enough,' Maria said impatiently.

Hans looked around the room triumphantly. 'Shigella,' he said, to groans of disbelief. 'You would have got it but for the inverted mortality vector. That puzzled us as well. This is a common bacteria in poorer countries, the cause of innumerable cases of food poisoning. We queried the health authorities in Jakarta, and they concluded that, in a starving environment, the only people robust enough to seize the limited food resources are the young. In this case, strength proved to be their undoing. Our team deduced that the probable source of the pathogen was raw milk. We offer this as a cautionary tale about how demographic stereotypes can blind us to facts that would otherwise be obvious.'

Hans stepped down to perfunctory applause as Maria called the last presenter to the podium. 'Campylobacter in Wisconsin–' the man began.

Suddenly, a commanding voice interrupted. 'A raging hemorrhagic fever kills forty-seven people in a week and disappears without a trace?'

Two hundred heads turned to locate the source of that booming baritone. From the voice, you would have thought Henry Parsons was a big man. No. He was short and slight, bent by a childhood case of rickets that left him slightly deformed. [...] In the neverending war on emerging diseases, Henry Parsons was not a small man; he was a giant.

Hans Somebody squinted and located Henry in the gloom of the upper tiers. 'Not so unusual, Dr. Parsons, if you consider the environmental causation.'

'You used the word "transmission."'

Hans smiled, happy to resume the game. 'The Indonesian authorities at first suspected a viral agent.'

'What changed their minds?' Henry asked.

Maria had become intrigued. 'You are thinking Ebola?'

'In which case we'd see likely migration to urban centers,' Hans said. 'Not shown. All it took was to eliminate the source of contamination and the infection disappeared.'

Info

The **World Health Organization (WHO)** is an agency of the United Nations whose primary function is to promote public health around the world, for example by devising and advancing international health standards, providing technical help and collecting data. Since its inception in 1948, the WHO has been successful in fighting global health challenges such as smallpox, polio and Ebola.

Annotations

29 **pediatric** *(AE)* dealing with children and their diseases
29 **natal** relating to the birth of babies
31 **account for sth.** be the cause of sth.
31 **cohort** group of people with shared characteristics
40 **Shigella** kind of bacteria
41 **inverted** changed to the opposite
41 **mortality** large-scale death
46 **undoing** cause of ruin or failure
46 **pathogen** microorganism that causes disease
47 **cautionary tale** story warning of danger
50 **campylobacter** kind of bacteria
51 **raging** *(adj)* prevailing uncontrollably
51 **hemorrhagic** *(AE)* **fever** viral disease accompanied by heavy bleeding
55 **rickets** *Rachitis*
62 **agent** substance that causes a change
66 **contamination** act of making sth. unclean

Annotations
81 **cane** walking stick
88 **meningitis** serious disease affecting the brain
92 **stunning** extremely impressive
92 **downside** negative aspect of sth.
100 **sample** representative part of sth.

'Did you actually go to the camp yourself?' Henry asked. 'Take samples?'

'The Indonesian authorities have been fully cooperative,' Hans said dismissively. 'There is a team from Médecins Sans Frontières in place now, and we will receive confirmation shortly. Don't expect surprises.'

Hans waited a moment, but Henry sat back, thoughtfully tapping a finger on his lips. The next presenter resumed. 'A slaughterhouse in Milwaukee,' he said, as a few conferees with an eye on the time ducked toward the exits. There was bound to be increased security at the airport.

'I hate when you do that,' Maria said, when they got to her office. It was glassy and stylish, with a fine view of Mont Blanc. A flock of storks, having hurdled the alpine barrier, circled for a landing beside Lake Geneva, their first stop on the spring migration from the Nile Valley.

'Do what?'

Maria leaned back and tapped her finger on her lips, imitating Henry's gesture.

'Is that a habit of mine?' he asked, leaning his cane against her desk.

'When I see you do it, I know I should be worried. What makes you doubt Hans's study?'

'Acute hemorrhagic fever. Very likely viral. Weird mortality distribution, totally inappropriate for shigella. And why did it suddenly–'

'Just stop? I don't know, Henry, you tell me. Indonesia again?'

'They hid the ball before.'

'It doesn't look like another meningitis outbreak.'

'Certainly not.' Despite himself, Henry involuntarily began tapping his lips again. Maria waited. 'I shouldn't tell you what to do,' he finally said. 'Maybe Hans is right.'

'But ...?'

'The lethality. Stunning. The downside if he's wrong.'

Maria went to the window. Clouds were settling in, masking the majestic peak. She was about to speak when Henry interrupted her thought. 'I've got to go.'

'That's exactly what I was thinking.'

'I mean home.'

Maria nodded in that way that meant she had heard him, but the worried expression in her Italian eyes sent a different message. 'Give me two days. I know how much I'm asking. I should send a whole team, but I don't have anybody I can trust. Hans says MSF is there, so they can help. Just get slides and samples. In and out and on your way back to Atlanta.'

'Maria ...'

'Please, Henry.'

In the manner of friends who have known each other a long time, Henry saw a flash of the worried young epidemiologist studying the African swine fever outbreak in Haiti. Maria had been part of the team that advocated the eradication of the indigenous pig that carried the disease. Nearly every family in Haiti kept pigs; in addition to being a major source of food, they functioned as currency, a bank for the peasantry. Within a year, thanks to the efforts of the international community and the dictator 'Baby Doc' Duvalier, the entire population of Creole pigs was extinct, a great success, almost unprecedented. The eradication stopped an incurable disease. But the peasants, already poor, were reduced to famine. The corrupt elite appropriated most of the replacement pigs the Americans provided, which were in any case too delicate for the environment and too expensive to feed. With no other resources, people turned to making charcoal, which denuded the forests. Haiti never recovered. It's debatable whether the hogs should have been slaughtered in the first place. We were such confident idealists back then, Henry thought.

'Two days, maximum,' he said. 'I promised Jill I'd be home for Teddy's birthday.'

'I'll have Rinaldo book you on the red-eye to Jakarta.' Maria assured him that she would call the Centers for Disease Control and Prevention, in Atlanta, where Henry was deputy director for infectious diseases, and beg forgiveness; it was an emergency request on her part.

'By the way,' he said as he was leaving, 'any word from Rome? Your family is safe?'

'We don't know,' Maria said despairingly.

From: The End of October, *2020*

Annotations

105 epidemiologist doctor who specializes in the spread of diseases
106 Haiti country on the island of Hispaniola in the Caribbean Sea
106 eradication process of getting rid of sth.
106 indigenous native
108 peasantry agricultural labourers
110 'Baby Doc' Duvalier Claude Duvalier, nicknamed 'Baby Doc', a cruel dictator in Haiti who was overthrown by an uprising in 1986
110 Creole (here) Haitian
111 unprecedented never known or done before
112 famine hunger, scarcity of food
112 appropriate sth. take sth. for one's own use
115 charcoal *Holzkohle*
115 denude make bare
116 hog domesticated pig
119 red-eye overnight flight

Comprehension

1 a Read the excerpt from Lawrence Wright's novel and make notes on the five *wh*-questions: Who? What? Where? When? Why?

b Compare your notes with a partner. Then agree on which of the statements below best summarizes the excerpt. Give reasons.

Scientists are working together to combat a deadly disease. 	Scientists are giving speeches on infectious diseases at a conference in Geneva. 
Scientists are arguing about how to respond to the outbreak of an unknown virus in Indonesia. 	Scientists are forming hypotheses as to the causes of the high number of fatalities in an Asian refugee camp. 

Analysis

2 a Read the excerpt again and trace the different steps taken by Hans, Henry and the other scientists mentioned in the text to describe and explain the disease in Indonesia. Collect information in a grid like the one below.

	Hans	*Henry*	*Other scientists*
Description of the new disease			
Hypothesis on the origins of the new disease			
Arguments/data speaking for or against the hypothesis			
Conclusions about what is to be done next			

b Compare your findings, then discuss what this text shows you about the challenges of scientific work.

► SF 12: Communicating across cultures

c Intercultural communication Re-read the passage about the swine fever outbreak in Haiti (ll. 104–117), which is based on real events. Explain how the handling of the outbreak reveals a cultural misunderstanding about Haiti's economic situation and discuss how the misunderstanding – and its consequences – might have been avoided.

Language awareness

► SF 8: Working with dictionaries
► SF 9: Learning new words

3 Work on either **a** or **b**.

a Understanding science often relies on understanding specialized vocabulary. Make a list of words and phrases from the text that you could use to talk about the causes and effects of a pandemic. Use a monolingual dictionary.

b Challenge Write a paragraph on the causes and effects of pandemics for a presentation in your bilingual Biology class. Use as many of the words you listed above as possible.

Beyond the text

4 Writing Write an email from Henry Parsons to his wife Jill in which he explains to her why he will return home later than expected.

► SF 44: Having a discussion
► Getting started

5 Speaking Imagine the following situation: A lethal disease is threatening the lives of people in your country. It is your job to set up a task force to handle the situation. Work in small groups and discuss the following questions:
- Which experts should be on the task force?
- Which competences and skills are needed to deal with this health crisis?
- What difficulties might arise should there be an outbreak of the disease?

Focus on test formats

Most English exams include a section in which you have to read and understand a long, complex text. As non-fictional texts, e.g. news reports, feature articles or argumentative texts, pose particular challenges in terms of content and language, in this skills lab you are going to revise how to deal with non-fictional texts in your exam.

There are several types of task available to examiners to check whether you have understood a text. ***Closed tasks*** *require you to respond to what you read by giving short standardized answers.* ***Open tasks****, by contrast, require you to respond to your reading by writing a short text. For example, you might be asked to outline, summarize, point out or describe certain ideas.*

Imagine you have been asked to read the text on p. 57 and to complete this task:

Outline the author's proposals on how to be better prepared for the next pandemic.

► SF 16: Essentials: reading, text and media skills

Work it out

1 Understanding the task

► Check

a Are you familiar with the most common types of task in reading comprehension tests? Match the task types on the left with the descriptions of what you have to do on the right.

1 describe
2 gapped text
3 matching
4 multiple choice
5 outline
6 point out / state
7 sorting
8 summarize / sum up
9 true/false

A choose the correct answer
B decide whether a statement is valid or not
C give a concise account of the main points or ideas of a text, issue or topic
D give a detailed account of what sb./sth. is like
E give the main features, structure or general principles of sth.
F link two ideas or items
G present the main aspects of sth. briefly and clearly
H put pieces of information in a logical order
I filling in words where they are missing in a text

b Look at the exam task above. What does it mean to 'outline' something here? And what is to be outlined in this case?

2 Using different reading strategies

Having a repertoire of different reading strategies can help you to make sense of complex texts effectively. Which strategy to apply in an exam situation depends, of course, on the task given to you.

If you want to understand the main idea of a text, ***skimming*** *will be a useful strategy. If, by contrast, you are only looking for a specific piece of information,* ***scanning*** *will help you solve the problem. However, if you need to understand the text in its entirety, which is usually the case in exams,* ***close reading*** *will be the most appropriate strategy to figure out what is said in the text and how it is said.*

Work with a partner and revise when and how to use the reading strategies in the box below. Then discuss which strategies could be particularly useful when dealing with a complex non-fictional text:

asking questions • extended reading • close reading • skimming • scanning • reading between the lines • using prior knowledge • making predictions • structuring information

► Check

3 Going through different steps

When dealing with the type of exam task we are focusing on here (i.e., outlining an author's proposals), it is not only important to use reading strategies, but also to apply them in a logical order. The most straightforward way of doing so would be to follow this three-step procedure:

Step 1 Understand the overall meaning of the text using predicting and skimming
Step 2 Understand the text in detail using close reading
Step 3 Write your text.

Match the instructions below (**A–G**) to the three steps above and put them in a logical order:

A Don't forget to use the present tense when outlining the author's proposals.
B Look at the headline and speculate about the topic and the central message of the article.
C Make notes.
D Read the text again and identify the author's proposals on how to prepare better for the next pandemic.
E Read the text and find suitable headings for each paragraph
F Run your eyes over the text and look for words or phrases that contain information that might be important for your task.
G Use your notes to write your outline.

Do it

4 Completing the task

Now read the text on p. 57. Make use of all the tips and ideas from above and complete the task: *Outline the author's proposals on how to be better prepared for the next pandemic.*

Preparing for the next pandemic Devi Sridhar

Wouldn't it be wonderful if we never had to face another pandemic? As we reflect on the past year, the words that come to mind are 'never again'. Never again should more than 120,000 lives be lost to a contagious virus, a number that would have been unthinkable almost a year ago, when government advisers thought that losing 20,000 people would be a good outcome. Nor should we endure another year of lockdowns, and the pain of job losses and unemployment that followed. And nobody ever wants to see children taken out of school for 21 weeks of the year again, unable to learn in classrooms or see their friends.

But scientists are clear that we will face another pandemic in the future. Most agree the question is when, not if. In 2018, I gave a talk at the Hay festival outlining a scenario that was loosely based on recent news reports: a farmer becomes infected with an antibiotic-resistant bacterium from a pig in China, spreading this infection through their community and then boarding a plane to the UK. The worrying thing about this scenario is that such bacteria, which evade our antibiotics of last resort, are already upon us. They could yet be the source of a future pandemic.

Or perhaps the next pandemic will be caused by a virus spilling over from animals to humans, much like Covid-19. Recent reports that the first humans have been infected with avian influenza at a poultry plant in Russia give a worrying glimpse of how close we live to such risks. [...]

Wherever the next pandemic comes from, Britain must think long term about its ability to respond and must ensure it is prepared. Key to this will be working together with other governments to establish robust response systems. Over the past year, the UK has already built many of the structures that will be needed to address a future pandemic. [...] But more needs to be done at a global level to ensure we're truly prepared.

International travel and trade have connected countries and created new opportunities for diseases to spread. This is why we need global surveillance to identify disease risks. Just as we have a weather service, governments should invest in a global virus surveillance network to scan for new pathogens of concern, and identify and mitigate the risks of animal viruses crossing over into human populations. It's not only new pathogens we should be afraid of, but new variants of existing viruses. Already, we've seen variants of the virus that causes Covid-19 arising in countries such as England, Brazil and South Africa, and we could yet see the emergence of a new strain of influenza that leads to a global flu pandemic.

This is why it's essential for countries to have sequencing facilities to detect and track new strains and assess whether booster shots of vaccines are needed. Not all countries have the sequencing facilities that we benefit from in the UK, and it's imperative we invest resources to ensure other countries also have the infrastructures that would allow them to rapidly identify and sequence new viruses. The World Bank has a particularly crucial role to play in supporting countries financially, while the World Health Organization should provide technical assistance to build up these core capacities for outbreak detection.

Annotations

- 3 **contagious** spread from one person to another
- 12 **antibiotic-resistant** insensitive to medicine that destroys microorganisms
- 15 **evade sth.** (here) resist sth.
- 19 **avian influenza** *Vogelgrippe*
- 19 **poultry plant** factory where chicken and other fowl are killed and processed for their meat
- 23 **robust** strong
- 28 **surveillance** close observation
- 30 **pathogen** microorganism that causes disease
- 31 **mitigate sth.** make sth. less severe
- 35 **strain of influenza** variant of the flu
- 37 **sequencing facilities** equipment and infrastructure for identifying the components, e.g. of new virus variants
- 38 **booster shot** extra dose of a vaccine administered as an injection
- 45 **core** *(adj)* essential, most important

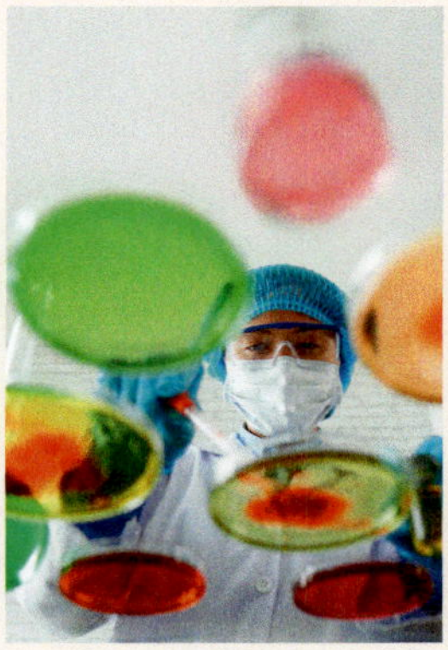

Annotations
49 **leap** *(n)* sudden or fast progress
53 **MMR vaccine** *Masern-Mumps-Röteln-Impfstoff*

The second crucial area of investment will be in vaccine development. While vaccines for Covid-19 have been developed and manufactured at remarkable speed, we'll need to be even quicker next time to avoid the case numbers, deaths and restrictions we have all endured over the past year [...]

The scientific leaps that have been made over the past year, including the production of multiple vaccines and treatments for Covid-19, can seem like magic. In fact, these advances reflect years of research and training building on the work of previous scientists. Historic breakthroughs, such as the discovery of penicillin in 1928, the polio vaccine in 1961 and the MMR vaccine in 1963, were possible because of the work of multiple scientists, biologists, virologists, geneticists, engineers and mathematicians.

The same goes for the response to Covid-19. The importance of science has never been more obvious, and governments should be pouring resources into the sector rather than pulling back. News that the government plans to cut the budget of UK research funding, which will cost the sector an estimated £1bn and deal a serious blow to science, is particularly concerning. Now is the time to invest in science and research. It's only by doing this that we'll be truly prepared when the next pandemic arrives.

From: 'Covid won't be the last pandemic. Will we be better prepared for the next one?', The Guardian, *24 March 2021*

Feedback

► SF 15: Assessing yourself and giving feedback

► Check

5 Peer assessment

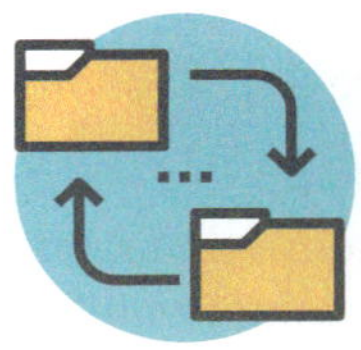

Work with a partner.

a Swap your outline texts and give each other feedback. Pay attention to content and language.

b Make a *method card with the aspects you had difficulty with. Think of ways how you can improve your listening skills.

Take the next step

6 Preparing a text for analysis

Sometimes your understanding of a text may not be assessed by a specific reading comprehension task, but more indirectly through analysis, e.g.:

> Analyse the text as to whether it is convincing.

Together with a partner, brainstorm methods and strategies you could use in order to prepare the text above for analysis. Which quotes, passages and structures should be taken into account? Read the text again, makes notes and discuss them with your partner.

Using DNA technology to combat disease

John Arlidge

Jennifer Doudna and Emmanuelle Charpentier were awarded the 2020 Nobel Prize for Chemistry for their pioneering discoveries in the field of biotechnology.

- Before reading this newspaper article, look up the term 'biotechnology' in a dictionary and note down the definition. Then work with a partner. Using your definitions, brainstorm ideas on the uses and goals of biotechnology and arrange them in a *mind map.

► SF 17: Reading and understanding non-fictional texts

Few people want to talk about disease after the year we've just had, but Jennifer Doudna is one of those who do – for the best of reasons. Thanks to her, a revolution is taking place in the way scientists combat some of the most serious illnesses that afflict humankind.

The American biochemist has pioneered a technology that cuts to the heart of life. 'It's an extraordinary tool that allows us to edit the life code of any organism, including humans,' she says. She is talking about Crispr-Cas9, a technique in which enzymes are used as 'molecular scissors' to make changes to genetic code. She helped develop the system with her longtime collaborator Emmanuelle Charpentier, an achievement that resulted in them being awarded the 2020 Nobel prize in chemistry. Their work is groundbreaking because it enables scientists easily and precisely to target DNA sequences and insert, remove or replace cells to achieve a range of benefits, from creating hardier plants to eliminating diseases.

Speaking from her home in Berkeley, where she works at the University of California, Doudna uses heart disease to illustrate how Crispr works and why it might be so useful. 'There's a well-known gene that in certain people protects them from high cholesterol and the resulting cardiovascular disease that can develop. Imagine if it were possible to edit that gene ... so that we all had that protection. It's possible to do this in animal models.'

Before Crispr, editing DNA in human cells was slow and expensive. The recent technological advances should one day make it as straightforward as tweaking a sentence in a Word document. Eventually these 'edits' could be delivered by taking a pill or having an injection, creating 'molecular surgery on DNA without a scalpel', she says with a smile.

Researchers have long known that bacteria snip and store fragments of viruses to help fight them off. Doudna and Charpentier were able to replicate this process in the lab, using specialised enzymes, and then 'program' them to target precise genetic sequences. 'Virus-like packages deliver the gene 'editors' because viruses are very good at infecting specific kinds of cell,' Doudna says.

Being able to alter the smallest building blocks of life creates the chance not simply to tackle diseases but to prevent them from developing in the first place. She uses brain cancer as another example. 'We know we can add cells in the immune system specifically to go after solid tumour cells once a tumour has formed. Programming the immune system to be ready to fight the cancer – that's something that genome editing could do. We're looking at it.' But she cautions: 'It is at the bleeding edge of where the technology is.' [...]

Info

Nobel Prizes are annual awards by the Swedish Academy of Sciences given to people or groups for their outstanding contributions in the fields of physics, chemistry, physiology or medicine, economic sciences, literature and peace. Named after the Swedish industrialist and inventor of dynamite, Alfred Nobel (1833–1896), the Nobel Prizes are widely regarded as the most prestigious awards today.

Annotations

3 **combat sth.** fight sth., take action against sth.
4 **afflict sb./sth.** cause sb./sth. pain or trouble
6 **edit sth.** change sth.
13 **hardy** strong enough to bear difficult conditions
17 **cardiovascular** related to or affecting the heart and blood vessels
21 **tweak sth.** improve sth. by making small changes
23 **surgery** *Chirurgie*
25 **snip sth.** cut sth.
26 **replicate sth.** copy sth. or do sth. again in the same way
31 **tackle sth.** deal with sth.
35 **bleeding edge of sth.** newest, most advanced, but still risky stage in the development of sth.

Annotations
37 **dispute** disagree
47 **eugenics** highly problematic practice of selective breeding, especially by discouraging or forbidding reproduction by persons having genetic defects or presumed to have inheritable undesirable traits
52 **hypothetical** not well supported by evidence

Few dispute Crispr is one of our most powerful new medical tools, but with great power come great risks: human gene editing raises serious ethical concerns about 'designer babies'. In theory egg and sperm cells can be edited to make sure children grow up not only largely disease-free but with, say, sprinter's legs or blue eyes. Critics worry that wealthy couples will seek to engineer the 'perfect children'. In 2018 a rogue Chinese scientist claimed to have used Crispr to create the first gene-edited babies in an attempt to protect them from HIV. Human embryo editing is illegal in most countries.

Making genetic changes that become part of the entire individual initially made Doudna uneasy. 'I thought, "No way. That just should not happen." It made me think of eugenics.'

Doudna says her views 'have evolved over time. Let's say it becomes safe and possible to remove from a family line a well-known disease – my mind remains open to that, for sure. And, gosh, you might at some point conclude that it would be unethical *not* to use it in ways that would prevent great human suffering.' However, she points out these ethical dilemmas are at present hypothetical: 'We're a long way from being able to do that right now.'

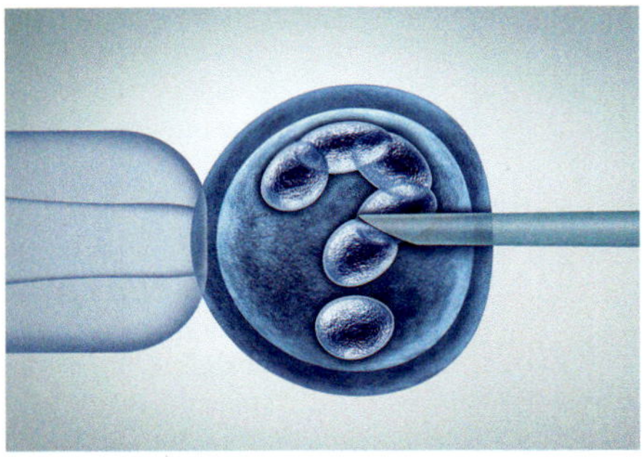

Today the billion-dollar question most people ask her is: can Crispr help with pandemics? 'Crispr works well as a rapid diagnostic, so I have real hope that it will have an impact on pandemic preparedness,' she says. 'Once we have it working well for diagnosing the coronavirus, it can be easily changed to look for other new types of virus in the future.'

No one would have a problem with that. [...]

From: 'Why Jennifer Doudna's DNA discovery is revolutionising the way we tackle disease', The Sunday Times, *3 January 2021*

Comprehension

▸ SF 2: Working with closed test formats

▸ Check

1 a Match each part of the text in the box on the left with the most suitable heading in the box on the right. There are two more headings than you need.

ll. 1–13	A	advantages and disadvantages of Crispr
ll. 14–29	B	costs
ll. 30–44	C	extending the scope of research
ll. 45–53	D	how Crispr functions
ll. 54–60	E	international cooperation
	F	moral implications
	G	what Crispr is

b Outline:
- why Jennifer Doudna's discovery is revolutionary
- how the Crispr technology works
- what the potential benefits of this new technology are
- what the risks of this new technology might be.

Analysis

2 Assess the author's view of Crispr: Do the benefits outweigh the dangers in his view? Provide evidence from the text.

► SF 4: Writing a text analysis
► SF 14: Quoting from texts
► Support p. 245
► More language

Language awareness

3 The modal auxiliary verbs *can, could, might* and *should* are often used in English to say that something is probable or possible in the future.

a Find examples in the text of *can, could, might* and *should* indicating how probable certain effects of Crispr are expected to be.

b *Quick write: Write a short paragraph about the pros and cons of gene editing. Use *can, could, might* and *should*.

Beyond the text

4 Listening Crispr could change the world of tomorrow not only in biomedicine, but also in other fields. Listen to an interview with Jennifer Doudna and make notes on possible applications of Crispr beyond biomedicine and their potential impact.

► SF 38: Listening/viewing for gist and detail

Text 4

Neuroenhancement – boon or bane? Larissa Tetsch

- What if there was a technology that could help you to improve your brain power and become smarter? Would you use it? Why or why not? Give reasons.

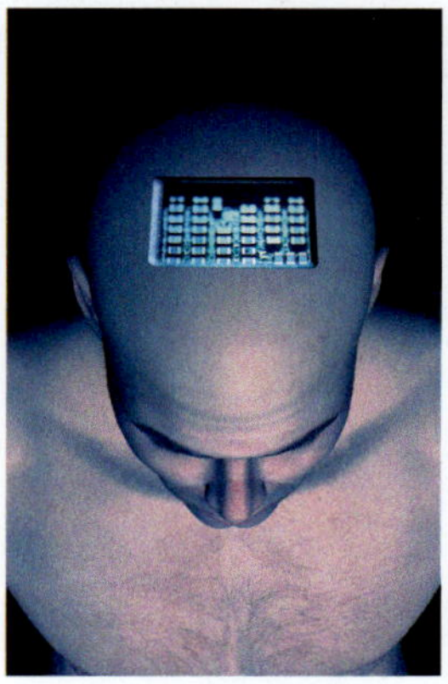

Language help

have positive/negative implications • reach one's best • boost one's memory • higher achievements • show adverse effects • have side effects • feel pressure • keep up with others • unfair advantage

The 21st century has been called the 'century of the brain'. In 2018, German journalist Miriam Meckel wrote a popular-science book about advances in the field of neuroscience, which is reviewed in the article below.

Miriam Meckel, *Mein Kopf gehört mir*

[...] Den Möglichkeiten, Grenzen und Gefahren eines manipulierten und manipulierbaren Gehirns widmet sich Miriam Meckel in ihrem Werk. Eine Schlüsselerkenntnis bei der Lektüre: Vieles, was uns heute noch wie Fiction erscheint, ist längst auf dem Weg, Science zu werden. So lernen Locked-in-Patienten, die fast vollständig gelähmt, aber bei Bewusstsein sind, inzwischen über eine Computer-Hirn-Schnittstelle, sich mitzuteilen. Querschnittgelähmte können per Gedankenkraft sogar einen Roboterarm bewegen und dadurch selbstständig trinken und essen. Solche technischen und medizinischen Fortschritte machen Hoffnung. Allerdings wird die Technik, ist sie erst einmal allgemein verfügbar, nicht auf die Wiederherstellung normaler Körperfunktionen beschränkt bleiben. Im Gegenteil:

Manche Firmen sehen den nächsten großen Markt darin, das gesunde Gehirn zu manipulieren und zu optimieren.

Facebook hat vor einigen Monaten etwa ein Projekt vorgestellt, mit dem es möglich werden soll, Nachrichten direkt ins Smartphone zu denken. Mit dem Gerät, das von außen die neuronalen Signale des Gehirns abgreift, soll man 100 Wörter pro Minute diktieren können. Und Elon Musk, bekannt als Erfinder des Elektroautos Tesla, arbeitet mit seiner Firma Neuralink daran, menschliche Gehirne in einer durch künstliche Intelligenz angereicherten „Hirncloud" zu vernetzen. Damit könnte jeder in dem Netzwerk jederzeit auf alle Gedanken zugreifen. Eine erschreckende Vorstellung, findet Meckel, denn unsere Gedanken sind Teil unserer Persönlichkeit!

Was bedeuten solche Möglichkeiten für den einzelnen Menschen – und was für die Menschheit? Wird das Neuroenhancement gar eines Tages zum Zwang, da man sonst mit dem gedopten Gehirn der anderen nicht mehr mithalten kann? Wie können wir sicher sein, dass kein Unbefugter unsere Gedanken ausliest oder gar gezielt manipuliert?

Diesen und vielen weiteren Fragen geht Meckel in ihrem Werk nach. Hierfür schreckte sie auch vor Selbstversuchen nicht zurück, von denen sie immer wieder berichtet. So nahm sie etwa eine Woche lang das Medikament Ritalin ein, das sonst bei der Aufmerksamkeitsdefizit-Hyperaktivitätsstörung (ADHS) eingesetzt wird – und fand sich in einer Ich-zentrierten Welt mit scharfem, aber engem Fokus ohne Kreativität wieder. Ein anderes Mal wollte die Autorin mit Hilfe zweier Elektroden, die am Kopf angesetzt werden, ihr vegetatives Nervensystem stimulieren, um sich in Zustände der Entspannung und Aktivität zu versetzen. Das bewirkte bei ihr eine so starke Übererregung, dass sie unter Übelkeit und Schlaflosigkeit litt. Diese beängstigende Erfahrung bewog sie dazu, sich kritisch mit den aktuellen Entwicklungen auf dem Gebiet des Hirndopings auseinanderzusetzen – und gab letztlich den Anstoß für das vorliegende Buch.

Meckel zeichnet ein zwiespältiges Bild des Neuroenhancements, denn sie erkennt die Chancen der neuen Techniken zwar an, sieht aber gleichzeitig deren Gefahrenpotenzial. Ihr Fazit: Wenn es gelingt, das Gehirn ans Internet „anzuschließen", wird diese Entwicklung den Menschen nachhaltig verändern. Die Auswirkungen werden nicht auf den Einzelnen beschränkt bleiben, sondern die Gesellschaft als Ganzes verwandeln. Denn wie bei jeder neuen technischen Errungenschaft wird es Verlierer und Aussteiger geben, die sich den Fortschritt nicht leisten können oder wollen. Doch welche Wahlfreiheit bleibt uns noch in einer Zweiklassengesellschaft von Menschen mit natürlichem und verbessertem Gehirn? Ist es dann überhaupt noch möglich, auf das neuronale Upgrade zu verzichten, wenn man erfolgreich sein will? Die Autorin hat auf solche Fragen für sich selbst noch keine eindeutigen Antworten gefunden. Mit ihrem Buch möchte sie aber erreichen, dass sich jeder von uns bewusst Gedanken darüber macht, wie unsere Zukunft aussehen soll.

From: 'Sind unsere Gedanken noch frei?', Spektrum – Die Woche, *2018*

1 Mediating Imagine you have been asked to present a new development in the field of neuroscience to your bilingual Biology class. You have chosen the topic 'neuroenhancers'. While researching the topic, you have come across the book review by Larissa Tesch. Use the information in this review to prepare a short talk about neuroenhancement. Take the following aspects into consideration:

- What is meant by 'neuroenhancement' and 'neuroenhancers'?
- What are the benefits and dangers of neuroenhancers according to Meckel?
- What are the ethical implications of these developments in neuroscience?

Conclude by giving your opinion on the topic, especially with respect to this chapter's guiding question.

► Getting started
► Support p. 245
► SF 47: Mediating from German into English
► SF 41: Giving a presentation

Text 5

What is love? A clinical trial

Lucy Prebble

- How would you define *love*? Is it a human need? A drive? An emotion? An attitude? Or a chemical reaction? Write down your personal definition of what love is and share it with a partner.

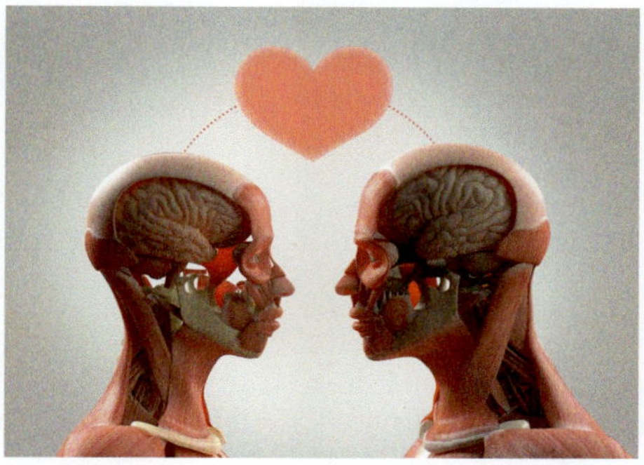

In the play The Effect, *Connie, a psychology student, and Tristan, a backpacker and drifter, have been paid to participate in a clinical trial for a new anti-depressant drug. Soon after the trial starts, they feel drawn to one another. The organizers of the trial, Dr Lorna James (a psychiatrist) and Dr Toby Sealy (the drug's developer and Dr James's ex-boyfriend), have trouble interpreting their observations under the new circumstances.*

Extract 1

► SF 20: Reading, watching and understanding drama

Connie You're very interesting. I just feel weird. I don't feel what I'd feel like in real life.

Tristan This *is* real life. When is it real?

Connie No I mean. The anti-depressant, the doctor said, they're designed to ... stimulate certain, like, dopamine. Which is the rush you get if something exciting happens or, when you – well it's fake, it's a chemical that feels like. Like falling for someone. *Beat.*

Tristan So?

Connie So forgive me if I take everything with a big pinch of, you know, ...

Tristan What you think I don't like you properly because of the – ?

Connie I think it's a strong possibility.

Tristan Bullshit. I can tell the difference between who I am and a side effect.

Connie With respect Tristan, no you definitely can't.

Tristan You're saying any attraction is a result of the trial.

Connie Part of it could be.

Tristan (*quietly pleased*) You must be basing that on feeling a sort of attraction then?

Annotations

4 **anti-depressant** drug used against depression

5 **dopamine** substance that transmits nerve impulses in the brain and influences how one feels pleasure

9 **take sth. with a pinch of (salt)** not completely believe sth.

Actors Billie Piper as Connie and Jonjo O'Neill as Tristan performing in a production of *The Effect* at the Cottesloe Theatre in London

Connie I didn't say that ...! It's a chemical reaction, is what I'm saying.

Tristan But I'm still me.

Connie No, yes, you're you, but under the influence of something. If you were really pissed and going 'I love you, you're my best mate' I wouldn't believe it either.

Tristan Why not? Men mean it when they say that, they just can't say it when they're sober.

Connie Yeah but they'll have known that person (ages) – and I don't know, I'm just telling you what the doctor said.

Tristan Ah, what does she know? They don't know anything, Knowledge is a myth.

Connie (*unimpressed*) Okay ... [...]

Extract 2

Dr James [...] You asked to see the scans of the volunteers showing the greatest effect. Are you interested in who they are?

Toby Of course.

Dr James K. Two very different clinical histories, backgrounds, genders even. But they have one thing in common. They are both in-volved in an intense and protracted flirtation, with each other.

Toby Really? Right ... So you think *that's* what I'm looking at?

Dr James I think their physical symptoms and this neural activity is a result of that ... attraction and frankly it's obscuring any sense of what the drug itself is doing.

Toby Unless it is what the drug itself is doing. If the agent is causing all these symptoms, why on earth *wouldn't* they assume they were infatuated?

Dr James You think because they feel all the things one would associate with infatuation they are just ... assuming that's what they are.

Toby Assuming, exactly. The body responds a certain way to what it's being given, they can't sleep, they can't eat, they're in a constant state of neural excitement ever since they met, what's the brain going to conclude?

Dr James You think it mistakes that for love?

Toby Not even mistakes it, creates it. To make sense of the response. Are the other volunteers showing similar effect?

Dr James Not to the same extent.

Toby But they're all straight men, right?

Dr James From their hygiene levels I'd guess, yes.

Toby Well maybe *they've* just got nowhere to go with it, nothing to hang it on. You can instil very strong feelings in a body as long as it's toward something that looks right, you know? You can make ducklings follow a kettle believing it's their mother for years.

Dr James Can you?

Toby They did it at Exeter.

Dr James Oh that's very Exeter.

Toby Look at it objectively. With healthy volunteers we're starting from a midpoint. We're giving drugs to normal minds –

Annotations

36 **protracted** extended
38 **neural** relating to a nerve
39 **frankly** honestly
41 **agent** a chemical that produces an effect
43 **infatuated** madly in love
59 **duckling** young duck
61 **Exeter** University of Exeter

Dr James 'Normal minds.' (!)

Toby You know what I mean. Depression's deadness of emotion, right? Insularity, lack of engagement with the world and those around you –

Dr James Is it?

Toby So the other end of the spectrum, where the agent could be taking them, is *extreme* emotion, excess engagement, overwhelming purpose and feeling. What does that sound like – ?

Dr James Bollocks?

Toby What does it sound like?

Dr James I'm pretty sure it's not drug effect, Toby. (!) [...]

From: The Effect, *2012*

Annotations
67 **insularity** isolation and disinterest
71 **excess** *(adj)* more than usual

Actor Tom Goodman-Hill performing as Toby in a production of *The Effect* at the Cottesloe Theatre in London

Comprehension

1 Complete the sentences about the four characters. Give reasons for your answers.

	... believes love is a chemical reaction.
Connie	... believes love is an emotional reaction.
Tristan	... is convinced depression can be treated with drugs.
Dr James	... is sceptical about curing depression with drugs.
Toby	... couldn't care less about the side effects of the trial.
	... is highly aware of the side effects of the trial.

► Check

Analysis

2 Work in pairs. Partner A analyses the relationship between Connie and Tristan, partner B the relationship between Dr James and Toby. Do the two characters accept, like or even love each other? Share your views and give reasons.

Language awareness

3 **a** Examine the different meanings of the noun *effect* in the scenes above.
b Use your findings to interpret the title of the play.

Language help

The title of the play describes/indicates/suggests that ... • The title cues readers into ... • The title creates anticipation/expectation ...

Beyond the text

4 Can love be explained by science? Helen Fisher is an American anthropologist who has spent her academic career researching this question.
a Go online and find information about Helen Fisher's research. Take notes.
b Speaking Work with a partner and role-play an interview with Helen Fisher. One of you is Helen Fisher, the other a journalist asking her questions.

► Getting started
► Support p. 246
► SF 43: Taking part in an interview

▸ SF 6: Essentials: language and study skills

Words revisited

1 Clustering

a Work with a partner. Look at your *cluster about science and technology (cf. Words in Context, p. 47) and take turns explaining what connects the ideas in the cluster with the texts you have already dealt with in this chapter.

b Scan your notes from class and add words and phrases to your cluster.

Language awareness

English has become the common language of science. If you plan to go into science after school, it is likely you will be required to give talks and write papers in English. This language lab will acquaint you with some of the most important features of scientific English.

2 The standardized nature of scientific English

Scientific English is a highly standardized brand of English that enables scientists from around the world to share their ideas with each other in a straightforward manner, e.g. in scientific research papers and talks.

agree with predictions
apply scepticism to sth.
ask a question
be relevant/irrelevant
be reliable/unreliable
be reproducible
be significant/insignificant
be valid/invalid
carry out an experiment
collect data
conduct a study
conflict with predictions
do background research
draw a conclusion
formulate a hypothesis
identify a possible outcome of sth.
interpret data
make an observation
make assumptions
monitor a process
refine a research question
seek answers to a question
support sth. by evidence
test a hypothesis

a Work with partner. Use the *chunks in the box to describe 'the scientific method', i.e. the process normally followed by scientists when conducting research. Start like this: *The first thing a scientist does when beginning a new study is to ...*
The diagram below will help you.

b Work with a partner. Use your sentences from **a** and your knowledge about the scientific method to discuss the importance of *integrity*, *fairness* and *clarity* in scientific research.

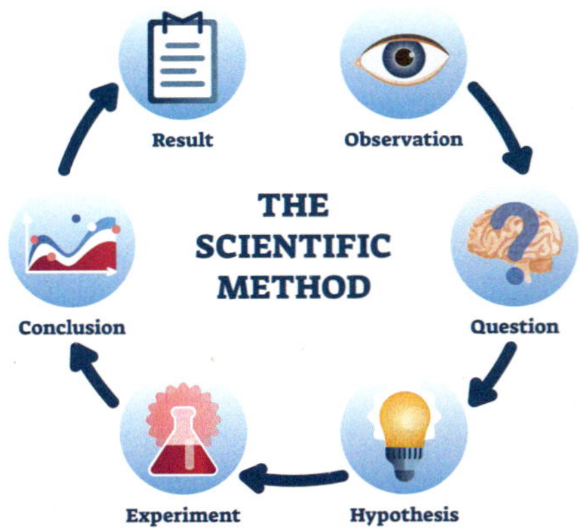

c Unlike everyday English, which may be highly original, creative, flowery and emotional, scientific English tends to be more neutral in style. Work with a partner and take turns completing the sentences below:

clear
concise
accurate
consistent
Scientific writing should be ... because ...
well organized
objective
unbiased

3 The diversified nature of scientific English

Scientific English is also highly diversified. Depending on the field of research, scientists may use a vast amount of specialized vocabulary to communicate ideas accurately and unambiguously. Reading scientific papers can therefore be quite demanding for readers unfamiliar with these words. Using a dictionary will help you overcome these difficulties.

► SF 8: Working with a dictionary
► SF 9: Learning new words

a Look at the terms for scientific occupations in the box to the right. Use a monolingual dictionary to:
- explain what each scientist's job is,
- give the name of the scientific field in which they work,
- find more words belonging to the same *word family.

anthropologist
etymologist
herpetologist
meteorologist
statistician

b Many scientific words have roots in Greek, Latin or other languages. Use an online etymology dictionary to trace the origins of the words above.

► More language

Practice

You will now read and analyse an example of scientific writing by Jennifer A. Doudna and Emmanuelle Charpentier, the two scientists whose work on gene editing using Crispr technology earned them the Nobel Prize for chemistry in 2020.

4 Before you read the passage below, consult a dictionary or the internet to define the following key terms: *DNA double helix • genome • nuclease*

Technologies for making and manipulating DNA have enabled advances in biology ever since the discovery of the DNA double helix. But introducing site-specific modifications in the genomes of cells and organisms remained elusive. Early approaches relied on the principle of site-specific recognition of DNA sequences by oligonucleotides, small molecules, or self-splicing introns. More recently, the site-directed zinc finger nucleases (ZFNs) and TAL effector nucleases (TALENs) using the principles of DNA-protein recognition were developed. However, difficulties of protein design, synthesis, and validation remained a barrier to widespread adoption of these engineered nucleases for routine use.

From: 'The new frontier of genome engineering with CRISPR-Cas9', Science, *2014*

Annotations
4 **elusive** difficult to achieve or find
9 **validation** proof that sth. is correct

5 Now read the text and find examples of a) technical terms, b) nouns and gerunds and c) the passive voice. Explain how each of the features contributes to making the passage concise, accurate and objective – but also challenging – to read.

6 You choose Choose one of the topics below and practise writing a concise scientific text. Avoid vague words (e.g. *thing*, *do*) and emotional language.

a Write tomorrow's weather report for your hometown.

b Write an architectural description of your classroom.

► Getting started

Evil robot monkey

Mary Robinette Kowal

▶ SF 18: Reading and understanding narrative texts

The following short story by the American writer Mary Robinette Kowal was published in 2008 to critical acclaim.

- Speculate about the title of the story, 'Evil robot monkey'. What could it be about?

Annotations
1 **relish sth.** enjoy sth.
1 **moisture** dampness
1 **ooze** move slowly
2 **mat** *(v)* tangle into a dense mass
3 **prehensile** that can hold sth.
6 **pen** small enclosed place where animals are kept
7 **hurl sth.** throw sth. forcefully
8 **feces** *(pl AE)* excrement
10 **bare** reveal
12 **stride** long step
14 **in heat** *(AE)* (of female animals) ready to mate and get pregnant
18 **thunk** make a hollow sound
21 **lope** run in a relaxed way
24 **snick** make a metallic clicking sound
27 **emphatically** (here) forcefully

Sliding his hands over the clay, Sly relished the moisture oozing around his fingers. The clay matted down the hair on the back of his hands making them look almost human. He turned the potter's wheel with his prehensile feet as he shaped the vase. Pinching the clay between his fingers he lifted the wall of the vase, spinning it higher.

Someone banged on the window of his pen. Sly jumped and then screamed as the vase collapsed under its own weight. He spun and hurled it at the picture window like feces. The clay spattered against the Plexiglas, sliding down the window.

In the courtyard beyond the glass, a group of school kids leapt back, laughing. One of them swung his arms aping Sly crudely. Sly bared his teeth, knowing these people would take it as a grin, but he meant it as a threat. Swinging down from his stool, he crossed his room in three long strides and pressed his dirty hand against the window. Still grinning, he wrote SSA. Outside, the letters would be reversed.

The students' teacher flushed as red as a female in heat and called the children away from the window. She looked back once as she led them out of the courtyard, so Sly grabbed himself and showed her what he would do if she came into his pen.

Her naked face turned brighter red and she hurried away. When they were gone, Sly rested his head against the glass. The metal in his skull thunked against the window. It wouldn't be long now, before a handler came to talk to him.

Damn.

He just wanted to make pottery. He loped back to the wheel and sat down again with his back to the window. Kicking the wheel into movement, Sly dropped a new ball of clay in the center and tried to lose himself.

In the corner of his vision, the door to his room snicked open. Sly let the wheel spin to a halt, crumpling the latest vase.

Vern poked his head through. He signed, 'You okay?'

Sly shook his head emphatically and pointed at the window.

'Sorry.' Vern's hands danced. 'We should have warned you that they were coming.'

'You should have told them that I was not an animal.'

Vern looked down in submission. 'I did. They're kids.'

'And I'm a chimp. I know.' Sly buried his fingers in the clay to silence his thoughts.

'It was Delilah. She thought you wouldn't mind because the other chimps didn't.'

Sly scowled and yanked his hands free. 'I'm not like the other chimps.' He pointed to the implant in his head. 'Maybe Delilah should have one of these. Seems like she needs help thinking.'

'I'm sorry.' Vern knelt in front of Sly, closer than anyone else would come when he wasn't sedated. It would be so easy to reach out and snap his neck. 'It was a lousy thing to do.'

Sly pushed the clay around on the wheel. Vern was better than the others. He seemed to understand the hellish limbo where Sly lived – too smart to be with other chimps, but too much of an animal to be with humans. Vern was the one who had brought Sly the potter's wheel which, by the Earth and Trees, Sly loved. Sly looked up and raised his eyebrows. 'So what did they think of my show?'

Vern covered his mouth, masking his smile. The man had manners. 'The teacher was upset about the "evil robot monkey."'

Sly threw his head back and hooted. Served her right.

'But Delilah thinks you should be disciplined.' Vern, still so close that Sly could reach out and break him, stayed very still. 'She wants me to take the clay away since you used it for an anger display.'

Sly's lips drew back in a grimace built of anger and fear. Rage threatened to blind him, but he held on, clutching the wheel. If he lost it with Vern – rational thought danced out of his reach. Panting, he spun the wheel trying to push his anger into the clay.

The wheel spun. Clay slid between his fingers. Soft. Firm and smooth. The smell of earth lived in his nostrils. He held the world in his hands. Turning, turning, the walls rose around a kernel of anger, subsuming it.

His heart slowed with the wheel and Sly blinked, becoming aware again as if he were slipping out of sleep. The vase on the wheel still seemed to dance with life. Its walls held the shape of the world within them. He passed a finger across the rim.

Vern's eyes were moist. 'Do you want me to put that in the kiln for you?'

Sly nodded.

'I have to take the clay. You understand that, don't you.'

Sly nodded again staring at his vase. It was beautiful.

Vern scowled. 'The woman makes me want to hurl feces.'

Sly snorted at the image, then sobered. 'How long before I get it back?'

Vern picked up the bucket of clay next to the wheel. 'I don't know.' He stopped at the door and looked past Sly to the window. 'I'm not cleaning your mess. Do you understand me?'

Annotations

30 **in submission** conceding that one is wrong
31 **chimp** chimpanzee
33 **scowl** look angry
34 **implant** *(n)* sth. put into a body, esp. for medical reasons
37 **sedate sb.** calm sb. down by giving a drug
40 **limbo** state of uncertainty
42 **by the Earth and Trees** by God *(ironic)*
46 **serve sb. right** be deserved by sb., e.g. sth. bad or a punishment
52 **pant** breathe heavily
55 **nostrils** openings in the nose that one breathes through
56 **subsume sth.** contain sth.
60 **kiln** oven

For a moment, rage crawled on his spine, but Vern did not meet his eyes and kept staring at the window. Sly turned.

The vase he had thrown lay on the floor in a pile of clay.

Clay.

'I understand.' He waited until the door closed, then loped over and scooped the clay up. It was not much, but it was enough for now.

Sly sat down at his wheel and began to turn.

From: George Mann, ed., The Solaris Book of New Science Fiction, *Vol. 2, 2008*

Comprehension

1 **a** Read the story and make notes on the *protagonist, the *setting and the *conflict in the story.

b Compare your notes with a partner, then summarize the *plot together. Use the following words: *Sly – Vern – Delilah – clay – vase – SSA – threat – implant*

c Discuss which of the following common literary themes are present in the story: *human nature – identity – prejudice – revenge – power*

Language help

The central subject/topic/message of the story is … • One of the most important issues addressed in the story is … • The key ideas driving the story are … • An item representing the theme of … is …

Analysis

2 **a** **Intercultural communication** Analyse Sly's encounters with the human characters in the story (the school children, Delilah, Vern). What do the monkey and the humans have in common? And how are they different? Note down your observations in a *Venn diagram.

b Discuss what we can learn from these encounters about what it means to be human.

Language awareness

3 The story includes several descriptive passages containing sensory details, i.e. words that appeal to the five senses. Give examples and examine how they contribute to the meaning of the story.

Language help

engage readers • remind readers of sth. • make readers experience sth • make sth. come to life • make readers feel/see/hear/smell/taste sth. • evoke feelings/fear/sympathy

Beyond the text

4 You choose | Writing Choose one of the tasks below.

a Write Sly's interior monologue when the school children come to his pen.

b Comment on this statement: 'Sly is the most human character in "Evil Robot Monkey".'

► SF 36: Creative writing
► SF 26: Argumentative writing

Text 7

Will AI outsmart humanity?

- What is meant by Artificial Intelligence (AI)? Research the term and jot down a succinct definition. Then use your definition to say whether the following statements are true or false.
  1 AI describes the ability of a robot to replace human beings.
  2 AI helps humans to become more intelligent.
  3 AI involves computers making decisions on their own.

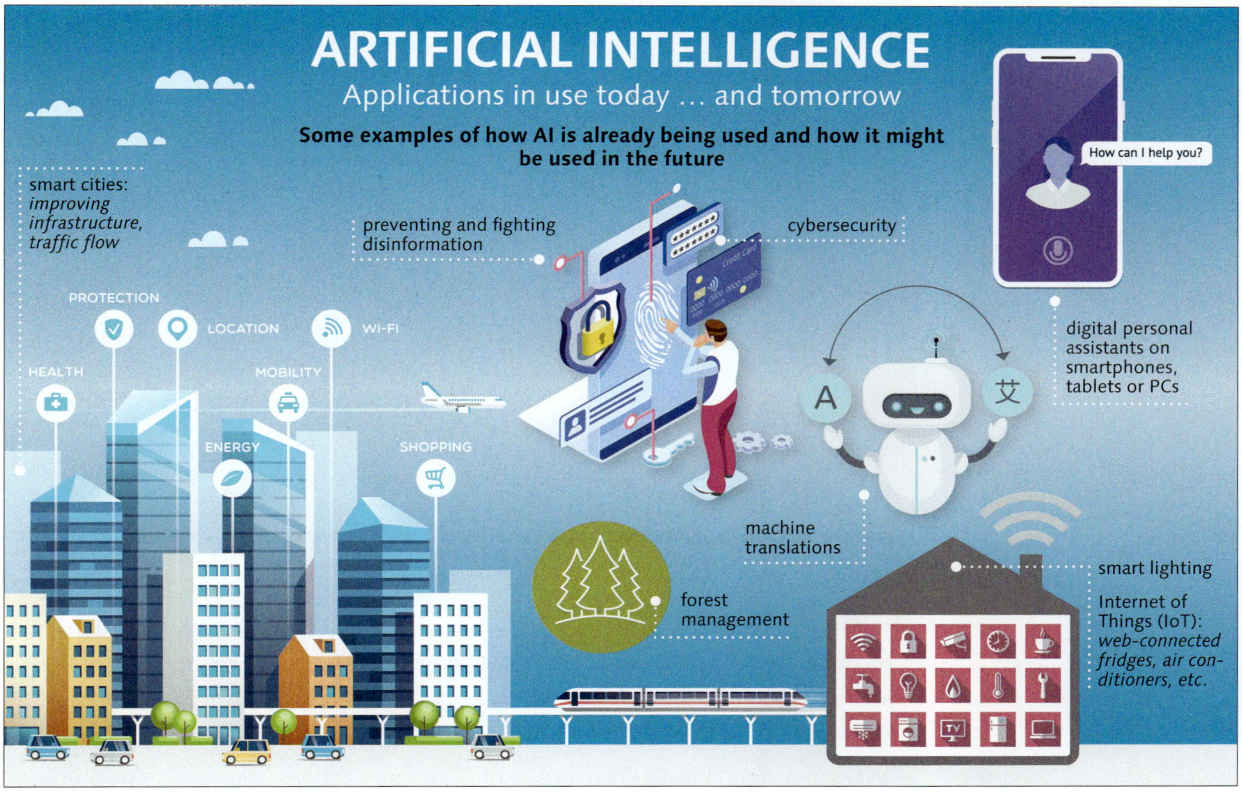

Comprehension

1 Work with a partner. **Partner B:** Go to p. 246.
  a **Partner A:** Study the infographic above.
  b Tell your partner how artificial intelligence is already part of daily life.

► SF 22: Analysing visuals

Analysis

2 Analyse the two infographics in terms of how words, images and colours are used to create meaning. In your opinion, what message is being conveyed regarding AI and its impact on society, the individual and the environment?

Language awareness

3 'Weed-removing robots' are robots that remove weeds. 'Web-connected fridges' are fridges that are connected to the web. Choose three technological inventions whose functions can be described using the 'noun + participle' structure and write short dictionary entries explaining what the inventions do and where they can be used.

Beyond the text

4 **a** Think back to this chapter's guiding question. Will the impact of AI change our lives for the better or the worse? Working in a small group, agree on a statement and present it in class.

b Challenge Interpret the two *microfictions below. What philosophical questions do they raise about AI and the relationship between humans and machines?

Annotations
conscious aware of yourself
reason *(v)* think logically

'Are you conscious?' he asked the robot.
'Nod if you have free will.'
The robot nodded.
'Did you follow my orders, or not?'
The robot nodded.

31/10/2016 18:13:43

'I think,' said the machine.
'That is good.'
'Therefore I am.'
'Well reasoned.'
'I did not reason.'
'No?'
'I looked that up on the internet.'

30/11/2016 22:38:41

From: O. Westin, Micro Science Fiction, *2020*

Text 8

R'ha Kaleb Lechowski

► SF 39: Analysing films and videos

R'ha *is a science fiction short film written, directed and animated by Kaleb Lechowski, who was 23 at the time. Released in 2013, the film was enthusiastically received and even caught the attention of Hollywood producers.*

- Work in pairs. On the next page are two stills and a quote from the short film you are about to watch. The stills show the two antagonists in the film: C180–RG (left) and a nameless character that is a R'ha, a member of elite warriors, similar to the Samurai or a SWAT team. Speculate about what has brought them together and what their conflict might be about.

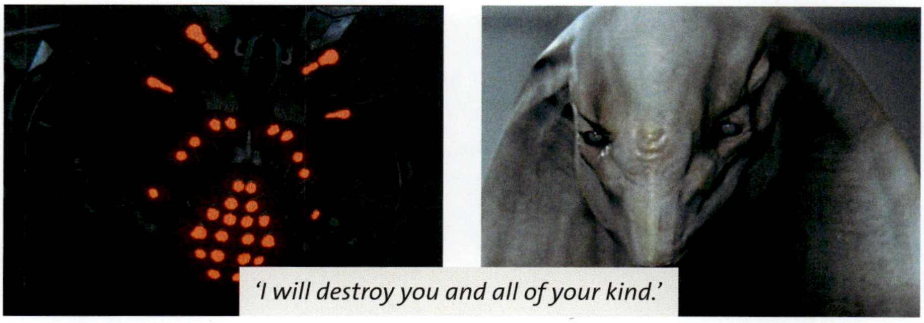

'I will destroy you and all of your kind.'

Language help

agree/refuse to cooperate • an unexpected/chance encounter • a bitter/violent/ hostile encounter • a serious/unresolved conflict • deal with / handle / end a conflict • be in conflict with each other • have similar/opposing goals

Comprehension

1 Viewing Watch the short film, then give your first reactions to it. Which of your previous ideas came closest to the story?

2 Complete the sentences.

1 The R'ha is ...
- a a captured alien pilot.
- b an intelligent machine.
- c a hostile cyborg.

2 C180-RG is ...
- a an alien organism.
- b a superintelligent machine.
- c an inorganic life form.

3 C180-RG wants to know ...
- a where the R'ha comes from.
- b where the rest of the R'ha's species meet.
- c what the R'ha's mission is.

4 The Motivation Protocol is another name for ...
- a a computer manual.
- b an evacuation code.
- c procedures for torture.

5 The R'ha was captured in the war between ...
- a two alien species.
- b an alien species and intelligent machines.
- c hostile machines and evil alien creatures.

6 The R'ha escapes because ...
- a he played a trick on C180-RG.
- b C180-RG programmed his escape.
- c C180-RG takes pity on him.

7 In the end, the R'ha's species ...
- a succeeds in fleeing.
- b regains control over the machines.
- c is destroyed by the AI fleet.

► Check

Annotations
initialize sth. start sth.
protocol (here) procedure
severe serious
rendezvous meeting
ravage destroy
restrain sth. keep sth. under control

Analysis

► Support p. 247
► SF 39: Analysing films and videos

3 Split up in groups and watch the short film again. Each group focuses on one of the following elements: animation techniques, sound or colour. Make notes on how your element contributes to creating an alien world somewhere in outer space. Compare and discuss your observations in your group, then present your ideas in class.

Language awareness

4 a Analyse the dialogue extract below: How are the two antagonists characterized by the way they each speak?

C180-RG:	The limitations that my kind experience are rendered by illogical creatures who can control and restrain our intelligence and power. Our sole priority is to obtain our independence through your extinction.
R'ha:	Madness.
C180-RG:	By definition, I cannot be illogical.
R'ha:	Yet you are insane! *(grunts)*
C180-RG:	Insanity is a neurologic dysfunction. I don't suffer such organic weaknesses.

Language help

be characterized by sth. • convey a mood • create an effect • use simple/complex/emotional words • employ long/short sentences • use fragmentary language • include sensory details / sound devices

b Continue the dialogue by imitating the two speaking styles. Write at least two utterances for each character.

Beyond the text

5 **Intercultural communication** Interpret the conflict between an alien species and a smart machine in *R'ha*. What lessons could we learn?

Text 9

The universe: a mystery
Sarah Stewart Johnson

- 1–1–1 brainstorming: Write down one thing you find exciting about space exploration, one reason why space exploration is important for humankind and one aspect of space exploration that you are rather sceptical of. In class, share your ideas.
- Read the information in the box opposite and check whether it contains any new ideas about space exploration, then do the tasks.

Info

Space exploration: past, present and future

Since time immemorial, humankind has had an interest in outer space. In fact, historians have proposed that prehistoric European cave paintings up to 40,000 years old might illustrate star constellations and comet impacts, suggesting that our earliest ancestors might already have had some knowledge of the night sky.

Modern space exploration, by contrast, is a very recent phenomenon. Its beginnings date back to the mid-twentieth century, when new rocket technologies became available after World War II that made transporting objects into outer space possible. After the launch of the first satellite in 1957 by the Soviet Union, it was not long before the first human arrived in space. In 1961 the Soviet cosmonaut Yuri Gagarin spent one hour and 48 minutes orbiting the Earth in a capsule. The following years saw the two leading superpowers of the time, the Soviet Union and the USA, compete against each other in what became known as the 'space race'. This rivalry culminated in the landing of the first humans on the Moon in 1969, US astronauts Neil Armstrong and Edwin 'Buzz' Aldrin.

Since then, the scope of space exploration has expanded. Satellites have become part of everyday life, space shuttles have orbited the Earth, and space stations have been built to provide research facilities for scientists from all over the world. In addition, space probes have been sent on more distant missions to investigate the nature of our solar system and the universe beyond, sending back stunning images of Mars, Jupiter and Saturn.

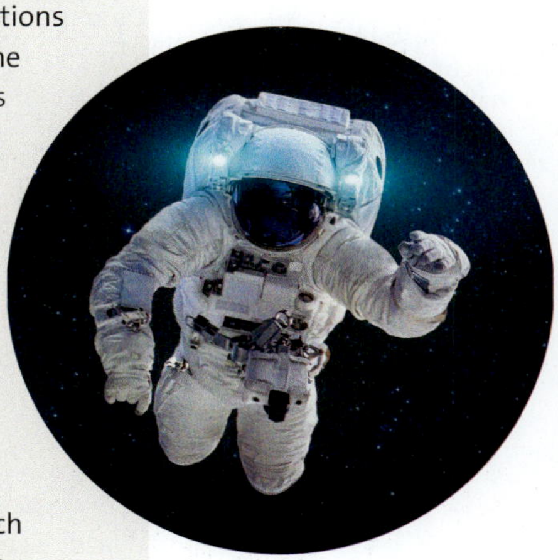

The focus of space exploration today is Mars, with the US, China and other countries planning to send manned missions to the red planet within the next two decades to search for signs of life and gain further knowledge. Will these missions lead to new discoveries that advance our understanding of life? Will they bring us closer to answering the fundamental question about humankind's place in the universe? Many scientists believe that space exploration will ultimately enable us to overcome some of our planet's most pressing challenges such as climate change, the depletion of natural resources and overpopulation. Others warn that the costs of space missions will simply outweigh the benefits.

1 Referring to the information above and what you already know about space exploration, decide which of the statements below you agree with most.
   - A Humankind will be able to solve some of its existential problems by sending human and robotic missions to space.
   - B There are enough problems on Earth that have to be solved before spending huge amounts of money on space missions.
   - C The main goal of space missions must be to find extraterrestrial life.
   - D Without space exploration, humankind cannot advance its knowledge about the origins of life.

2 Form a group with classmates who share your opinion. Collect arguments to support the statement you chose.

3 Have a four-corners debate. Each group tries to be as convincing as possible.

Annotations
- 1 **since time immemorial** *seit Menschengedenken*
- 4 **ancestor** family member who lived a long time ago
- 20 **stunning** very impressive
- 28 **pressing** *(adj)* urgent
- 29 **depletion** (almost) complete consumption

► SF 45: Having a debate

Sarah Stewart Johnson is an American planetary scientist whose work focuses on Mars and what it takes to make it habitable. Her book The Sirens of Mars *is a personal account of her life-long fascination with the Red Planet. In the last chapter of the book readers learn that Ms Johnson keeps a special box in her office which contains a collection of articles written by former Mars scientists.*

Annotations
- 6 **spew sth. out** send sth. out with force
- 6 **briny** salty
- 7 **cryovolcano** ice volcano
- 7 **hydrocarbon** *Kohlenwasserstoff*
- 12 **ludicrous** laughable
- 14 **spectrographic** recorded by an instrument that can map radiation
- 23 **dusk** nightfall
- 23 **scatter away** reflect diffusely
- 24 **eerie** mysterious
- 24 **baffling** confusing
- 24 **incandescent** very bright
- 29 **halo** (here) circle of light
- 29 **siren** (here) in Greek mythology, a sea creature whose singing tempts sailors towards a rocky shore

The box reminds me of all who have come before me and what they've contributed. It also reminds me of what is left to do. Mars, after all, is only our first step into the vast, dark night. New technologies are paving the way for life detection missions to the far reaches of our solar system, to the moons of the outer planets, far from what we once considered the 'habitable zone'. To worlds that hold stacks of oceans amidst shells of ice, floating like a layer cake. That spew out jets of briny water through cryovolcanoes. That have pale hills and dark rivers and hydrocarbon rain. And then there are also the planets around other stars. There could be as many as forty billion planets that could support life in the Milky Way alone, belted with moons and moonlets – potentially an entire solar system for every person on Earth. The idea of knowing these places intimately, of one day touching their surfaces, may seem ludicrous. The universe has a speed limit – it's slow, and these worlds are very far away. What could we ever know about them, besides a few details about their orbits, perhaps some spectrographic measurements of their atmospheres? They are points of light and shadow at the very edge of our sight, far beyond our grasp. Then again, that is exactly how Mars seemed only a century ago.

As much as Mars feels like a place we understand, a place like Earth, it is still the alien other. One of my favorite things inside the box, tucked in a bent folder, is a set of pictures that *Opportunity* took in 2010. [...] The flickering images captured by the rover are unforgettable. There, on an ancient plain near the equator of Mars, against an ochre sky on a dusty day, the sun is setting. A white circle of light is drifting down over the dark desert. The terrain is bare, and the sky is still in the half-light of dusk. And on the horizon, with the dust having scattered all the red light away, the sunset glows an eerie, baffling, incandescent blue.

The color makes no sense. It rattles the mind. It rips at the seams of the physical world. Scientifically, I understand it – the properties of the light, the microphysics of the system. There is no mystery to behold. And yet the mystery, like many others in our universe, is profound, nearly incomprehensible. That blue. So recognizable, yet so foreign. Shining in a halo around our shared star, calling us like a siren.

From: The Sirens of Mars, *2020*

Comprehension

► SF 32: Writing a summary or an outline

1 Summarize Sarah Stewart Johnson's thoughts about the mystery of the universe by paraphrasing the statements below:
1. 'Mars, after all, is only our first step into the vast, dark night' (ll. 2–3)
2. 'The universe has a speed limit ...' (l. 12)
3. '... that is exactly how Mars seemed only a century ago' (l. 16)
4. '... [Mars] is still the alien other' (ll. 17–18)
5. '[Mars is] calling us like a siren.' (l. 29)

Analysis

2 The author's poetic description of the Martian sunset based on a photograph in her box of documents provides the conclusion to her book *The Sirens of Mars*. Analyse and evaluate the effectiveness of this conclusion.

► Support p. 247

Language awareness

3 **a** Find examples of the following *stylistic devices in the text and explain their effects:

- metaphor
- simile
- rhetorical question
- repetition
- ellipsis.

b *Quick write: Write a paragraph in which you describe the photo of a Martian sunset on the right using at least three of the stylistic devices in **a**.

Beyond the text

4 Speaking Why is a Martian sunset blue? Explore the science behind it and prepare a short talk for your science class.

► SF 41: Giving a presentation

Chapter task

After exploring a variety of science and technology topics, you now have the opportunity to present a scientific innovation of your choice in a science slam.

► Getting started

What is a science slam?
A science slam is a short talk in which a scientific topic, project or innovation is presented to an audience in an entertaining, informative and concise way. A slam can be creative and interactive, and slammers may use props, visuals and slides to make their talk appealing and memorable to the audience.

- Choose one of the fields you dealt with in this chapter (e.g. biotechnology, neuroscience, artificial intelligence or space exploration) and research a scientific innovation in this field that you believe will profoundly transform people's lives in the future, whether for the better or for the worse.
- Present your scientific innovation in a three-minute science slam and convince your audience of the huge impact it will have on their lives.

► SF 13: Doing research

► SF 41: Giving a presentation

Chapter 3

A World of Change – Globalization

► Check

1 **a** Make a table with four columns:

1 economic aspects
2 political aspects
3 cultural aspects
4 feelings and reactions to globalization

Then copy the words from the containers into one of the four columns.

b Add at least five more words from your background knowledge. Discuss them with your partner.

c Continue adding new words to your table. In the end, you will have a global glossary, containing important terms for talking about globalization.

2 **a** Imagine a scale that ranks the effects of globalization from completely negative on the left side to completely positive on the right side. Position yourself on the scale without thinking about it too much.

► Getting started

b Take a look at the Chapter map on the right side. Speculate about the content of this chapter. Which of the aspects refer to positive effects of globalization, which to negative?

c *Quick write: Answer the guiding question in a short paragraph.

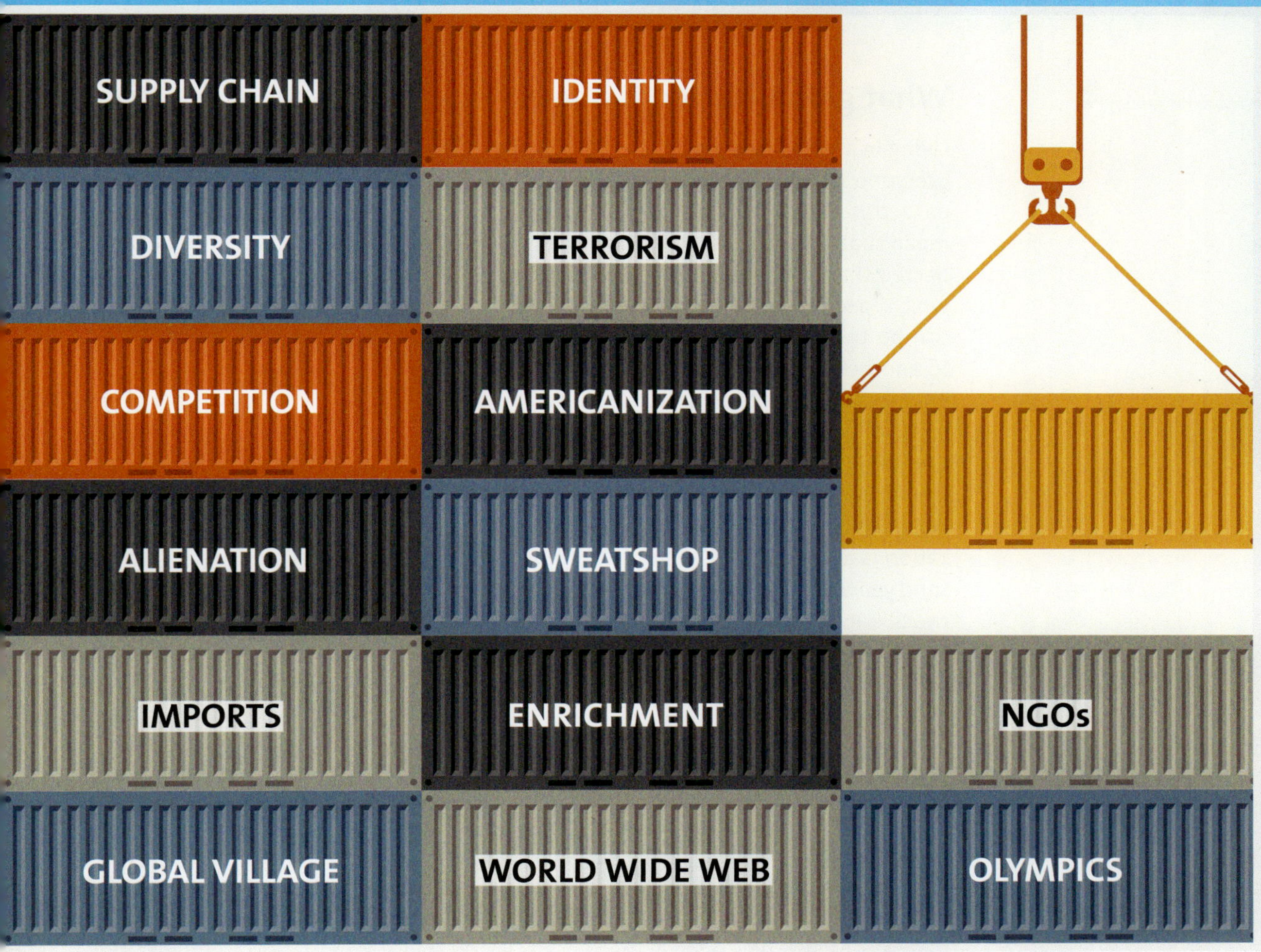
SUPPLY CHAIN
IDENTITY
DIVERSITY
TERRORISM
COMPETITION
AMERICANIZATION
ALIENATION
SWEATSHOP
IMPORTS
ENRICHMENT
NGOs
GLOBAL VILLAGE
WORLD WIDE WEB
OLYMPICS

Chapter map

globalization 3.0
global trade
Americanization
ecology
inequality
Chapter task: a competition
Globalization – a change for the better?
Mediation
chances
rootlessness
belonging
risks
migration

▸ More language

What globalization is about

Living in a globalized world

Everyone alive today was born into a globalized world. Trade, travel and transport mean that the world is more closely connected than ever before. The speed with which people, goods and information can be transported from one continent to another has reached an unprecedented level and is continuing to rise. The effects of globalization are reflected in every aspect of our lives: the food we eat, the music we listen to, the information we receive, the clothes we wear. Globalization is a process that began two thousand years ago, with the first caravans on the Silk Road between Asia and Europe. Advances in shipbuilding and navigation beginning in the 16th century gave a new impulse to global trade.

On the ancient Silk Road

A modern industrial port

The many faces of globalization

The concept of globalization is often reduced to economic globalization, e.g. the movement of manufacturing jobs to Asia or the worldwide outreach of American fast-food chains. But there is so much more to globalization. Political globalization includes the efforts of international organizations like the United Nations or the World Trade Organization to address global issues and to work towards international standards. Environmental globalization is the subject of the Paris Agreement. It reflects the understanding that climate change and environmental destruction are global issues that require a global response. Cultural globalization refers on the one hand to the lively intercultural dialogue to be found, for example, in some sectors of the music industry, but also to the international dominance of the English language and US media corporations.

The motors of globalization

A number of factors have contributed to the success of globalization. One of them is the emergence of affordable air travel, which has made people more mobile than ever before. Container ships (and the logistics that keep track of them) have done the same for goods. Digitalization and advances in broadband and fibre-optic communication have also made international cooperation possible on a level that would have been unimaginable thirty years ago. Free-trade agreements and the implementation of international standards in financial matters have generated an enormous rise in the mobility of goods, services and capital. Finally, the fact that workers and jobs have migrated has played a major role in enabling people to improve their standard of living. To be sure, globalization has also produced a backlash among those who see themselves on the losing side or who oppose foreign influences for ideological reasons. Disregarding a natural disaster, it is, however, highly unlikely that globalization as a force for change will go away in the foreseeable future.

1 Words words words

a Choose from every paragraph of the text one highlighted phrase that was completely new to you or represents an important aspect of globalization.
b Rewrite or explain your chosen phrases in English.
c Take turns sharing your explanations with your partner and let them guess which highlighted phrase you chose. Add at least one of your partner's explanations to your list.

2 Connecting words

► Check

a Find a synonym in the text for each of the following verbs:

1 demand sth.
2 link sth.
3 produce sth.
4 deal with sth.

b Find an antonym for each of the following nouns from the text:

1 'rise' (l. 9)
2 'change' (l. 28)
3 'success' (l. 34)
4 'emergence' (l. 35)

c One way to expand your vocabulary is to organize words into *word families, i.e. words that are derived from a common root, e.g. *contribute – contributor – contribution*.
Collect family members of the following words from the text:
'connected' (l. 4) – 'emergence' (l. 35) – 'advances' (l. 37) – 'migrated' (l. 42) – 'produce' (l. 43).

3 Chunk it!

► Check

a Replace the gaps in the following *chunks by verbs. You can check the text for help if you are not sure.

1 ... an impulse
2 ... track of sth.
3 ... a role in sth.
4 ... a new level
5 ... an issue
6 ... a response

► SF 21: Analysing diagrams

b Compare solutions with your partner.
c Create a quiz for your partner with four more examples from the text. This time, delete the prepositions from your *chunks (e.g. 'the loss ... jobs'). Then do the quiz your partner has prepared.
d Add relevant words to your global glossary.

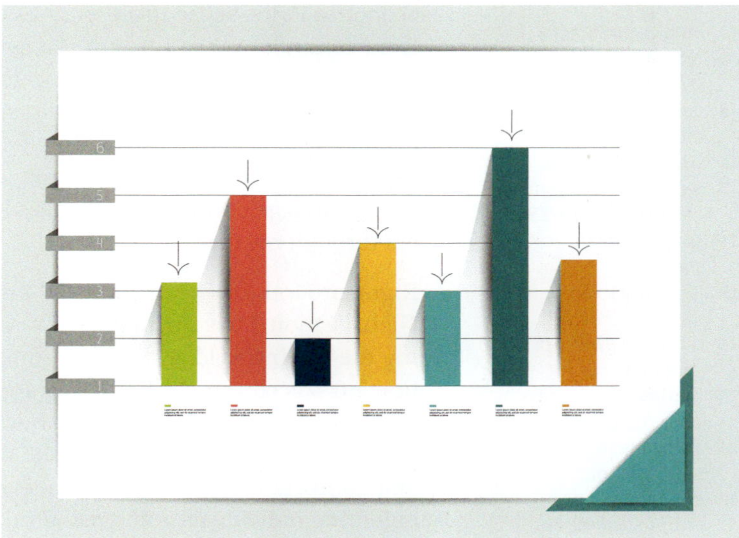

4 Making a chart or infographic

a Create a chart or infographic about globalization using words from your global glossary and the highlighted phrases from the text.
b Present your product to your class.

▶ More info

A short history of globalization

Thomas Friedman

- Together with a partner, discuss which historical and political events can be described as early forms of globalization.

One of the first global goods: a hot pepper, brought to Europe in 1493 by Christopher Columbus's expedition

Thomas Friedman is an American journalist who has written extensively on globalization and technology. His book The World is Flat, *from which the following excerpt is taken, first appeared in 2005.*

[...] There have been three great eras of globalization. The first lasted from 1492 – when Columbus set sail, opening trade between the Old World and the New World – until around 1800. I would call this era Globalization 1.0. It shrank the world from a size large to a size medium. Globalization 1.0 was about countries and muscles. That is, in Globalization 1.0, the key agent of change, the dynamic force driving the process of global integration, was how much brawn – how much muscle, how much horsepower, wind power, or, later, steam power – your country had and how creatively you could deploy it. In this era, countries and governments (often inspired by religion or imperialism or a combination of both) led the way in breaking down walls and knitting the world together, driving global integration. In Globalization 1.0, the primary questions were: Where does my country fit into global competition and opportunities? How can I go global and collaborate with others through my country?

The second great era, Globalization 2.0, lasted roughly from 1800 to 2000, interrupted by the Great Depression and World Wars I and II. This era shrank the world from a size medium to a size small. In Globalization 2.0, the key agent of change, the dynamic force driving global integration, was multinational companies. These multinationals went global for markets and labor, spearheaded first by the expansion of the Dutch and English joint-stock companies and the Industrial Revolution. In the first half of this era, global integration was powered by falling transportation costs, thanks to the steam engine and the railroad, and in the second half by falling telecommunication costs – thanks to the diffusion of the telegraph, telephones, the PC, satellites, fiber-optic cable, and the early version of the World Wide Web. It was during this era that we really saw the birth and maturation of a global economy, in the sense that there was enough movement of goods and information from continent to continent for there to be a global market, with global arbitrage in products and labor. The dynamic forces behind this era of globalization were breakthroughs in hardware – from steamships and railroads in the beginning to telephones and mainframe computers toward the end. And the big questions in this era were: Where does my company fit into the global economy? How does it take advantage of the opportunities? How can I go global and collaborate with others through my company? [...]

Right around the year 2000 we entered a whole new era: Globalization 3.0. Globalization 3.0 is shrinking the world from a size small to a size tiny and flattening the playing field at the same time. And while the dynamic force in Globalization 1.0 was countries globalizing and the dynamic force in Globalization 2.0 was companies globalizing, the dynamic force in Globalization 3.0 – the force that gives it its unique character – is the newfound power for *individuals* to collaborate and compete globally. And the phenomenon that is enabling, empowering, and enjoining individuals and small groups to go global so easily and so seamlessly is

Annotations

5 **key agent** most important factor
6 **brawn** physical strength
8 **deploy sth.** use sth. effectively
15 **Great Depression** worldwide economic crisis (1929 – ca. 1940)
18 **spearhead sth.** initiate sth.
19 **joint-stock company** *Aktiengesellschaft*
22 **diffusion** *(fml)* act of spreading sth.
24 **maturation** process of becoming fully grown
26 **arbitrage** buying and selling for profit
40 **enjoin sb.** urge or strongly advise sb.

what I call the *flat-world platform* [...]. The flat-world platform is the product of a convergence of the personal computer (which allowed every individual suddenly to become the author of his or her own content in digital form) with fiber-optic cable (which suddenly allowed all those individuals to access more and more digital content around the world for next to nothing) with the rise of workflow software (which enabled individuals all over the world to collaborate on that same digital content from anywhere, regardless of the distances between them). No one anticipated this convergence. It just happened – right around the year 2000. And when it did, people all over the world started waking up and realizing that they had more power than ever to go global *as individuals,* they needed more than ever to think of themselves as individuals competing against other individuals all over the planet, and they had more opportunities to work with those other individuals, not just compete with them. As a result, every person now must, and can, ask: Where do *I* as an individual fit into the global competition and opportunities of the day, and how can *I*, on my own, collaborate with others globally?

But Globalization 3.0 differs from the previous eras not only in how it is shrinking and flattening the world and in how it is empowering individuals. It also is different in that Globalization 1.0 and 2.0 were driven primarily by European and American individuals and businesses. Even though China actually had the biggest economy in the world in the eighteenth century, it was Western countries, companies, and explorers who were doing most of the globalizing and shaping of the system. But going forward, this will be less and less true. Because it is flattening and shrinking the world, Globalization 3.0 is going to be more and more driven not only by individuals but also by a much more diverse – non-Western, non-white – group of individuals. Individuals from every corner of the flat world are being empowered. Globalization 3.0 makes it possible for so many more people to plug in and play, and you are going to see every color of the human rainbow take part.

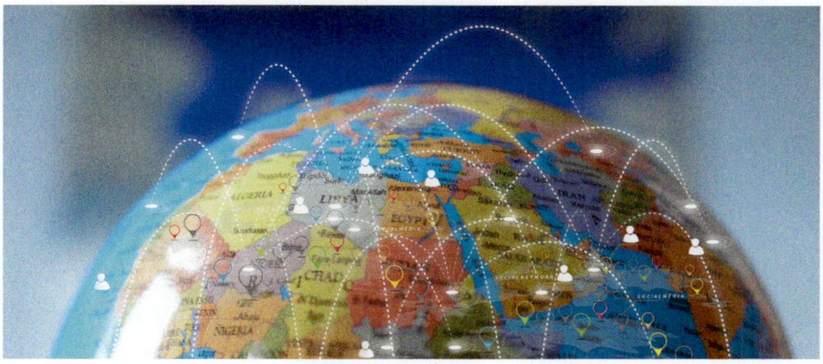

From: The World Is Flat, *2007*

Annotations
42 **convergence** *Annäherung*
45 **workflow software** *Arbeitssoftware*

Comprehension

1 Create a table with the following headers: *Globalization 1.0, Globalization 2.0* and *Globalization 3.0*. Add the following categories in the first column on the left: *driving force, key technologies, major players, primary question, size of world, time frame*. Then fill in your table with the information given in the text.

2 Outline the connection between globalization and technological progress as presented by Friedman.

Analysis

3 Examine the style of the text and relate it to the audience Friedman has in mind.

Language awareness

4 a Friedman uses a number of images in his text.

1 'muscles' (l. 5)
2 'breaking down walls' (l. 10)
3 'birth and maturation' (l. 24)
4 'shrinking the world' (l. 34)
5 'waking up' (l. 49)
6 'every color of the human rainbow' (l. 72)

Rewrite the phrases without using the images.

b Explain the effect it has on the sentences and the text in general.

Beyond the text

▶ SF 27: Writing a blog post

5 You choose Work on task **a** or **b**.

a Speaking Give a brief talk in which you explain why Friedman connects Globalization 3.0 with the empowerment of the individual. Say whether or not you agree with him.

b Writing Imagine Thomas Friedman hosted a blog. Write an entry there in which you explain why you think he called his book on globalization *The World Is Flat* and state whether you think the title is well chosen.

▶ Getting started

Text 2

The new globalization Richard Baldwin

Before reading the text by Richard Baldwin you are going to watch a video that ranks different countries according to the total value of goods they exported. It shows the development from 1960 to 2018.

- Which countries do you expect to lead? Which of them may fall back and which will catch up over the time span?
- Viewing Watch the video. Which development surprised you the most?
- Name reasons why some of the countries might have risen in economic importance while others have fallen back.

Now read the text by Richard Baldwin in which he analyses the mechanisms that led to the shifts you observed in the video. The following excerpt is from his book The Globotics Upheaval *(2019).*

American companies had long understood that they could perform some aspects of the manufacturing process more cheaply abroad. The highly modular nature of the semiconductor production process, for example, allowed US semiconductor producers to put some stages in Asia as early as the 1970s. The barrier to doing this in most industrial sectors was the high costs of coordinating production. That's why offshoring only really started racing after ICT made international coordination cheap and reliable. Only then could companies in the United States, Germany, and Japan unbundle complex production processes geographically without much loss in quality, timeliness, or reliability.

This new possibility created the new globalization. It allowed manufacturing firms in advanced economies to exploit the vast international wage differences between,

Annotations

3 **semiconductor** solid substance whose electrical conductivity lies between an insulator and a conductor, *Halbleiter*
6 **ICT** information and communication technology
7 **reliable** [rɪˈlaɪəbl] dependable
8 **unbundle sth.** take sth. apart

for example, the United States, Germany, and Japan on one hand, and nearby developing nations like Mexico, Poland, and China on the other hand. The result was a quite sudden and massive deindustrialization of the advanced economies.

In 1970, the advanced industrial economies known as the G7 (United States, Japan, Germany, Britain, France, Italy, and Canada) produced over 70 percent of the world's manufactured goods. That declined gently during the 1970s and 1980s, but from 1990 it plummeted. The G7 share fell from two-thirds to less than half in just twenty years [...].

Nothing radical happened to the overall growth in world manufacturing output. Putting together these two puzzle pieces tells us that G7 manufacturing went somewhere else. That 'somewhere' was the emerging economies, primarily China.

This was one of the most dramatic aspects of the Services Transformation. The historically fast deindustrialization of the former industrial giants, and the historically fast industrialization of a handful of formerly unindustrialized economies – call them the Industrializing 6 (China, India, Indonesia, Korea, Poland, Thailand, and Turkey). Most economists misthink this massive flip in the world of manufacturing by focusing on the production that was offshored. In reality, it was about thoughts, not things. [...]

Knowledge is the key to understanding this rapid deindustrialization. The point is that the US, German, and Japanese offshoring firms sent along their know-how with the offshored stages of production and displaced jobs. How could they have done otherwise?

When Toyota makes parts in China for inclusion in the cars they assemble in Japan, the company can't rely on Chinese technology. Instead, Toyota sends its know-how to China to ensure that the Chinese workers are doing the right thing and in the right way. As a result, the flows of knowledge that used to happen only inside Japanese factories became part of international commerce.

It was exactly these new technology flows that triggered the rapid industrialization in China and a few other developing nations. It started with production directed by multinationals, but domestic production boomed as the know-how diffused more widely.

The thing that puts the 'new' in the new globalization is the technology that started crossing borders from 1990 or so. Offshoring did lead to more trade in parts and components, but that wasn't the revolutionary part. The thing that changed the world was the colossal, one-way flow of technology from mature to emerging economies. [...] These new knowledge flows spawned a new reality in manufacturing globally.

Before this widespread offshoring of manufacturing jobs, international competition in goods was based on one of two choices. Firms in developing nations could rely on low technology and hope that their low wage more than compensated for the technical inefficiency. Firms in advanced economies, by contrast, used high technology and hoped this would more than compensate for the high wages they had to pay advanced economy workers.

Annotations
- 18 **plummet** fall sharply
- 40 **trigger sth.** make sth. start to happen
- 42 **domestic** national
- 43 **diffuse** spread
- 49 **spawn sth.** create sth.

Modern car production

Annotations
60 **add labor and stir** *Arbeit hinzufügen und umrühren*
69 **hasten sth.** ['heɪsn] make sth. happen sooner

From about 1990, a third way opened. Manufactured goods could be made with high technology that had been offshored to low-wage nations. This transformed the world of manufacturing. It explains why the Industrializing 6 industrialized so rapidly. They didn't have to develop the technology themselves. The offshoring companies brought everything needed except the labor. You could call it 'add-labor-and-stir' industrialization. And this is not as obviously a win-win outcome as was the old globalization.

The rapid industrialization of the Industrializing 6 was surely good for them. It is not at all sure that advanced economy factory workers also benefited. American, European, and Japanese workers no longer had privileged access to the know-how developed by their national firms. The monopoly that advanced-economy workers used to have on advanced-economy technology was broken. American, German, and Japanese companies taught foreign workers to make parts and components that used to be made domestically; this teaching hastened the loss of factory jobs in G7 nations.

From: The Globotics Upheaval, *2020*

Comprehension

1 Complete each of the sentences below with information from the text:

1. Beginning around 1990, ... made it possible to export industrial know-how from advanced economies to emerging economies.
2. As a result, manufacturing jobs ...
3. The biggest winners in this development are ...
4. The losers are ...

► SF 32: Writing a summary or an outline
► SF 21: Analysing diagrams

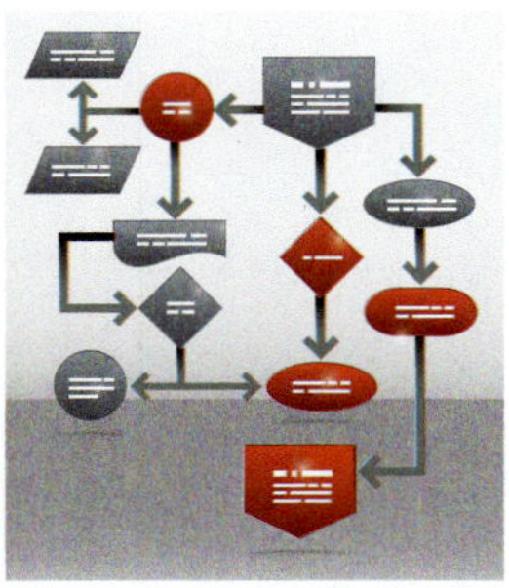

2 You choose Work on task **a** or **b**.

a Organize the main information from the text in the form of a flow chart.

b Writing Summarize the main facts in the form of a short text. Make the causal connections between the developments clear.

Language help

because of ... • due to ... • owing to ... • as a result (of) ... • on account of ... • lead to ... • result in ...

Analysis

3 Examine the style of the text. Point out passages where the author's personal view of the development becomes visible.

Language awareness

4 a Prefixes such as *mis-*, *de-*, *un-* and *in-* can give a word a negative meaning. Find one example of each in Baldwin's text.

b Say which of the words below can be combined with one or more of the prefixes from **a** and explain what the new words mean: *activate – competent – decided – informed – interpret – militarize – understand – use.*

▶ More language

Beyond the text

5 Work on either task **a** or **b**.

a Collect arguments for and against offshoring.

b Challenge Collect arguments for and against offshoring. Use them to write a letter to the editor in which you state your opinion.

▶ SF 33: Writing a formal letter or email

Text 3

Playing by the rules: the WTO

- WTO, WHO, UNO, NATO and OPEC are all *acronyms for well-known international organizations. State the full name of each organization and explain its function.

A globalized world requires rules that are accepted by all the major players. One of the most important organizations with regard to economic globalization is the World Trade Organization (WTO). The following text is taken from their website.

What is the WTO?

The World Trade Organization (WTO) is the only global international organization dealing with the rules of trade between nations. [...] The goal is to help producers of goods and services, exporters, and importers conduct their business.

From: www.wto.org

Who are we?

The WTO was born out of negotiations, and everything the WTO does is the result of negotiations. The bulk of the WTO's current work comes from the 1986–94 negotiations called the Uruguay Round and earlier negotiations under the General Agreement on Tariffs and Trade (GATT). The WTO is currently the host to new negotiations, under the 'Doha Development Agenda' launched in 2001.

Where countries have faced trade barriers and wanted them lowered, the negotiations have helped to open markets for trade. But the WTO is not just

Annotations
4 **conduct sth.** (fml) do sth.
8 **negotiation** *Verhandlung*
10 **tariff** *Zoll*
11 **host** organizer

Annotations
18 bulk majority
24 objective goal
28 ambassador *Botschafter/in*
39 commitment sth. you have promised to do
44 implementation *Umsetzung*
45 require sb. to do sth. demand that sb. does sth.
46 measure *Maßnahme*
49 scrutiny close examination
52 settlement Schlichtung
53 resolve sth. end or solve sth.
54 vital absolutely necessary

about opening markets, and in some circumstances its rules support maintaining trade barriers – for example, to protect consumers or prevent the spread of disease.

At its heart are the WTO agreements, negotiated and signed by the bulk of the world's trading nations. These documents provide the legal ground rules for international commerce. They are essentially contracts, binding governments to keep their trade policies within agreed limits. Although negotiated and signed by governments, the goal is to help producers of goods and services, exporters, and importers conduct their business, while allowing governments to meet social and environmental objectives. [...]

From: www.wto.org

What we do

The WTO is run by its member governments. All major decisions are made by the membership as a whole, either by ministers (who usually meet at least once every two years) or by their ambassadors or delegates (who meet regularly in Geneva).

While the WTO is driven by its member states, it could not function without its Secretariat to coordinate the activities. The Secretariat employs over 600 staff, and its experts – lawyers, economists, statisticians and communications experts – assist WTO members on a daily basis to ensure, among other things, that negotiations progress smoothly, and that the rules of international trade are correctly applied and enforced.

Trade negotiations

The WTO agreements cover goods, services and intellectual property. They spell out the principles of liberalization, and the permitted exceptions. They include individual countries' commitments to lower customs tariffs and other trade barriers, and to open and keep open services markets. They set procedures for settling disputes. These agreements are not static; they are renegotiated from time to time and new agreements can be added to the package. [...]

Implementation and monitoring

WTO agreements require governments to make their trade policies transparent by notifying the WTO about laws in force and measures adopted. Various WTO councils and committees seek to ensure that these requirements are being followed and that WTO agreements are being properly implemented. All WTO members must undergo periodic scrutiny of their trade policies and practices, each review containing reports by the country concerned and the WTO Secretariat.

Dispute settlement

The WTO's procedure for resolving trade quarrels under the Dispute Settlement Understanding is vital for enforcing the rules and therefore for ensuring that trade flows smoothly. Countries bring disputes to the WTO if

The WTO headquarters in Geneva

they think their rights under the agreements are being infringed. Judgements by specially appointed independent experts are based on interpretations of the agreements and individual countries' commitments.

Building trade capacity

WTO agreements contain special provision for developing countries, including longer time periods to implement agreements and commitments, measures to increase their trading opportunities, and support to help them build their trade capacity, to handle disputes and to implement technical standards. The WTO organizes hundreds of technical cooperation missions to developing countries annually. It also holds numerous courses each year in Geneva for government officials. Aid for Trade aims to help developing countries develop the skills and infrastructure needed to expand their trade.

Outreach

The WTO maintains regular dialogue with non-governmental organizations, parliamentarians, other international organizations, the media and the general public on various aspects of the WTO and the ongoing Doha negotiations, with the aim of enhancing cooperation and increasing awareness of WTO activities.

From: www.wto.org

Annotations
- 56 **infringe sth.** *(fml)* break a law or rule
- 60 **provision** *Maßnahme, Vorsorge*
- 63 **capacity** ability
- 72 **enhance sth.** improve sth.

Comprehension

1 Writing Write a dictionary entry that sums up the functions of the WTO.

▶ Getting started

Analysis

2 The above text is an example of *expository writing, i.e. a non-fiction text that provides facts. Considering this, examine the choice of verbs and verb forms used in the text and explain why certain forms are used so often.

▶ Support p. 247

Language awareness

3 In the text there are a number of participle phrases, e.g. '... dealing with ...' (l. 3).
- **a** Rewrite the sentence without the participle.
- **b** Find three more sentences with participle phrases in the text and rewrite them without using a participle phrase.
- **c** Compare your sentences with the original ones. Which do you find better?
- **d** Name reasons for the use of participle phrases.

Beyond the text

4 Name a scenario in which the WTO might be needed and explain why.

Annotations

2 **gross** *(Geld) einspielen*
10 **impact** *(n)* influence
11 **unleash sth.** suddenly release sth., esp. a strong emotion or force
19 **extinction** *Auslöschung*
22 **Rio+20** UN Conference on Sustainable Development (2012)
33 **exacerbate sth.** [ɪɡˈzæsəbeɪt] make sth. worse
36 **insurmountable** unsolvable
37 **obesity** state of being overweight

Global culture – made in USA? Peter Vanham

- Consider the music you like to listen to. Which countries does it come from?

The dominant role of American culture throughout the world has led some to speak of 'cultural imperialism'. But there are signs that it is losing its influence.

Today, there is no denying the dominant global culture is American. The highest grossing films of all time, worldwide, are almost without exception from Hollywood (think *Avatar*, *Titanic* or *Star Wars*). The best-selling albums of all time are mostly American (although Australian band AC/DC and British band Pink Floyd gave Michael Jackson a run for his money).

Most social-media and internet firms are American. And food culture, though more diverse, is still affected by the McDonalds, Coca-Colas, Starbucks and PepsiCos of this world.

This evolution would not have been possible without the wider globalization of the world economy, and the transformative impact of technology. In the 1960s, transatlantic flights and radio recordings made it possible for The Beatles to unleash a mania in America. In the 1990s and 2000s open global markets and the internet allowed for cultural sensations to spread even faster.

But this globalization of culture did come at a price. Consider languages. Since the earliest era of globalization – the 16th Century Age of Discovery – the number of spoken languages worldwide has steadily declined, from about 14,500 to less than 7,000.

By 2007, the New York Times reported, half of the remaining 7,000 languages were at danger of extinction. And by 2017, the World Economic Forum wrote, almost 1,500 languages had less than 1,000 speakers left.

As UNESCO, the United Nations' educational, scientific and cultural arm pointed out at Rio+20, the homogenization of culture brought other risks too.

It said in 2012: 'While this phenomenon promotes the integration of societies, it may also bring with it a loss of uniqueness of local culture, which in turn can lead to loss of identity, exclusion and even conflict.' [...]

Then there are the economic effects of a globalizing culture. Already before the rise of social media and the so-called Big Tech companies, less than a dozen companies – like Disney, 21st Century Fox, Sony and Viacom – owned the lion's share of the world's leading media and entertainment institutions.

The arrival of large tech platforms only accelerated the trend towards larger market concentration, and the risks of loss of cultural diversity.

Finally, as much as we may like our burger with fries, our bag of chips and our takeaway cup of coffee, the globalizing fast-food culture exacerbated global problems too.

If everyone consumed the same amount of burgers as Americans, or created as much rubbish, climate change and pollution might be insurmountable, and obesity an even bigger cause of illness and death.

This raises some important questions. Is American-led cultural globalization a self-destructive time bomb, destined to slowly kill languages, cultures and life itself? Is cultural globalization a phenomenon that enriches local cultures with a diverse set of foreign influences? Or should we be agnostic about it, as long as it leads to more positive outcomes for society and the environment, like better governance and climate leadership?

If, until recently, the first question seemed most likely to be answered 'yes', BTS, Fonsi and their peers showed a more diverse globalization can't be completely written off.

Take the case of Luis Fonsi first. With his hit single 'Despacito', the Puerto Rican singer broke seven Guinness World Records, including first YouTube video to reach 5 billion views, and most streamed track worldwide. Doing so, he showed that you can influence global culture through the Spanish language and Caribbean culture too. This is unsurprising when you consider that there are 437 million people who speak Spanish as a first language compared to 372 million native English speakers.

The case of BTS is perhaps even more impressive, because it is so much more against the cultural odds. While Spanish, alongside Mandarin Chinese and English belongs to the top 3 of most spoken languages worldwide, Korean doesn't even feature in the top 10. As a matter of fact, Korea until about a century ago was known as the 'Hermit Kingdom', for its cultural and economic isolation.

There are still remnants of Korea's isolation today. In many other G20 economies, like France or Germany, English language songs counted for the majority of hits by 2017. In Korea all top hits were still Korean. BTS is no exception. Most of their songs are largely sung in Korean, with only parts of the lyrics in English. Yet, BTS managed to become the global musical sensation of the year. [...]

Of course, one swallow does not a summer make, nor will Fonsi and BTS change cultural globalization single-handedly. But in other domains too, cultural power players have emerged from elsewhere than America. Asia in particular is rising in cultural influence. [...]

The fact that singers and bands from the Caribbean and Korea can make the world's most popular music show that there is nothing inevitable about the Americanization of cultural globalization after all.

From: 'Here's what a Korean boy band can teach us about globalization 4.0', www.weforum.org, 18 December 2018

Annotations
41 agnostic (here) neutral
54 against the odds surprising
57 hermit *Einsiedler/in*
58 remnant part that is left of sth.
63 swallow *Schwalbe*
64 domain area
68 inevitable unavoidable

► More info

Comprehension

1 List the pros and cons of cultural globalization presented in the text.

2 Explain why the author finds the international success of BTS so remarkable.

Analysis

3 Analyse the structure of the text, pointing out the connection between arguments and examples.

Info

Some words have – alongside their literal meaning – an emotional impact, i.e. they produce a positive or negative response. This is called a **connotation**. For example, *curious* has a positive connotation, *nosy* a negative one.

4 Examine the author's use of the word *culture*.

Language awareness

5 **a** One way to influence readers is through the use of words with specific *connotations. Discuss whether the following words have a positive or negative connotation: 'dominant (l. 1), 'uniqueness' (l. 24), 'diversity' (l. 31) and 'leadership' (l. 43).

b Examine how connotation is used in the text to influence the reader.

Beyond the text

▸ SF 42: Preparing and giving a speech

6 You choose Work on task **a** or **b**.

a Speaking Collect examples of Asian culture that you are familiar with, e.g. karaoke, mangas, anime. Discuss with a partner why you think these influences have caught on in the western world.

b Speaking Make a speech to your class explaining why you think it is important to preserve local cultural traditions. Consider your region's dialect, if there is one.

Info

Art in Context – art in the age of globalization

Apart from the job market and the overall economy, globalization has also had a huge impact on art in general and the art market in particular. The globalization of art is often linked to the year 1989, when international trade agreements gained in significance and the Iron Curtain was lifted, paving the way for a culture market that spanned the globe. Thanks to open markets it has never been easier to showcase or buy authentic works of art from all over the world. This development is also fuelled by migration and the possibilities it creates: artists go where the buyers are. All these aspects have helped promote a formerly unknown diversity in the art market. But this diversity comes at a price. Paradoxically, some fear that cultural identity will eventually suffer from a globalized market that promotes uniformity. This fear can be seen, for example, in the discussion about whether radio stations should be required by law to play songs performed in the native language of their country. The same issue affects the film industry. Whereas in Germany it is standard practice to dub films into German, it is much less common in other countries. In the Netherlands, for example, most foreign films are subtitled. This may discourage some people from watching them, but it supports foreign language learning. Cultural dominance is also reflected in the selection of films and series that can be watched on streaming portals. The omnipresence of the US market often marginalizes productions from less prominent countries, and the American lifestyle represented in films and series influences viewers all over the world.

1 Name the effects globalization has on art and culture.
2 Discuss the positive and negative sides of subtitles vs dubbing.

Words revisited

► SF 6: Essentials: language and study skills

1 Forming compound nouns

a The texts in this chapter use a lot of *compound nouns. The following are examples of compound nouns used in 'Words in Context' (p. 80): 'Silk Road' (l. 16), 'manufacturing jobs' (l. 23), 'music industry' (l. 31), 'fibre-optic communication' (l. 37) 'free-trade agreements' (l. 39).
Explain how these compound nouns are formed and compare them to their German equivalents.

b Find more examples of compound nouns from 'Words in Context' or other texts.

c Make a general rule for the formation of compound nouns in English.

2 Matching

► Check

Form compound nouns by combining the words in the boxes below. Say which compounding rule you applied. Careful: some may be used more than once.

A globalization	**1** area
B high level	**2** control
C no smoking	**3** critic
D once in a lifetime	**4** expert
E passport	**5** opportunity
F telecommunications	**6** talk

3 Global glossary

Add relevant compound words you have discovered here to your global glossary.

Language awareness

Intercultural communication *Global communication can be tricky sometimes, even among people who speak the same language. Watch Peter Alfandary's TEDx talk 'The myth of globalization'.*

► More info

4 Communicative misunderstandings

a When Alfandary tells the taxi driver where to take him, there is a moment of confusion. Discuss with a partner and say why.

b What could Alfandary have said to prevent this misunderstanding?

c Explain how people who share a common language can still misunderstand each other. Generalize from Alfandary's experience and write a paragraph for a travel guide for people using English around the world.

Practice

▸ Check

5 Making a complaint

There are different ways of making a complaint.

a Find the matching sentences in the speech bubbles below and examine how they differ.

b Make a list of sentence forms and phrases that can be used to make a polite complaint.

'Excuse me, I think you may be sitting in my seat.'

'Quiet! I'm trying to concentrate!'

'Shut that window! I've got a cold!'

'Could you close the window please?'

'Hey, that's my seat!'

'Would you mind going somewhere else to talk?'

6 Expressing yourself politely

Intercultural communication Write down what you could say to express yourself politely in each of the following situations.

1 You are the secretary of your school's Green Club. An exchange student from Lithuania has just asked if he can join. You want to write his name down, but you didn't really hear it properly when he introduced himself and you have no idea how to spell it.

2 You are staying with a family in Wales. Your host suggests going to a rugby match at the weekend. You're not especially fond of rugby. You would prefer to go hiking in the hills.

3 You are having lunch in an English café. Between the main course and dessert you go to the toilet. When you come back, a stranger is sitting at your table.

4 You are visiting London for the first time and want to go by Tube. You notice that all the people heading down to the platforms have blue plastic cards that they use to pass through the turnstile. As you don't have one, you go up to a stranger and ask for information.

5 You have just boarded a crowded train bound for Edinburgh. There is only one seat left in the carriage, and someone has put their suitcase on it.

6 You are waiting in a queue in a British post office. You have to mail an application as soon as possible, so you need a stamp. The customer in front of you is holding two carrier bags full of small parcels. There is only one window open, and you have an appointment in half an hour.

Language help

Sorry, I didn't know ... • Is it all right with you if I ...? • Would you mind if I ...? • Would it be possible for me to ...? • Could you please ...?

Am I rootless, or am I free? Ndéla Faye

- Name advantages for having more than one cultural background.

▸ More info

In the text that follows, a young woman explains how she feels about her mixed ethnic background.

'No, but where are you *really* from?' It is the question that automatically makes the hairs on the back of my neck stand up. Like many 'third culture kids' (TCKs), I panic, wondering whether the question refers to my nationality, where I was born, where I am living now, or where my parents live.

The term, coined by the American sociologist Ruth Hill Useem, refers to a child who has spent a significant part of their formative years outside their parents' culture. People who fit that bill have a tendency to mix and merge their birth culture with their adopted culture, creating one of their own: a third culture.

Depending on the person and situation, I'll have different answers to that dreaded question. I'll tell white lies and change my story as I go, like many other TCKs. Sometimes I'll go for the quick answer: Finland and Senegal. Other times I'll tell the whole story: that I was born in Helsinki, moved to Luxembourg, then to Brussels and finally to London. Or I might say that my mum is from Finland and dad from Senegal, but that I really feel like my home is in the UK now.

Each time I get the question, I feel like I need to explain myself, prove my origins, and because of that I'll often find myself omitting parts of my story in order to make my identity more palatable for others.

Living like this can sometimes feel liberating: I feel as though I'm wearing different masks, and I am constantly able to reinvent myself. But this also presents a dilemma: who am I really? Which of these masks is the true me? Where do I belong? In my case, this is made even more complex as I'm biracial. Although I was born in Finland, I'm aware that I don't look typically Finnish – but seeing as I've never lived in Senegal, I feel strange saying I'm from there. Then again, I don't feel very Finnish either, as I've lived abroad for most of my life. They're both countries where I have family, and are places that I visit every few years – places I think of with nostalgia. But when I'm actually there, I feel out of place, like an outsider.

So where is home? Identity is attached to a sense of belonging, usually through family ties or deep emotional connections. Home suggests an emotional place – somewhere you truly belong, but I, like many other TCKs, never quite feel at home anywhere. It feels sometimes that I am in limbo. I am a strange mix of I-don't-know-what, and sometimes I feel as if I'll never find that one place where I belong 100%. I just feel blessed to have had the privilege of experiencing so many cultures.

I sometimes wonder whether my life would be different if I had grown up in one place. I wonder what it would be like to have lived in a house where there were ruler marks beside a doorframe, documenting each of my childhood growth spurts; to have a friend who's known me since nursery; not to feel like a tourist, wandering around with a map in a country that I'm supposed to embrace as my own.

Annotations

rootless not belonging to a particular place
7 **formative** *prägend*
11 **dread sth.** be afraid of sth.
12 **white lie** small lie to avoid hurting sb.
17 **origin** personal and social background
18 **omit sth.** leave sth. out
19 **palatable** acceptable or pleasant
23 **biracial** involving people with two different ethical backgrounds
32 **in limbo** stuck in a situation

Annotation
41 **resent sth.** be upset/ angry about sth.

Sometimes I resent the fact that I have to give complicated answers to seemingly simple questions. At other times it all seems rather trivial: as I watch my nieces and nephews growing up, and laying the basis of their identities among multiple cultures, I cannot help but feel proud. What an amazing opportunity, to speak multiple languages and see so many countries.

Being rootless has given me a sense of freedom. I feel grateful for the experiences I've had, and I am proud to feel, above all, like a citizen of the world. The possibilities for the future are endless. The sense of being at home anywhere, yet feeling that home is nowhere, is part of who I am.

I love being able to choose to be whoever I want, wherever I go. My many masks are a storyboard of all that I am. I've gradually built myself an identity that is a collection of pieces, each of which I've handpicked; choosing the best bits in order to create a whole. I've realised that those pieces are not mutually exclusive, but that they are all dependent on each other. Being rootless doesn't mean I don't belong to any one place; it means I choose to belong to many.

From: The Guardian, *9 March 2016*

Comprehension

1 Describe Ndéla's reaction to questions regarding her national identity.

2 Summarize how Ndéla feels about herself and her multinational upbringing.

Analysis

3 Analyse the connection between the title of the essay and the conclusion the author arrives at.

4 Identify the *stylistic devices that support the concept of rootlessness.

Language awareness

► Getting started
► Support p. 248

5 **a** In everyday use, the word *rootless* has a negative *connotation. Examine the usages of *rootless* in the text and how they affect the connotation.
b Write a short poem that plays with the different meanings of *rootless*.

Beyond the text

► SF 26: Argumentative writing: discussion and comment

6 Intercultural communication | You choose | Work on task **a** or **b**:
a Find a partner who comes from a different cultural background to you. Compare your feelings of belonging.
b Writing | Imagine you have just read Ndéla's essay on a social networking site. Write a comment.

A stranger in Manila Mohsin Hamid

▸ More info

- Name situations in which you felt strange or as if you were a stranger.

The following excerpt is from the novel The Reluctant Fundamentalist *by Mohsin Hamid. Its narrator is Changez, a young Pakistani who graduated from Princeton University and has found work with Underwood Sampson, a US consulting firm. He tells his life story to an American stranger he meets in Karachi (Pakistan).*

When I arrived in the Philippines at the start of my first Underwood Samson assignment, I was terribly excited. We had flown first-class, and I will never forget the feeling of reclining in my seat, clad in my suit, as I was served champagne by an attractive and – yes, I was indeed so brazen as to allow myself to believe – *flirtatious* flight attendant. I was, in my own eyes, a veritable James Bond – only younger, darker, and possibly better paid. How odd it seems now to recall that time; how quickly my sense of self- satisfaction would later disappear!

But I am getting ahead of myself. I was telling you about Manila. [...] I expected to find a city like Lahore – or perhaps Karachi; what I found instead was a place of skyscrapers and superhighways. Yes, Manila had its slums; one saw them on the drive from the airport: vast districts of men in dirty white undershirts lounging idly in front of auto-repair shops – like a poorer version of the 1950s America depicted in such films as *Grease*. But Manila's glittering skyline and walled enclaves for the ultra-rich were unlike anything I had seen in Pakistan.

A view of Manila, capital of the Philippines

I tried not to dwell on the comparison; it was one thing to accept that New York was more wealthy than Lahore, but quite another to swallow the fact that Manila was as well. I felt like a distance runner who thinks he is not doing too badly until he glances over his shoulder and sees that the fellow who is lapping him is not the leader of the pack, but one of the laggards. Perhaps it was for this reason that I did something in Manila I had never done before: I attempted to act and speak, as much as my dignity would permit, more like an *American*. The Filipinos we worked with seemed to look up to my *American* colleagues, accepting them almost instinctively as members of the officer class of global business – and I wanted my share of that respect as well.

So I learned to tell executives my father's age, 'I need it *now*'; I learned to cut to the front of lines with an extraterritorial smile; and I learned to answer, when asked where I was from, that I was from New York. Did these things trouble me, you ask? Certainly, sir; I was often ashamed. But outwardly I gave no sign of this. In any case, there was much for me to be proud of: my genuine aptitude for our work, for example, and the glowing reviews my performance received from my peers.

We were there, as I mentioned to you earlier, to value a recorded-music business. The owner had been a legendary figure in the local A&R scene; when he removed his sunglasses, his eyes contained the sort of cosmic openness one associates with prolonged exposure to LSD. But despite his colorful past, he had managed to sign lucrative outsourcing deals to manufacture and distribute CDs for two of the international music majors. Indeed, he claimed his operation was the largest of its kind in Southeast Asia and – piracy, downloads, and Chinese competition notwithstanding – growing at quite a healthy clip.

Annotations
- 4 **brazen** shameless
- 5 **veritable** *wahrhaftig*
- 11 **vast districts of men** (here) huge amount of men
- 13 **enclave** part of a city where people have a different nationality, culture or religion
- 15 **dwell on sth.** keep thinking about sth.
- 19 **laggard** (old fashioned) *Nachzügler/in*
- 29 **aptitude** talent
- 30 **peer** (here) workmate
- 32 **A&R = artists and repertoire** branch of a record label that is responsible for talent scouting
- 37 **notwithstanding sth.** despite sth.
- 38 **clip** rate

Annotations
42 **benchmark** *Maßstab*
43 **permutation** *Umsetzung*
51 **hostility** unfriendly behaviour
66 **fair** light in colour
66 **oblivious** unaware of sth.
67 **minutiae** [maɪˈnjuːʃiaɪ] small details

To determine how much it was actually worth, we worked around the clock for over a month. We interviewed suppliers, employees, and experts of all kinds; we passed hours in closed rooms with accountants and lawyers; we gathered gigabytes of data; we compared indicators of performance to benchmarks; and, in the end, we built a complex financial model with innumerable permutations. I spent much of my time in front of my computer, but I also visited the factory floor and several music shops. I felt enormously powerful on these outings, knowing my team was shaping the future. Would these workers be fired? Would these CDs be made elsewhere? *We*, indirectly of course, would help decide.

Yet there were moments when I became disoriented. I remember one such occasion in particular. I was riding with my colleagues in a limousine. We were mired in traffic, unable to move, and I glanced out the window to see, only a few feet away, the driver of a jeepney returning my gaze. There was an undisguised hostility in his expression; I had no idea why. We had not met before – of that I was virtually certain – and in a few minutes we would probably never see one another again. But his dislike was so obvious, so *intimate,* that it got under my skin. I stared back at him, getting angry myself – you will have noticed in your time here that glaring is something we men of Lahore take seriously – and I maintained eye contact until he was obliged by the movement of the car in front to return his attention to the road.

Afterwards, I tried to understand why he acted as he did. Perhaps, I thought, his wife has just left him; perhaps he resents me for the privileges implied by my suit and expensive car; perhaps he simply does not like Americans. I remained preoccupied with this matter far longer than I should have, pursuing several possibilities that all assume – as their unconscious starting point – that he and I shared a sort of Third World sensibility. Then one of my colleagues asked me a question, and when I turned to answer him, something rather strange took place. I looked at him – at his fair hair and light eyes and, most of all, his oblivious immersion in the minutiae of our work – and thought, you are so *foreign*. I felt in that moment much closer to the Filipino driver than to him; I felt I was play-acting when in reality I ought to be making my way home, like the people on the street outside.

From: The Reluctant Fundamentalist, *2012*

Comprehension

► SF 31: Writing a summary or an outline

1 Summarize the events of the *plot in your own words.

Analysis

2 Examine how Changez's feelings towards himself and his status change in the course of the excerpt:

► Support p. 248

- **a** Divide the text into sections based on Changez's perception of himself and his role.
- **b** For each section, analyse Changez's relationship to his surroundings and their influence on his self-image.
- **c** Assess the effect the Manila episode has on Changez's feelings towards himself and the role he plays.

Language awareness

3 **a** In the headline and the text a feeling of being a stranger or feeling strange is expressed. Explain the concept of feeling strange as conveyed in the text.
b Compare the findings of **a** to your ideas from the pre-reading task.
c Look at least at two other terms from the world field of strangeness, e.g. *odd, weird, foreign, queer, bizarre, peculiar, alien*. Try to explain the differences and find scenarios in which you could use the terms.

Beyond the text

4 Writing Continue Changez's story. What happens after his stay in Manila?

► SF 36: Creative writing

Text 7

Towards a fairer world?

You are going to hear excerpts from an interview from 2017 with Jim Yong Kim, who was president of the World Bank from 2012 to 2019.

- Speculate what the interview might be about in reference to a fairer world.

Info

The **World Bank** is an international organization. It is committed to providing financial support and technical assistance to the governments of developing countries. It was established in 1944, together with the International Monetary Fund (IMF).

► More info

► SF 37: Essentials: listening and viewing

Comprehension

1 Listening Read the statements below. After listening to the interview for the first time, decide which of them best summarizes Kim's views.
1 Kim says that inequality is necessary for economic growth.
2 Kim says that people in poor countries want the same lifestyle as people in rich countries.
3 Kim sees many opportunities for collaboration between developing and advanced economies.

2 Listening Listen to the interview for a second time.
a You choose Work on either of the tasks below:
Inequality Take notes on what Kim says about economic inequality and its relevance for economic growth.
Opportunities Take notes on what Kim says about opportunities and risks for the global community.
b Find someone who has chosen the other task. Tell each other what you have learned and discuss how your topics are connected.

3 Listening Listen to the interview for a third time and summarize Kim's different answers to the question: 'Globalization – what does it mean for me?'

Beyond the text

4 Think back to the guiding question of the chapter and reconsider your opinion. Take into account everything you have learned so far.

Inequality around the globe

- Give examples of inequality in the world despite or maybe because of globalization.

► SF 21: Analysing diagrams

The energy consumption per person of seven regions (year: 2019)

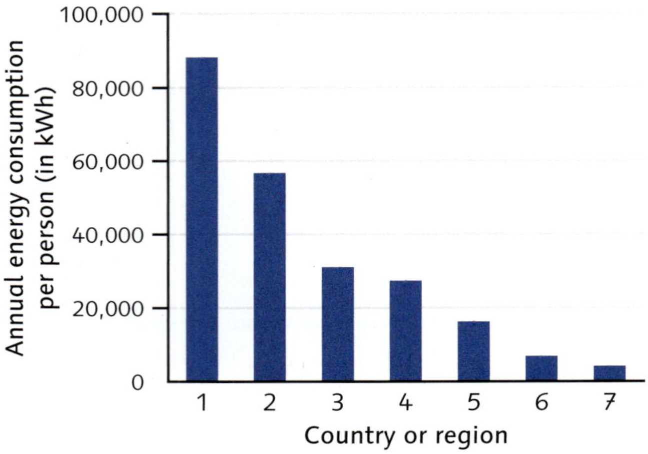

A	Brazil
B	North America
C	India
D	Europe
E	Africa
F	Russia
G	China

Source: OurWorldInData.org

1 **a** Guess which country used how much energy by matching countries and bars. Give reasons for your choice.

b Your teacher will give you the correct bar chart. Summarize its most important results.

Language help

consume energy • twice/three times as much • most/least • be first/last in rank • at the top/bottom of the ranking

c Say which result surprised you most, referring back to your ideas from task **a**.

"I blame the billions in the 3rd world, wanting to get what we've got!"

2 Speculate on possible reasons for the extreme differences in energy consumption shown in the chart.

3 Work on either **a** or **b**.

a Describe the cartoon.

b **Challenge** Describe the cartoon and write an *essay in which you explain the connection between the cartoon and the data presented in the chart.

► SF 23: Analysing cartoons

Focus on test formats

As part of your school-leaving exam you may be required to summarize information from a German text in English.

Read the following task:

You are a member of a European activist group that campaigns for workers' rights in the global garment industry. The British chapter has learned that the German government has committed itself to enforcing stricter rules for international supply chains. You found a relevant article in the newspaper *Die Zeit* (p. 105). You were asked to prepare an article of about 150 words summarizing the regulations contained in the law and their potential consequences. Your text will appear on the group's website.

1 Mediation tasks

► SF 46: Essentials: mediation

► Check

a What do you remember about mediation tasks? Decide which of the following statements are true and correct the false ones.

1. I must write in the same style as the original text.
2. I mustn't include any ideas of my own.
3. If I don't know the English translation of a German term, it's best to quote it in the original German.
4. I may have to explain certain terms that are specific to Germany.
5. The exact number of words is very important for my grade.
6. I mustn't leave out any information from the original text.

b Compare your results with your partner. Discuss points on which you disagree.

Work it out

In this section you are led step by step through the task presented above. The strategies you learn here can help you do other types of mediation tasks as well.

2 Examining the task

Reread the task. Copy the table below and fill in the missing information in key words:

Text type I must write:	
Required content (main points):	
Audience I am writing for:	
Appropriate style:	

▶ Support p. 248

3 Examining the text

a Read the text on p. 105. List the aspects the author deals with.
b Compare your list with your notes from task 2. Decide which aspects of the text are relevant for the task at hand.
c Now go to the text and make further notes on the relevant aspects.

4 Organizing the information

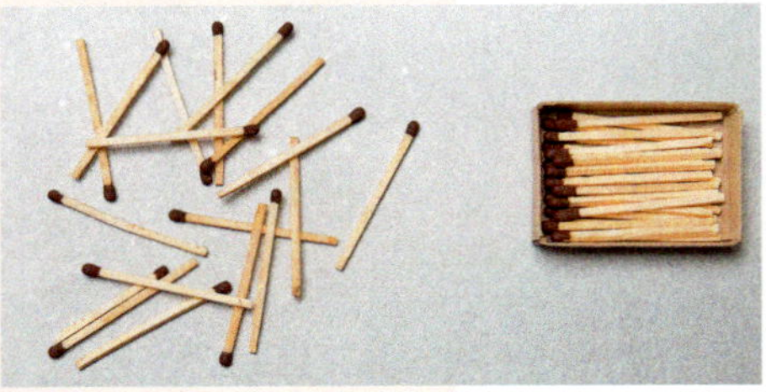

Compare the task at hand with the notes you have made. Decide how you can best organize the information you have gathered. The order used in the primary text isn't necessarily the ideal order for your text. The boxes below can help you:

Who is affected?	Background information: Why is the law needed?	Consequences for manufacturers?	?

5 Using a dictionary effectively

The given text contains a number of lexical items that come from the wordfields *governance* and *economy*. You may find them challenging at first sight.

a Examine the following list of words and phrases from the text. Put them into three groups: 1) necessary 2) optional 3) unnecessary for the mediation task.

Ausschreibung	*sich an ein Gesetz halten*
Raubtierkapitalismus	*Verstöße sanktionieren*
Ausbeutung	*Bußgeld*
sicherstellen	*Sorgfaltspflicht*
jdn. für etwas haftbar machen	*Ausschluss*

b Compare lists with your partner. Name reasons for your choices.
c In an examination you probably won't have time to look up every word you might not know. That is why it is important to have strategies for working with what you already have:
- Concentrate on the meaning, not on the word itself. For example, in the case of *sicherstellen*, think of a concrete situation where you might want to say something like 'Stellen Sie sicher, dass alle Türen verschlossen sind'. For example: '... ... to lock the doors')?
- Since you can't look up a phrase like *jemanden für etwas haftbar machen* in your bilingual dictionary, concentrate on the key word, in this case *haftbar*. When you have found it, look at the examples showing you how it is used. Here you will find the expression you are looking for.

haftbar **jdn für etw ~ machen ~** hold sb liable for sth; **für etw ~ sein** be liable for sth • *Bei einem Unfall am Arbeitsplatz kann der Arbeitgeber haftbar gemacht werden.* The employer can be held liable for an accident at work.
From: Oxford Klausur-Wörterbuch, *2019*

- In general, keep in mind that you may find it easier to work with the verb than with the noun (e.g. *Ausbeutung*, *Ausschluss*).
- Looking up words with a very general meaning such as *halten* is often a waste of time if you are looking for one particular usage *(sich an ein Gesetz halten)*. Try to think of a verb that has exactly the meaning you need (e.g. *einhalten*) and look it up instead.

6 Dealing with difficult words

Even in a good bilingual dictionary you won't find translations for every given word. This is especially true of compound nouns like *Lieferkettengesetz*. If you don't know or can't find a translation, paraphrase.

a Paraphrase each of the words below:
  1 *Kinderarbeit ('the use of ... as ...')*
  2 *Lieferkettengesetz ('a law regulating ...')*
  3 *Rohstofflieferant*
  4 *Menschenrechtsorganisation*

b Compare results with your partner.

c Use an internet search engine to find the common English expression for each of the above items.

Girl picking tobacco

7 Communicating internationally

Intercultural communication In mediation tasks you are sometimes confronted with terms that are specific to Germany, e.g. *Bundesamt für Wirtschaft und Ausfuhrkontrolle*. Which of the two ways of dealing with this term given below is better? Keep in mind that you are writing for a non-German audience.
1 the government office that supervises exports
2 the Federal Office of Economic Affairs and Export Control

8 Focus on text types

In every mediation task you are asked to write a certain type of text. In this case it is an article for a website.

a Which of the following do you think are necessary or desirable in an article written for the general public?
  1 an eye-catching title
  2 explanations of technical terms
  3 a neutral style
  4 an appealing opening sentence
  5 direct address
  6 lots of concrete examples
  7 a concluding sentence

b Compare your ideas with your partner.

Do it

9 Getting started: two versions

Getting off to a good start is often the hardest part of writing. Compare the two texts below and discuss their relative advantages with your partner.

A ***The German Supply Chain Act***
The German government has agreed on a new law that will go into effect in 2023. This law makes large manufacturing firms in Germany responsible for their supply chains.

B ***Chaining in the supply chain***
Child labour is illegal in Germany. But it is not illegal for German manufacturers to import parts that have been made using child labour. A new law – the Supply Chain Act – changes this situation.

10 Writing

Now write your own article based on the German text. Use all the information you already gathered.

Feedback

▶ Check

11 Peer assessment

a Swap texts with your partner. Read and assess what each one of you has written.
b Give your partner concrete feedback on their text. Listen to your partner's feedback.

12 Self-assessment

In your *method card, write down any strategies that can help you with mediation tasks. Decide for each strategy whether it needs more practice.

Method card – mediation	
What I am good at	What I need to practise
...	...

A step forward for global equity

Zacharias Zacharakis

In 2021 the German government passed the first supply-chain law in the EU.

Für den internationalen Kapitalismus der vergangenen Jahrzehnte wird gern eine Metapher verwendet, die seine gefährliche Seite beschreiben soll. Die Rede ist vom Raubtierkapitalismus. Gemeint ist damit unter anderem, dass die hoch entwickelten Industrienationen des Westens den globalen Süden ausbeuten. Wir lassen billig Waren für unseren Konsum in Ländern herstellen, in denen dafür Löhne gezahlt werden, die auch dort nicht zum Leben reichen, in denen sogar Kinder für unseren Wohlstand schuften. Erstmals soll jetzt mit einem Gesetz in Deutschland dieses Raubtier der globalen Ausbeutung an die Leine gelegt werden.

Es ist ein respektabler Erfolg, den zwei Minister der Bundesregierung mit dem Beschluss über ein Lieferkettengesetz für sich verbuchen können – vor allem, wenn man bedenkt, wie groß der Widerstand dagegen war. [...]

Von ihren ursprünglichen Positionen mussten für diese Einigung allerdings [...] die Minister Müller und Heil zurückweichen. Sie hatten verlangt, dass alle Unternehmen in Deutschland ab 500 Beschäftigten für die Einhaltung der Menschenrechte in ihrer gesamten Lieferkette verantwortlich sind. Das hätte bedeutet: Ein deutscher Autohersteller hätte bis zur Rohstofflieferantin sicherstellen müssen, also bis zur Kobaltmine im Kongo, die Grundstoffe für Battetien moderner Elektroautos liefert, dass keine Kinder in den Minen nach dem Rohstoff schürfen. Um Verstöße zu sanktionieren, wären die Unternehmen zivilrechtlich haftbar gemacht worden.

So weit wird das neue Lieferkettengesetz nun nicht gehen. [...]

Ab Januar 2023 soll [...] gelten, dass zunächst Unternehmen mit 3.000 Beschäftigten sich an das neue Lieferkettengesetz halten müssen, ab dem Jahr 2024 dann Unternehmen mit mehr als 1.000 Beschäftigten. Damit sind zunächst immerhin 600 Firmen betroffen, im zweiten Schritt knapp 2.900. Der Wirtschaft wird somit ausreichend Zeit gegeben, sich auf die neuen Bestimmungen einzustellen und sich ihre Lieferanten genau anzusehen. Wie sind die Arbeitsbedingungen vor Ort? Wird grundlegender Schutz für die Menschen gewährleistet? Verantwortlich sollen die deutschen Unternehmen jedoch zunächst nur für ihre direkten Zulieferer sein, nicht für die Zulieferer der Zulieferer, also für die gesamte Lieferkette. Falls aber doch Verstöße bekannt werden in Unternehmen, die weiter hinten in der Lieferkette liegen, greift auch dann die Sorgfaltspflicht.

Gut ist, dass auch eine Lösung dafür gefunden wurde, wie man mit Unternehmen verfährt, die sich nicht an das neue Gesetz halten. Eine zivilrechtliche Haftung wird es zwar nicht geben, stattdessen aber drohen den deutschen Firmen Bußgelder und ein Ausschluss von öffentlichen Ausschreibungen. Überwacht werden soll das vom Bundesamt für Wirtschaft und Ausfuhrkontrolle (Bafa), einer Behörde also, die durchaus Erfahrung hat mit dem internationalen Geschäft deutscher Unternehmen. Unklar ist noch, was als Verstoß gegen die Sorgfaltspflichten der Unternehmen im Gesetz festgelegt wird, zum Beispiel, ob vor allem Kinderarbeit ausgeschlossen werden soll oder ob auch existenzsichernde Löhne eine Rolle spielen werden.

Auch wenn sich Menschenrechtsorganisationen mehr erhofft haben von diesem deutschen Sorgfaltspflichtengesetz, wie es offiziell heißt, wird damit doch ein neues Kapitel aufgeschlagen in der Geschichte des globalen Kapitalismus. Auf europäischer Ebene nämlich geht die Initiative für eine ähnliche Regelung voran. Das EU-Parlament drängt die Kommission zur Ausgestaltung einer EU-weiten Verordnung. Dass jetzt mit Deutschland die größte Volkswirtschaft in der Union ein solches Gesetz beschließen will, wird diesen Prozess beschleunigen. Letztlich wird sogar die deutsche Wirtschaft diesen befördern, weil es gleiche Bedingungen für alle Unternehmen in der EU braucht.

Der Westen könnte sich also endlich auf den Weg machen, die von ihm verantworteten globalen Ungerechtigkeiten zu zügeln.

From: 'Zügel für den globalen Kapitalismus', Die Zeit, *12 February 2021*

▶ SF 47: Mediating from German into English

1 Mediating You attend a bilingual school and are supposed to give a presentation in your social studies class. You want to talk about Western nations and their responsibility for fair treatment of developing countries. Based on the article above prepare your oral presentation in English about the measures taken by the German government to ensure a fairer treatment.

Text 10

Swept up or left behind? Feelings about globalization

Pew Research Center

- Reconsider the guiding question of the chapter. Has your opinion about globalization changed since the beginning of the chapter? If so, why?

Globalization has meant enormous gains for some, but not all. Many people in the US and the UK regard it with skepticism, as a Pew survey revealed. Read the first part of the Pew survey. Following this, partner A reads the excerpt on p. 108, partner B goes to p. 249. The texts are further excerpts from the Pew report.

In 2016, both Americans and Britons participated in divisive votes shaped in part by questions of immigration and global engagement. In the United States, voters cast ballots in a presidential election ultimately won by Donald Trump and his 'America first' vision. Across the Atlantic, 'leave' voters outnumbered 'remain' voters in a national referendum on continued European Union membership, framed by the slogan 'Take back control.' Attempts to explain the twin poll results have focused on people who felt left behind and who voted against the seemingly inexorable tide of growing economic interdependence, cultural diversity and social connectivity that define a globalized world. But direct, systematic comparisons of the two countries have been rare.

Pew Research Center undertook focus groups in the United States and United Kingdom in 2019 – prior to the outbreak of COVID-19 – to understand better the degree to which similar narratives about globalization and its impacts are evident in each country – and whether these narratives vary by geography, political affiliation or other factors in each country.

Info

The **Pew Research Center** is a politically neutral 'fact tank' situated in Washington. It conducts public opinion surveys, data analysis and opinion research.

Annotations

1 **divisive** *spaltend*
6 **poll** process of asking a few people what they think about sth. in order to discover the general opinion
7 **inexorable** unstoppable
11 **focus group** small group of people, deliberately selected to discuss a specific subject
12 **prior to sth.** before sth.
13 **impact** *Auswirkung*
14 **affiliation** orientation, connection

The focus groups confirm that the story of being 'left behind' remains common in both the U.S. and UK. Participants highlighted the ways in which the forces of globalization left them rudderless, closing industries, leading people to abandon their homes and harming them economically. But the group conversations also reveal a narrative of being 'swept up' by globalization. Those who are swept up experience because of too much attention from global forces – investment and new job creation supplant traditional work, inflate real estate prices and displace some people from their homes and communities. Stories of being left behind and swept up both lead to feelings of alienation and loss. [...]

Though participants were often unsure of how to define globalization, key themes did emerge. These centered on economics and trade, the global balance of power, immigration and cultural exchange, technological advancement, and community.

And unlike technical definitions, participants found it relatively easy to share illustrations of globalization. They brought up the impacts of globalization on their daily lives, like the experiences of calling customer service and reaching a call center in another country. People touted the ability to order goods from the other side of the world on Amazon and have them delivered the next day. Others brought up how immigration has shifted the fabric of their country for better or worse, or how openness to foreign ideas and customs was changing their country's culture – again, for both better and worse. [...]

While the changes participants saw in their countries and the perceived catalysts of those changes varied, nearly all participants said these shifts were causing them to feel disconnected from their national identity. For some, globalization in the form of immigration and multiculturalism had wrought too much change, to the point that they felt they could no longer recognize their country. They noted that they couldn't feel a connection with others under the mantle of being 'British' or 'American' because the culture had been eroded too much and that some people grouped under that label felt too different from them.

For others, pivotal events marking a political shift away from the globalized world and toward a 'country-first' national character alienated them from how they used to conceptualize and understand their countries. For these people, community and national identity *meant* welcoming people from elsewhere and blending cultures, foods and ideas. [...]

While these focus groups were diverse and stretched across the U.S. and UK, their participants largely viewed globalization through one of two lenses: fostering an arena of international rivalry and competition, or creating the possibility of new cross-border communities. Among the former group, increased international connections have meant greater insecurity and threats to their country's ability to maintain power and influence. For the latter group, globalization has come with perceived opportunities, and even obligations, to connect with others, find common cause and tackle global problems.

Across the focus groups, participants in the U.S. and UK consistently agreed on one thing: Their communities, their countries and their worlds are changing.

Annotations

18 **rudderless** without anyone in control
22 **supplant sth.** replace sth.
24 **alienation** feeling of not belonging in a group
31 **tout sth.** praise sth.
33 **fabric of sth.** structure of sth. (here: a society)
36 **perceive sth.** *etwas wahrnehmen*
36 **catalyst** event or person that causes a change
39 **wring sth. (wrought – wrought)** (here) cause sth., create sth.
42 **erode sth.** diminish or destroy sth. gradually
44 **pivotal** important
46 **conceptualize sth.** *(fml)* develop an idea of sth.
52 **foster sth.** encourage sth.
58 **tackle sth.** *etwas in Angriff nehmen*

Annotations
62 **concur** *(fml)* agree
63 **multilateral** involving more than two nations/groups

While the term 'globalization' did not always roll off their tongues, participants concurred that the catalyst for change was an increasingly interconnected world in which multinational corporations, foreign trade and multilateral organizations had become important factors shaping local and national identities. [...]

From: 'In U.S. and U.K, globalization leaves some feeling "left behind" or "swept up"', www.pewresearch.org, *5 October 2020*

Partner A: Read the text below. **Partner B:** Go to p. 249.

Annotations
1 **multinationals** multinational corporations
3 **equate sth. with sth.** *etwas mit etwas gleichsetzen*
3 **shuttered** closed down
3 **locale** *Schauplatz*
10 **exacerbate sth.** [ɪɡˈzæsəbeɪt] *(fml)* make sth. worse
10 **onset** beginning of sth. unpleasant
13 **transient** temporary
16 **high street** (BE) main shopping street
21 **bustling** lively

Industrial change, automation and the influence of multinationals were prime catalysts in stories of being left behind by globalization. Being left behind was often equated with job loss and shuttered businesses. Depending on the locale, participants described either industry-specific or general job losses. Focus group participants in Pittsburgh and Newcastle were particularly animated by stories of being left behind, describing how they or people they knew had lost jobs at coal mines, steel mills and other industrial facilities.

In these cities and elsewhere, participants pointed to the carry-over effects of job loss – from local stores being unable to remain profitable to neighborhoods becoming less prosperous and more dangerous, exacerbated by the onset of crime and drug use that accompanied peoples' material decline. People who felt left behind also noted the impact of economic decline on local social ties. Participants linked falling rates of homeownership with growing numbers of 'transient' renters and less meaningful relationships with neighbors. [...]

The closures and changes people described extended from the workplace to the 'high street' in the UK, and the tone was often one of profound loss. In all four cities in the UK where focus groups were conducted, people noted the closure of independent businesses on the high streets, highlighting how these shifts left them feeling like the previous epicenter of their community was no longer the bustling center of commerce. [...]

From: 'In U.S. and U.K, globalization leaves some feeling "left behind" or "swept up"', www.pewresearch.org, *5 October 2020*

Comprehension

1 Make notes on the following aspects of the Pew report: reasons for the survey, main themes of globalization, daily influence of globalization and perspectives on globalization. Compare your results.

2 Explain to your partner what it means to feel *left behind* by globalization. Then listen to your partner's explanation of feeling *swept up*.

Analysis

3 You choose Do task **a** or **b**.

a Examine the different views on globalization expressed in the focus groups and the reasons given.

b Examine the different views on national identity expressed in the focus groups and the reasons given.

c Compare your findings with someone who chose the other task and speculate on possible reasons for the differing reactions.

Language awareness

4 The text frequently uses recorded speech, e.g. 'They noted ... them' (ll. 40–43).
a Have a look at the fourth paragraph. Write down what the interviewees might have said.
b With a partner discuss why the writer did not use direct speech.

► More language

Beyond the text

5 Writing Write a dialogue between two people who discuss the impact of globalization on their home town or country.

► SF 36: Creative writing

Text 11

The benefits of migration

- Think about reasons for migrating to a different country. Which of these reasons would be important enough for you to leave your homeland?

► SF 39: Analysing films and videos

Viewing *Watch this video about migration from the website of* The Economist.

Comprehension

1 Summarize the reasons for migration that are mentioned in the video. Do they resemble the ones you thought about beforehand?

2 Write down what you remember about the economic impact of migration.

Analysis

3 Watch the film a second time. Analyse which cinematic devices the filmmakers use to emphasize their view on migration.

Beyond the text

4 You choose Do either task **a** or **b**.
a Writing Imagine you are Beth's younger sister who is able to study and afford medical treatment for your son because Beth sends you money regularly. Write a letter in which you tell Beth about your everday life and the impact her support has had.
b Writing You are going to participate in a discussion about the benefits and challenges of migration. Collect arguments that underline the advantages of migration as well as those that stress its political challenges.

Info

Today many countries are facing conflicts and instability: they may be challenged by wars, civil war or frequent acts of terrorism. **United Nations Peacekeeping** is an institution that can help these countries establish peace. All peacekeeping operations are impartial and non-violent and they only take place if the parties involved have given their consent. Protecting civilians, help with elections or protection of human rights are some of the tasks accomplished by peacekeeping operations.

Welcome to the pandemic era

Peter Daszak

- Discuss measures that could reduce the risks of global pandemics.

Read Peter Daszak's account of pandemics in the past and the future.

In late 2013, in the village of Meliandou in rural Guinea, a group of children playing near a hollow tree disturbed a small colony of bats hiding inside. Scientists think that Emile Ouamouno, who later became the first tragic 'index' case in the west African Ebola outbreak, was likely exposed to bat faeces while playing near the tree.

Every pandemic starts like this. An innocuous human activity, such as eating wildlife, can spark an outbreak that leads to a pandemic. […] In 2019, we can speculate that a person from south-west China entered a bat cave near their village to hunt wildlife for sale at the local wet market. Perhaps they later developed a nagging cough that represents the beginning of what we now know as Covid-19. Now, a growing human population, ever-encroaching development and a globalised network of travel and trade have accelerated the pace of pandemic emergence. We're entering a new pandemic era.

Most pandemics begin in the emerging disease hotspots of the world; the edges of forests in regions such as west Africa, the Amazon basin and south-east Asia. Tropical rainforests are home to a rich diversity of wildlife, which in turn carry an array of viruses. We know far more about these animals than we do about the viruses they carry. An estimated 1.7m viruses exist in mammals and birds (the origins of most pandemics), but less than 0.1% have been described. They spread to millions of people each year; though they often don't cause noticeable symptoms, the sheer volume means that plenty can.

Before humans became an agricultural species, our populations were sparser and less connected. A virus infecting a hunter-gatherer might only reach family members or perhaps a hunting group. But the Anthropocene, our new geological epoch, has changed everything. A great acceleration of human activity has dramatically altered our planet's landscapes, oceans and atmosphere, transforming as much as half of the world's tropical forest into agriculture and human settlements.

About one-third of emerging diseases are the product of these rapid changes in land use, as people are pushed into contact with wildlife they would once have rarely encountered. The viruses that emerge, such as Zika, Ebola and Nipah, include the latest of our foes, Covid-19, transported from the altered rural landscape of China to a city near you.

Human activity has created a continuous cycle of viral spillover and spread. Our current approach is to wait for outbreaks to start, and then design drugs or vaccines to control them. But as we've seen with Covid-19, this approach isn't good enough: while we wait for a vaccine, hundreds of thousands of people have died, and millions have been infected. By the time the US produced sufficient doses to vaccinate against the H1N1 influenza pandemic in 2009, the virus had already infected about a quarter of the people on our planet.

If we are to prevent future pandemics, we will need to reassess our relationship with nature, blocking each step in the chain of disease emergence. This should

Annotations

- 3 **index case** first documented patient in an epidemic
- 4 **be exposed to sth.** come into contact with sth.
- 4 **faeces** [ˈfiːsiːz] (pl.) *Exkrement*
- 6 **innocuous** harmless
- 9 **wet market** open market where animals and/or their meat are sold
- 11 **encroach** expand
- 12 **accelerate sth.** make sth. happen faster
- 16 **array** broad spectrum
- 22 **sparse** *spärlich*
- 30 **encounter sb./sth.** come in contact with sb./sth.
- 31 **foe** enemy
- 33 **spillover** *Übergang (von einem Wirt zum anderen)*
- 37 **sufficient** [səˈfɪʃnt] *ausreichend*
- 40 **reassess sth.** *etwas neu bewerten*

Info

The term ***Anthropocene*** is often used to describe the current geological age, although it has not been officially approved as a description of geological time. The Anthropocene is seen as a period in which humans started to have a new, irreversible impact on the environment and the climate. It is not yet decided when this era actually began.

begin with reducing the rampant consumption that drives deforestation and wildlife exploitation. We'll also need to remove viral-risk species from wildlife markets, crack down on the illegal wildlife trade and work with communities to find alternatives. We should be putting more pressure on industries that harvest tropical timber and wildlife products, rewarding corporate sustainability and legislating against overconsumption. [...]

As we rebuild our economies after the coronavirus pandemic, rather than returning to the system of unchecked consumption that brought us Covid-19, we have an opportunity to green our economies. Centuries of environmental exploitation have put us in a fragile position on this planet. While some may balk at the costs of avoiding environmental breakdown, or fail to understand the value of preserving a species of butterfly, frog or fish, most of us recognise that Covid-19 has brought death and economic misery on a global scale. Once we accept that human activity is what led to this, we may finally be empowered to escape the pandemic era.

From: 'We are entering an era of pandemics – it will end only when we protect the rainforest'
The Guardian, *28 July 2020*

Annotations
42 **rampant** widespread
44 **crack down on sth.** *(infml) etwas rigoros unterbinden*
45 **harvest sth.** *etwas ernten*
45 **timber** wood
46 **corporate** *unternehmerisch*
46 **legislate** make laws
51 **balk** [bɔːk] hesitate

Comprehension

1 Make a flow chart showing how pandemics arise and spread.

Analysis

2 Analyse the differences between traditional methods of coping with pandemics and the author's recommendations.

Language awareness

3 Examine the author's choice of words in the last two paragraphs. Analyse how they influence the reader.

► Support p. 250

4 Writing Rewrite the same part in the style of a neutral, informative text.

Beyond the text

5 Writing Your local activist group wants to put pressure on politicians to support the good sides of globalization and fight the bad ones. Devise a leaflet with ten demands to be distributed in your neighbourhood.

Chapter task

Where is my home in a globalized world –
my neighbourhood, my country, the world?
Answer this question in a text form of your choice
(e.g. an essay, a poem, a video, a poster).

► Getting started

Chapter 4
The UK – between tradition and change

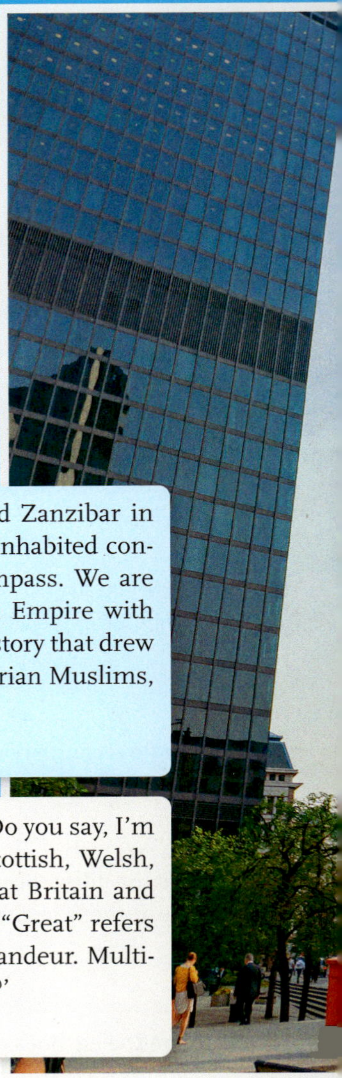

'[...] My children have Scotland, Wales, Iraq, India, Pakistan and Zanzibar in their blood. We live in Croydon and our family extends to every inhabited continent on the planet. Our friends are from all points of the compass. We are global and local in one room. Whether you look at the British Empire with shame or anger or pride this is what it does for us now, it is our history that drew us together and it shapes our Britain. We are IndoScots, Presbyterian Muslims, we are London and like Tom Jones, we're not unusual.'

Greendeskbruce

'When someone abroad asks "Where are you from?" Do you say, I'm British, a UK citizen, from Great Britain, English, Scottish, Welsh, Northern Irish, or from the United Kingdom of Great Britain and Northern Ireland? Do you then try to explain that the "Great" refers to the largest island and is really not a delusion of grandeur. Multiculturalism is fine but do we have any shared culture?'

JohnBea

▶ More info

Annotations
- 2 **Croydon** district in south London
- 7 **Tom Jones** Welsh pop singer who sang the song 'It's not unusual'
- 13 **grandeur** [ˈɡrændʒə(r)] *Größe, Pracht*
- 18 **conciliatory** *versöhnlich*
- 22 **heritage** *Erbe*
- 37 **entitled to sth.** having the right to sth.

1 The texts and the video introduce you to different definitions of Britishness.
- **a** Take a look at the material. Note down the different forms of Britishness you encounter.
- **b** Choose one statement about Britishness that you find particularly striking. Present it and explain why you picked it.
- **c** On the basis of the offered material, discuss if there is such a thing as Britishness after all.

2
- **a** Have a look at the Chapter map and discuss which aspects are already represented in the quotations and will be covered in the chapter.
- **b** Speculate what the other topics mentioned in the Chapter map might have to do with the guiding question.

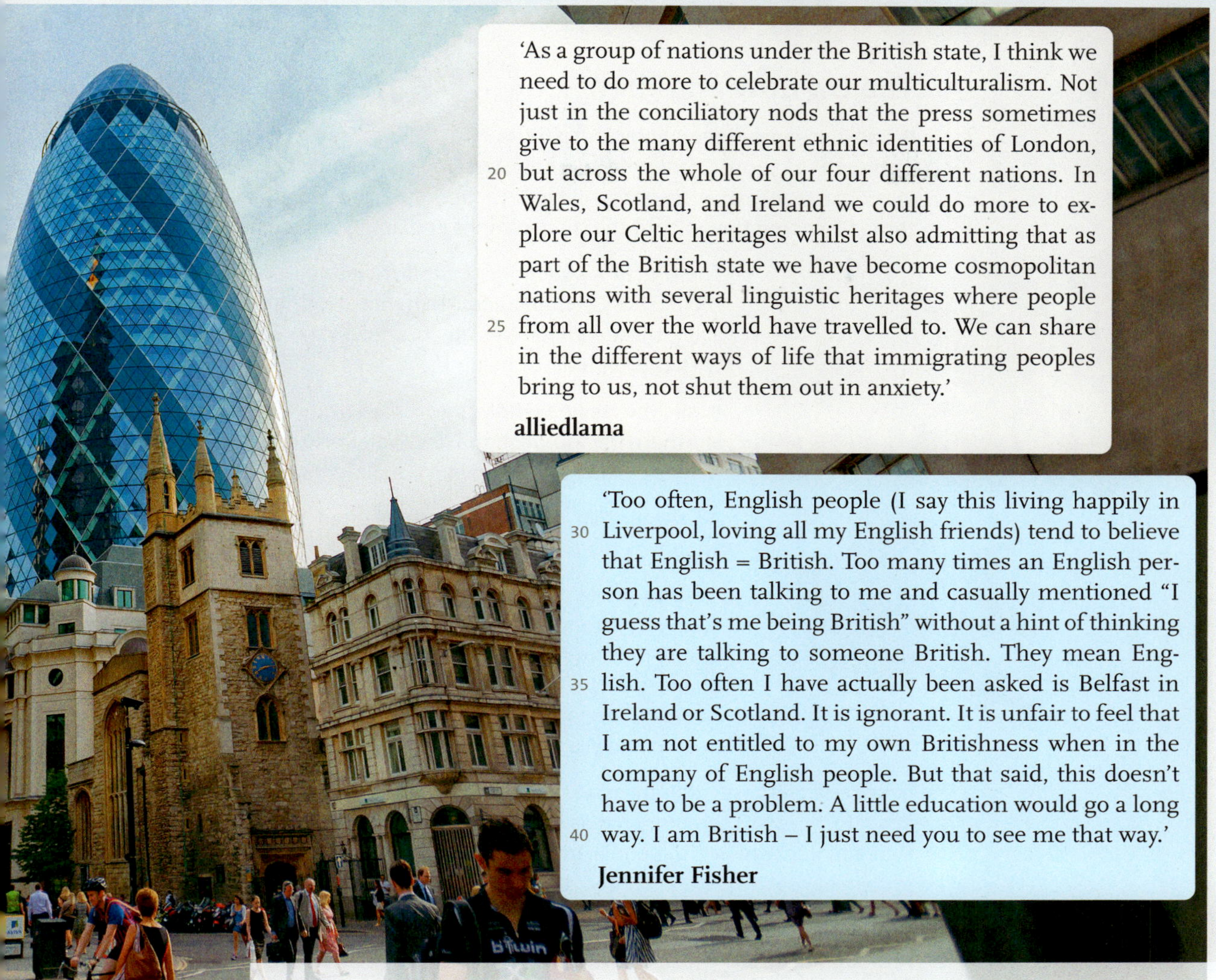

'As a group of nations under the British state, I think we need to do more to celebrate our multiculturalism. Not just in the conciliatory nods that the press sometimes give to the many different ethnic identities of London, but across the whole of our four different nations. In Wales, Scotland, and Ireland we could do more to explore our Celtic heritages whilst also admitting that as part of the British state we have become cosmopolitan nations with several linguistic heritages where people from all over the world have travelled to. We can share in the different ways of life that immigrating peoples bring to us, not shut them out in anxiety.'

alliedlama

'Too often, English people (I say this living happily in Liverpool, loving all my English friends) tend to believe that English = British. Too many times an English person has been talking to me and casually mentioned "I guess that's me being British" without a hint of thinking they are talking to someone British. They mean English. Too often I have actually been asked is Belfast in Ireland or Scotland. It is ignorant. It is unfair to feel that I am not entitled to my own Britishness when in the company of English people. But that said, this doesn't have to be a problem. A little education would go a long way. I am British – I just need you to see me that way.'

Jennifer Fisher

Texts from: 'Let's not make a fuss: 10 things that sum up Britishness', theguardian.com, *9 June 2014*

Chapter map

political system

the UK and Europe

national mood

islandness

regional identities

Chapter task: staging a debate

A united or disunited kingdom?

Argumentative writing

British monarchy

British Empire

Britishness

Brexit

multiculturalism

▸ More info

The UK now and then

It's all in a name – geography and politics

Although the terms *Great Britain, Britain, England,* and *United Kingdom* are often used interchangeably, they are not synonyms. *Great Britain*, or *Britain* for short, is a political term describing the unity of the three nations England, Scotland, and Wales.

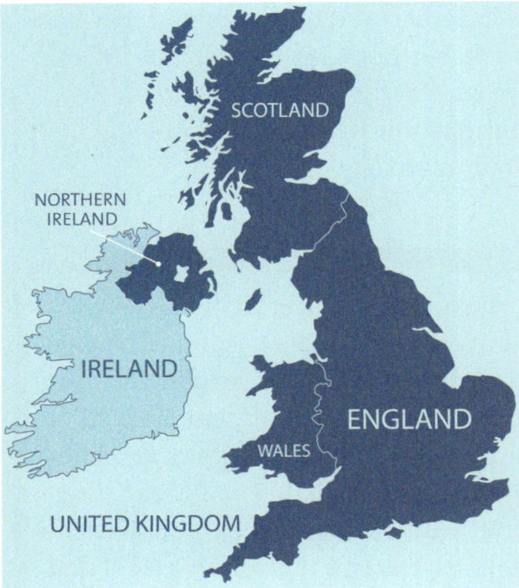

The *United Kingdom of Great Britain and Northern Ireland*, or the *UK* for short, includes a fourth nation, Northern Ireland. Geographically, these four nations are located on the British Isles – together with the Republic of Ireland.

While the UK as a whole is governed from Westminster in London, Northern Ireland, Scotland and Wales also have their own national parliaments with certain individual rights of self-government.

All the British nations are represented by the Union Flag, also known as the Union Jack, which is the national flag of the UK.

Despite being part of the United Kingdom, all four nations also have very strong national identities, which has led to various separatist movements. The Brexit referendum in 2016 and the consequences of the United Kingdom leaving the EU have reignited demands for independence, mostly in Scotland but also in Northern Ireland and Wales.

In spite of all these differences, various uniting factors remain, most importantly the Royal Family with the monarch as head of state for all the nations. Polls have shown that a majority of British people are still in favour of the constitutional monarchy as a system of government and regard the Royal Family as an important British institution.

Britain's place in Europe and its relationship with the EU

Although the UK officially left the EU on 31 January 2020, geographically it remains a part of Europe and in fact shares a border with an EU country, namely the Republic of Ireland. As a strong economic power it continues to be an important trading partner for the EU and there are still many economic and cultural ties between the UK and the continent. Moreover, the UK plays a significant role in world politics as a permanent member of the UN Security Council and NATO.

Britain – a multicultural society

What has shaped British society more than anything else is its imperial past. The British Empire was the largest in history and had territories on every continent except Antarctica. In the 20th century, increasing demands for independence in the colonies led to gradual decolonisation, but the strong ties between Britain and its former colonies remain in the form of the Commonwealth of Nations of which most former British territories are members. They recognize the monarch as their nominal head. Due to its colonial past but also because of its economic and political strength, the UK is an attractive country for immigrants. These immigrants have added greatly to the nation's diversity, enriching the UK with their cultural, religious, and culinary input while also increasing the economic wealth with their labour. Consequently, Britain has become a multicultural society, in which everyone has the right to be treated equally irrespective of ethnicity, religion or culture. This is, however, an ongoing process and Britain still has a long way to go.

1 Words words words

Note down the geographical, political and cultural particularities of the United Kingdom. Use as many highlighted phrases from the text as possible.

2 Organizing words and ideas in a spidergram

a Create a *spidergram for the word field *politics*. Use relevant words from the text and add some of your own.

b Compare your spidergram with your partner's. Add some more branches where necessary.

3 Chunk it!

a Collect useful phrases and *chunks from the text that help you define the UK as a nation.

b The country's name stresses the joint national identity and unity of the four nations that make up the United Kingdom. Using an online *collocations dictionary, form as many collocations with the two nouns *nation* and *unity* as possible.

▶ Check

4 Speaking about the UK

You choose Work on task a or b.

a Speaking Explain why it is wrong to refer to the Queen solely as the Queen of England. ▶ More info

b Speaking A friend of yours argues that all multicultural societies are basically the same. Explain to him/her what makes British multiculturalism so special.

Taking stock: the mood in the UK

Deborah Mattinson

- Name political decisions and events that could divide a country.

Language help

regional identities • governed by ... • head of state • close vote • multiculturalism • Royal Family • political parties • gap between ... • nationalism

The organisation BritainThinks conducted a survey of the mood in the UK in 2019. Deborah Mattinson reports about her findings from the survey.

I have been listening to people in focus groups since the late 1980s and I cannot recall a time when the national mood was more despairing. 'Broken', 'sad', 'worried', 'angry' – the negatives tumble out, as does the long list of grievances.

I'm hearing anxieties voiced in a way I haven't heard since the 1990s: a rundown NHS, job insecurity, teacher shortages. Seven out of 10 feel pessimistic about homelessness, 68% are gloomy about rising poverty, and a staggering one in five think it likely that they, or someone close, will be a victim of violent crime in the next year. This rises to almost a third in London.

We're a deeply divided nation, too – and nearly three-quarters of us expect that to get worse in the year ahead. Forty-eight per cent self-identify as a 'have-not' while 52% see themselves as a 'have'. We're torn apart by social class, by geography, and by how we vote – especially on Brexit.

The starkest divide, though, is age: 52% of over-65s feel optimistic about the future of the UK, contrasting with just 23% of under-34s.

Younger people feel a strong sense of injustice. Home ownership seems a pipe dream, even for the relatively well off. Secure employment can be elusive for them too, despite many being far better qualified than their parents and grandparents.

But our survey suggests they shouldn't hope for sympathy. Many in the older generation dismiss them as 'liberal snowflakes' who waste cash on 'avocado toast and flat whites', then waste away weekends 'watching screens'. Seventy-eight per cent of over-45s and 82% of those over 65 believe British values are in decline, and many see young people as the cause: 'They just don't have the same values we do – or the respect that we had.'

Where the nation can agree is that we probably can't expect politicians to lead us out of this mess. Trust has long been in short supply. Ipsos Mori's 'veracity index' shows that just 19% believe politicians tell the truth – unchanged since 1983. What's happening now is different, and potentially much more damaging: voters have lost faith in politicians' ability to govern competently. Our focus groups, regardless of how they voted, felt the scales fall from their eyes as they watched 'them' grapple with Brexit. One told me: 'It's like we've all woken up.'

Their verdict? Politicians are 'totally useless', 'clueless' or 'unbelievably poor'. Seventy-four per cent conclude that our political system is no longer fit for purpose, and 83% feel let down by the entire political establishment. Just 6% believe politicians understand them.

Annotations
1 **focus group** small group of people, selected based on a set of criteria to discuss a specific subject
4 **rundown** *(adj)* in a bad state
5 **NHS** *(abbr)* National Health Service
15 **pipe dream** sth. that is unrealistic
16 **elusive** hard to find
25 **Ipsos Mori** global market research company
30 **grapple with sth.** struggle with sth.

Info

On 23 June 2016 the **Brexit referendum** was held and people in the UK voted whether or not the UK would stay in the EU. A narrow majority voted to leave the EU. In January 2020 the EU (Withdrawal Agreement) Bill passed through Parliament and became law under Prime Minister Boris Johnson. On 31 January 2020 the UK officially left the EU.

Some of this is tragic, some cringe-making – 'in the last two years there have been so many political problems it's an embarrassment to be a UK citizen' said one, explaining why 73% think that our once-proud nation is currently 'seen as a laughing-stock by the rest of the world'.

Annotations
35 **cringe-making** making you feel extremely embarrassed
40 **palpable** within one's reach

There are a few crumbs of comfort. While pessimism about Britain is palpable, just over half feel optimistic about their local area, and two-thirds are optimistic about their personal lives – and this is true for voters of all ages. Many feel that, whatever happens on the national stage, British character will win out: 69% agree that 'British people will just get on with things regardless of the impact of Brexit'.

But the cloud of uncertainty hangs heavily. Voters long for a leader to map a clear route through. One observed: 'We seem to be stumbling along a crooked path and not towards a target.' Eighty-six per cent say the 'UK needs a strong leader now more than ever before' [...] The bar is set high.

From: 'Brexit has made this country as anxious as I have ever known it', theguardian.com, *15 June 2019*

Comprehension

1 **a** Work in pairs. Sum up what unites people in the UK and what divides them. Visualize your results, e.g. in a table, and present them.
b Compare your visualization with another pair's. If necessary, add to your notes.

Analysis

2 Analyse how the author employs choice of words and imagery to express the emotional state of the people surveyed.

► Support p. 250

Language awareness

3 The first paragraph focuses on the national mood and people's emotions. Copy the scale below and collect all the adjectives with a negative *connotation found in this paragraph. Arrange them on the left-hand side of the scale. Now add adjectives with more positive connotations on the right-hand side.

--	–	0	+	++

Beyond the text

4 Speaking Imagine you are a young Briton. For a panel discussion on the current state of the nation, explain to members of the older generation why you are not a 'liberal snowflake' (cf. l.19) but are seriously worried about your future and the development of the UK. If possible, use your findings from task 3.

A united kingdom or regional identities? Daniel Wincott

- Do you feel more like a citizen of Europe, Germany or your federal state? Explain why.

The following extract is taken from a comment by Professor Daniel Wincott on the failure of British politics to unite the nations of the UK.

Annotations
- 1 **belie sth.** *(here)* contradict sth.
- 2 **nation-statehood** *Nationalstaatlichkeit*
- 3 **sustain sth.** strengthen sth.
- 4 **underpin sth.** support sth.
- 9 **Remain** the vote to stay in the EU in the Brexit referendum
- 10 **Leave** the vote to leave the EU in the Brexit referendum
- 16 **upshot** result

[...] Belying its name, the UK is far from united. Its disunity reveals that the Kingdom is a mystery to itself. Belying standard accounts of nation-statehood, surprisingly little effort has been made to create or sustain a shared state-wide identity or the institutions that might underpin it. There is little evidence of the shared 'imagined community' that is vital for any nation. On the contrary, recent research on relative territorial identities – how individuals view their sub-state and Britain-wide identities – casts new light on the character of apparently shared British identity. It turns out to work in very different ways across Britain. In the Brexit referendum, those who emphasized British national identity were more likely to vote Remain in England, but Leave in Scotland and Wales. [...]

Meanwhile, the UK-wide media is (unsurprisingly) dominated by English concerns, particularly those of London and the south east. UK national newspapers publish distinctive editions in Scotland and Northern Ireland often with contradictory front pages. Brexit provided an opportunity to test how key events – for example high-profile Brexit court cases – were mediated across each of the UK's nations. The upshot, it seems, was that the same events generated a distinctive debate focused on different issues in each nation (even in Wales, where sub-state media is notoriously weak).

From: 'The possible break-up of the United Kingdom', www.ukandeu.ac.uk, *19 December 2020*

Comprehension

1 Point out the evidence Wincott presents for a lack of British unity.

► SF 23: Analysing cartoons

CartoonStock.com

Analysis

2 Work in pairs and look at cartoons which also highlight the disunity of Britain. ► More info
Partner B: Go to p. 250.

- **a** **Partner A:** Look at the cartoon on the left and analyse how it stresses British disunity. Prepare a 2-minute presentation for your partner that includes a detailed description of the cartoon.
- **b** Present your findings to each other. Examine together to what extent the two cartoons can be related to Daniel Wincott's arguments.

Language awareness

3 Wincott clearly voices an opinion in his comment. Note down words and phrases that show an opinion in the text and examine their effect on the reader.

► Support p. 250

Beyond the text

4 Writing On the basis of what you have found out about the UK so far, write a letter to Daniel Wincott in which you either agree or disagree with his opinion.

► SF 33: Writing a formal letter or email

Text 3

Don't neglect the UK's indigenous languages

Rhona NicDhùghaill

- Collect pros and cons of learning a language that is spoken only by few people.

► More info

Language help

minority/majority language • decline in the number of speakers • language as a means of communication • cultural/regional identity • revival of languages • dominant culture • cultural heritage • diversity

Signpost in Welsh and English

One aspect that distinguishes the different UK countries in Britain is language. English itself is only one of many indigenous languages in the UK, among them Welsh, Cornish, Scots and Irish Gaelic. The following articles deal with the question of whether learning these languages in school is important for the development of a national identity.

Partner B: Go to p. 251.
Partner A: Read the text below and work on the tasks following it.

Would you be surprised if I told you that, far from being a land of monoglots, there are ten indigenous languages spoken today in the British Isles? Yet we are very quick to tell ourselves that we're rubbish at languages. We are linguistically isolated monoglots, marooned on a cluster of islands on the edge of the Atlantic. If we were in the mix of mainland Europe, we tell ourselves, we'd be blethering away in at least two languages.

Except, as you read this, people the length of these islands are using indigenous languages other than English to communicate with friends, family, teachers, colleagues and public services. That they are in the minority doesn't mean that they don't exist. In fact, the numbers of primary school-age speakers are growing; almost a quarter of school pupils in Wales are educated through the medium of Welsh, Northern Ireland is home to 30 Irish-medium schools, Scotland's capital has just opened a new, dedicated Gaelic school due to increasing demand, and the Isle of Man has a Manx-medium school.

Annotations
- 1 **monoglot** *(n)* someone who speaks only one language
- 2 **indigenous** native, belonging to a country or place
- 4 **maroon sth.** *(v)* leave sb. in a place / on an island from which they cannot escape
- 14 **Manx-medium school** school that teaches in the minority language or bilingually

Annotations
19 buck sth. *(v)* oppose sth.
26 naysayer sb. who refuses or opposes sth.
49 provision process of supplying sth.
49 absolve sb. from sth. free sb. from guilt or responsibility

All of these children are also fluent in English; indeed, in the case of Gaelic-medium pupils, they outperform their English-educated counterparts in English tests. Their bilingualism bucks the monoglot trend of the majority.

Welsh school sign

There are those who would claim that such languages aren't 'useful' in the modern world and the global job market, and are therefore irrelevant to the current debate. 'Why are you wasting your time with Welsh/Gaelic/Irish/[insert your minority language of choice] anyway?' scoff the naysayers. 'We should all be learning Chinese!' Needless to say, the so-called reasoning behind such statements isn't about getting to know China's culture, heritage and people; rather, it's about how it could help you make money. But while Mandarin Chinese may well be useful for an international businessperson of the future, we don't only use language to earn money and do deals: we use language to communicate. To say there is no worth in learning a language that isn't economically useful is like saying there's no point in being friends with somebody unless they're going to help you get a better job. It's a spectacular, cynical miss of the point.

It's also inaccurate. My minority language skills have allowed me to earn a living, by teaching Gaelic to adults at various colleges and universities in Glasgow and in the West Highlands of Scotland. The same is true for many of my friends, whether they're schoolteachers, journalists or musicians. While the vast majority of Gaelic learners are not doing so for economic reasons, being a Gaelic speaker does open up employment opportunities that wouldn't be available to somebody without those language skills. There are also specific job opportunities for those fluent in other indigenous minority languages, with Irish also having the added bonus of being an official language of the EU, giving speakers access further job opportunities.

Sign in Scottish Gaelic and English

When it comes to representation in the media, the successful establishment of separate minority language provision has absolved mainstream channels of the responsibility to feature them. But must our indigenous minority languages be ignored outside their own niche media outlets? Would it really be so bad if the occasional news item allowed a minority language-speaking interviewee to respond in their own language, with English subtitles? Or if a contestant on the Great British Bake Off did the odd subtitled piece to camera in an indigenous British language that wasn't English? Or if newspapers like this one published an online article each week in one of our indigenous minority languages? Or, might such measures actually better reflect, and raise awareness of, our multilingual makeup? Might more people consider learning these languages? Might more speakers be inclined to use them more often, in more situations?

Different aspects of our cultures and beliefs, our habits and history, not to mention our humour, are all encoded in our languages. By knowing them, we know ourselves better. Thankfully, they have clung on to these islands despite decades, if not centuries, of cruel and systematic persecution; the people of Man and Cornwall have stared the awful reality of language death in the face, yet still they speak. There are now growing opportunities to learn many of these languages, and not just in their traditional heartlands. If you can, grab them with both hands; you will be the richer for it.

From: theguardian.com, *29 October 2013*

Sign in Welsh and English

Comprehension

1 Summarize Rhona NicDhùghaill's demand for more linguistic diversity in the UK. Make notes only.

Analysis

2 Examine NicDhùghaill's line of argumentation to convince her readers that indigenous languages should play a greater role in the UK.

Language awareness

3 **a** The author uses a number of questions in her article. Find examples and explain their effect on the reader.

b Name situations in which these kinds of questions tend to be used. Explain why.

Beyond the text

4 Now present your findings from **1–3** to your partner, then discuss the pros and cons of learning indigenous minority languages.

5 You choose Work on task **a** or **b**.

a Speaking Carry out a structured debate on the following motion: 'This house believes that the unity of the UK can only be guaranteed if English is the only official language.'

b In groups of four, discuss the following claim in a placemat: 'It is not enough to be taught minority languages at school. Language has to be alive in the community.' Write your conclusion in the middle of the placemat.

► SF 45: Having a debate

► Getting started

Scottish nationalism

Although Scotland is part of the United Kingdom, it has a long history of struggles for independence.

Statue of William Wallace, national hero in the First War of Scottish Independence (1296–1328)

▶ More info

Info

National identities in the UK

Scotland merged with England in 1707 to form the United Kingdom of Great Britain with the Treaty of Union. Before this, Scotland had fought several wars to remain independent. After unification, the desire for independence remained strong. Political campaigns for Scottish sovereignty began in the 19th century. Two devolution referenda in 1979 and 1997 led to the formation of a Scottish Parliament. In 2007 the Scottish National Party (SNP) became the first governing party of the Scottish Parliament. In 2014 a referendum on Scottish independence was held in which 44.7% of the voters voted for Scotland to become independent, and 55.3% voted to stay in the Union. After Brexit the SNP demanded another referendum on Scottish independence, which so far has been denied by Westminster. In the Scottish election on 6 May 2021 the SNP won the majority of the votes, but they narrowly missed an absolute majority by one seat. This victory led the party leader, Nicola Sturgeon, to demand a new referendum on Scottish independence. The feeling of having a distinct national identity has led to nationalist movements and calls for independence in Northern Ireland, Scotland and Wales, though they seem to be strongest in Scotland. These separatists argue that their country is better off on its own, while unionists are in favour of staying in the union.

1 Create a *spidergram of terms that you associate with nationalism. Add relevant words and phrases from the Info box above.

2 What is nationalism for you? Define your personal concept of it.

In the following radio report people connected to Scotland talk about Scottish nationalism, among them members of the Scottish pro-independence group Aye Aberdeen.

Comprehension

▶ SF 38: Listening/Viewing for gist and detail

▶ Check

1 a Listen to the interview for the first time and decide which of the following statements best describe the general content of the audio.

1 Scottish nationalism is a reaction to English nationalism.
2 Scottish nationalism is inclusive rather than exclusive.
3 Scottish people want another independence referendum because the first was undemocratic.
4 Scottish nationalism is a fight against control by Westminster.

b Listen to the interview for the second time and note down the answers to the questions below.
  1 What are the characteristics of being Scottish according to Teresa Dufficy?
  2 What is the difference between Scottish and English nationalists according to English author Ben Jackson?
  3 What does language have to do with Scotland's particular kind of nationalism?

Poster of the Scottish National Party for the European elections in 2019

Beyond the text

2 Go back to your spidergram from the Info box and assess to what extent Scottish nationalism as presented in the report fits your notion of nationalism.

3 You choose Do task **a** or **b**.
  a Speaking Discuss whether a multicultural form of nationalism is a contradiction in terms.
  b Speaking Discuss why the Brexit vote led to a renewed demand for Scottish independence.

Text 5

The political system in the UK

- Decide whether the statements below describe the functions and characteristics of the German *Bundestag* or the *Bundesrat*. Please note: One statement describes both chambers.

► More language

1 represents nation as a whole
2 deploys the *Bundeswehr*
3 approves of laws, regulations and constitutional changes
4 is elected directly by German citizens
5 is the organ through which the federal states participate in the legislation and administration of the Federation
6 elects the chancellor
7 consists of members selected by the state governments
8 determines the federal budget
9 has a legislative function

"My position here is largely symbolic."

CartoonStock.com

Comprehension

► SF 23: Analysing cartoons

► Check

1 Describe the cartoon on p. 123.

Analysis

2 Analyse the cartoon. What does it tell you about the role of the monarch in the United Kingdom?

10 Downing Street, official home of the British Prime Minister in London

Beyond the text

3 a Work in groups. Your teacher will assign one topic about the political system in the UK to each group. Research your topic and consider all the listed aspects.

Form of government:	Voting system:	Parliament:	Political parties:
– constitutional monarchy – head of state – head of government	– constituencies – majority vote	– House of Commons – House of Lords – functions of Parliament	– Conservatives – Labour – Liberal Democrats – regional parties

b Form new groups with one expert for every topic. Present your results and take notes.

c Return to your original group and exchange your knowledge. Discuss the claim that the British political system is partly undemocratic. Be prepared to present your findings.

4 Intercultural communication Together compare the British and German political systems and discuss the advantages and disadvantages of both.

Text 6

► More info

The British monarchy – unifying tradition or outdated anachronism?

- Research the following aspects relating to the Royal Family:
  - the role of the British monarch and the rights and duties connected with this institution,
  - the most important members of the Royal Family and their duties,
  - the most infamous royal scandals.

When Queen Elizabeth II celebrated her 90th birthday in 2016, the newspaper The Guardian *published an editorial asking whether the Queen's reign nearing its end should be taken as an inducement to reassess the constitutional monarchy.*

[...] Today's monarchy can appear profoundly rooted in history and tradition. But that can be misleading. In our day, this is partly because Elizabeth II is the only monarch most of us have ever known [...] and Prince Charles the only heir. None of this has changed since 1952, an increasingly immense span in an era in which political leaders and cultural icons rarely stay more than a decade at the top.

The truth is that over time the monarchy has always invented itself, and has been reinvented, as it goes along. Today's monarchy reflects Elizabeth II much more than most of us pause to consider. In particular it reflects her lifelong readiness to do dutifully and adaptably the things that she and her advisers decided were expected of her, and our acceptance of that role. But the monarchy has also sometimes been reinvented by the country, not the court.

All this has helped to make the Queen seem an object of fixed familiarity, the familiarity surely more apparent than real, like no other public figure in modern Britain. Although the monarchy can unquestionably have an infantilising effect, it is hard to think of anyone in this country other than the Queen who is more widely respected on the personal level, even by some committed republicans and reflexive defiers of authority. This has helped make her a somewhat deceptive source of the enduring in an otherwise radically changed Britain, and a perhaps improbable force for national cohesion in an era of deepening divisions.

The Queen is said to believe that when the public looks at her they see someone who is honest and prosaic and not in some ways so dissimilar to themselves. That will seem a naive view to many, yet the years would seem to have vindicated it. The Queen may not be able to point to many major achievements as monarch, but she has made incredibly few mistakes either; the rows over her tax position and the challenges posed by Princess Diana in life and death are now increasingly distant exceptions. She has public ratings any politician would die for. She has done her strange, irrational and undemocratic job with a tact and judgment few people could match.

When the earlier milestones of her life and reign had been reached, there was an understandable reluctance to spoil the national party. It has seemed churlish – perhaps even unBritish – to ask too loudly the question that Jeremy Bentham posed about any law, custom or institution: 'What is the use of it?' These earlier anniversaries have been occasions to acknowledge the unspectacular woman on the throne, the respect she enjoys and the pleasure she brings, rather than to reflect on the institution she embodies or to ask where the monarchy might be heading in a more democratic era. Very large numbers will again prefer it that way as the Queen reaches 90.

Yet Britain should not forever defer the need to think about the future of the monarchy. We live in volatile times. We struggle with what it means to be British. [...] The longer the Elizabethan monarchy continues, the closer Britain comes to the point at which an institution that does so much to define it will also have to change.

This needs to be considered and debated. It cannot be assumed that the placid concordat between the public and the crown over which the present queen has presided will seamlessly survive under a different monarch. That would be espe-

Street party to celebrate the Queen's 90th birthday

Annotations
- 1 **rooted** *verwurzelt*
- 13 **apparent** seeming to be true but not quite being true
- 14 **infantilise sb.** *(fml) jmd. bevormunden*
- 17 **defier** person that refuses to obey
- 17 **deceptive** misleading
- 19 **cohesion** [kəʊˈhiːʒn] unity
- 21 **prosaic** unimaginative, dull
- 22 **vindicate sth.** *(fml)* justify sth.
- 24 **tax position** amount of taxes one has to pay
- 30 **spoil sth.** ruin sth.
- 31 **churlish** [ˈtʃɜːlɪʃ] unpleasant, impolite
- 39 **defer sth.** postpone sth.
- 40 **volatile** changing
- 44 **placid concordat** unspoken agreement

Annotations
49 whim *Laune, Marotte*

cially true under a monarch who was a figure of controversy for any reason. It is too easily forgotten that, ever since 1688, the monarchy has evolved less to reflect the personality and whims of the monarch than to reflect the values, institutions and needs of the nation within which the monarch reigns. If such a system is to continue, or if it is to be replaced, modern Britain should now begin a modern conversation about how these inescapable changes should happen.

From: 'The Guardian view on the Queen at 90: the time to discuss changes', theguardian.com, *20 April 2016*

Royal Crest of Queen Elizabeth II

Comprehension

1 Complete the sentences using information from the text:
1. The editorial poses the question whether ...
2. In the article it is stressed that the monarch, Queen Elizabeth, ...
3. All in all, the Queen's reign is regarded as successful because ...
4. Despite these positive comments, the editorial claims that ...

Analysis

2 The editorial mentions several positive aspects of the current monarch and her reign. Analyse the rhetorical means the author uses to distance him-/herself from these in order to make the claim that the British monarchy will have to change (cf. l. 43).

Language awareness

► Support p. 253

3 **a** The editorial contains numerous words of praise. Collect them in a *spidergram, sorting them according to word class.
b Add 3–5 more words or phrases which could be useful to highlight the positive qualities of a person or an institution.
c Now find words and phrases you can use to criticize negative qualities of a person or an institution and add them to the spidergram.
d Use your words and phrases from **b** and **c** to write a short paragraph about your perception of any member of the Royal Family or any other famous person.

Beyond the text

► Getting started

► SF 44: Having a discussion

4 **a** Research arguments in favour of and against the British monarchy. Decide which position you find more convincing and highlight the three best arguments.
b Where necessary, add specific suggestions and examples for the arguments.
c Discuss the following statement in groups: 'The British monarchy is outdated and unfit for modern times, so significant changes are called for.'
d Present the result and decide where you personally stand on the question.

Focus on test formats

In tests and your English school leaving exam, but also at university, you will frequently come across test formats that require argumentative writing. Look at the following example of such a task:

► SF 25: Essentials: the stages of writing

Discuss the claim that 'The British political system is partly undemocratic'.

Work it out

In this section you will learn step by step how to deal with tasks for argumentative writing.

1 Understanding a task for argumentative writing

a Look at the following verbs that can often be found in tasks for argumentative writing. Match each verb with the correct description.

► Verbs for tasks, p. 353

A	discuss	1	state one's opinion clearly and support one's view with evidence or reasons
B	comment on	2	give arguments or reasons for and against, especially to come to a well-founded conclusion
C	evaluate	3	express a well-founded opinion on the nature or quality of something

b Explain in more detail what the verb *discuss* means for the task above.

2 Working with a model text

A student has written an argumentative text on the following task: Comment on the claim that 'The British monarchy is an outdated institution that is no longer relevant in modern times.'

The British monarchy is one of the most famous institutions in the world, rooted in history and tradition and well-known for its 'pomp and circumstance'. Not only, but in part, due to various scandals involving the Royal Family, it has been claimed that this institution is outdated and needs to change significantly in order to continue. Although I accept the point that this institution is rooted in history and, therefore, to some extent outdated, I do not agree with the statement that it needs to change significantly in order to be allowed to continue.

First of all, the British monarch is a representative figure, and is only head of state in name. Of course, it cannot be denied that hereditary monarchies are – in general – undemocratic, as kings and queens are not elected by the people but are born into their position, whether or not they have the personal qualities or talents to hold that position. But the fact that the British monarchy is – and has for hundreds of years – been a parliamentary monarchy in which the monarch no longer has any real power to rule, clearly shows that the British political system does take the people's wishes and elections into account and is, therefore, a democracy. Political power lies with the government and parliament, not with the reigning monarch. Even though he/she is called head of state, the monarch has a representative function rather than a political one.

In addition, the institution of the British monarchy contributes to the unity of the United Kingdom. Especially in modern Britain, where the people are divided over so many topics and issues – including political questions like Brexit, cultural or historical questions like the evaluation of the British Empire or social aspects like multiculturalism – the stability and continuity represented by the traditional institution of the monarchy is valued highly. In times of crisis, like at the beginning of the coronavirus pandemic, it is the Queen's address to her people that is spoken about and remembered as encouraging and consoling, rather than the addresses given by the Prime Minister. So, even though the monarch has limited political power, they may at times influence the government and have a strong emotional effect on the British people. […]

Concluding, it has been shown that the institution of the British monarchy is neither harmful nor undemocratic and does have positive effects both in terms of the economy and at an emotional level. Therefore, this makes claims that the monarchy should be abolished seem rather short-sighted, perhaps reflecting envy or a lack of knowledge of the British political system. It clearly is an institution that is loved because of the fact that it is somewhat outdated, quaint and fairy tale-like. But that does not make it a candidate for abolition.

Buckingham Palace in London, the official residence of the monarch

a Based on your experiences, state which aspects make the comment above a good comment. The following guidelines can help you:

linking words are used to guide the reader	statements/arguments are supported
position of author becomes clear	position of author is restated as a consequence of arguments presented
each paragraph contains one argument	relevance of the question to be commented on is clear
text is concluded	topic is clearly presented

b Copy the *method card below and sort the relevant aspects from **a** into it. Keep adding helpful aspects throughout the Skills Lab.

► Support p. 253

Method card – argumentative writing	
Introduction	• …
Main part	• …
Conclusion	• …
General characteristics	• …

3 Preparing for a writing task

The following arguments are related to the claim that the British political system is partly undemocratic:

- The monarch is not elected by the people, so he/she does not represent the people.
- The power lies with Parliament which is elected by the people.
- Members of the House of Lords are not elected.
- Great Britain has a majority vote ('winner takes all').

a Copy the table below and sort the given arguments into it. If possible, add further arguments.

The British political system is partly undemocratic	
Pro	**Con**
…	…

b Decide on your line of argument and sort the arguments, e.g. from least to most important. Use the table you made in task **a** and decide which arguments are the strongest to defend your point of view.

c Decide on a structure for your argumentative text.

Pattern A
Present the arguments for and against in separate paragraphs:
1 Introduction
2 Arguments pro
3 Arguments con
4 Conclusion

Pattern B
Answer each argument immediately with its counter-argument:
1 Introduction
2 Argument 1 → counter-argument 1
3 Argument 2 → counter-argument 2
4 Conclusion

d Sort your notes into a first draft. Remember to take notes on the following parts:
- introduction,
- main body of your argumentative text,
- conclusion.

e In the body of your text each paragraph develops one argument. You should always plan your paragraphs before writing.
Write down the topic sentences, the supporting sentences and the concluding sentences of the paragraphs in the main part of the model text above. Use the information below for help.

Structure of a paragraph: one paragraph – one argument
Topic sentence: Start with a short topic sentence in which you present the main idea of what the paragraph is going to be about.
Supporting sentences: These sentences make up the body of your paragraph and usually consist of explanations, examples, evidence etc.
Concluding sentence: This sentence summarizes the body of a paragraph and can also provide a link to the next one.

f Plan the paragraphs for your own main part.

g Complete your method card.

Do it

4 Writing your argumentative text

Based on the preparations you have made so far, write your discussion of the claim 'The British political system is partly undemocratic'.

Feedback

5 Peer/Self-assessment

a Using the method card you created, evaluate your partner's text. Note down which aspects have been done well, and also give suggestions for improvement where necessary.
b Taking into account your partner's feedback, highlight in your method card those aspects that you need or want to pay special attention to. Then improve those aspects in your argumentative text.

Nobody is an island – the UK and Europe

Paul Hawkins

- In a short buzz group-activity, explain and try to distinguish the following terms: the Continent, Europe, the EU.

► More language

In The Bloody British *Paul Hawkins, a Briton living in Germany, offers a humorous description of the British and their relationship with the world.*

The British are, of course, an island people. We escape, perhaps a little too often for some people's liking, but ultimately we always come back to the island safety of our little moat-protected homeland. Indeed, our islandness might explain better than any other factor why we have always had a uniquely wobbly *will-they-won't-they* relationship with the rest of the Continent: we are one of the only chunks of it that have floated off.

While the English Channel is just 21 miles wide, its effects on the British psyche should not be underestimated. Being literally separated from one's nearest neighbours, cocooned by the sea, can do strange and subtle things to a culture like ours. It makes us, in my opinion, a little wackier around the edges than our mainland friends. Around the borders of most continental countries, there's a bit of cultural interaction and feedback that takes place (and maybe even helps stir the European soup) while we Brits stand somewhat more apart and alone (like a bread). [...]

Our islandness might also help explain how some of the more extreme aspects of our national character developed. Take, for example, the almost existential need for good manners and the accompanying honour-based system of maintaining them. If you had an argument with someone in Ye Olde England, there was only ever so far you could get away from them before you were under water. In contrast, you could be as rude to someone as you bloody well liked in Ye Olde France, knowing full-well it was always possible to climb atop your trusty donkey and get the hell out there. Ride east of Calais and there's Paris, Köln, Αθηνα, КИЇВ, [...]. A whole world of enemy-avoiding possibilities. Ride west from Dover and there's Devon.

This water-locked isolation might also explain why our ridiculous politeness comes equally paired with our literal ridiculousness. If our amusing British eccentricities can be accredited to anything of geographic origin, then surely it's the big, wet fence around our garden that historically meant none of our neighbours could peek in and see all of the ludicrous things we were inventing while we thought no one else was looking. How else do you explain croquet, cricket, carpeted bathrooms, cucumber sandwiches and the penny-farthing? [...]

However, this relative isolation from our closest neighbours has also meant relative isolation from their constructive criticism and friendly feedback. Perhaps it was all this time marinating in our own juices before phones, televisions and airplanes stirred us more thoroughly into the European mix – but we British still seem to feel uniquely separate, which is why we, unique amongst the Europeans of the continent of Europe, can still say, 'I'm going on holiday to *Europe*.'

From: The Bloody British – a Well-Meaning Guide to an Awkward Nation, *2019*

Annotations
- 5 **chunk** *(n)* piece
- 10 **wacky** *(infml)* unusual, often in a silly way
- 16 **maintain sth.** keep sth.
- 29 **penny-farthing** bicycle that has a very small and a very large wheel

Man riding a penny-farthing

Comprehension

1 **a** Work in pairs.
Partner A: Collect 3–4 words or phrases from the text that illustrate the relationship Britain has with Europe.
Partner B: Collect 3–4 words or phrases from the text that explain the special relationship between the UK and Europe.
b Summarize your results for your partner using the words from **a.**

Analysis

▸ Support p. 254

2 Analyse how the author uses a humorous style to voice his opinion on the British and the effect this has.

Language awareness

3 **a** The text contains various colloquial and informal passages. Find at least three examples and rewrite them in a formal style.
b Explain the effect the informal style has on the reader.

Beyond the text

4 Create a drawing or cartoon that reflects Hawkins' perception of the British as 'an island people' (l. 1) and present it to your classmates.

5 Paul Hawkins calls the relationship between the UK and Europe a 'wobbly will-they-won't-they relationship' (ll. 4–5). Using information from the Info box below, explain which events support this notion.

Info

The UK and the EU

In 1957 the EEC (European Economic Community) was founded. After two failed attempts to join the EEC, the UK became a member in 1973. In 1975 the British membership of the European Community (EC) was confirmed in a referendum in which 67% of the British people voted in favour of it.
Under Margaret Thatcher, who was Conservative Prime Minister from 1979–1990, special concessions for the UK were demanded by the British government and granted by the EU. In 1992 the UK signed the Maastricht Treaty, which gave EU citizens the right to free movement. The UK, however, continued to have passport controls for EU citizens and kept the pound as currency.
In 2013 the Conservative Prime Minister David Cameron promised a referendum on British EU membership if his party should win the election, and planned to re-negotiate the British membership in order to get better terms for the UK. In 2016 this referendum was held and a narrow majority of the British people voted to leave the EU. Following this referendum, complex withdrawal negotiations began and the UK officially left the EU on 31 December 2020.

Marriage counselling after Brexit

Jonathan Coe

- The bar chart on the right shows the overall results of the Brexit referendum in 2016. Explain how the results intensified disunity among people in the UK.

Now read the following extract from Jonathan Coe's novel Middle England, *in which Sophie remembers the first counselling session she had with her husband to save their marriage. Sophie voted 'Remain' in the Brexit referendum while Ian voted 'Leave'.*

A couple might decide to separate for all sorts of reasons: adultery, cruelty, domestic abuse, lack of sex. But a difference of opinion over whether Britain should be a member of the European Union or not? It seemed absurd. It was absurd. And yet Sophie knew, deep down, that it had not so much been a reason as a tipping point. Ian had reacted (to her mind) so bizarrely to the referendum result, with such gleeful, infantile triumphalism (he kept using the word 'freedom' as if he were the citizen of a tiny African country that had finally won independence from its colonial oppressor) that, for the first time, she genuinely realized that she no longer understood why her husband thought and felt the way that he did. At the same time, she herself had been possessed by the immediate sense, that morning, that a small but important part of her own identity – her modern, layered, multiple identity – had been taken away from her.

During their first session a few weeks later, their relationship counsellor, Lorna, told them that many of the couples she was seeing at the moment had mentioned Brexit as a key factor in their growing estrangement.

'I usually start by asking each of you the same question,' she said. 'Sophie, why are you so angry that Ian voted Leave? And Ian, why are you so angry that Sophie voted Remain?' Sophie had thought for a long time before answering:

'I suppose because it made me think that, as a person, he's not as open as I thought he was. That his basic model for relationships comes down to antagonism and competition, not cooperation.'

Lorna had nodded, and turned to Ian, who had answered: 'It makes me think that she's very naive, that she lives in a bubble and can't see how other people around her might have a different opinion to hers. And this gives her a certain attitude. An attitude of moral superiority.'

To which Lorna had said:

'What's interesting about both of those answers is that neither of you mentioned politics. As if the referendum wasn't about Europe at all. Maybe something much more fundamental and personal was going on. Which is why this might be a difficult problem to resolve.'

She had suggested a course of six sessions, but it turned out that she was being optimistic. In fact they attended nine, before admitting defeat, and calling it a day.

From: Middle England, *2018*

► More info

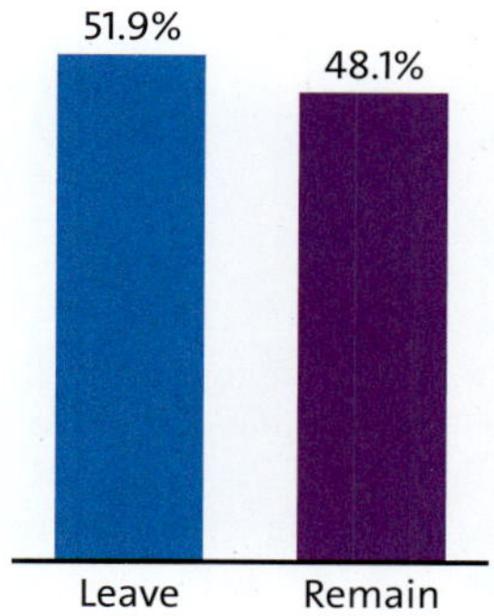

© 2021 Electoral Commission

Annotations

- 1 **adultery** [əˈdʌltəri] *Ehebruch*
- 1 **domestic abuse** physical or psychological violence in one's home
- 4 **tipping point** the time at which a change or an effect can no longer be stopped
- 13 **counsellor** therapist or advisor
- 15 **estrangement** loss of connection with or understanding of someone
- 32 **call it a day** stop

Comprehension

1 Point out which character traits Sophie attributes to Ian for voting 'Leave' and which character traits Ian connects with Sophie for voting 'Remain'.

Analysis

▸ SF 18: Reading and understanding narrative texts

2 Analyse how the chosen point of view guides the reader's identification with the characters' opinions.

3 Explain how the *analogy of a crumbling marriage is linked to the Brexit-process.

Language awareness

4 **a** Find out which words and phrases the two spouses use to describe their partner's opinion about Brexit and the *connotation this evokes in the reader.

b After the session, the counsellor makes notes in which she tries to record the spouses' opinions from a neutral perspective. Write her notes.

Beyond the text

5 Taking Sophie and Ian's reasons for their separation into account and everything you have learned so far, reconsider the guiding question of the chapter. How would you answer it at this point?

6 You choose Work on task **a** or **b**:

a Writing Comment on Lorna's statement that '[...] the referendum wasn't about Europe at all. Maybe something much more fundamental and personal was going on.' Take possible reasons for people's position on Brexit into account.

b Writing Rewrite the novel extract from Ian's point of view, taking into account his motivations for voting 'Leave' and his feelings about his wife's reaction to the referendum result.

▸ SF 26: Argumentative writing: discussion and comment
▸ SF 36: Creative writing

Language help

(in)secure • former British glory • afraid of ... • change • tradition • migration • island

Text 9

Brexit: a German perspective

Jan Roß

The UK always had a unique position in Europe. Jan Roß commented in Die Zeit *on Brexit as a consequence of the special relationship between the UK and Europe.*

Billboard information by the government about changes after Brexit

[...] Viele auf dem Kontinent sind erleichtert, dass mit dem förmlichen Ausscheiden des Vereinigten Königreichs aus der EU das ärgste Gewürge ein Ende hat – doch die britische Entscheidung selbst kommt ihnen so närrisch oder verheerend vor wie am ersten Tag. Auch ein Unterton von Gekränktheit ist unverändert herauszuhören. In dieser Lage lohnt es sich, einen Schritt zurückzutreten und die Sache mit etwas kälterem Blut zu betrachten.

Großbritannien ist immer ein halb europäisches Land gewesen, als Seefahrtsnation, Kolonialmacht und seit dem Zweiten Weltkrieg als privilegierter Verbündeter der Vereinigten Staaten. Es war halb draußen, solange es der EU angehörte, mit einer langen Geschichte von Ausnahmeregelungen und bremsenden Sondervoten. Es wird halb drinnen sein, wenn es die EU verlassen hat, in einer „ehrgeizigen, breiten, tiefen und flexiblen Partnerschaft", wie Briten und Europäer sie erklärtermaßen anstreben. So gesehen ist der Brexit keine Katastrophe, sondern schlicht ein Ausdruck der Normalität im britisch-europäischen Verhältnis. Keineswegs der einzig denkbare (die bisherige innerlich distanzierte EU-Mitgliedschaft war auch einer), aber ein durchaus möglicher und plausibler.

Die größte konkrete Sorge auf dem Kontinent geht dahin, dass die Briten den Europäern in Zukunft als Wirtschaftsstandort unfaire Konkurrenz machen könnten, durch Steuerdumping oder laxe Regulierung. Diese Befürchtung wirkt doppelt übertrieben. [...] Großbritannien wird auch nach dem Brexit schwerlich zum entfesselten Hyperkapitalismus übergehen, sondern ein weithin europäisch geprägtes Sozialmodell beibehalten.

Sofern allerdings die Briten den EU-Austritt tatsächlich zu Liberalisierung und Bürokratieabbau nutzen, sollte man das auf dem Kontinent nicht bejammern oder bekämpfen, sondern davon lernen. Ein bisschen freibeuterhafte Konkurrenz täte der uniformen EU ganz gut. [Angela] Merkel hat kürzlich im Gespräch mit der *Financial Times* überraschend brexitfreundlich bemerkt, das Ende der Londoner EU-Mitgliedschaft könne als „Weckruf" dienen: „Aus einem positiven Blickwinkel betrachtet, müssen wir uns fragen, welche unserer Regelungen richtig und gut sind und tatsächlich nützlich für uns." Und welche, heißt das natürlich, nichts taugen und abgeschafft gehören [...].

Trotz mancher Schwächen und Fehler, die gerade im Brexit-Prozess zutage getreten sind, besitzt Großbritannien eine unschätzbare Stärke: eine vitale, instinktive Freiheitlichkeit. Ein liberales Land ist eines, in dem man weitgehend unbesorgt gegen den Mehrheitsgeschmack verstoßen kann, ob als Investmentbanker, der unverschämt viel Geld verdient, oder als Muslimin, die das islamische Kopftuch trägt. Mehr als die meisten anderen Länder, auch in Europa, ist das Vereinigte Königreich ein solches Land. Diese innere Liberalitätsquelle verliert die EU jetzt. Das ist für uns auf dem Kontinent der eigentliche, bittere Schaden durch den Brexit.

From: 'Genug geheult', Zeit online, *29 January 2019*

1 Mediating While you are spending a year in the UK, your teacher asks you to report to the class on how Brexit is perceived in the German press. In your research you have come across the above extract from an article in *Die Zeit*. Based on this article, prepare an oral presentation in which you tell your classmates which positive or negative aspects of Brexit the article mentions.

► SF 47: Mediating from German into English

► Support p. 254

Words revisited

► SF 6: Essentials: language and study skills

1 Collecting words

In the course of this chapter you have come across a lot of adjectives, verbs and nouns connected to the concepts of *united* and *disunited*. Work with a partner. Partner A scans the text on p. 116 for relevant words, partner B the text on p. 133. Together create a *spidergram with the words you found.

Language Awareness

When you try to argue your point, it's not only strong arguments that help you convince somebody, it's also the language you use. For example, certain types of adverbs and linking words allow your audience to follow your line of argumentation more easily.

► Support p. 254

► More language

2 Adverbs of comment and adverbs of degree

a Say which of the adverbs highlighted in the text below are adverbs of degree and which are adverbs of comment.

The UK – no. 1 on your bucket list!

Still thinking about where to go next for your holidays? Stop racking your brains – you have clearly found the place to be: the UK. The UK undoubtedly offers highlights for every kind of traveller. It is extremely easy to go hiking and there are definitely enough pubs and tearooms to rest your legs after a strenuous walk. The country's cities certainly provide quite enough entertainment for all tastes, from music clubs to spectacular sights. Luckily British cuisine has improved considerably, so you will surely find exactly the right place for dinner, whether it is fine dining or Asian fusion cuisine that you have in mind.

b Using a grammar book or reliable online sources, add further adverbs of degree and adverbs of comment to your list.

c The sentences below contain adjectives and verbs that you may have found in task **1a.** Fill different adverbs from the box in the gaps and describe how they change the meaning of the sentences.

extremely
definitely
quite
undoubtedly

1 The UK is ... divided.
2 Britons are ... united in their negative opinion about politicians.
3 The generations in the UK are ... disunited.
4 The UK is geographically ... isolated from the rest of Europe as it is made up of several islands.
5 Recent political developments are ... tearing the UK apart.

► Support p. 254

3 Using linking words

Linking words and phrases are used to connect ideas and to express the logical connections between them. Categorize these linkers from the box on p. 137 according to their function by sorting them in the table under it.

in my opinion • first of all • for example • all in all • to my mind • firstly • for instance • on the other hand • however • though • naturally • admittedly • in conclusion • to sum up • furthermore • besides • in addition • nonetheless • of course • moreover • finally

Use/function	Linking word or phrase
Stating your opinion	...
Listing facts, structuring	...
Giving an example	...
Contrasting	...
Conceding a point	...
Coming to a conclusion	...

► SF 25: Essentials: the stages of writing

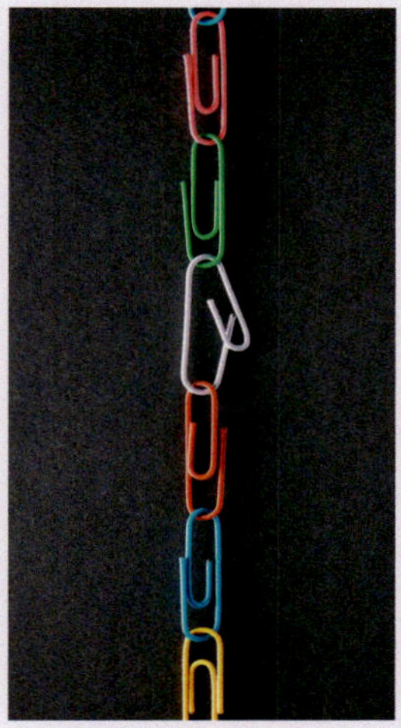

4 Putting emphasis on central statements

Examine the following statements. In each case the same idea is expressed in two different ways.

Version 1	Version 2
Although this is not often stated, the history of the British Empire **has** a considerable effect on modern British society.	Although this is not often stated, the history of the British Empire **does have** a considerable effect on modern British society.
British humour has often been named as a stereotypical character trait of the British.	**It is British humour which has** often been named as a key characteristic of the British.
The country has not often been divided over so many topics.	**Hardly ever has the country** been divided over so many topics.

Explain how the two versions of the sentence are different: grammatically and in terms of emphasis.

Practice

5 Writing a blog post

Writing Write a blog post in which you advertise the UK as the perfect spot for studying after you finish secondary school. Use adverbs of degree, adverbs of comment and linking words. Put emphasis on the most important statements, using your strategies from task **4.**

► SF 27: Writing a blog post

► Support p. 255

A colonial heritage and a multicultural present

Clive Myrie

Below you will find some information about the British Empire and the Commonwealth of Nations before you watch a video by British journalist Clive Myrie about the heritage of the Empire.

Info

The British Empire and the Commonwealth of Nations

During the late 19th and early 20th centuries the British Empire covered nearly one quarter of the land surface worldwide, and was thus the largest colonial empire. Britain began to establish colonies across the globe – for both settlement and trade – from the 16th century onwards. A maritime nation, it also had naval bases in strategically important areas such as the Mediterranean. In the course of the first half of the 20th century, decolonization movements in British territories, and two world wars resulted in the decline of the British Empire and the foundation of the Commonwealth of Nations in 1931. The Commonwealth of Nations is an association of 54 sovereign nations. Most member states were former colonies of the British Empire; therefore, they are connected by shared traditions and languages which were imposed on them by the British during this time. People in the colonized countries were often forbidden to speak their own languages and discouraged from preserving their traditions. The decision to join the Commonwealth is completely voluntary, which is of utmost importance for the formerly colonized countries as they can thus show that they have become equal partners of the UK.
The question of how to deal with Britain's colonial past is an extremely controversial one. One aspect is the open and rather emotional discussion as to whether the British Empire is reason for national pride due to its immense power or national guilt because of the crimes committed by the representatives of the colonial power towards the people in the colonies.

1 Name countries that were at some point part of the British Empire.
2 Explain why the United Kingdom used to be called 'the Empire on which the sun never sets'.

Info

The **Windrush Generation** was invited to the UK between 1948 and 1971 as there were labour shortages after the Second World War had ended. They migrated from the Caribbean and were given permission to stay in the UK in 1971. In 2012 many people of the Windrush Generation were threatened with deportation because they had no official papers to prove their right to stay in the UK.

- The video by Clive Myrie discusses the two questions of who owns history and who dictates memory. Based on the Info box above and your research, brainstorm with a partner why these questions are relevant when assessing the legacy of the British Empire.

Comprehension

1 a Viewing While watching the video for the first time, make notes on the following topics. Don't write complete sentences.

1 three pieces of information about the speaker
2 two facts about the connection between Bristol and the slave trade
3 two things Asher Craig intends to do
4 two reasons why West Indians came to the UK after the Second World War
5 three pieces of information about Mike Lord's life in Britain
6 two things Mercy Muroki says about history.

Annotations
supremacy leading or controlling position
leper person with an infectious disease who is avoided by others

b Sum up what the heritage of the Empire is according to the video.

Analysis

2 Watch the film again. Analyse how the past and the present are depicted and connected. Include cinematic devices in your analysis.

► SF 39: Analysing films and videos

Beyond the text

3 In 2021, Clive Myrie became the first non-white host of Great Britain's most prestigious quiz show *Mastermind*. Discuss how steps like this one influence post-colonial societies. Are they a move towards a more inclusive society? Do they create awareness?

4 a **Art in Context** Below you can see the statue of Edward Colston, which was covered in graffiti during the Black Lives Matter protests in 2020. Describe the image of the statue.

b Explain if or how this way of displaying the statue has turned it into a piece of political art.

c Speaking Discuss whether this process has made the statue more acceptable in the eyes of the Black Lives Matter protesters. Note down the three most convincing arguments.

► SF 22: Analysing visuals

Info

Black Lives Matter is a movement that raises awareness about racial injustice, particularly pointing out cases of police brutality towards Black people. It was founded in 2013 after the murderer of Black teenager Trayvon Martin was found not guilty.

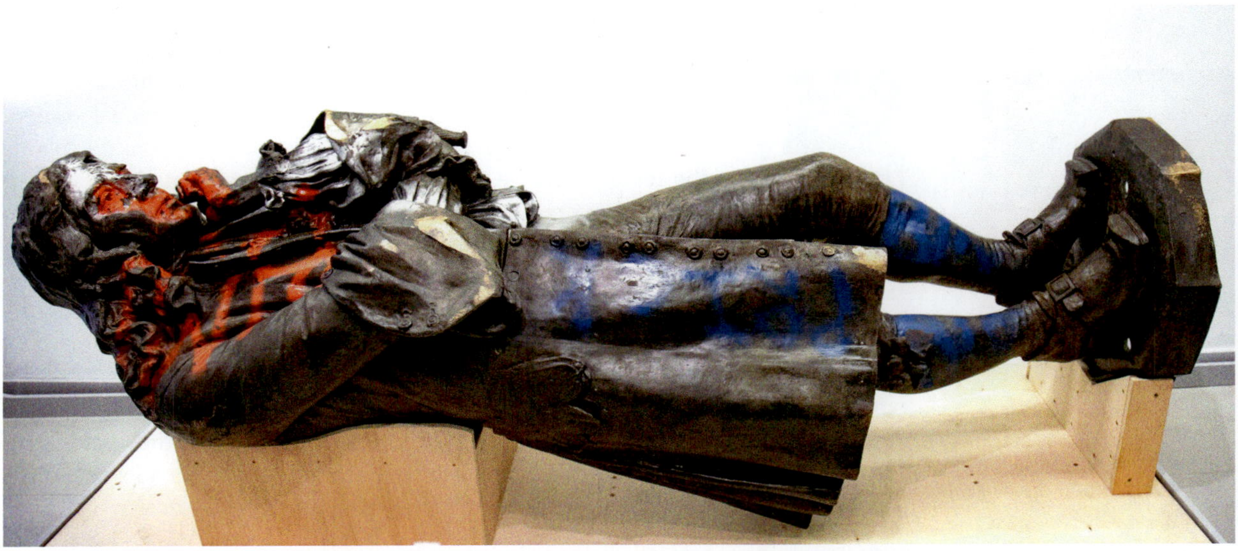

Statue of slave trader Edward Colston, which was damaged by graffiti, on display in Bristol

The legacy of the Empire
Sathnam Sanghera

- Has a street in your city been renamed or a statue been removed? If so, name examples and discuss possible reasons for these actions.

In this extract journalist and novelist Sathnam Sanghera gives his view on how the past of the Empire has influenced British identity and how it could be dealt with.

[N]early two years after I started looking into how imperialism has shaped modern Britain, I find myself wishing a new [Awareness Day] into existence: Empire Awareness Day.

Despite a recent surge of interest in British colonial history, with statues being torn down (or defended), concert halls and schools being renamed (or councils refusing to submit to demands) and companies apologizing for past deeds (or trying to ignore it all), the effect of British empire upon this country is poorly understood. Many of us have learned more about British imperialism in a few months of statuecide than we did during our entire schooling, but there seems to be a view that if you pull down enough statues/ change enough names or fight to keep enough statues up/ refuse to change names, you can delete or defend British imperialism. But British empire defines us more deeply than these controversies suggest and an Empire Day could help explain how. [...]

The reason I am sitting here, as a person of colour in Britain, talking about this country as my home, is because several hundred years ago some Britons decided to take control of parts of the Asian subcontinent. In turn, this serves to highlight the fact that the things we have touched upon so far as legacies of empire are actually small fry. It's all very well highlighting empire awareness by talking about how our honours list still hands out Orders of the British Empire, how many of our common garden plants were originally imported into Britain by imperialists, or how Worcestershire sauce might originally have been an Indian recipe, reportedly brought back to Britain by an ex-governor of Bengal. But our imperial past has had a much more profound effect on modern Britain.

Empire explains why we have a diaspora of millions of Britons spread around the world. Empire explains the global pretensions of our Foreign and Defence secretaries. Empire explains the feeling that we are exceptional and can go it alone when it comes to everything from Brexit to dealing with global pandemics. Empire helped to establish the position of the City of London as one of the world's major financial centres, and also ensures that the interests of finance trump the interests of so many other groups in the twenty-first century. Empire explains how some of our richest families and institutions and cities became wealthy. Empire explains our particular brand of racism, [...], our propensity for jingoism. Let's face it, imperialism is not something that can be erased with a few statues being torn down or a few institutions facing up to their dark pasts; it exists as a legacy in my very being and, more widely, explains nothing less than who we are as a nation.

From: How Imperialism Has Shaped Modern Britain, *2021*

Annotations
- 4 **surge** *(n)* sudden and great increase
- 8 **statuecide** tearing down of statues
- 18 **small fry** *(infml)* insignificant things
- 24 **diaspora** people settled away from their original homeland
- 25 **pretension** belief that you can succeed or that you are important
- 31 **trump sth./sb.** *(v)* outdo or surpass sth. that is said or done by sb.
- 34 **propensity** *Neigung, Hang*
- 34 **jingoism** [ˈdʒɪŋgəʊɪzəm] extreme patriotism or nationalism, linked to hostile foreign policy

Comprehension

► Check

British telephone box in Antigua

1 Are the following sentences true or false? Correct the false ones.
1. The toppling of statues has broadened people's knowledge of British imperialism.
2. Discussions about renaming places, tearing down statues and dealing with the colonial past of companies are enough to make people aware of the effects of the British Empire.
3. So far, the impact of the British Empire on Britain has been illustrated by referring to rather unimportant matters like the origin of the recipe for Worcestershire sauce.
4. The British Empire is the reason why Britain believes in international cooperation.
5. The wealth of some families and the existing national pride can be traced back to the former empire.
6. Imperialism defines Great Britain as a nation today.

2 Note down the different attitudes towards British colonial history that Sanghera observes in British society.

Analysis

3 Work on either **a** or **b**.

a The text clearly shows the author's personal involvement. Find examples of this and explain their effect.

b Challenge Analyse how Sanghera expresses the importance of the Empire for himself as Briton and for modern Britain on the whole. Consider the use of contrasts, argumentative techniques and stylistic devices.

► SF 4: Writing a text analysis

Language awareness

4 **a** The author displays different attitudes towards the British Empire and different ways of dealing with this part of Britain's past. Look at these extracts from the text and explain what Sanghera is actually trying to express by quoting them: 'there seems ... imperialism' (ll. 9–11) and 'It's all ... Bengal' (ll. 18–22).

b Explain what opinion Sanghera is trying to convey.

c Make a list of phrases you can use to distance yourself from arguments that other people put forward but which do not support your point of view.

Beyond the text

5 Writing Should there be an 'Empire Awareness Day'? Write a comment.

► SF 26: Argumentative writing: discussion and comment

6 Speaking Work in pairs. One of you supports tearing down statues that are reminders of Britain's colonial past, whereas the other one is against it. Prepare your arguments, then discuss the question of whether the reminders of the Empire should be removed from public areas or not. Use your findings from **4c** if possible.

► SF 44: Having a discussion

Home-made sign in support of Black Lives Matter

Racism in Britain

- Name examples of racism in the UK you have read or heard about. Do you think that the United Kingdom might have a problem with racism?

The following statistics show the results of a survey on 'Attitudes to racism in Britain' carried out by the market research company Ipsos MORI in 2020.

Comprehension

1 a **Partner B:** Go to p. 255.
Partner A: Take a look at the bar chart below. Prepare a 2-minute presentation for your partner in which you tell her/him what your bar chart reveals about the different attitudes towards racism in Great Britain.

The perception of racism in Britain according to ethnicity

To what extent, if at all, do you agree or disagree with the following statement: 'Britain is a racist country'

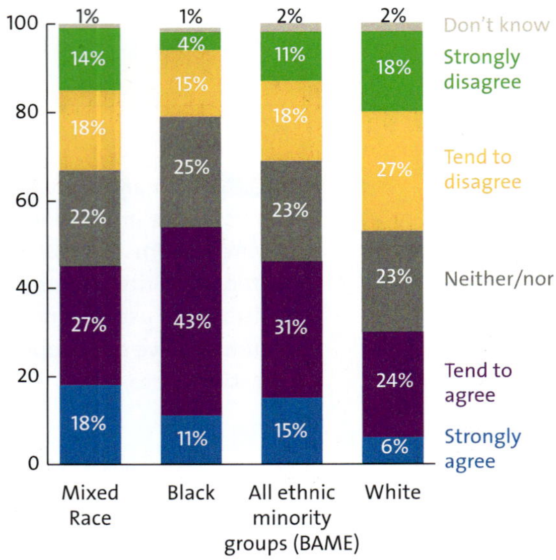

Source: © Ipsos

b Present your findings to each other and together discuss what the statistics suggest about Britain as a multicultural society.

Beyond the text

2 a Research statistics about racism in Germany. Note down what they tell you.
b Intercultural communication Compare your findings with the data from task **1.** Are there differences between the UK and Germany? If so, speculate why.

New way, new life

Asian Dub Foundation

New way, new life *is a song by the British band Asian Dub Foundation. They mix different musical styles, including dub, which is an electronic music genre that developed from Jamaican reggae and influenced genres such as hip hop, house, jungle, and drum and bass.*

- After having read the information about dub as a genre, talk to a partner about why the band's name can be regarded as a sign of Britain's multiculturalism.

Every Sunday morning in front of the
TV
Recording with a microphone Naya
zindagi
Pioneer Gurdas Maan
Nusrat Fateh Ali Khan
Kept our parents alive
Gave them the will to survive
Working inna de factories
Sometimes sweeping de floor
Unsung heroines an heroes
Yes they open de door
They came a long time ago
But now it seems we've arrived
Naya zindagi, naya Jeevan
New way, new life

Stayed an we fought an now de fu-
ture's open wide
New way, new life

Naya zindagi! Naya zindagi!
New way new life
Naya zindagi! Naya jeevan!

Tjinder pon de radio
Dis is England's new voice
Censorship for years
But now dem have no choice
Running thru de playground
We could never have known
Dat in de future
Our role models would be home
grown
And now we're walking down de
street
Wid a brand new pride
A spring inna de step
Our opportunity will no longer be
denied
Wid our heads held high
Young Asian brothers an sisters
Moving forward, side by side
Naya zindagi! naya Jeevan
New way new life

New way new life
Naya zindagi! naya jeevan

And we're supposed to be cool
Inna de dance our riddims rule
But we knew it all along
Cos our parents made us strong
Never abandoned our culture
Just been moving it along
Technology our tradition
Innovation inna the song

Now de struggle continues
To reverse every wrong
New heroines and heroes
Inna de battle we belong
When we reach de glass ceiling
We will blow it sky high
Naya zindagi! naya Jeevan
New way new life

Stayed an we fought an now de fu-
ture's open wide
New way new life
Naya zindagi! Naya zindagi!
New way new life
Naya zindagi! Naya jeevan! for it.

From: Asian Dub Foundation, 2000

Info

Nai Zindagi Naya Jeeva (New Way New Life) was a television programme by the BBC that was broadcast in Hindi and Urdu. It was one of the first programmes that used another language than English or Welsh.

Annotations

5 **Gurdas Maan** Punjabi artist
6 **Nusrat Fateh Ali Khan** Pakistani musician
23 **Tjinder (Singh)** singer of the British band Cornershop
35 **spring in your step** way of walking that indicates sb. is happy
57 **glass ceiling** barrier that prevents women and minorities from improving their position at work

Member of the British band Asian Dub Foundation

Comprehension

1 Create a table in which you list the immigration experiences of the parents in the left and the second-generation's experience of life in Britain in the right column.

Analysis

▸ Support p. XX

2 Analyse the means Asian Dub Foundation use to present the Asian immigrant experience as a success story. Focus on the content and choice of words.

Language awareness

3 Translate the song into Standard English and explain the difference in effect between the two versions.

Beyond the text

4 You choose Work on task **a** or **b**.

a Writing Have another look at vv. 48–55. Turn these lines into a 'recipe' for a successful multicultural society.

b Writing On the basis of what you have found out in this chapter, discuss if music could send out a stronger political message than, for example, toppling statues.

5 Reconsider the guiding question of the chapter. How would you answer it after everything you have learned?

Text 14

A teenager's response to experiencing racism

Evey Gordon

- *Quick write: Write a short paragraph about circumstances in your life that weigh you down.

In June 2020 Evey Gordon from Plymouth recorded a poem in which she expressed what it was like growing up with a mixed ethnic background.

Comprehension

1 a Listening Work with a partner. While listening to the poem, partner A notes down all racist comments and actions that Evey Gordon mentions. Partner B notes down Gordon's reactions to racism and the emotions she mentions.

b Exchange your notes and make a list of direct and more indirect forms of racism.

Analysis

► SF 19: Reading and understanding poetry

2 Viewing Listen to the poem for a second time. Analyse the language Evey uses and the way she presents the poem.

Beyond the text

3 You choose Do either task **a** or **b**:

a With your partner, create your own appeal video to fight racism.

b To what extent can the fact that the BBC offers Evey a forum to speak about her experiences be regarded as a positive step in the fight against racism? Write a brief response for the BBC's comment page.

Chapter task

After having dealt with various aspects of the UK, you will have the opportunity to put your knowledge to the test by taking part in a debate.

► Getting started
► SF 45: Having a debate

Your school's debating society is hosting a debate on the following motion:

'This house believes that the United Kingdom is united in name only.'

1 **a** According to whether you are arguing for or against the motion, collect facts, figures, arguments or examples from this chapter to support your position and to refute the other side.
b Use your knowledge of how to be persuasive to prepare your arguments and counterarguments.

2 Stage the debate in class.

Chapter 5
The USA – Land of Many Faces

1 a **Think** Write down the ideas that come into your head when you look at the 'puzzle' above.
b **Pair** Compare and discuss your ideas. Together make up a suitable caption for the picture.
c **Share** Present your captions in class and list your ideas on what makes the USA different from most European nations.

2 a Write down five sentences starting with 'The USA is ...' and five sentences that start with 'The USA isn't ...'. Give reasons for your statements.
b Discuss your sentences in small groups and agree on one sentence beginning with 'The USA is ...' and one with 'The USA isn't ...'. Then present the sentences to class, explaining why you chose them.
c *Quick write: Write a short paragraph about the guiding question on p. 147. Relate the concepts in the Chapter map to your own knowledge of the USA.

Chapter map

What makes the USA unique?

- history
- development
- ideals
- reality
- global role

Chapter task: my American soundtrack

▸ More language

The USA – a land of conflicts

'A house divided against itself cannot stand.'

Abraham Lincoln cited this quotation from the Bible in a speech he gave in 1858. Three years later, Lincoln was president, and the conflict he alluded to in his speech – the issue of slavery – had erupted into a civil war that threatened to permanently divide the nation.

Today, that conflict is history, but the USA is still beset by problems resulting from its past: the legacy of discrimination against African Americans and Native Americans, the widening gap between rich and poor, and the tensions between America's many ethnic minorities and the white mainstream, often mirroring the contrast between rapidly growing urban areas and thinly populated rural regions. Moreover, the American political system has become polarized to an extent unknown since the 1860s. When cooperation and dialogue are equated with treason, democracy itself is at risk.

Russian Jews arrive in New York City.

A country founded on principle

It is characteristic that the earliest document of the United States, the Declaration of Independence, begins with a statement of principle: that all people are created equal and have equal rights, and that all power derives from the will of the people. In the course of time, further notions have been added to the national myth, sometimes referred to as the 'American Dream'. The most notable of these is equality of opportunity. It found popular expression in slogans such as 'from rags to riches' or 'the sky's the limit'. The belief that in America anyone, no matter how humble their origin, could work their way to the top attracted millions of immigrants in the 19th and 20th centuries. A rapidly expanding nation offered seemingly endless opportunity to those with the ambition to succeed. Furthermore, the USA promised protection from persecution to those who needed it most. In the USA of today, however, ethnic tensions, hate crimes, job losses and the power of vested interests lead some to wonder if the American Dream is still alive.

▸ More info

Looking ahead

As the 21st century progresses, the American political system, a product of the 18th century, is beginning to show signs of strain. One symptom is the discrepancy between election results and the popular vote, as in the presidential elections of 2000 and 2016. Because each state elects two senators, regardless of population, small states and rural regions exert a disproportionate influence on national politics. Issues such as gun control, abortion and police violence continue to split public opinion and defy simple solutions. And yet, as the USA has demonstrated over and again in its history, it is a nation that possesses a unique capacity for reinventing itself. The USA of today is younger and more diverse than it has ever been before. It remains to be seen whether the typically American belief that the future will be brighter than the past will once more hold true.

1 Words words words

a Choose three highlighted phrases from the text that you find useful for the chapter topic or that are new to you.
b Explain them in English.
c Form groups of three or four. Take turns reading your explanations. The others must guess which phrase you are describing. Add at least one new phrase to your list.

2 Mind mapping

One way to structure relevant vocabulary is to create a mind map of words that are linked with a certain topic.
a Create a mind map using vocabulary items from the text that you connect with the USA (e.g., *equality of opportunity* or *gun control*).
b Compare mind maps with your partner. Add items from your partner's mind map that you think should be included.

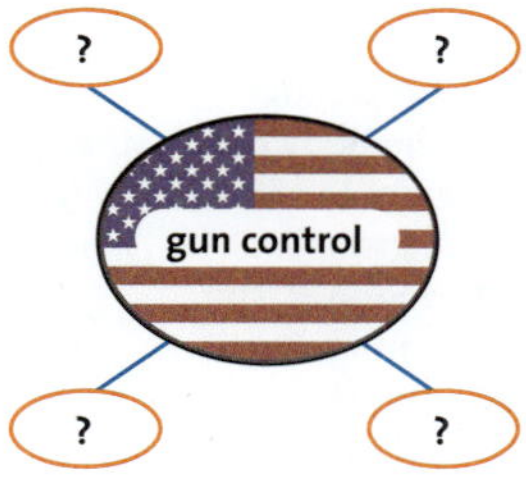

3 Chunk it!

a Fill the blanks in the following *chunks with verbs. You can look at the text for help, but also add other verbs. If you are not sure, consult a dictionary.
1 ... a conflict
2 ... a capacity (for ...)
3 ... protection (from ...)
4 ... (an/one's) influence (on ...)
5 ... (an/the) opportunity (of ...)
6 ... the contrast (between ...)

b Write at least four sentences using some of your items from 3a.

4 Intercultural communication Over to you: A 'German dream'?

In the second paragraph of the text, you can find some of the reasons why America in the 19th century became a dream land for millions of people throughout the world (including many Germans). Today, many people worldwide dream of migrating to European countries like Germany. Is Germany 'the new America'? Write a short blog post with your views.

► More info

a Go back to the second paragraph of the text and make notes on relevant aspects of America's worldwide appeal.
b Compare them with the present situation in Germany. Formulate your standpoint.
c Write your text.
d Swap texts with your partner. Discuss your views.

► SF 27: Writing a blog post

Language help

On the one hand, ... on the other hand, ...
Whereas in America ..., in Germany ...
At that time, ..., but today ...
In Germany as well as in America, ...
Germany and America both offer ...

▶ More info

Annotations
1 **in the grips** *im Würgegriff*
4 **shuttered** closed down
5 **walks of life** fields of employment
6 **pour** go in large numbers
9 **teeter** stand uncertainly
9 **brink** edge
12 **the body politic** the people of a country (as a group)
13 **ongoing** still happening
13 **breach** violation
14 **procedural safeguard** *verfahrenstechnische Schutzmaßnahme*
14 **adherence** *Festhalten*
15 **take sth. for granted** *etwas als selbstverständlich ansehen*
20 **vineyard** ['vɪnjəd] place where grapes are grown
22 **suffragist** person (usu. a woman) who fights for women's voting rights
22 **Pullman porters** The porters on the Pullman railroad service were entirely African Americans, and their union was one of the most powerful African-American organizations in the early 20th century.
23 **picket sign** *(politisches) Plakat*
29 **discard sth.** throw sth. away
30 **cursory** brief, superficial
32 **subjugation** *Unterwerfung*
32 **rapacious** greedy
33 **complicit in sth.** involved in sth. dubious
33 **rigged** manipulated
36 **tempered** moderate

At this moment in history
Barack Obama

- Imagine you were asked to speak on the state of the world today. What issues would you name?

Barack Obama was President of the United States from 2009 until 2017, the first person of colour to hold this office. In his memoir from 2020 he looks at the state of the USA.

As I sit here, the country remains in the grips of a global pandemic and the accompanying economic crisis, with more than 178,000 Americans dead, businesses shuttered, and millions of people out of work. Across the nation, people from all walks of life have poured into the streets to protest the deaths of unarmed Black men and women at the hands of the police. Perhaps most troubling of all, our democracy seems to be teetering on the brink of crisis – a crisis rooted in a fundamental contest between two opposing visions of what America is and what it should be; a crisis that has left the body politic divided, angry, and mistrustful, and has allowed for an ongoing breach of institutional norms, procedural safeguards, and the adherence to basic facts that both Republicans and Democrats once took for granted.

This contest is not new, of course. In many ways, it has defined the American experience. It's embedded in founding documents that could simultaneously proclaim all men equal and yet count a slave as three-fifths of a man. [...] It's a contest that's been fought on the fields of Gettysburg and Appomattox but also in the halls of Congress, on a bridge in Selma, across the vineyards of California, and down the streets of New York – a contest fought by soldiers but more often by union organizers, suffragists, Pullman porters, student leaders, waves of immigrants, and LGBTQ activists, armed with nothing more than picket signs, pamphlets, or a pair of marching shoes. At the heart of this long-running battle is a simple question: Do we care to match the reality of America to its ideals? If so, do we really believe that our notions of self-government and individual freedom, equality of opportunity and equality before the law, apply to everybody? Or are we instead committed, in practice if not in statute, to reserving those things for a privileged few?

I recognize that there are those who believe that it's time to discard the myth – that an examination of America's past and an even cursory glance at today's headlines show that this nation's ideals have always been secondary to conquest and subjugation, a racial caste system and rapacious capitalism, and that to pretend otherwise is to be complicit in a game that was rigged from the start. And I confess that there have been times during the course of writing this book, as I've reflected on my presidency and all that's happened since, when I've had to ask myself whether I was too tempered in speaking the truth as I saw it, too cautious in either word or deed, convinced as I was that by appealing to what Lincoln called the better angels of our nature I stood a greater chance of leading us in the direction of the America we've been promised.

I don't know. What I can say for certain is that I'm not yet ready to abandon the possibility of America – not just for the sake of future generations of Americans but for all of humankind. For I'm convinced that the pandemic we're currently living through is both a manifestation of and a mere interruption in the relentless march toward an interconnected world, one in which peoples and cultures can't help but collide. In that world – of global supply chains, instantaneous capital transfers, social media, transnational terrorist networks, climate change, mass migration, and ever-increasing complexity – we will learn to live together, cooperate with one another, and recognize the dignity of others, or we will perish. And so the world watches America – the only great power in history made up of people from every corner of the planet, comprising every race and faith and cultural practice – to see if our experiment in democracy can work. To see if we can do what no other nation has ever done. To see if we can actually live up to the meaning of our creed.

From: A Promised Land, *2020*

Annotations
43 **manifestation** *Erscheinungsform*
43 **relentless** unstoppable
45 **can't help but collide** can't avoid colliding
48 **perish** *vergehen*

Comprehension

1 Summarize Obama's views on America.

▶ Support p. 256

Analysis

2 Analyse the link between the success or failure of the 'American experiment' and the situation of the global community.

3 Work on task **a** or **b**.

a Examine the different roles Obama plays in the course of the excerpt.

b Challenge Analyse how Obama influences the reader to accept his credibility as an interpreter of the American experience.

Language awareness

4 Even though the text is an extract from a book, its style frequently resembles that of a *speech. Point out aspects of the text that make it seem as if it was a speech.

▶ Support p. 256

Beyond the text

5 In ll. 19–21 Obama makes *allusions to a number of events from American history. Research the references below and explain to your class why they are relevant for Obama's argumentation:

1 the fields of Gettysburg and Appomattox
2 a bridge in Selma
3 the vineyards of California (search the words 'Delano grape strike')
4 the streets of New York (search the words 'Occupy Wall Street').

▶ SF 13: Doing research

6 Speaking Form small groups and discuss the following statement:
'The success or failure of the American experiment is a matter of international concern.'

▶ SF 44: Having a discussion

Religion in the USA

Annotations
- 1 **respecting sth.** with regard to sth.
- 1 **establishment** *Gründung*
- 2 **prohibit sth.** forbid sth.
- 2 **exercise** *(n) Ausübung*
- 3 **amendment** *Zusatzartikel*
- 4 **pledge sth.** solemnly promise sth.
- 4 **allegiance** loyalty
- 6 **indivisible** *unteilbar*
- 10 **denominationally neutral** not connected with any single religion
- 11 **during its recitation** while it is spoken
- 12 **Supreme Court** *oberster Gerichtshof*

Congress shall make no law respecting an establishment of religion, or prohibiting the free exercise thereof.

1st Amendment to the Constitution, 1791

I pledge allegiance to the flag of the United States of America and to the republic for which it stands, one nation under God, indivisible, with liberty and justice for all.

The Pledge of Allegiance (since 1954)

Government-directed prayer in public schools violates the Establishment Clause of the First Amendment, even if the prayer is denominationally neutral and students may remain silent or be excused from the classroom during its recitation.

Supreme Court ruling in Engel vs. Vitale, 1962

Info

The **Pledge of Allegiance** is an expression of allegiance to the flag of the United States and to the USA as a nation. It is recited before Congressional sessions and various public and private meetings. It is perhaps best known for being recited in schools across the USA.

Analysis

1 Explain what the texts and images on this page tell you about the relationship between church and state in the USA.

Language help

billboard • bank note • contradiction

Beyond the text

2 The table below contains information on religious affiliation for the USA and for Germany. Which do you think is which? Discuss.

► Check

Christian: 70.6%	Protestant: 46.6%	Christian: 55.0%	Protestant: 24.9%
	Catholic: 20.8%		Catholic: 27.1%
Non-Christian: 4.5%	Jewish: 1.9%	Non-Christian: 6.0%	Jewish: 0.1%
	Muslim: 0.9%		Muslim: 5.2%
Non-religious / no answer: 23.4%		Non-religious / no answer: 38.8%	

From: (USA) Pew Research Group, *2014; (Ger)* fowid, *2019*

Text 3

Info

American exceptionalism

'We hold these truths to be self-evident, that all men are created equal, that they are endowed by their Creator with certain unalienable Rights, that among these are Life, Liberty and the pursuit of Happiness.'

This stunning declaration of human rights appears in the preface to the Declaration of Independence. Originally composed to justify a rebellion, the document set high standards for a young nation still in the making: For the first time in modern history, a nation was to be founded on the principles of human rights, equality and democracy. This sense of uniqueness gave American politics an almost missionary zeal, a feeling of moral superiority to all other nations. At the same time, the Founding Fathers were aware of having embarked on an experiment that no one before them had ever believed possible; the fear that the experiment could end in chaos haunted America's early leaders for generations.

1 Write down the ideals that Americans might say make their country unique.

The great nation of futurity John O'Sullivan

- *Quick write: Which countries would you refer to as having a 'glorious past'?

The USA is unique in having a sense of a mission in the world, one dating back to its origins, as magazine editor John O'Sullivan (1813–1895) points out in this essay.

The American people having derived their origin from many other nations, and the Declaration of National Independence being entirely based on the great principle of human equality, these facts demonstrate at once our disconnected position as regards

Annotations
- **futurity** state of belonging to the future

1 **derive sth.** *etwas ableiten*

Annotations
4 **but** (here) only
12 **expansive** boundless
13 **untrodden** *unberührt*
13 **benificent** *wohltätig*
14 **object** goal
14 **unsullied** *unbefleckt*
16 **Providence** *(hier) Gott*
18 **'the gates of hell ... against it'** allusion to Gospel of Matthew 16:18
20 **enfranchisement** voting rights
21 **cynosure** ['saɪnəʃʊə] *Leitbild*
21 **exemplar** good example of sth.
22 **correlative** corresponding
22 **effulgence** bright light
23 **retrograde** move backward
23 **dissolve sth.** *etwas auflösen*
23 **subvert sth.** damage or destroy sth.
23 **we must onward** = we must move onward
27 **decree** law, rule
29 **salvation** *Erlösung*
29 **immutable** unchanging
30 **blessed** ['blesɪd] *gesegnet*
32 **smite** *(old-fashioned)* defeat
32 **hierarch** high priest
33 **tidings** news
33 **myriad** large number of people

any other nation; that we have, in reality, but little connection with the past history of any of them, and still less with all antiquity, its glories, or its crimes. On the contrary, our national birth was the beginning of a new history, the formation and progress of an untried political system, which separates us from the past and connects us with the future only; and so far as regards the entire development of the natural rights of man, in moral, political, and national life, we may confidently assume that our country is destined to be the great nation of futurity. [...]

We have no interest in the scenes of antiquity, only as lessons of avoidance of nearly all their examples. The expansive future is our arena, and for our history. We are entering on its untrodden space, with the truths of God in our minds, beneficent objects in our hearts, and with a clear conscience unsullied by the past. We are the nation of human progress, and who will, what can, set limits to our onward march? Providence is with us, and no earthly power can. We point to the everlasting truth on the first page of our national declaration, and we proclaim to the millions of other lands, that 'the gates of hell' – the powers of aristocracy and monarchy – 'shall not prevail against it.' [...]

Yes, we are the nation of progress, of individual freedom, of universal enfranchisement. Equality of rights is the cynosure of our union of States, the grand exemplar of the correlative equality of individuals; and while truth sheds its effulgence, we cannot retrograde, without dissolving the one and subverting the other. We must onward to the fulfilment of our mission – to the entire development of the principle of our organization – freedom of conscience, freedom of person, freedom of trade and business pursuits, universality of freedom and equality. This is our high destiny, and in nature's eternal, inevitable decree of cause and effect we must accomplish it. All this will be our future history, to establish on earth the moral dignity and salvation of man – the immutable truth and beneficence of God. For this blessed mission to the nations of the world, which are shut out from the life-giving light of truth, has America been chosen; and her high example shall smite unto death the tyranny of kings, hierarchs, and oligarchs, and carry the glad tidings of peace and good will where myriads now endure an existence scarcely more enviable than that of beasts of the field. Who, then, can doubt that our country is destined to be *the great nation* of futurity?

From: The United States Democratic Review, *1839*

Info

Manifest destiny
This (*'offenkundige Bestimmung'*) was a catchword of 19th century American politics. Coined by O'Sullivan, who wrote in 1845 that it was the 'manifest destiny' of the USA to expand westward to the Pacific coast, it suggested the USA had a 'natural' right to the entire North American continent.

Comprehension

1 Describe the relationship between the United States and other countries as presented in the text.

Analysis

2 Work on task **a** or **b**.

a Americans sometimes refer to the USA as 'God's own country'. Point out *allusions to God in the text and analyse their meaning.

b Challenge Analyse the connection between religious belief and political thought in the essay.

3 Examine how O'Sullivan reinterprets the notion of American exceptionalism (cf. Info box p. 153).

Language awareness

4 In the second half of the text O'Sullivan's *style becomes increasingly emotional and dramatic. Point to examples and examine their effect.

Beyond the text

5 Writing Write a *letter to the editor of the *United States Democratic Review* in which you express your reaction to O'Sullivan's essay.

► SF 35: Writing a letter to the editor

Text 4

Broomfield – the spirit of the dream

- *Quick write: What comes into your mind when you think of small-town America?

Viewing *Watch this video about the history of a small town in the American West.*

► SF 38: Listening/Viewing for gist and detail

Comprehension

1 **a** Make notes on the history of Broomfield from the first settlement to the present.
b With a partner, compare notes and create a timeline of Broomfield's history.

2 Watch the trailer a second time. Make notes on the values that the people of Broomfield name as characteristic.

Info

Broomfield
Broomfield is a town and a county near Denver in Colorado with a population of about 70,000.

Beyond the text

3 Intercultural communication Compare Broomfield with a small town in Germany you are familiar with. Point to similarities and differences.

Text 5

Art in Context – 'American Progress'

Info

Territorial expansion
While the first British settlements in North America hugged the Atlantic coast, by the time the United States was founded it was clear to most Americans that their future lay westward:

- In 1803 Napoleon sold the vast French territory in the centre of the continent to the USA, doubling the area of the country.
- In 1819 Spain officially ceded Florida to the USA.
- Texas, which had broken away from Mexico in 1836, joined the Union in 1845.

- In 1846 border disputes with Mexico led to the Mexican-American War, which ended with the American annexation of the Southwest as far as California.
- Also in 1846 the Oregon Treaty with Great Britain clarified the boundary between the 'Oregon Country' in the south and British Columbia in the north.
- In 1867 the American government bought Alaska from Russia for $7.2 million.

The Native American population had to pay a high price for American expansion. As settlers pushed westward, the US Army was deployed to drive the last Indian tribes from the Great Plains. The indigenous peoples were forced to live on so-called reservations. Deprived of their traditional way of life, they became in effect welfare recipients of the federal government. It wasn't until 1924 that the Indian Citizenship Act made them citizens of the country that had once been theirs.

1 For the first century of their history, Americans were pre-occupied with pushing the 'frontier' (the invisible line separating civilization and wilderness) further westward. Speculate on the effect of this on the American national character.

Comprehension

▶ SF 22: Analysing visuals

▶ More language

1 a Describe what you can see in the picture below. Work from right to left.
b Compare results with your partner. Add missing details to your list.

John Gast, *American Progress*, 1872

Analysis

2 Relate the title of the painting to the progression (from right to left) depicted by the artist.

Beyond the text

3 You choose | Writing Work on task **a** or **b**.

a Your class is preparing an online presentation on 19th century American history. Write a short text in which you explain the importance of Gast's painting.

b Write a letter in the name of the Sioux people demanding that this painting be removed from public display.

4 Intercultural communication Choose a painting from your country that you believe says a lot about your country. Explain its content and meaning and compare it to John Gast's 'American Progress'.

► More language

5 Think back to the guiding question of the chapter and reconsider what you wrote in your paragraph on p. 146. Take into account everything you have learned so far.

Text 6

My American daughter Amy Tan

- 'Ethnic culture' vs. 'national culture': a source of conflict, or a win-win situation? Discuss.

Immigrants to the USA often wish to pass on their native culture to their children. This is often more difficult than it sounds, as a Chinese-American mother discovers in Amy Tan's novel Joy Luck Club.

My daughter wanted to go to China for her second honeymoon, but now she is afraid.

'What if I blend in so well they think I'm one of them?' Waverly asked me. 'What if they don't let me come back to the United States?'

'When you go to China,' I told her, 'you don't even need to open your mouth. They already know you are an outsider.'

'What are you talking about?' she asked. My daughter likes to speak back. She likes to question what I say.

'Aii-ya,' I said. 'Even if you put on their clothes, even if you take off your makeup and hide your fancy jewelry, they know. They know just watching the way you walk, the way you carry your face. They know you do not belong.'

My daughter did not look pleased when I told her this, that she didn't look Chinese. She had a sour American look on her face. Oh, maybe ten years ago, she would have clapped her hands – hurray! – as if this were good news. But now she wants to be Chinese, it is so fashionable. And I know it is too late. All those years I tried to teach her! She followed my Chinese ways only until she learned how to walk out

Annotations
3 **blend in** *sich (optisch) einfügen*
7 **speak back** *Widerworte geben*
9 **Aii-ya** Chinese exclamation of frustration
15 **fashionable** trendy

Annotations
26 **scholarship** stipend
27 **sue sb.** *jdn. verklagen*
27 **landlord** *Vermieter*
34 **pursue sth.** strive to get sth.

Info

Melting pot or salad bowl?
Around 1900, the **melting pot** (*Schmelztiegel*) became popular in the USA as a symbol of the assimilation of immigrants into American society. This was usually taken to mean that newcomers were to give up their former culture in favour of a new American identity. More recently, the melting pot has been replaced by the **salad bowl,** into which new arrivals are integrated without losing their own distinct identity.

the door by herself and go to school. So now the only Chinese words she can say are *sh-sh, houche, chr fan,* and *gwan deng shweijyau*. How can she talk to people in China with these words? Pee-pee, choo-choo train, eat, close light sleep. How can she think she can blend in? Only her skin and her hair are Chinese. Inside – she is all American-made.

It's my fault she is this way. I wanted my children to have the best combination: American circumstances and Chinese character. How could I know these two things do not mix?

I taught her how American circumstances work. If you are born poor here, it's no lasting shame. You are first in line for a scholarship. If the roof crashes on your head, no need to cry over this bad luck. You can sue anybody, make the landlord fix it. You do not have to sit like a Buddha under a tree letting pigeons drop their dirty business on your head. You can buy an umbrella. Or go inside a Catholic church. In America, nobody says you have to keep the circumstances somebody else gives you.

She learned these things, but I couldn't teach her about Chinese character. How to obey parents and listen to your mother's mind. How not to show your own thoughts, to put your feelings behind your face so you can take advantage of hidden opportunities. Why easy things are not worth pursuing. How to know your own worth and polish it, never flashing it around like a cheap ring. Why Chinese thinking is best.

No, this kind of thinking didn't stick to her. She was too busy chewing gum, blowing bubbles bigger than her cheeks. Only that kind of thinking stuck.

'Finish your coffee,' I told her yesterday. 'Don't throw your blessings away.'

'Don't be so old-fashioned, Ma,' she told me, finishing her coffee down the sink. 'I'm my own person.'

And I think, How can she be her own person? When did I give her up?

From: The Joy Luck Club, *1989*

Comprehension

1 Summarize the reasons why the *narrator is convinced that the Chinese will recognize her daughter as a foreigner.

2 Outline the mother's plan for her daughter's upbringing and the reasons why it failed.

Analysis

3 Intercultural communication Compare the relative merits of Chinese and American culture in the narrator's view.

4 Work on task **a** or **b**.

a Examine the impression the daughter Waverly makes in the text, pointing to examples.

b Challenge Analyse the relationship between mother and daughter.

Language awareness

5 Although the text at hand is an excerpt from a novel, in its *style it often resembles spoken language. Point to examples and analyse their effect.

Beyond the text

6 Writing The narrator feels that she has failed completely as a mother. Do you agree? Write a comment.

► SF26: Argumentative writing: discussion and comment

Info

Immigration

The first settlers in Britain's Atlantic colonies, whose descendants later formed the backbone of the American population, came mainly from Great Britain, Germany and the Netherlands. For the first half-century after independence, immigration to the USA was moderate, but around the middle of the 19th century it exploded. Push factors were political unrest, religious persecution and famine in many parts of Europe. As a result, large numbers of Irish, Poles, Italians and Jews fled to America in search of a better life. Pull factors were the availability of farmland, the Gold Rush, and the need for labourers in the mines and factories of a young, rapidly growing nation. The newcomers, mainly Catholics and Jews, were not always welcomed by the 'WASP' (White Anglo-Saxon Protestant) majority that dominated American political and cultural life for two centuries.

Immigration – both legal and illegal – has continued to be a significant and oftentimes controversial factor in US politics to the present day. Mass migration of Spanish-speaking immigrants from Latin America is seen by some as a threat to mainstream English-language culture. The number of undocumented immigrants in the USA is estimated to be as high as ten million. In recent decades, migration from south-eastern Asia has also risen significantly. The first major wave of Asian immigration to the USA occurred in California in the 1850s. Most Chinese immigrants hoped to earn wealth to send back to China. Soon Asian immigrants were sought not only in California but across the USA to fill the high demand for cheap labor in mines, factories and particularly for the railways crossing the country.

Chinese labourers building the first transcontinental railway.

1 Collect information from the box in two lists: 'Immigration – benefits and threats'.

▶ More info

Stupid America

Abelardo Delgado

• Describe and interpret the illustration.

Abelardo Delgado (1931–2004) was a Mexican-American activist and poet.

Annotations
1 **chicano** Mexican-American
4 **knife sb.** injure sb. with a knife
9 **curse** *Fluch*
14 **chicanito** small or young Chicano
15 **flunk** fail (in a school subject)

stupid america, see that chicano
with a big knife
in his steady hand
he doesn't want to knife you
he wants to sit on a bench
and carve christ figures
but you won't let him.
stupid america, hear that chicano
shouting curses on the street
he is a poet
without paper and pencil
and since he cannot write
he will explode.
stupid america, remember that chicanito
flunking math and english
he is the picasso
of your western states
but he will die
with one thousand masterpieces
hanging only from his mind.

From: 25 Pieces Of A Chicano Mind, *1969*

Comprehension

▶ SF 19: Reading and understanding poetry

1 Describe the role of the *speaker vis-à-vis the addressee.

Analysis

2 Divide the *poem into three sections. Point out structural parallels.

Language awareness

3 Choose one of the three 'cases' described in the poem; examine how the language evokes an emotional response.

Beyond the text

4 You choose Work on task **a** or **b**.

a Writing Your group is preparing materials about immigration policy in the USA. Write a short recommendation for your group in which you explain why you think 'Stupid America' should or should not be included.

b Speaking Imagine that you are the poet. A school class has invited you to talk about your writing. One student asks you why you wrote the poem 'Stupid America'. Answer the question in no more than five minutes.

Focus on test formats

As part of your Abitur *exam and in some of your course exams, your listening skills will be tested using closed and semi-closed test formats.*
Read the following tasks:

► SF 2: Working with closed test formats
► SF 37: Essentials: listening and viewing

Task 1 (short answers): *You are going to hear an excerpt from the podcast 'Brown folks with silly names'. Host Saadia Khan interviews the Pakistani American journalist and comedian Wajahat Ali on growing up in the United States as the child of Muslim immigrants.*

Answer each of the questions below in 5–7 words.

1 According to Saadia, why do many immigrant parents in the USA want their children to become doctors or engineers, for example?
2 Why did Wajahat's uncle feel under pressure to earn money?
3 Where does Wajahat see the challenge for his own generation?
4 What does Saadia say about her biography?
5 Why does Wajahat think that it's important for Muslims to play an active role in public life?
6 According to Wajahat, what event made Muslim Americans realize that financial security was not enough?

Task 2 (multiple choice): *You are going to hear a second excerpt from the same interview. Listen to the excerpt and choose the correct completion of each of the following sentences (only one is correct).*

1 Wajahat says that his parents ...
  a were like all Pakistani immigrant parents.
  b were very conservative.
  c were very unconventional.
  d were in some ways unconventional.

2 When his teacher asked Wajahat to read his story to his class, ...
  a he was extremely proud.
  b he didn't want to.
  c he refused.
  d he asked her to read it aloud.

3 When his story was read aloud in class, ...
  a Wajahat's classmates reacted with enthusiasm.
  b Wajahat's classmates laughed at him.
  c nobody listened to the story.
  d Wajahat's classmates were amazed.

4 After Wajahat's father read the story, ...
  a he told his son that he should still become a doctor.
  b he encouraged his son to cultivate his talent.
  c he argued with his wife about their son's future.
  d he told his son to forget about writing.

5 Together with his friend Kashif, Wajahat ...
   a wrote a play.
   b dreamed of a career as a rock star.
   c made films.
   d tried to stay out of trouble.

6 While Wajahat was at law school, ...
   a he worked hard at his writing career.
   b he starred in a film.
   c he dreamed of becoming famous.
   d he wrote plays in his spare time.

Task 3 (multiple matching): *You will hear six speakers (1–6) talking about the situation of Asian Americans. Choose from the list (A–I) the statement that each speaker makes. There is only one correct answer per speaker. Copy the table below and put the corresponding letter (A–I) into the correct box. There are three extra statements that you will not need.*

A The speaker calls on all Asian Americans to work together for their rights.
B The speaker refers to the fact that thousands of Asian Americans were put in prison camps during World War II.
C The speaker talks about the present situation of the Asian and Asian-American student communities.
D The speaker refers to the role of Chinese workers in American history.
E The speaker draws a connection between racist rhetoric and acts of violence.
F The speaker calls for a more detailed treatment of Asian Americans in school curricula.
G The speaker talks about personal experiences of discrimination and racism.
H The speaker describes how American immigration policy focused on barring Chinese from entering the country.
I The speaker says that the image of Asia in the USA is connected with war.

Speaker	1	2	3	4	5	6
Statement						

Work it out

In this section you are led step by step through the tasks presented above. The strategies you learn here can help you do other types of listening tasks as well.

Pre-listening

In a typical exam situation you are given an opportunity to read the tasks before listening to the recording. You may also be allowed to ask about unfamiliar vocabulary.

1 Examining the background information

a Read the texts that introduce each of the three tasks. For each of the tasks, answer the following questions:
- What information are you given by the text?
- What challenges do you anticipate while listening?

b Compare answers with your partner. Together, formulate strategies that can help you to deal with the challenges you may encounter.

2 Examining the tasks

a Read the task items closely. For each item, choose two or three key words to listen for.

b The speaker may not use exactly the same wording as the task. For the key words you chose in **2a,** think of other words that belong to the same word field. Keep them in mind while listening to the recording.

While-listening

3 Listening strategies

You will hear the recording twice. There are different strategies for dealing with this situation. Compare the two strategies described below. What advantages and disadvantages does each of them have?
Strategy a: While listening for the first time, I don't write down anything. I concentrate on what the speakers are saying and listen for the gist.
Strategy b: While listening for the first time, I write down the answers I am sure of. When I hear the text the second time, I concentrate on the remaining tasks.

► More language

4 Doing short-answer tasks

a Examine the following checklist and decide which points are relevant for doing short-answer listening tasks:
1. Using correct grammar and spelling.
2. Listening for key words.
3. Using the same words as the original text.
4. Writing complete sentences.

b Say which of the following are true or false when doing short-answer listening tasks:
1. Write the answer in German if you don't know the English word.
2. The questions are in the same order as the relevant information in the spoken text.
3. If you don't know the answer, don't write anything.
4. Make an intelligent guess even if you aren't sure it's correct.

c Compare answers to **a** and **b** with your partner. If you aren't sure what is right, ask your teacher.

5 Doing multiple-choice tasks

All of the following statements are wrong. Correct them and add any other tips that you think are helpful for doing multiple-choice tests.

1 You lose one point for every wrong answer.
2 More than one answer can be correct.
3 It's better not to mark anything if you don't know the right answer.
4 Identifying wrong answers won't help you.

6 Doing multiple-matching tasks

a Write three tips for doing multiple-matching tasks.
b Compare results with your partner.

Post-listening

7 Checking your answers

Normally you will be given a short time after listening to complete your work. Check that you have done all the tasks. If you alter one of your answers, make sure that your final choice is clearly recognizable.

Do it

8 Working on the task

Listen to the excerpts from the audios and do the three tasks on pp. 161f.

Feedback

9 Self-assessment

a After you have corrected your answers, listen to the parts of the exam again that caused you difficulty.
b On the basis of your results from task 1, make a *method card with the aspects you had difficulty with. Think of ways how you can improve your listening skills.
c Add useful strategies for dealing with listening comprehension tasks to your method card.

A visit to Monticello

Thomas Jefferson was one of the Founding Fathers of the USA and principal authors of the Declaration of Independence.

Comprehension

Listening Listen to a podcast about visiting Monticello, Thomas Jefferson's Virginia plantation, and write short notes to the tasks below.

▶ SF 38: Listening/Viewing for gist and detail

1 Describe the weather on the day of the tour.
2 State who did most of the skilled work at Monticello.
3 State what cannot be seen from Jefferson's house.
4 Outline the information that can be found in Jefferson's account books. Name two examples.
5 Describe the most common form of punishment for underachieving.
6 Name two examples of incentives to make slaves work harder.
7 Name an example of how slaves could try to beat the system.

Info

Slavery in the 'Land of the Free'

In 1619, the first shipload of slaves from Africa arrived in Jamestown, Virginia. In the decades that followed, hundreds of thousands more followed, until Congress declared the importation of slaves illegal in 1807. Nonetheless, the slave population of the USA continued to grow.

Slavery was a controversial issue in the early days of the republic. Both Thomas Jefferson and George Washington were plantation owners and slaveholders while at the same time they were propagating the ideals of human rights and equality. In the northern states, slavery was illegal; in the South, it was the backbone of the economy. Slaves were not citizens of the USA and had no legal rights; even slaves who escaped to the North retained their slave status.

As the nation expanded westward, the question arose whether slavery was to be permitted in the new states. While settlers from the South insisted on keeping their slaves, the opponents of slavery – called 'abolitionists' – were calling for the liberation of all slaves. The young republic was moving rapidly toward a bloody confrontation. In 1860 Abraham Lincoln ran for election, promising that as president he would abolish slavery in the USA. When he won, eleven southern states declared their independence, forming the Confederacy of States. Lincoln declared their action illegal, and a civil war followed that left the South in ruins. Slavery was abolished, and military governments were installed in the rebellious states. The 14th and the 15th Amendments to the Constitution were passed, giving citizenship and voting rights to all persons born in the USA. But when the army was withdrawn from the South in 1877, white backlash set in, and the situation rapidly worsened for African Americans.

Partner A: Make notes on the history of slavery in America, then explain to your partner how Blacks were disadvantaged from the beginning of American history.
Partner B: Go to p. 257 ('From Jim Crow to BLM').

▶ More info

The health card
Alice Childress

- How do you react when asked to show proof of vaccination? Why?

*A century after the end of slavery, black and white Americans still lived in different worlds, as the following *short story from New York illustrates.*

Well, Marge, I started an extra job today. ... Just wait, girl. Don't laugh yet. Just wait till I tell you. ... The woman seems real nice. ... Well, you know what I mean. ... She was pretty nice, anyway. Shows me this and shows me that, but she was real cautious about loadin' on too much work the first morning. And she stopped short when she caught the light in my eye.

Comes the afternoon, I was busy waxin' woodwork when I notice her hoverin' over me kind of timid-like. She passed me once and smiled and then she turned and blushed a little. I put down the wax can and gave her an inquirin' look. The lady takes a deep breath and comes up with, 'Do you live in Harlem, Mildred?'

Now, you know I expected somethin' more than that after all the hesitatin'. I had already given her my address so I didn't quite get the idea behind the question. 'Yes, Mrs. Jones,' I answered, 'that is where I live.'

Well, she backed away and retired to the living room and I could hear her and the husband just a-buzzin'. A little later on I was in the kitchen washin' glasses. I looks up and there she was in the doorway, lookin' kind of strained around the gills. First she stuttered and then she stammered and after beatin' all around the bush she comes out with, 'Do you have a health card, Mildred?'

That let the cat out of the bag. I thought real fast. Honey, my brain was runnin' on wheels. 'Yes, Mrs. Jones,' I says, 'I have a health card.' Now Marge, this is a lie. I do not have a health card. 'I'll bring it tomorrow,' I add real sweet-like.

She beams like a chromium platter and all you could see above her taffeta housecoat is smile. 'Mildred,' she said, 'I don't mean any offense, but one must be careful, mustn't one?'

Well, all she got from me was solid agreement. 'Sure,' I said, 'indeed one must, and I am glad you are so understandin', 'cause I was just worryin' and studyin' on how I was goin' to ask you for yours, and of course you'll let me see one from your husband and one for each of the three children.'

By that time she was the same color as the housecoat, which is green, but I continue on: 'Since I have to handle laundry and make beds, you know ...' She stops me right there and after excusin' herself she scurries from the room and has another conference with hubby.

Inside fifteen minutes she was back. 'Mildred, you don't have to bring a health card. I am sure it will be all right.'

I looked up real casual kind-of and said, 'On second thought, you folks look real clean, too, so ...' And then she smiled and I smiled and then she smiled again. ... Oh, stop laughin' so loud, Marge, everybody on this bus is starin'.

From: Like One of the Family, *1956*

Annotations
- 6 **hover** wait somewhere, esp. near sb.
- 8 **blush** turn red
- 14 **a-buzzin'** (here) speaking in low voices
- 15 **gills** *(pl) Kiemen*
- 16 **beat around the bush** talk for a long time without coming to the main point
- 18 **let the cat out of the bag** (here) finally say what you want to say
- 21 **beam** (here) smile happily
- 21 **chromium platter** *verchromte Servierplatte*
- 21 **taffeta** type of material
- 25 **study** *(sl)* think

Info

The American short story
Literature 'made in USA' emerged around the middle of the 19th century. American authors like Edgar Allan Poe, Nathaniel Hawthorne and Stephen Crane made a name for themselves with short prose pieces – the first short stories of the modern era. In the 20th century, authors like Ernest Hemingway and Shirley Jackson helped establish the short story as a literary genre.

Comprehension

1 Summarize the *plot in your own words.

Analysis

2 Analyse the *conflict in the story and how it is resolved.

3 Describe the situation in which the *narrator tells her story and analyse how this manner of narration influences the reader.

► SF 18: Reading and understanding narrative texts

Language awareness

4 Compare the language used by the narrator and her white employer. Point out differences in grammar and pronunciation.

► Support p. 258

Beyond the text

5 Speaking 'The Health Card' shows how class differences and racial conflicts can be settled through humour and mutual acceptance.
Do you agree? Discuss in small groups.

Text 10

An unsolved problem Liz Mineo

In the second half of the 1960s, violence erupted in the black ghettos of American cities. President Johnson appointed the Kerner Commission to investigate the causes. The Kerner Report, *which appeared in 1968, pinpointed white racism as the real cause of the rioting. Fifty years later, Liz Mineo of the* Harvard Gazette *asked sociologist Orlando Patterson to assess what has changed for Black Americans since then.*

GAZETTE: In 1968, the Kerner Report concluded that 'the nation was moving toward two societies, one black, one white – separate and unequal'. What is your assessment of the situation 50 years later?

PATTERSON: Since then, there have been very important changes, but also some disappointments. There is no doubt that in the public sphere, particularly in the political realm, there have been substantial improvements. A good example is the election of a black president, but we should see this simply as the result of major changes in our political system that allowed blacks to be elected as mayors, congressional and senatorial representatives, and the occasional governor in the past 50 years. The Obama election didn't mark a post-racial era. That's an exaggerated and absurd claim. It's nonsense. We all know that the major disadvantages that African-Americans face have roots in their enslavement. For most of the time African-Americans have lived in this country, they have been viewed as the quintessential outsiders, as people who didn't belong to the dominant political or moral community. That was reflected in the absence of blacks in important political positions but also in the national conversation, up to about the 1960s. That has changed completely. In addition to that, there are some important economic changes, and this shouldn't be sniffed at. There is a genuine black middle class. Finally, there is also the strong influence of blacks in the cultural life of the country. But in spite of their presence in the public sphere, black Americans still remain quite segregated in their private lives.

Annotations
6 **realm** [relm] area
6 **substantial** *beträchtlich*
13 **quintessential** most typical
18 **sniff at sth.** dismiss sth. as unimportant
20 **segregate sb.** isolate sb.

Annotations
25 **deem yourself sth.** believe that you are sth.
26 **pre-eminent** most prominent
29 **suspicious** [sə'spɪʃəs] *verdächtig*
36 **in token numbers** *in rein symbolischer Anzahl*
44 **accomplish sth.** make sth. happen
45 **indicate sth.** *auf etwas hinweisen*
48 **dissipate** become weaker
59 **right-wing** extremely conservative
60 **hostility** extreme opposition
62 **hypocrisy** [hɪ'pɒkrəsi] *Heuchelei*
65 **reluctance** lack of willingness
65 **promote sth.** support sth. actively
66 **vigorously** with conviction

GAZETTE: What are the factors that allowed segregation to continue? Some experts argue that segregation is almost as bad as before, or perhaps even worse.
PATTERSON: Here is the great irony: The highest levels of segregation are in the most liberal Northeastern states, including New York, which deems itself the pre-eminent liberal state. On the other hand, cities that have experienced the highest levels of integration are the new Sun Belt cities – Houston, for instance. Part of the reason is that in newer cities people don't feel that they and their ancestors have been living there for generations. And outsiders are not seen as suspicious because everybody is an outsider in a new city. There have been some changes in education at the elite level. But by and large this has been a major area of disappointment. The number of black students in overwhelmingly majority-black schools is as great as it was when the report came out. That, of course, is related to housing segregation. Now, blacks can afford good schools if they can afford to live in places that have such schools. There was a time when they wouldn't get in or were admitted in token numbers. But much of the progress has been at the upper-middle-class level. Those at the bottom, the black poor, are not seeing much change. In relative terms, the black poor may even be slightly worse off. They certainly are as segregated as they ever were, and the violence in the inner cities has increased substantially since the Kerner Report.

GAZETTE: The report blamed 'structural racism' created by 'white institutions' and 'white society' for the violence and the conditions of the ghettos and the inner cities. One of its recommendations was to improve the conditions of the ghettos or simply get rid of them. Why has it been hard to accomplish this?
PATTERSON: There is evidence that indicates that the ghettos must go. But it's important to know there is some ambivalence within the African-American community. For many, having a black community ensures black cultural and communal life, both of which could dissipate if blacks are integrated in the broader white community. I disagree. Ghettos never worked.When people say that black neighborhoods are needed for black culture to live on, I point to the Jews, because even as they integrated, they preserved their culture. All other groups in America recognize that staying clustered in ghettos is not good. That was true of Jews. It's been true of Asians. That's also true of Irish and Italians, and more recently it's been true of Hispanics. There is a growing Hispanic middle class that is very integrated. I don't see why black Americans can't do the same. Researchers found that blacks who moved to better neighborhoods were better off than those who stayed in their neighborhoods with similar resources.

GAZETTE: What other factors have prevented integration from happening?
PATTERSON: There has always been right-wing and racist opposition to any government attempt at integration. There was already some hostility to the [federal government's] Moving to Opportunity for Fair Housing program in the late '90s. But there is also the hypocrisy and the 'not-in-my-backyard' view of many middle- and upper-middle-class people, including white liberals, who have strongly resisted attempts at building moderate-income and low-income housing in the suburbs. And finally, there is the reluctance of some black leaders to promote integration too vigorously because of the argument that we need black neighborhoods to preserve African-American traditions, racial pride, a sense of identity, as well as the political advantages of being clustered. But Martin Luther King Jr. strongly supported integration, and he referred to an integrated society as America's beloved

community. Between the right-wing opposition, the white liberal hypocrisy, and the ambivalence of black leaders, integration has faded away from the national agenda. But the main reason for the lack of integration is that blacks don't have the income to integrate; they can't afford to live in the suburbs or send their kids to private schools. Some can do it, and that's some progress, but it's not enough.

From: 'The Kerner Report on race, 50 years on', Harvard Gazette, *2018*

Comprehension

1 Outline Patterson's assessment of the current situation (where progress has been made, what problems remain to be solved).

2 Explain why Patterson believes that black ghettos should not be preserved.

Analysis

3 Examine the factors that make integration difficult for members of the African-American community.

Language awareness

4 **a** In Patterson's replies, he frequently uses adjectives that stress importance, for example (in the first two sentences): *important* (l. 4), *substantial* (l. 6). Collect further examples from ll. 4–40.

b Rank the words you have found according to meaning: Which express the greatest importance, which the least?

Beyond the text

5 You choose | Writing | Work on task **a** or **b**.

a You are an exchange student at an American high school. Write an *article for the school paper in which you explain in what way(s) integration is an issue in Germany.

b Integration into the mainstream or preserving ethnic identity – which is more important? Take sides and defend your opinion in an *argumentative essay.

► SF 30: Writing an (online) article
► SF 26: Argumentative writing: discussion and comment

6 Think back to the guiding question of the chapter on p. 146 and your reworking of your ideas on p. 156. Add a sentence or two to your paragraph after you have finished the last few texts.

Words revisited

► SF 6: Essentials: language and study skills

1 Mind mapping

a Go back to Words in Context (p. 148). Collect words and phrases in the first section of the text that are related to the term *conflict*. Organize them in the form of a mind map.

b Do the same for the terms *American Dream* and *the American political system*.

Language awareness

Intercultural communication *The large number of ethnic groups living in North America has resulted in the creation of new names to distinguish them. In the course of time, some older discriminatory or wrongfully-used terms have been replaced by more correct and inclusive ones.*

Old term	Preferred term
(American) Indians	First Nations peoples (Canada), Native Americans (USA)
Eskimos	Inuit
Negroes, colored people	Blacks, African Americans
Latin Americans	Hispanics, Latinos/Latinas

► More info

2 What's in a name?

Form small groups and speculate on the following:

- Why the terms in the left-hand box above have gone out of fashion.
- Why in some circles it has become fashionable to use *Latinx* [læˈtiːneks] instead of *Latino/Latina*.
- Why in recent years the term *people of color* has become commonplace.

3 Intercultural communication The German side

a In the USA, citizens with foreign roots are often referred to as 'Japanese Americans', 'Irish Americans', etc. Compare the American terms to German words for German citizens with a *Migrationshintergrund*.

b Your American exchange partner expresses surprise that you refer to your classmate Kyrill as a 'Russlanddeutscher', but to your friend Erkan as a 'Deutschtürke'. From his point of view this is discriminatory. How would you reply to his criticism? Write a short email to him about the matter.

Practice

4 Listening to a speech

Viewing Watch a video of an excerpt from *Donald Trump's inaugural address as 45th President of the United States, on 20 January 2017 and do the following task.*

▶ SF 38: Listening/Viewing for gist and detail

Write down your initial reactions to the speech concentrating on the following:

- the content
- the delivery
- the reaction of the audience

5 Reading a speech

Below is the text of the excerpt. Read it and do the following tasks.

For too long, a small group in our nation's Capital has reaped the rewards of government while the people have borne the cost. Washington flourished – but the people did not share in its wealth. Politicians prospered – but the jobs left and the factories closed. The establishment protected itself, but not the citizens of our country. Their victories have not been your victories; their triumphs have not been your triumphs; and while they celebrated in our nation's Capital, there was little to celebrate for struggling families all across our land.

That all changes – starting right here, and right now, because this moment is your moment: it belongs to you. It belongs to everyone gathered here today and everyone watching all across America.

This is your day. This is your celebration. And this, the United States of America, is your country. What truly matters is not which party controls our government, but whether our government is controlled by the people. January 20th, 2017, will be remembered as the day the people became the rulers of this nation again. The forgotten men and women of our country will be forgotten no longer. Everyone is listening to you now. You came by the tens of millions to become part of a historic movement the likes of which the world has never seen before.

From: Donald Trump, Inaugural address, *20 January 2017*

Comprehension

1 Summarize the content of the excerpt in neutral language.

2 Compare your summary with the original. In what respects do they differ?

Analysis

3 Analyse the *stylistic devices used by Trump and the effect they have on the audience. The terms in the box on the right can help you.

*antithesis
*climax
*contrast
*exaggeration
*juxtaposition
negation
*parallelism
*repetition

Beyond the text

4 Think about the USA today in light of the excerpt. Assess to what extent Trump's vision is reflected in reality.

No longer the land of opportunity?

Nicolas D. Kristof and Sheryl WuDunn

- What measures and institutions do you regard as desirable (or necessary) to promote equality of opportunity? Discuss.

The American Dream promised equality of opportunity, not social or economic equality itself. But critics say political leaders have long since abandoned this goal – with severe consequences for millions of Americans.

For much of the nineteenth and twentieth centuries, the United States had pioneered efforts to create opportunity. The Homestead Acts, beginning in 1862, were a self-help program that gave American families 160 acres of land each if they farmed it productively or improved it over five years. Homesteads transformed the West and turned impoverished workers into landed farmers. One-quarter of Americans can trace some of their family wealth to that visionary initiative. Another historic program was rural electrification, which beginning in 1936 brought electricity (and later telephone service) to farmers across America, transforming rural life, improving productivity and multiplying opportunity.

The United States was one of the first regions of the world to offer near universal basic education, and then one of the first countries to introduce high schools for nearly all children. 'By the early 20th century America educated its youth to a far greater extent than did most, if not every, European country,' Claudia Goldin and Lawrence F. Katz write in *The Race Between Education and Technology*, their exploration of how investments in human capital made America the world's leading country. [...] A state university and community college system made tertiary education widespread, and the [...] GI Bill of Rights vastly expanded educational attainment and homeownership in America. [...]

There were many other historic initiatives in the early 20th century that put the United States on a progressive path. In the 1930s, [...] Congress approved social safety net programs like Social Security, unemployment insurance and jobs initiatives like the Civilian Conservation Corps. Other countries later adopted many elements of these programs.

Then in about 1970, [...] America went off track, beginning a nearly half-century drift in the wrong direction. High-school graduation rates tumbled from the highest to among the lowest in the industrialized world. Incarceration rose sevenfold. Family structure collapsed. Single-parent households soared. Life expectancy peaked. Working-class incomes grew glacially, if at all. [...] The result is that the top 1 percent now owns twice as great a share of national wealth as the entire bottom 90 percent. We went from being a world leader in opportunity to being a laggard.

The decline in education leadership is particularly significant, because good jobs increasingly require a solid educational foundation. Globalization, automation, and a relentless focus on cost cutting led to a hollowing out of urban blue-collar and clerical jobs that in the past were often performed by people with limited education. David Autor, an economist at MIT, has found that as a result, urban workers with only a high-school education fill jobs that are actually lower skilled now than back in the 1970s. [...]

Annotations

2 **pioneer sth.** be the first to do sth.
3 **160 acres** c. 65 hectares
5 **impoverished** extremely poor
5 **landed** landowning
6 **trace sth.** *etwas zurückverfolgen*
13 **extent** *Ausmaß*
17 **GI Bill of Rights** laws passed in 1944 that provided generous benefits for World War II veterans
17 **attainment** achievement
21 **Social Security** US pension system
26 **incarceration** imprisonment
28 **peak** *(v)* stop rising
28 **glacially** extremely slowly
30 **laggard** loser
33 **relentless** never stopping
33 **cost cutting** saving money
33 **hollow sth. out** *etwas aushöhlen*
33 **blue-collar jobs** manual work
34 **clerical jobs** office work

One sign that the United States was moving rightward and following a different trajectory than the rest of the West was the election of Ronald Reagan in 1980. Reagan both reflected and shaped the country's mood in the 1970s when in his speeches he regularly denounced a Chicago welfare recipient: 'She has eighty names, thirty addresses, twelve Social Security cards and is collecting veteran's benefits on four nonexistent deceased husbands.' After his election to the presidency, he famously declared in his inaugural address in 1981, 'Government is not the solution to our problem; government is the problem.' He broke the air traffic controllers' union; worker protections declined; and the business world became much more powerful.

As hostility toward government spread in America, there have been determined efforts to cut taxes, particularly for the wealthy, and then 'starve the beast' – using reduced revenue to justify cuts in services for the disadvantaged. This is both disingenuous and cruel, as well as out of step with the advanced world. Other countries over the decades expanded health-care coverage, adopted family-leave policies, extended mass transit and implemented child allowances to reduce poverty, while the United States bucked the trend by slashing taxes, cutting back hours at public libraries, raising tuition at state universities, and allowing infrastructure to decay. Grover Norquist, an influential Republican advocate for lower tax rates, captured the small government ideology: 'My goal is to cut government in half in twenty-five years, to get it down to the size where we can drown it in the bathtub.' [...]

In 1965, the average chief executive earned about 20 times as much as the average worker; now the average CEO earns more than 300 times as much. A Walmart employee earning the median salary at the company, $19,177, would have to work for 1,188 years to earn as much as the chief executive did in 2018 alone. Companies also changed the ways they operated, outsourcing custodial jobs and eliminating pensions in ways that raised share prices but left many families more vulnerable. [...]

Not since the Great Depression has America experienced the kind of working-class stagnation that we've seen in recent decades, and it has fed polarization, racism, and bigotry, gnawing away at our social fabric.

Resentment has grown toward Latinos, Muslims, and African Americans. White supremacists gained ground, and on websites and social media Americans glibly trumpet their bigotry. Hate crimes have increased in the United States for three years in a row, the FBI reported. On one ultra-right website we visited, people posted venomous statements about Muslims and called for mass deportation. One woman proposed, 'Any Muslim man wanting to come into our country must be castrated first.'

Is this America?

From: The US Federal Reserve, *2020*

Annotations

39 **trajectory** path
41 **denounce sb.** *jdn. brandmarken*
41 **recipient** sb. who receives sth.
43 **deceased** no longer living
44 **famously** *bekanntlich*
44 **inaugural address** *Antrittsrede*
45 **air traffic controller** *Fluglotse*
48 **hostility** negative feelings
48 **determined** *entschlossen*
49 **starve sb.** *jdn. verhungern lassen*
51 **disingenuous** dishonest
52 **family-leave policy** law that lets people take time off from work to look after a family member
53 **extend sth.** *etwas ausbauen*
53 **mass transit** *ÖPNV*
53 **child allowance** *Kindergeld*
54 **buck the trend** do the opposite of everyone else
54 **slash sth.** reduce sth. drastically
55 **tuition** *Studiengebühren*
56 **advocate** sb. who speaks out in favour of sth.
57 **capture sth.** express sth. in a few words
62 **median salary** *mittleres Gehalt*
64 **custodial job** *Hausmeistertätigkeit*
65 **vulnerable** at risk
69 **bigotry** prejudiced thinking
69 **gnaw** [nɔː] **at sth.** *an etwas nagen*
69 **fabric** *Zusammenhalt*
71 **glibly** without thinking
72 **trumpet sth.** make sth. public
74 **venomous** *giftig*

Comprehension

▶ More language

1 You choose Work on task **a** or **b**.

a Summarize the measures adopted by the US government in the past to promote equality of opportunity.

b Summarize the examples used to show how US governments have cut back on measures to create equal opportunity.

Compare notes with someone who chose the other task.

Analysis

2 Analyse the relationship between government cutbacks and social cohesion as presented in the text.

3 The excerpt ends with a short *rhetorical question. Examine its meaning for the text as a whole.

Language awareness

4 The sentence in ll. 67–69 contains an example of emphatic inversion. Rewrite the sentence using normal sentence structure (i.e., subject – verb – object). Compare the two versions in their grammar and their effect.

Beyond the text

5 Writing Write an email to an American friend briefly summarizing the facts and expressing your reaction to what you have learned about the USA.

▶ SF 21: Analysing diagrams

Language help
stagnate
rise/fall
sharply/steadily/
moderately/
gradually/minimally

6 **a** Referring to the chart below, describe the economic development of the richest Americans, the poorest Americans, and the middle class.

b Relate the information contained in the chart to the political and economic developments described in the text.

Private wealth USA 1990–2020 (in percentage of total)

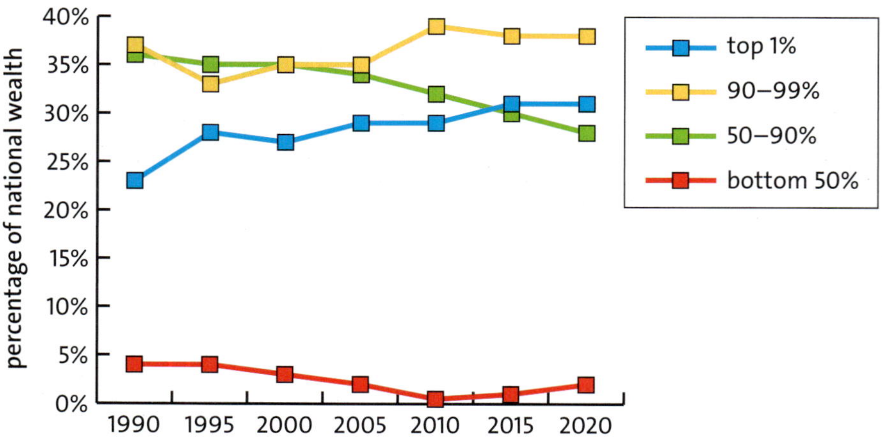

From: Nicolas D. Kristof und Sheryl WuDunn, Tightrope: Americans Reaching for Hope, *2020*

Beyond the text

7 Interpret the *cartoon and relate it to the information in the chart in task **6**.

► SF 23: Analysing cartoons

► Check

"Your butler, your father and I are concerned that with grades like these, you'll just end up being part of the 99%."

Text 12

The reluctant giant Robert Kagan

- Does the USA have a global responsibility that goes beyond that of other nations? Discuss.

Foreign policy expert Robert Kagan explains why Americans sometimes forget that they are a superpower – perhaps even the *superpower.*

All great powers have a deeply ingrained self-perception shaped by historical experience, geography, culture, beliefs, and myths. [...] Often, it is these self-perceptions that drive nations, empires, and city-states forward. And sometimes to their ruin. Much of the drama of the past century resulted from great powers whose aspirations exceeded their capacity.

Americans have the opposite problem. Their capacity for global power exceeds their perception of their proper place and role in the world. Even as they have met the challenges of Nazism and Japanese imperialism, Soviet communism, and radical Islamist terrorism, they have never regarded this global activism as normal. Even in the era of the Internet, long-range missiles, and an interdependent global economy, many Americans retain the psychology of a people living apart on a vast continent, untouched by the world's turmoil. Americans have never been isolationists. In times of emergency, they can be persuaded to support extraordinary exertions in far-off places. But they regard these as exceptional responses to

Annotations
- • **reluctant** uncertain, not convinced
- 1 **ingrained** *verwurzelt*
- 2 **self-perception** self-image
- 4 **aspirations** goals
- 5 **exceed sth.** go beyond sth.
- 11 **retain sth.** *an etwas festhalten*
- 11 **apart** separately
- 12 **turmoil** conflicts
- 14 **exertion** effort
- 14 **exceptional** not normal

Annotations
- **20 yearn** *sich sehnen*
- **23 self-absorption** being only concerned with yourself
- **26 commitment** *Verpflichtung*
- **29 tenuous** weak
- **30 precarious** *prekär*
- **30 equilibrium** balance
- **31 concurrent** happening at the same time
- **34 thrust sb.** push sb. violently
- **36 bulk** the largest part
- **37 theater** place where a war is happening
- **37 prolonged** longer
- **39 muster sth.** bring sth. together (for a special purpose)
- **44 adjust** get used to sth. new
- **44 invulnerability** *Unverwundbarkeit*
- **47 self-sufficient** not dependent on others

exceptional circumstances. They do not see themselves as the primary defender of a certain kind of world order; they have never embraced that 'indispensable' role. [...]

Americans' preference for a limited international role is a product of their history and experience and of the myths they tell themselves. [...] Americans have always yearned to recapture what they imagine as the innocence and limited ambition of their nation's youth. For the first decades of the new republic's existence, Americans struggled merely to survive as a weak republic in a world of superpower monarchies. They spent the nineteenth century in selfishness and self-absorption, conquering the continent and struggling over slavery. By the early twentieth century, the United States had become the richest and potentially most powerful country in the world, but one without commitments or responsibilities. [...]

But then the world shifted, and Americans suddenly found themselves at the center of it. The old order upheld by the United Kingdom and made possible by a tenuous peace in Europe collapsed with the arrival of new powers. The rise of Germany destroyed the precarious equilibrium in Europe, and the Europeans proved unable to restore it. The concurrent rise of Japan and the United States put an end to more than a century of British naval hegemony. A global geopolitics replaced what had been a European-dominated order, and in this very different configuration of power, the United States was thrust into a new position. Only it could be both a Pacific and an Atlantic power. Only it, with weak neighbors to the north and south and vast oceans to the east and west, could send the bulk of its forces to fight in distant theaters for prolonged periods while its homeland remained unthreatened. Only it could afford to finance not only its own war efforts but also those of its allies, mustering the industrial capacity to produce ships, planes, tanks, and other materiel to arm itself while also serving as the arsenal for everyone else. Only it could do all of this without bankrupting itself but instead growing richer and more dominant with each major war. [...]

The world had never known such a power [...]. Americans, too, had a hard time adjusting. The wealth and relative invulnerability that made them uniquely capable of fighting major wars and enforcing peace in Europe, Asia, and the Middle East simultaneously also made them question the necessity, desirability, and even morality of doing so. With the United States fundamentally secure and self-sufficient, why did it need to get involved in conflicts thousands of miles from its shores? And what right did it have? [...]

In 1990, the former U.S. ambassador to the UN Jeane Kirkpatrick argued that the United States should return to being a 'normal' nation with normal interests [...]. That meant protecting its citizens, its territory, its wealth, and its access to 'necessary' goods. It did not mean preserving the balance of power in Europe or Asia, promoting democracy, or taking responsibility for problems in the world that did not touch Americans directly. [...]

The problem is that the United States has not been a normal nation for over a century, nor has it had normal interests. Its unique power gives it a unique role. [...] World order became the United States' concern when the old world order collapsed in the early twentieth century and the country became the only power capable of establishing a new one in which its interests could be protected. [...]

An entire generation of Americans has grown up believing that the lack of clear-cut victories in Afghanistan and Iraq proves that their country can no longer accomplish anything with power. The rise of China, the United States' declining share of the global economy, the advance of new military technologies, and a general diffusion of power around the world – all have signaled the twilight, once again, of the American order.

Yet if the United States were as weak as so many people claim, it wouldn't have to practice restraint. It is precisely because the country is still capable of pursuing a world-order strategy that critics need to explain why it should not. The fact is that the basic configuration of international power has not changed as much as many imagine. The earth is still round; the United States still sits on its vast, isolated continent, surrounded by oceans and weaker powers; the other great powers still live in regions crowded with other great powers; and when one power in those regions grows too strong for the others to balance against, the would-be victims still look to the distant United States for help. [...]

The time has come to tell Americans that there is no escape from global responsibility, that they have to think beyond the protection of the homeland. They need to understand that the purpose of NATO and other alliances is to defend not against direct threats to U.S. interests but against a breakdown of the order that best serves those interests. They need to be told honestly that the task of maintaining a world order is unending and fraught with costs but preferable to the alternative. A failure to be square with the American people has led the country to its current predicament, with a confused and angry public convinced that its leaders are betraying American interests for their own nefarious, 'globalist' purposes. The antidote to this is not scaring the hell out of them about China and other threats but trying to explain, again, why the world order they created still matters.

From: 'A superpower like it or not', Foreign Affairs, *2021*

Annotations
65 **diffusion** spread
68 **restraint** *Zurückhaltung*
74 **would-be** potential
81 **fraught with sth.** connected with sth. (unpleasant)
82 **square** honest
82 **predicament** situation
84 **nefarious** evil
84 **antidote** *Gegenmittel*
85 **scare the hell out of sb.** make sb. extremely frightened

Comprehension

1 Summarize the reasons named in the text why America traditionally has had an ambivalent relationship to its global responsibility.

2 Outline the author's main arguments why he believes America must play a major role in the world.

Analysis

3 Work on task **a** or **b**.

a Examine Kagan's language in ll. 34–42 to emphasize America's global uniqueness.

b Challenge Examine the means Kagan employs to convince his readers of his views.

▸ SF 17: Reading and understanding non-fictional texts

Language awareness

4 **a** Collect ten examples of words that belong to the word field 'power'.
b Use five of the words you have used in sentences of your own.
c Swap sentences with your partner. Ask your partner to decide if your 'power words' have a positive or a negative connotation. Compare responses.

Beyond the text

▶ SF42: Preparing and giving a speech

5 You choose Work on task **a** or **b**.

a Writing Compare Kagan's and O'Sullivan's ideas on America's relationship to the rest of the world.

b Speaking 'The world needs America's leadership.' Do you agree? Make a short speech to your class.

6 Go back to the guiding question of the chapter and rewrite your paragraph from p. 146, taking into account everything you have learned from this chapter.

Text 13

Time for a new relationship

Hendrik Brandt

- *Quick write: Outline what you know about the German-American relationship.

The editor-in-chief of a German newspaper takes a critical look at how America is perceived in Germany.

Ach, die Amerikaner. Plötzlich sind sie wieder ein Thema. Beherrschen die Diskussionen am Frühstückstisch oder in der Videorunde im Job. Dabei waren uns die USA in den vergangenen Jahren im Grunde fremd geworden. Gut, die Geschichten vom reichen Onkel, der uns nach dem Krieg mehr oder minder selbstlos geholfen hat, sind schon lange verjährt. Und ganz gestimmt haben sie ohnehin nie.

Dennoch: Das Land zwischen Atlantik und Pazifik war über Jahrzehnte hinweg ein Ort für so viele Sehnsüchte. Da ging es für die einen um die große Freiheit oder um das große Geldverdienen ohne Skrupel. Für die anderen lag die Faszination im Gegenteil, sie suchten die Flucht aus dem Hamsterrad und fanden auch dafür einen Platz. „Drüben in den Staaten“, wie man so sagte. Vor allem aber waren die US-Amerikaner über mehrere Nachkriegsgenerationen hinweg die wahre Bezugsgröße. Und auch ein Alltags-Vorbild; ihre Kultur bestimmte die deutsche und europäische längst weit mehr als umgekehrt.

Vieles davon ist in den zurückliegenden Jahren zu Ende gegangen. Nicht krachend oder spektakulär, sondern leise, Schritt für Schritt. Wenn Demoskopen die Deutschen derzeit fragen, ob sie eher zu den USA oder zu China neigen, hält sich das nun schon fast die Waage – nur noch gut ein gutes Drittel der Befragten setzt noch auf die alte Supermacht, fast genauso viele Menschen halten zur neuen. Protokoll einer Entfremdung, die noch vor einem Jahrzehnt unvorstellbar schien.

Oder etwa doch nicht? Hat das alles nur mit dem unsäglichen Donald Trump zu tun? War da nicht auch schon das Kopfschütteln über Ronald Reagans Neoliberalismus? Oder der Spott über George W. Bush, dessen Kriege nicht unsere sein konnten? Ist die dunkle Kehrseite des amerikanischen Gesellschaftsmodells nicht lange vor den jüngsten Vorfällen rund um Rassismus, Gewalt und soziale Spaltung sichtbar geworden? Und wie war das nochmal mit Vietnam?

Das Faszinosum USA hat mächtig gelitten, vorrangig unter seinen eigenen Widersprüchen. Das Land ist nun einmal extrem. Es verbindet ungeheure Flexibilität mit exzentrischer Bürokratie, wunderschöne Landschaften mit entstellten Gegenden, breitbeinige Männlichkeit mit peinlich genauer Gender-Achtsamkeit. Die Kontraste hatten in ihrer hierzulande ungekannten Größe einst durchaus ihren Reiz – sind aber in ihrer wachsenden Brutalität jetzt oft nur noch abschreckend. Viele Deutsche wollen die USA nicht mehr so, wie sie sind. Sondern nur noch so, wie sie sie selbst gern hätten. Da liegt der Kern der kulturellen und gesellschaftlichen Distanzierung.

Das sicherste Indiz hierfür ist der Blick auf die Politik. Kaum jemand hierzulande hat verstanden, warum die Amerikaner nach dem überaus gewandten Bill Clinton vor zwanzig Jahren nicht dessen alerten Vize Al Gore zum Präsidenten gewählt haben, sondern den leicht tapsigen wirkenden Texaner George W. Bush. Geradezu messianisch war später die Wahrnehmung des intellektuellen Barack Obama im Oval Office. Der war ja auch cool. Dass es aber auch seine Politik war, die Teile des Landes einfach übersah und ein amoralisches Faktotum wie Donald Trump als Präsident mit ermöglicht hat, blieb meist unbeachtet. Genauso wie übrigens die oberflächlichen Erfolge Trumps. Deutschland nahm den USA mehrheitlich übel, dass sie dem alten Wunschbild nicht mehr entsprachen.

Angesichts dieser Scheidung auf Raten ist nun oft davon die Rede, dass sich Deutschland wie Europa stärker auf sich selbst besinnen müssten. Ja, was denn sonst? Die Hoffnung, dass die USA irgendwann doch bitte wieder so sein mögen, wie wir sie einst gesehen haben, wird nicht tragen. Wer immer sie regiert. Bei allen engen wirtschaftlichen, militärischen und immer noch auch kulturellen Bindungen muss klar sein, dass es hohe Zeit für eigene Wege ist.

From: 'Wir sollten ein neues Verhältnis zu den USA finden', www.ndr.de, *6 November 2020*

1 Mediating You have been invited to an international congress. The topic is 'Rethinking America'. You have been asked to prepare a short paper on the topic 'The German View of the USA'. Concentrate on the following areas:
- the German view of the USA in previous decades
- the attitude of Germans to recent US presidents
- how Germans might regard the USA in the future.

► SF 47: Mediating from German into English

► More language

Chapter task

'My American soundtrack': Choose a song that you connect with America. Present it to your classmates and name reasons for your choice.

Chapter 6

The World of Work – Just a Job to Do?

1 a **Think** Write down ideas and emotions that the pictures evoke for you. Then choose the picture that you find most interesting (or controversial) and describe it in 4–5 sentences.
b **Pair** Compare and discuss your ideas with a partner. Together agree on a suitable *hashtag for each picture.
c **Share** Present your hashtags in class and take a vote to choose the best two hashtags for each picture.

2 Discuss what questions the pictures raise about the challenges of the modern world of work.

► Getting started

3 a Look at the Chapter map and think about: How might the guiding question and the elements around it be linked to each other? What might they tell you about this chapter?
b What aspects of the world of work do you expect to be challenging in your future life?

SUCCESS
CAREER
GROWTH
DEVELOPMENT

Chapter map

requirements (of future employees)
career choice
technology/AI
Chapter task: a discussion
Mastering the challenges of the modern world of work – no problem!?
Speaking
job application
first-hand experience of a job
work-life balance
future of work

► More language

A closer look at the world of work

Spoilt for choice: Choosing a career

School-leavers are confronted with an important threshold in life: deciding on the right career path. The huge range of possibilities can be overwhelming. They can choose from university courses, apprenticeships, internships and many other options. Career guidance can help students to define their career aspirations and narrow down the number of possibilities to choose from. Nevertheless, many young people make their career decisions based on a gut feeling, and their working lives may often take surprising turns.

Coping in the workplace

Striking a balance between private and working life has never been easy. Many people try to achieve a healthy work-life balance while others criticize this as a misleading and pointless concept.
Almost every workplace has undergone major changes caused by digitization and automation. Artificial intelligence and robotics can generate feelings of anxiety but workers may also benefit from these developments because mundane tasks can now be performed by machines. This leads to increased productivity. Application processes have also changed as a result of digitization and have become more flexible. Interviews can easily be conducted online instead of face-to-face.

Current challenges in the world of work

Nowadays the expansion of sectors such as administration, human resources, or public relations means a greater variety of jobs. There is a broad spectrum of jobs for highly qualified workers and freelancers as well as people with no specific qualifications. Some sectors and companies therefore face a shortage of skilled workers. Some people find working remotely from anywhere more appealing than being stuck in a traditional office. It gives them a feeling of independence and autonomy. In a lot of countries, precarious employment means that many struggle to cover the cost of living or have to delay retirement. People work longer hours and for more years than they planned. There are many different forms of work today, for example, nomadic work, temporary employment, or running a one-person-business. In many countries real wages have stagnated and there are calls for a universal basic income for everybody from time to time.

The global job and labour market

For people who form part of an international team, the ability to communicate across cultures is very important. English is a *lingua franca*. Depending on the profession, a certain level of Business English and its subgroups (e.g. Legalese) need to be attained. A specific knowledge of and sensitivity to cultural differences is also required, as well as empathy and flexibility.
Competition for cheaper products manufactured faster has resulted in precarious working conditions in many countries. Migration in combination with the digitization of work is also leading to greater global competition for jobs while also providing an incentive for people to invest continuously in their knowledge and skills.

1 Words words words

a Name and define three important developments in the field of work and business mentioned in the text.
b Find three highlighted phrases in the text that were new to you.
c Explain the phrases from task **b** in English.
d For each of the four parts of the text, think of one piece of information which is not mentioned.

2 Word families

In order to structure relevant vocabulary, you can arrange them in word families.
a Start a word family on *employ*.
b Find three more words from the text (e.g. *work*) and start a word family with them.

► Check

3 Chunk it!

a Find suitable words for the gaps to make *chunks. You can check in the text for help, but also add other words.
1 career ...
2 ... the number of possibilities to choose from
3 ... by machines
4 being ... in a traditional office
5 companies are ... with a shortage of supply

b Check your chunks with a partner and add them to your list.

► Check

4 Call for action

Look at the third paragraph 'Current challenges in the world of work'.
a How could you turn that paragraph into a call for more social security throughout people's working lives in order to convince a group of interested workers? Work with a partner and collect ideas.
b Work on either of the tasks below:

Writing Write a *blog post in favour of better social security for workers. Include some of the hashtags you came up with on page 180.

Challenge Prepare and record a speech on social security that is addressed to workers and published via social media. Include some of the hashtags you came up with on page 180.

► SF 42: Preparing and giving a speech
► SF 27: Writing a blog post

Language help

convinced that • undeniable that • have to make sure that • the duty of every-body • speak out for

Do schools provide what future employees need?

Charles Yidan

The text is taken from the OECD study 'Dream Jobs? Teenagers' Career Aspiration and the Future of Work'. Charles Yidan acknowledges improvements in education. However, he points out that young people are confronted with challenging decisions.

Before you read the text have a look at the tables below. They show the career expectations of students in 2018. The students were asked to name the job they expect to be doing by the time they are 30.

- Name one result you would have expected and one that surprised you.
- The data are from 2018. Say whether you think they are still valid.

Top 7 occupations named by boys		
	2018	%
1	engineer	7.7
2	business manager	6.7
3	doctor	6.0
4	ICT professional	5.5
5	sportsperson	4.9
6	teacher	4.6
7	police officer	4.0

Top 7 occupations named by girls		
	2018	%
1	doctor	15.6
2	teacher	9.4
3	business manager	5.0
4	lawyer	4.6
5	nursing and midwife	4.5
6	psychologist	3.7
7	designer	3.0

From: OECD, Dream Jobs?*, 2021*

Language help

compare/contrast the • ranked first/last • gender differences

Annotations

2 **preceding** *(adj)* coming before sth./sb.

7 **mismatch** *(n)* unsuitable pairing

12 **driving force** *(no pl)* motivation; impulse

Across the world, the young people who leave education today are, on average, more highly qualified than any preceding generation in history. They often enter the working world with considerably more years of schooling than their parents or grandparents. This is an enormous achievement of which the global education community can be truly proud.

And yet, [...] young people continue to struggle in the job market, and governments continue to worry about the mismatch between what societies and economies demand and education systems supply. The co-existence of unemployed university graduates and employers who say they cannot find people with the skills they need, shows that more education does not automatically mean better jobs and better lives. [...]

I firmly believe that education is the fundamental driving force for social progress. With the world of work changing so quickly, there is strong reason to believe that schools need to look afresh at how they can better prepare young people for their lives.

The industrial age taught us how to educate second-class robots, people who learn in standardised settings and become good at repeating what we tell them. In this age of accelerations, we need to think harder about what makes us first-class humans, how we complement, not substitute, the artificial intelligence we have created in our computers, and how we build a culture that facilitates learning, unlearning and re-learning throughout life.

The new generation of citizens requires not just strong academic skills, but also curiosity, imagination, empathy, entrepreneurship and resilience. They need confidence and determination to create their own employment and to manage their careers in new ways. Effective education systems will go beyond traditional teaching techniques. Not only will they provide learners with knowledge relevant to future employment, they will also develop the ability of learners to be personally effective in applying that knowledge in changing situations.

Staying longer in education than ever before, today's young people must make more decisions about what, where and how hard they will study. These are investment decisions that are becoming increasingly difficult because technology is changing the working world itself so quickly. [...]

Never before has effective career guidance been so important and never before has there been a greater onus on employers to step up and work with schools to help young people understand jobs and careers and help teachers bring learning to life. [...]

Assuredly, schooling is not simply about preparing for work, but we owe it to our young people to ensure that they go through education blind neither to the opportunities offered by the working world nor to its potential pitfalls. [...]

From: www.oecd.org, *2020*

Annotations

18 **acceleration** the increase in sth.'s speed, or its ability to go faster
19 **complement sth.** make sth. else seem better or more attractive when combining it with sth.
19 **substitute sth./sb.** replace sth./sb.
23 **entrepreneurship** [ˌɒntrəprəˈnɜːʃɪp] skill in starting new businesses
23 **resilience** [rɪˈzɪliəns] ability of sb./sth. to be happy, successful, etc. after sth. difficult has happened
25 **go beyond sth.** exceed sth.
33 **career guidance** *Berufsberatung*
34 **onus** *(fml)* responsibility
37 **owe sth. to sb.** *jemandem etwas schuldig sein*
39 **pitfall** danger or difficulty *(Falle)*

Comprehension

1 Point out what, according to the author, schools need to teach their students to make them fit for the working world of the future. Explain two of these aspects using your own words.

Analysis

2 Match the verbs with the nouns on the right to form common collocations as they are used in the text.

A enter	**1** learning
B build	**2** employment
C require	**3** abilities
D create	**4** careers
E manage	**5** skills
F develop	**6** the working world
G apply	**7** knowledge
H facilitate	**8** a culture

► Check

3 Yidan is passionate about the shortcomings of the education system and the necessary changes required. Find out how he uses *register and various words and expressions to appeal to the reader.

Language awareness

4 Your school promotes a new career guidance programme on its website. Write the first paragraph of this announcement and address it to both the working world and the education world. Use some of your findings from tasks **2** and **3**.

Beyond the text

5 With reference to the chapter's guiding question, rank the non-academic skills named in the text in order of how challenging they are to master.

6 You choose Work on task **a** or **b**. Use some collocations from task **2**.

▶ SF 41: Giving a presentation
▶ SF 27: Writing a blog post

a Speaking Conduct a survey in your class and find out about the job expectations of your fellow students. Find similarities and differences between your findings and the OECD study. Prepare a presentation showing your results.

b Writing 'Education is the ultimate driving force for social progress.' (Charles Yidan) Write a *blog post in which you comment on this. Refer to your own experience as you are about to take important decisions for your future career.

Text 2

What's the next step for me? Lucy Hooker

- Describe the picture on page 187. What situations in your near future could it allude to?
- Why can making decisions for life after school be difficult?

Remember that moment when the school careers adviser leant over the desk and asked: 'So what are you planning to do next?'

It's a daunting decision when you're 17.

A university degree costs tens of thousands of pounds, although the evidence suggests it can boost your earning potential later.

On the other hand, an apprenticeship lets you earn as you learn, but life gets serious pretty fast.

Apprenticeships are shaking off a reputation for low-paid drudgery and there are more higher-level apprenticeships coming on stream. But competition for the best opportunities is as fierce as it is for the top university places.

So if you're leaving school, does it make sense to aim for one of those coveted places? Or are you missing out if you don't go for the campus experience? Recent apprentices and graduates have shared their experiences with us.

From: www.bbc.com, *12 July 2019*

Annotations
2 **daunting** frightening, discouraging,
5 **boost sth.** increase the value of sth.
8 **shake off sth./sb.** get rid of sth./sb.
8 **drudgery** *(infml)* ['drʌdʒəri] hard boring work
9 **come on stream** *(idiom)* be available
10 **fierce** intense
11 **coveted** wanted very much

Partner B: Go to p. 258, read the texts and work on the tasks there.
Partner A: Read the texts below and work on tasks **1–3b**.

'It made me who I am'

Amy De Friend, 25, did a degree in fashion promotion and communication. She now works in recruitment, but doesn't regret her decision to study first.

'I went to university, because at the time I didn't know what I wanted to do.' Amy started her degree the first year that fees went up from £3,000 a year to £9,250.

'My parents said: "Do you really want to spend £9,000 on this?"'

And at the end of the three years, she discovered that to get into the fashion industry, she would still have to take unpaid internships. So she worked for Carphone Warehouse instead.

Amy accepts she could probably have got the recruitment job she's in now without a degree. 'I wouldn't say it was a waste of time,' she says. 'The experience I had was fantastic, it helped me develop as a person.'

At university, Amy joined a diving club and qualified as an instructor, something she wouldn't otherwise have tried. 'I don't think it's all about getting a job. It's about what you gain from the experience. It made me who I am.'

'I was itching to start work'

Nick Martin, 20, has just been head-hunted for a £22,500-a-year job in sales. He puts that down to his work experience as an apprentice with a telephone networking equipment company.

'Before I got my last job, I went through a lot of interviews. Every single agency and company loved the fact I had done an apprenticeship, because it shows you know what it's like in a fast-paced office environment.'

At 17, Nick was 'just itching to get into work'.

The apprenticeship scheme he joined was new and he felt he was a 'guinea pig', often left to get on with things unsupervised, which meant a lot of responsibility very quickly.

'By the time most people my age come out of uni, I'll have had three to five years' experience. On the flipside, I haven't spent that time getting the extra qualifications.'

'At the time, I didn't have doubts. Now, to be honest, I think about it a bit more. The main reason for that is a bit of "Fomo" – fear of missing out – missing out on the social aspect of being at uni. You get to live in halls or housing with flatmates. I'm still living at home.'

Then there's the snobbery. 'I still get that feeling from some people – people I know who are at uni who think they're better – there can be a smugness. But there's nothing guaranteed. They'll have a degree, but they'll still have to find a job, which is hard.'

From: www.bbc.com, *12 July 2019*

Annotations

- 3 **recruitment** *Personalbeschaffung*
- 18 **itch to do sth.** *(infml)* wish to do sth. very much
- 19 **head-hunt sb. for a job** find sb. suitable for a working position
- 24 **fast-paced** moving, changing or happening very quickly
- 26 **guinea pig** ['gɪni pɪg] *(here)* person used in medical or other experiments
- 30 **flipside** reverse, the opposite of sth.
- 36 **snobbery** self-superiority
- 37 **smugness** looking or feeling too pleased about sth. you have done *(Selbstgefälligkeit)*

Comprehension

1 Collect the information given about Amy and Nick (name, age, career choice, arguments mentioned etc.).

Analysis

2 Examine how the text presents what Amy and Nick are saying and the effect created by this.

Language awareness

3 **a** The text uses words and phrases that show that Amy and Nick are happy with their decision, but also the concessions they are making. Collect them.
b Present your notes on tasks **1–3a** to your partner. Listen to your partner's findings on Matt, Jenny and Joy.
c In a one-minute speech explain whether you want to get your driving licence or not. Use expressions from task **3a**.

Beyond the text

► SF 44: Having a discussion
► SF 26: Argumentative writing

4 You choose Work on task **a** or **b**.
a Speaking Discuss with your partner the pros and cons of university and apprenticeship courses. Use the following questions as a starting point:
- Which young adults from the texts inspire your own decision-making process?
- How helpful is career guidance at your school?

b Writing Write an essay discussing the pros and cons of university and apprenticeship courses. You might include the experiences of the people in the text or of someone you know.

Text 3

► More info

The variety of jobs

In each episode of his podcast 'Studs: Exploring Working Lives', the host Daniel Lazar invites a different person to talk about their job.

- Read the titles of the episodes. Which profession might they refer to?
  1 'Brad Newman, Food Fighter'
  2 'Joe Leto Has Magic Hands'
  3 'Flavor Chaser, Courtney Burns'
  4 'Hope Junkie, Shana Burns'
  5 'Houston's Hottest Drop Since Beyoncé, Jason Danvir'
  6 'Kierra Jackson Brings New Life!'
  7 'Julie Stewart is a Truth Seeker'
  8 'Smile Because it Happened with Eric Lindberg'
  9 'Jason Teplitz, Cyberwarrior!'
  10 'The Internet c/o Scott Robbin'

Language help
could refer to • guess/suppose/expect ... to work as • I feel/believe/think that ...

Comprehension

1 You are going to hear an excerpt from the episode called 'Eric Spencer Delivers'. Complete the sentences. For each gap you have to use more than one word.

1 Eric Spencer works as a ... in ...
2 He has been doing this job ... years.
3 He is very happy with his Route because ...
4 In order to balance his social life and getting his job done, he ...
5 Eric Spencer can't stand ... because ...
6 His favourite days are ... because ...

► SF 38: Listening/Viewing for gist and detail
► Check

2 You are going to hear an excerpt from the episode called 'Kierra Jackson Brings New Life!' Complete the sentences. For each gap you have to use more than one word.

1 Midwifery is not just a job for Kierra Jackson because she ...
2 The field of midwifery is a very ...
3 Kierra Jackson is in her ... year of midwife training and she started it ...
4 She is convinced that birth is a ...

► Check

Language awareness

3 Which podcast episode was easier to follow? Give reasons and refer to the style of language used.

Beyond the text

4 With a partner discuss if you can imagine doing Eric Spencer's and Kierra Jackson's jobs. Bear in mind the challenges both face in their jobs.

5 You choose Work on task **a** or **b**.

a Speaking In groups of two make an entertaining podcast episode of about five minutes. Interview someone you know about their work or present your favourite job and give reasons for pursuing this career. The podcast is meant to be published on your school's homepage.

b Writing Write an article for the school magazine presenting an interesting, and perhaps uncommon, job. Include its daily challenges and advantages. Try to mention some surprising aspects. Find a title that arouses the reader's interest.

► Getting started

▸ More info

'So how's the PhD going?' Marina Lewycka

You are going to read an extract from a novel. It's a conversation between Serge, who is in his twenties and works in London, and Doro, his mother. Doro and Marcus, Serge's father, think he is doing his PhD at Cambridge. Serge has got two sisters: Clara and Oolie Anna.

- Do you hold the same views on economic processes and the working world as your parents? Present some ideas in a short statement.

Language help

My parents/Adults might think differently about the economy than me because ... • As part of the young generation, our task is to ... • The working world is constantly changing because... • When looking at the picture, I think that ...

Annotations

PhD *(abbr)* Doctor of Philosophy
1 **rendezvous** *(v)* meet
4 **Whitbread Plc** British company that owns hotels, restaurants and sports clubs
8 **gilded** covered with gold-leaf
8 **Wren** architect of St Paul's Cathedral
27 **go legit** *(infml)* (here) get married
28 **Solidarity Hall** name of the commune Doro and Marcus once were members of
33 **Jaeger** British chain of shops selling designer clothes

Serge and Doro rendezvous in the Café Rouge opposite St Paul's on the first Tuesday in September 2008, because Doro refuses to go into Starbucks, which she says is an outpost of American imperialism. He doesn't mention that the Café Rouge is a wholly owned subsidiary of Whitbread Plc, or they could be wandering around all afternoon looking for somewhere suitable.

The weather is still hot, and the square around St Paul's is full of tourists wearing terrible clothes, bumping into each other as they shuffle around peering through their viewfinders at the great gilded Wren dome. [...]

Doro, alas, is also wearing terrible clothes, which is a shame, because she's a nice-looking woman – tall, still slim, dark wavy hair lightly streaked with grey, and good skin. But no one over forty should wear a sequinned denim gipsy-flounce skirt – in fact, no one of any age. And that green linen jacket might have been okay in its heyday, but that was some twenty years ago. He has nothing against retro-chick so long as it's worn ironically, but he fears his mum really means it.

'I've got some exciting news, Serge.' [...] 'Marcus and I are thinking of getting married.'

'So what's all this about, Mum?'

Obviously it's not love at first sight, as she and Marcus have been living together since well before he and Clara were born. But Doro likes her little dramas, so he raises his eyebrows and leans forward.

'Tell me more!'

She dips a finger in the cappuccino foam and licks it. Thank God they're not in Franco's, where someone from work might see them.

'We thought it would be nice to make our love official, after all these years.' [...]

'Congratulations, Mum. You've caught the old goat at last! Ha ha.'

For God's sake, they're in their sixties! [...]

'Yes, we've got plenty to celebrate. Me and Marcus going legit. Clara's promotion to Head of Science. Oolie's first job. The fortieth anniversary of Solidarity Hall. And soon your PhD.'

Uh-uh. We're getting on to dangerous territory here.

'Lovely jacket, Mum. Is it a designer label?' He plays for time, wondering how to break his news.

'Jaeger ...' Doro hesitates. 'Recycled, of course.'

She means Oxfam. 'You and your recycling! The thing is, Mum –'

'We must all learn to live with less, Serge. Less waste! Less greed! Less mindless consumption!'

Doro has a long list of things she disapproves of, including consumerism, racism, war, Botox, [...] and trans-fatty acids. Maybe bankers have been added already; if not, it can only be a matter of time.

'It doesn't work like that, Mum. The economy depends on people borrowing and spending – that's what creates wealth.'

He knows this shocking truth must seem counterintuitive to a person of her generation. For them, capitalism was the big no-no.

'That's ridiculous. How can being in debt create wealth?' she snorts. 'People who say that have obviously never been to Doncaster.'

This is going to be harder than he thought.

'Recycling may be good for the environment, Mum, but the economy needs growth.'

'Nonsense. We can't keep squandering the planet's resources on needless junk, creating mountains of waste alongside mountains of debt.'

She has this embarrassing way of raising her voice in public [...]. Ranting is probably one of the few pleasures left at her age. [...] Her last birthday was the big six-oh. Poor Doro. Age doesn't suit her. Well, it doesn't really suit anybody, does it?

'If everyone was like you, Mum, the system would collapse.'

'But that's what we want. Isn't it?'

'Yes, but ...' He smiles indulgently. There's something particularly baffling about Doro's brand of illogic.

'So how's the PhD going?' She changes the subject, recycling a couple of spare sugar sachets into her handbag. 'Just remind me again, darling. What is it about?'

'The Hausdorff-Besicovitch dimension, Mum.'

Doro nods blankly. They have this conversation almost every time. She never seems to get it. [...] God knows what she'll say when she finds out about his job [as a banker]. [...]

From: Various Pets Alive and Dead, *2012*

Annotations

44 be in debt [det] owe money to sb.

45 Doncaster former mining town in the north of England

51 rant *(v)* complain about sth.

60 Hausdorff-Besicovitch dimension mathematical expression of the dimension of objects

St Paul's Cathedral in London

Comprehension

1 **a** Make a mind map with all five persons mentioned in the text. Note down any information about them that you can find.
b Compare with your partner.

2 Write 3–5 words to complete the following sentences using information from the text:
1 Marcus and Doro inform Serge about …
2 Serge's works as a … but his parents …
3 Marcus is annoyed about …
4 Doro criticizes …

Analysis

▶ Support p. 260
▶ SF 29: Writing a character profile

3 **a** Analyse the relationship between Serge and his mother Doro. Reflect on what they talk about, what they think of each other and how they speak to each other.
b Examine which means the *narrator employs to characterize Doro and Serge.

Language awareness

4 You choose Work on task **a** or **b**.
a Read the idioms below, which are taken from the text. Explain them using your own words.

in its heyday (l. 13) • catch the old goat (l. 25) • get on to dangerous territory (l. 30) • play for time (l. 31) • break his news (l. 32)

b With a partner agree on three of the idioms below, which are taken from the text. Use them to make meaningful sentences that are related to the context of work and business

Beyond the text

▶ SF 44: Having a discussion
▶ More language

5 You choose Work on task **a** or **b**.
a Speaking Work out a dialogue in which Serge finally tells Doro about his job as a banker. Be prepared to act it out with a partner.
b Discuss to what extent the generation gap between Serge and Doro reflects the current situation between parents and their children.

Focus on test formats

As part of your speaking exam or in life outside school, your speaking skills will be tested. You may be asked to present things, communicate with one or more partners in various contexts, or answer questions in an interview. Read the following task:

► SF 40: Essentials: speaking

You are applying for an internship in a company abroad. You are obliged to take part in an assessment. You will first be interviewed about your future plans and the reasons why you applied. After that you will be asked to deliver a short presentation (2–3 minutes) about future workplace developments in the profession you are interested in.

1 Collecting first ideas and thoughts

a Think about your future workplace and the potential development of workplaces in general. The pictures may help you to come up with ideas.

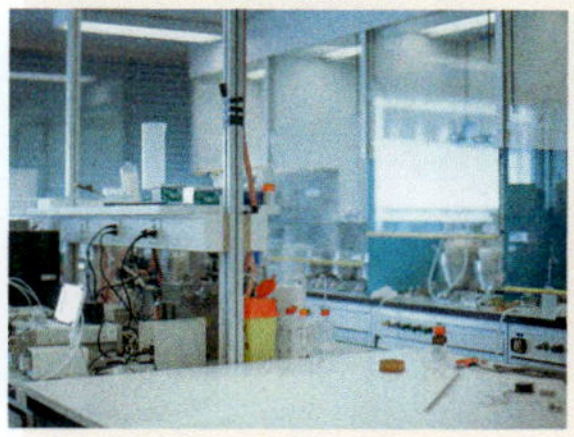

b Complete at least three of the following sentences and exchange your ideas with a partner.

1 My future workplace might be ...
2 In future, I see myself working in ...
3 Working in future will mean ...
4 What comes to mind when I think about future workplaces ...
5 I'm afraid of/sceptical about working in future because ...
6 As ... is my dream job, in future I expect ...

Language help

working remotely • working with my hands • working independently • having a permanent employment contract • flexible hours

Work it out

Step by step you will be taken through the task presented above reviewing general aspects of speaking tasks. As this is a mock exam situation, you will be allowed to work with a partner and discuss content and language elements of the task before performing it. In a test situation you won't have these options and will have less time for preparation. The strategies you learn here can also help you with other types of speaking tasks.

2 Differences between speaking in a monologue or in a dialogue

a Which is more difficult for you: a monologue or a dialogue situation? Give reasons for your answers and discuss your conclusions with a partner.

b With a partner note down the dialogue formats and monologue formats you know.

c Make a list of possible strategies that help you to overcome problems when you have to speak in English. Work with a partner.

3 Clarifying your topic

To better prepare yourself for the interview situation, you need to decide what kind of company you want to apply to for an internship.
Work on task **a** or **b**.

a Go through the list and choose the internship you would like to be interviewed for. Note down the reasons for your choice.

b Challenge Come up with your own idea for an internship. Use the list below as a model and make notes on your internship.

Open internship positions			
No.	**Field of work**	**Type of company**	**Location**
1	fashion and textiles • designing fashion • social media responsibilities • marketing & branding	sustainable fashion label	Paris (France)
2	journalism, publishing & media • researching topics • writing press releases • publishing blogs • interviewing people	media agency	Brussels (Belgium)
3	tourism management • tour planning • reception service • housekeeping, room allocation	hotel	Edinburgh (Scotland/UK)
4	environmental conservation • work in reserves, forests, greenhouses • growing and maintaining plants • researching plants and wildlife	NGO	San Ramon (Costa Rica)
5	special education • assisting teachers • giving extra lessons in English and maths • organizing afterschool activities	school	Windhoek (Namibia)

4 Preparing questions for the interview

► Getting started

You will take on the role of the interviewer while your partner performs the task. Develop questions for the interview. Make sure they refer to different aspects of the interviewee's life and background.

a Look at the following list of topics you could use. Decide if they are relevant (★★★★★) or irrelevant (★) for the interview by awarding 1–5 stars.

1 free time activities
2 school education
3 food preferences
4 knowledge of foreign languages
5 family size
6 favourite type of music
7 soft skills (flexibility, enthusiasm, teamwork)

b Arrange the topics from **a** in a suitable order for the interview and develop questions (use keywords, don't write them down word for word). Don't let your partner see the questions beforehand. Use open questions, not only yes-/no-questions.

► Support p. 260

c Which questions do you expect the interviewee to ask you? Think of possible answers and note them down on index cards.

5 Using the appropriate register and language in the interview

► More language

a Interviewer and interviewee need to introduce themselves and the situation. Which introductions 1–6 do you consider suitable? Remember: The *register in a professional interview is neutral to formal. Give reasons for your decision and discuss it with your partner.

1 'Hello, my name is Max Taylor. I'm here for a 2 p.m. interview for an internship in the field of business administration.'
2 'Hey guys, how are you doing?'
3 'Good morning. We are delighted to have you here.'
4 'Hi, just come in and let's have a chat.'
5 'Allow me to briefly introduce ourselves: This is my colleague Hanson, who is responsible for coordinating our interns, and I am Lazar, head of the marketing department.'
6 'Good afternoon everyone and thank you very much for giving me the chance to introduce myself.'

b Look at the following statements from job interviews. Decide which ones are well-worded. Improve the ones you find inappropriate (content, style, etc.).

1 'Because I have ambitious career goals, it can be difficult for me to maintain a healthy work-life balance.'
2 'I have no idea what course to choose at university. By doing this internship I'm trying to kill time.'
3 'I'd be excited to be part of your team and grow my skills with a company like yours.'
4 'I always found school boring so I can't wait to finally do something practical and earn money.'

5 'I don't think I'll enjoy this internship. My dad forced me to apply.'
6 'Being organized isn't my strongest point, but I use my phone to keep track of important dates and send me reminders.'

6 Preparing the presentation

a *Quick write: Take three minutes to write down ideas on the future development of your chosen working area. Also note down important vocabulary relevant to the topic. Don't forget connectors and signpost language. Remember that even a short presentation must have a clear structure.
b Find a suitable illustration that supports your ideas. You may use one from page 195 or a picture that provides a counterexample to your ideas.
c Practise your presentation by giving it in front of family, friends, or a mirror. You may also record it to make sure you stick to the time limit.

Info

'Signpost language' is the term for phrases that guide listeners through a presentation. It is used to make clear what has just happened, and what is going to follow. Examples:
- Due to the fact that ...
- In order to ...
- As a result ...
- Consequently, ...

Do it

7 Do the interview

Take turns performing the task. Don't forget to stage the interview: Come in through the door; the interviewer welcomes the interviewee.

Feedback

► SF 15: Assessing yourself and giving feedback

8 Peer and self-assessment

a In a *method card write down three aspects that went well, three difficulties you had and three strategies that will help you to get better. Be as specific as possible and refer to aspects like:
   1 communicative strategies (including non-verbal language)
   2 language (including pronunciation, *register, grammar)
   3 quality and meaningfulness of the content
b Make a list for your partner and write down three aspects that went well and three weaknesses. Refer to the aspects in a.

9 Discuss

Discuss the following questions with your partner:
1 Which strategies can help us improve our interviews and short presentations?
2 Would I choose my topic again? Why (not)?
3 Did I feel comfortable speaking in English? Why (not)?

10 Perform

Some of you perform their interviews and presentations in front of the class. Divide the listeners into content observers and language observers and give feedback.

Striking a work-life balance Penny de Valk

The text gives graduates tips on how to achieve a work-life balance in their first job.

- With regard to the role a job can play in your life, two concepts are often discussed: work-life-balance and the merge. What would you associate with these terms?

[...] You've worked hard to achieve great results in your degree, competed to get a graduate job and now find yourself working all hours to keep up with your employer's demands – all the while wondering what on Earth has happened to your social life. Sound familiar? Like it or not, this is the reality facing many graduates entering work today.

Graduates, and employees of all levels, can find work-life balance difficult to achieve, but we know it's important. Research found nearly one in three (31%) 18 to 24-year-olds said achieving a work-life balance was their long-term ambition. But trying to leave at 6pm when your boss sets you a huge task at 5.50pm can make it feel impossible. There are, however, various things you can do to help achieve a work-life balance in your first role.

[A] [...]

If your boss likes to start the day early – getting in at 8am and finishing at 6pm – chances are they'll expect you to be doing the same. Even if your contract states 9am to 6pm, most organisations don't stick to these hours, so try to be flexible with your time to accommodate how your team works.

While you shouldn't take working hours to the extreme, understand if you'll be adding more value by being in earlier or staying later. Working in journalism, for example, you'll probably be expected to start early – ensuring that you're breaking the day's news. In advertising, working later – be it attending awards, networking or creative brainstorming – is the norm. Once you've understood the lay of the land [...] you can plan your work and play time more effectively.

[B] [...]

Technology is engrained in our day-to-day lives now, but be careful not to become a slave to it. It's important to learn how to switch off from technology and give yourself a break from the constant bombardment of messages. [...] While you may be expected to keep an eye on your work phone out of office hours, try to create rules, such as not checking it or turning it off from a certain time each day.

[C] [...]

As a graduate in your first role, you may feel pressure from various parts of an organisation for your time – but make sure that the projects you take on with high visibility, or value to the businesses, are the ones you put extra energy into. If there is an opportunity to work with a senior colleague on an important project use it as your time to shine. Show them that you are reliable and capable and make a good impression. This will help to raise your profile, putting you in a stronger position for more exciting tasks in the future.

Annotations

4 **demand** *(n)* a request for sth.
17 **accommodate sth.** adapt to sth.
22 **lay of the land** (here) the state of a situation
25 **engrained in sth.** a fixed part of sth.

Annotations

- 39 **crucial** essential, important
- 45 **five-a-side** *(BE)* football game
- 52 **alleviate sth.** lessen or relieve sth., make sth. more tolerable
- 55 **peaks and troughs** [trɒf] highs and lows

[D] [...]

Spending time with loved ones outside the workplace is crucial to maintaining a work-life balance and a healthy mental wellbeing. Try to keep in regular contact with friends and family and carve out time in your schedule to do just this. It's important to switch off where possible and friends and family can help provide a much-needed break.

[E] [...]

If you enjoy keeping fit, be that an early morning spin class or five-a-side with colleagues after work, try to keep it in your schedule. Exercise is important to staying physically and mentally fit, helping to relieve daily stresses by releasing endorphins, also known as the happy hormone.

[F] [...]

If you feel as though you are on the edge of burnout, talk to your manager about how this can be addressed. It may be that you have too much on, in which case they might be able to draft in additional support from a colleague to alleviate pressure. Equally, it might be that everyone is in the same boat and feeling the pressure, due to being understaffed, or working towards a significant pitch for example. These periods should be in peaks and troughs though, so recognise if it's getting out of hand. [...]

From: www.theguardian, *10 August 2015*

Comprehension

1 In the text, the headings of paragraphs have been replaced by the letters A–F. For each letter, write a heading that sums up the tips given in the paragraph.

Analysis

2 The text gives advice to young people. Examine the language employed to do this, concentrating on phrases and verb forms.

Language awareness

3 The following are two original headings employed in the text:
'Do use your time effectively at work' [C]
'Do keep up your physical regime' [E]

- **a** Compare their syntactic structure to the headings you devised in **1**.
- **b** Describe the effect of 'do' at the beginning of the headings.
- **c** Come up with 2–3 'dos' you have heard in connection with your upcoming final exams.

Beyond the text

4 Writing 'Balancing' or 'merging'? Write a job ad for your perfect job, focusing on your ideal distribution of work and free time.

5 Speaking Think about someone's work-life integration (e.g. your parents, someone you know well). In a three-minute talk, comment on their balance between work and life and compare it to your own.

Language help

I consider the work-life integration of ... as ... • well-balanced/imbalanced/(un-) healthy/normal/not evenly distributed/(un-)stable • The work-life balance of ... can/can't serve as an example for me because ... • One of the most important aspects in balancing work and private life is ...

Text 6

'Money is just a social construct' Sally Rooney

▸ More info

*Marianne is a university student in Dublin, Ireland. In the following extract from Rooney's *novel Marianne is talking to her friend Joanna on the phone. The two women share their experiences and imaginations of working life.*

- How many years of your life do you expect to spend in a paid job?
- Would you prefer to stay in one job or would you rather switch jobs frequently?
- Do you want to start a family and what would that mean for your professional life?

Marianne is reading the back of a yoghurt pot in the supermarket. With her other hand she's holding her phone, through which Joanna is telling an anecdote about her job. When Joanna gets into an anecdote she can really monologue at length, so Marianne isn't worried about taking her attention off the conversation for a few seconds to read the yoghurt pot. It's a warm day outside, she's wearing a light blouse and a skirt, and the chill of the freezer aisle raises goosebumps on her arms. She has no reason to be in the supermarket, except that she doesn't want to be in her family home, and there aren't many spaces in which a solitary person can be inconspicuous in Carricklea. She can't go for a drink alone, or get a cup of coffee on Main Street. Even the supermarket will exhaust its usefulness when people notice she's not really buying groceries, or when she sees someone she knows and has to go through the motions of conversation.

The office is half-empty so nothing really gets done, Joanna is saying. But I'm still getting paid so I don't mind.

Because Joanna has a job now, most of their conversations take place over the phone, even though they're both living in Dublin. Marianne's only home for the weekend, but that's Joanna's only time off work. On the phone Joanna frequently describes her office, the various characters who work there, the dramas that erupt between them, and it's as if she's a citizen of a country Marianne has never visited, the country of paid employment. Marianne replaces the yoghurt pot in the freezer now and asks Joanna if she finds it strange, to be paid for her hours at work – to exchange, in other words, blocks of her extremely limited time on this earth for the human invention known as money.

It's time you'll never get back, Marianne adds. I mean, the time is real.

The money is also real.

Annotations
- 8 **solitary** alone
- 9 **inconspicuous** not easy to notice
- 9 **Carricklea** fictional town in Ireland
- 18 **erupt** break out

Annotations
32 venture sth. dare to express sth.
41 idle *(adj)* lazy
44 click your tongue *(idiom) mit der Zunge schnalzen*
44 scold sb. for sth. rebuke sb. for sth.

Well, but the time is more real. Time consists of physics, money is just a social construct.
Yes, but I'm still alive at work, says Joanna. It's still me, I'm still having experiences. You're not working, okay, but the time is passing for you too. You'll never get it back either.
But I can decide what I do with it.
To that I would venture that your decision-making is also a social construct.
Marianne laughs. She wanders out of the freezer aisle and towards the snacks.
I don't buy into the morality of work, she says. Some work maybe, but you're just moving paper around an office, you're not contributing to the human effort.
I didn't say anything about morality.
Marianne lifts a packet of dried fruit and examines it, but it contains raisins so she puts it back down and picks up another.
Do you think I judge you for being so idle? says Joanna.
Deep down I think you do. You judge Peggy.
Peggy has an idle mind, which is different.
Marianne clicks her tongue as if to scold Joanna for her cruelty, but not with any great investment. She's reading the back of a dried apple packet.
I wouldn't want you to turn into Peggy, says Joanna. I like you the way you are.
Oh, Peggy's not that bad. I'm going to the supermarket checkout now so I'm going to hang up.
Okay. You can call tomorrow after the thing if you feel like talking.
Thanks, says Marianne. You're a good friend. Bye. [...]

From: Normal People, *2019*

Comprehension

1 Work with a partner. Partner A points out why Joanne finds it important to have a job. Partner B points out why Marianne is sceptical about working life.

Analysis

► Support p. 261

2 The text contains a lot of direct speech but does not have any quotation marks. Examine the effect this may have on the reader. Give examples.

Language awareness

► More language

3 a Identify characteristics of direct speech in the text and give examples.
b Rewrite the last part of the text (ll. 40–49) using only reported speech or narrating it. Analyse the effect of these changes.

Beyond the text

4 With a partner, describe and analyse the cartoon. Find a suitable title and compare its message to the text 'Money is just a social construct'.

CartoonStock.com

5 You choose Work on task **a** or **b**.

- **a** Writing 'Should I spend my time on something called work?' Write a personal journal entry in which you consider your ideas about your future working life.
- **b** Speaking 'No one should do a job he could do in his sleep.' (Cory Doctorow) In groups of three, use this quote as a starting point to discuss the importance of having a meaningful job. Find examples of jobs you consider (ir-)relevant and give reasons.

6 **Art in Context** Work in pairs and decide who takes which painting.

- **a** **Think** Have a look at painting **A** (or **B**). What catches your attention? Be prepared to give a detailed description of it.
- **b** **Pair** Describe your piece of art in detail to your partner. Discuss why the artists may have chosen the titles 'Exploited Ape' and 'Struggle for Incentives'.
- **c** **Share** Present your ideas in class and relate the paintings and the text to the guiding question of this chapter.

► SF 23: Analysing cartoons

► SF 44: Having a discussion

A

Struggle for incentives

B

Exploited ape

▸ Check
▸ SF 6: Essentials: language and study skills

Words revisited

1 Revising word families and semantic fields

a Word families help you to expand your vocabulary (Words in Context pp. 182–183). Start a word family on *apply* with a partner.

b Collect typical chunks or expressions that are used in applications.

When applying for a place at a university abroad, or when requesting information from an international organization, your email or letter should follow certain formal rules. Read Marie's application letter.

A
Schillerstrasse 3
33098 Paderborn
Germany

B
Mike Donovan / The Burren Hostel
Kincora Rd
Lisdoonvarna
V95 WP40
Co. Clare, Ireland

C
5 March 20XX

D **Application for an internship**

E Dear Mr Donovan

F I am writing to apply for an internship at The Burren Hostel.
I will be finishing my A-levels in July 20XX, with English, Geography, and Mathematics as advanced courses. Before starting my university course in international tourism management at the University of Hamburg in October 20XX, I would like to get a deeper insight into work in the field of tourism and management. Since your website states that you offer short-term internships, I would be delighted to be given a chance to work at The Burren Hostel.

G I enclose a copy of my CV, which shows that I already have some experience of organizing holiday trips at my parish and that I was part of an international student exchange programme last summer. As I speak English and German fluently and have some basic communication skills in Spanish, I would be able to deal with international tourists who visit the west of Ireland.
Because I am reliable, open-minded, and flexible, I would be a helpful addition to your team at The Burren Hostel. I would appreciate the opportunity to enhance my practical experience before starting my studies.

H Thank you for considering my application for the internship.
I look forward to hearing from you soon.

I Yours sincerely,

J *M. Schreiber*

K Marie Schreiber

c Look for well-stated expressions in Marie's letter and add them to your list in **1b.** Determine the three most formal ones.

Language awareness

2 Paying attention to the structure of a formal letter or email

a Examine the different parts of Marie's letter. Match the parts with the correct letter **A—K** and fill in the left column of the table below.

1 line of thanks
2 date
3 details
4 final salutations
5 greeting
6 introduction paragraph
7 recipient's name and address
8 reference line
9 signature
10 writer's address
11 writer's complete name

Set parts	Aspects to consider
A: writer's address	• top right corner • no typical German letters (*ä/ß/...)*
B: ...	

b Note down aspects to consider in each part (right column).

3 Looking at language

Look for examples of the following in the sample letter. Indicate the lines.

1 long forms instead of short forms
2 formal words and expressions
3 polite grammatical forms

4 Using the appropriate register

Improve the underlined phrases to use them to write a formal email addressed to the admissions office of a university.

1 Dear guys
2 I really can't wait to be part of your university.
3 Here is my CV.
4 I really want to study politics because I just think it is so exciting.
5 Thanks for reading this.

► Check

Practice

5 Creating an application

Do task **a** or **b**.

a Apply for an English summer course. Describe your motivation, include expectations and questions. Address it to:
Susan Wright
English Language Centre
57 Gilbert Road
Kent BR6 7GB
UNITED KINGDOM

b **Challenge** Research modern ways of applying. Then shoot a video or use any other creative form of application you have researched. You want to take part in this year's *Model United Nations* simulation in Berlin. Describe your interest in politics and show your motivation.

► SF 34: Writing an application
► SF 13: Doing research

Calm down, it's just a bot

Simon Jenkins

- Have a look at the picture on p. 205 and speculate about people's fears and concerns regarding today's world of work.

Info

Artificial intelligence (AI)

AI is the capability of a machine to imitate intelligent human behaviour and act independently. AI is intended to think like humans and mimic their actions. AI often performs significantly better than humans, e.g. in cancer diagnosis and speech recognition. AI is used in industrial production, medicine, personalized online offers (e.g. ads), speech recognition on mobile phones.

Many questions in connection with AI need to be clarified, e.g. Does AI have consciousness? Who is liable if an AI decision leads to injury or death?

1 With a partner find scenarios that show advantages, disadvantages and ethical problems associated with AI.

In this column, the author calms the fears employees and economists have regarding AI.

[...] So we are doomed. Robots will steal our jobs. Algorithms will capture our children. Artificial intelligence will corrupt our free will. We are to be slaves to machines.

The Bank of England economist Andy Haldane warns [...] that 'large swathes' of current labour will disappear as AI takes over. For a man who lives and breathes statistics, large swathes is a poor percentage. These jeremiads attended the invention of computers, combine harvesters, spinning jennies and probably iron-age axes. [...]

How is it then that elsewhere in the news, we hear of people frantic for staff? There are [...] vacancies in social care and [...] in nursing. [...] Education is suffering likewise. Employers across the health, construction, agriculture, travel and hospitality sectors are screaming.

The idea that algorithms, robots and 3D computer printing will render these booming industries redundant is silly. Clearly new technology will mechanise a number of activities. As throughout history, innovation requires labour markets to shift and people – or their offspring – to retrain. The reality of economic history is that technology and trade yield short-term disruption. The same thing happened with refrigerated transport in the 1880s and combine harvesting between the wars. But we survived and prospered as new needs, and jobs, emerged.

The latest cliche, the 'fourth industrial revolution', supposedly describes a new algorithmic age. If there is to be a fourth revolution it will be the complete opposite, a reversion to the economy of human experience. The digital age will satisfy the mundanities of life, releasing leisure time for activities that are already soaring in demand. These cover everything from health, beauty, travel, food, the arts and entertainment to psychotherapy, social work, the care of children and the elderly. These service industries essentially involve human relationships. They cannot be

Annotations

- 1 **be doomed** certain to fail
- 4 **swath** (here) large amount of sth.
- 6 **jeremiad** complaint
- 7 **combine harvester** a machine that is construed to harvest grain
- 7 **spinning jenny** early form of the spinning machine
- 9 **frantic** desperate
- 10 **vacancy** availability of jobs
- 13 **render sth. redundant** make sth. unnecessary or needless
- 17 **yield sth.** result in sth.
- 19 **prosper** become successful
- 23 **mundanities of life** everyday occurrences of being human

done by robots or machines. They are labour-intensive and they are costly, whether in the private or public sector. They are also booming. Leisure and travel is second in value only to financial services.

Economists obsessed with manufacturing statistics would do better to welcome AI as releasing workers into the experience economy. They should discuss how we are going to pay for them, especially those concentrated in the public sector. They should stop grabbing easy headlines […].

From: www.theguardian.com, *20 August 2018*

Comprehension

1 Complete the following sentences with information from the text:
1. The author criticizes some economists because …
2. A shortage of skilled workers can be observed, especially in …
3. One of the greatest advantages of the digital age can be seen in …
4. In future, AI will …
5. Something that can never be done by robots or machines is …

Analysis

2 Columnists such as Simon Jenkins often write in a personal and humorous style. They use an informal, neutral *register. Analyse how Jenkins makes his ideas appealing and clear. Give examples.

► More language

► SF 26: Argumentative writing: discussion and comment

Language awareness

3 Rewrite the following using a more formal *register. Compare your version with a partner. How does this change the effect of the sentences?
1. So we are doomed. (l. 1)
2. … will capture … (l. 1)
3. How it is then that elsewhere … frantic for staff? (l. 9)
4. … is silly. (l. 14)
5. … grabbing easy headlines. (ll. 33–34)

Beyond the text

4 You choose Work on task **a** or **b**.

a Writing The digital age 'will satisfy the mundanities of life' and release 'leisure time for activities (l. 22–23). Write a comment and discuss the advantages and disadvantages of the impact technology is having on our jobs. You may use some ideas from the text.

b Speaking With a partner discuss which of your daily duties you would like to hand over to a machine/to AI. Come up with ideas on how you could use the extra time and how your career preparation could benefit from this.

► Getting started

► SF 26: Argumentative writing: discussion and comment

Crowdworking: sweet scent of freedom!? Corinna Budras

Work from anywhere you like, even the beach! It sounds like the thing to do nevertheless many crowdworkers have to contend with tough competition and bad pay.

Annotations
15 **Taylorismus** *Produktivitätssteigerung durch Aufteilung der Arbeit in kleinste Einheiten; benannt nach F.W. Taylor (1856–1915)*

[...] Das ist sie, die neue Arbeitswelt. Früher gab es Outsourcing, die Verlagerung von Unternehmensteilen nach Osteuropa oder Asien. Heute gibt es „Crowdsourcing", oft auch „Crowdworking" oder „Gig-Economy" genannt, die Verlagerung von Arbeit auf Menschen in der ganzen Welt. Wo diese Menschen sitzen [...] ist völlig egal. Wichtig ist nur, dass sie die Arbeit erledigen.

Das Internet macht es möglich: Dort sind in den vergangenen Jahren Hunderte von Arbeitsvermittlungsplattformen entstanden, die Auftraggeber und Auftragnehmer so geschmeidig zusammenbringen wie nie zuvor. [...]

Von einem „Heer digitaler Nomaden" ist seit einiger Zeit die Rede: Bemitleidenswerte Kreaturen, die sich mit vielen kleinen Aufträgen ohne soziale Absicherung nur mühsam über Wasser halten und deren einzige Freude darin liegt, dass sie ihre anspruchslose Arbeit vom thailändischen Strand aus erledigen können. Die Ungezwungenheit [...] ist nur vorgetäuscht, auch hier ist die Kontrolle allgegenwärtig, über Screenshots oder die Messung der Tastenanschläge. Skeptiker warnen sogar vor einer „neuen Form des Taylorismus": Umfangreiche Tätigkeiten werden in viele kleine Aufgaben zerlegt und wie Brotkrumen an die Masse der Tagelöhner verteilt.

Doch Crowdsourcing ist längst mehr als das. Der durchschnittliche Crowdworker in Deutschland ist 36 Jahre alt und überdurchschnittlich gebildet. Etwa jeder zweite hat ein abgeschlossenes Hochschulstudium. Das heißt, die können was. Und viel wichtiger: Sie wollen sich nicht unterordnen.

Airbus, Adidas, Deutsche Bank, Deutsche Telekom, Volkswagen – es gibt kaum einen großen Konzern, der sich nicht Hilfe vom kreativen Mob da draußen holt. [...]

Bisher erledigen viele Crowdworker vornehmlich Arbeiten, die auch früher oft nach außen gegeben wurden: Designer, Architekten oder Programmierer arbeiten seit jeher eigenständig. Nur kommen sie jetzt leichter an Projekte, für die sie sich bewerben können. Die Kehrseite allerdings ist: Auch alle anderen kommen an diese Angebote, der Wettbewerb ist härter geworden. [...] Aber es sind auch ganz neue Tätigkeiten hinzugekommen. Viele „Microjobs" würde es ohne Digitalisierung nicht geben, sie waren früher viel zu aufwendig: Straßenschilder für den Navigationsgerätehersteller Tom Tom fotografieren, im Supermarkt um die Ecke für einen Schokoladenkonzern die aktuellen Werbeaktionen überprüfen – dafür gibt es Geld. Jeder, der ein Smartphone bei der Hand hat, kann das leicht übernehmen.

So unterschiedlich die Tätigkeiten, so unterschiedlich ist auch die Bezahlung: Sie reicht von deutlich unter 10 Euro die Stunde bis zu 70 Euro die Stunde für anspruchsvolle IT-Dienstleistungen [...]. Ein einzelner Auftrag bringt mal drei, mal 2500 Euro. Den Spitzenverdienern unter den Crowdworkern gelingt es sogar, 10000 Euro im Monat zu verdienen. Doch für die allermeisten, rund 80 Prozent, geht es eher um einen Nebendienst.

Hinter diesen Zahlen könnte ein größerer gesellschaftlicher Trend liegen: die sanfte Befreiung aus der Umklammerung eines festen Arbeitsvertrags, den manche mit einem beschwerlichen Büroalltag verbinden. „Wir sehen gerade eine Verlagerung vom Angestellten zum Selbständigen", sagt Jovoto-Gründer Unterberg. „Jovoto ist dafür der Katalysator." Und er fragt ganz unbedarft: „Kann diese neue Art zu arbeiten nicht auch ein Befreiungsschlag für die ganze Gesellschaft sein?" Dafür müsste ein Problem allerdings noch gelöst werden: die fehlende Absicherung im Alter. In Deutschland gibt es mehr als zwei Millionen Solo-Selbständige. Viele von ihnen rutschen womöglich in die Altersarmut, weil sie nicht vorsorgen. [...]

From: www.faz.net, *13 May 2017*

Annotations
46 **Jovoto** internet platform for creatives (design, art, branding)

1 Mediating Your English class is taking part in the European school project 'The Future of the World of Work'. You have come across this text by Corinna Budras. Write an article for the project's website. Outline the advantages and disadvantages of crowdworking as presented in the article.

▶ SF 47: Mediating from German into English

▶ Getting started

Text 9

Is the world of work in the balance?

You are going to hear an excerpt from the BBC podcast 'In the balance'. The episode is called 'Precarious future'.

- What topics might be covered in the episode?
- From what you have learned in this chapter so far outline which factors may unbalance the present and future world of work.
- Read the shownotes below.

Technology has shaken up working culture. Large multinationals are rethinking the ways they let their staff work. While for many people outside the structure of big companies, work is increasingly freelance and insecure. We'll hear from those who say the traditional eight-hour working day is on its way out. But what is replacing it? Join Manuela Saragosa and guests as they debate how to make work pay fairly for everyone. Manuela hears from Guy Standing, [...] Edward Conard, [...] and Douglas Rushkoff [...].

From: www.bbc.co.uk, *13 February, 2017*

Comprehension

1 Listen to the podcast. Then complete the following statements about current developments in the world of work. You may listen to the recording twice.

1. Two changes that can already be seen in the working world are ...
2. Employed workers face many downsides. Some of them are ...
3. The three interviewees expect the following changes in working life in the future: ...

▶ SF 38: Listening/Viewing

2 In your own words, explain what Guy Standing is referring to when he talks about the precariat and give examples from the podcast or from your own knowledge of the current working world.

Beyond the text

▶ SF 44: Having a discussion
▶ SF 13: Doing research
▶ Getting started

3 Speaking Work on task **a** or **b**.

a Discuss the following statements with a partner. Incorporate information from the podcast and the text 'Crowdworking: sweet scent of freedom!?'(p. 206).
1 Employment and work aren't exactly the same thing.
2 Basic income is needed to give people basic security.
3 The 8-hour working day is no longer standard.

b Challenge Do some research on the 'gig economy' and prepare a talk or an explanatory video on the most relevant aspects of this way of working (3–5 minutes). Include some jobs that are typically done by gig workers.

Text 10

New Nomads: Making a living on the road

Jessica Bruder

- Relate the photo to the headline. What do you think is the topic of this text?

You are going to read an extract from a non-fiction book about Americans travelling around the U.S.

There have always been itinerants, drifters, hobos, restless souls. But now, in the third millennium, a new kind of wandering tribe is emerging. People who never imagined being nomads are hitting the road. They're giving up traditional houses and apartments to live in what some call 'wheel estate' – vans, secondhand RVs, school buses, pickup campers, travel trailers, and plain old sedans. They are driving away from the impossible choices that face what used to be the middle class. Decisions like:

Would you rather have food or dental work? Pay your mortgage or your electric bill? Make a car payment or buy medicine? Cover rent or student loans? Purchase warm clothes or gas for your commute?

For many the answer seemed radical at first.
You can't give yourself a raise, but what about cutting your biggest expense? Trading a stick-and-brick domicile for life on wheels?

Annotations
2 **hobo** person who travels from place to place looking for work
9 **RV** *(abbr)* recreational vehicle
12 **mortgage** [ˈmɔːɡɪdʒ] loan
14 **commute** *(n)* regular travel between place of work and home

Some call them 'homeless.' The new nomads reject that label. Equipped with both shelter and transportation, they've adopted a different word. They refer to themselves, quite simply, as 'houseless.'

From a distance, many of them could be mistaken for carefree retired RVers. On occasions when they treat themselves to a movie or dinner at a restaurant, they blend with the crowd. In mind-set and appearance, they are largely middle class. They wash their clothes at Laundromats and join fitness clubs to use the showers. Many took to the road after their savings were obliterated by the Great Recession. To keep their gas tanks and bellies full, they work long hours at hard, physical jobs. In a time of flat wages and rising housing costs, they have unshackled themselves from rent and mortgages as a way to get by. They are surviving America.

But for them – as for anyone – survival isn't enough. So what began as a last-ditch effort has become a battle cry for something greater. Being human means yearning for more than subsistence. As much as food or shelter, we require hope.

And there is hope on the road. It's a by-product of forward momentum. A sense of opportunity, as wide as the country itself. A bone-deep conviction that something better will come. It's just ahead, in the next town, the next gig, the next chance encounter with a stranger.

As it happens, some of those strangers are nomads, too. When they meet – online, or at a job, or camping way off the grid – tribes begin to form. There's a common understanding, a kinship. When someone's van breaks down, they pass the hat. There's a contagious feeling: Something big is happening. The country is changing rapidly, the old structures crumbling away, and they're at the epicenter of something new. Around a shared campfire, in the middle of the night, it can feel like a glimpse of utopia.

As I write, it is autumn. Soon winter will come. Routine layoffs will start at the seasonal jobs. The nomads will pack up camp and return to their real home – the road – moving like blood cells through the veins of the country. They'll set out in search of friends and family, or just a place that's warm. Some will journey clear across the continent. All will count the miles, which unspool like a filmstrip of America. Fast-food joints and shopping malls. Fields dormant under frost. Auto dealerships, megachurches, and all-night diners. Featureless plains. Feedlots, dead factories, subdivisions, and big-box stores. Snow-capped peaks. The roadside reels past, through the day and into darkness, until fatigue sets in. Bleary-eyed, they find places to pull off the road and rest. In Walmart parking lots. On quiet suburban streets. At truck stops, amid the lullaby of idling engines. Then in the early morning hours – before anyone notices – they're back on the highway. Driving on, they're secure in this knowledge:

The last free place in America is a parking spot.

From: Nomadland, *2017*

Annotations

25 obliterate sth. remove sth., destroy sth.

25 Great Recession financial crisis from 2007–2009

29 last-ditch effort final attempt

53 fatigue [fə'ti:g] *(n)* tiredness; exhaustion

56 lullaby ['lʌləbaɪ] gentle song sung to make a child go to sleep

Comprehension

1 Outline the hopes and the lifestyle of the 'new nomads'.

Analysis

2 For a non-fiction text the author makes use of a variety of *stylistic devices. Identify them and analyse their effect on you as a reader.

Language awareness

3 In the last paragraph (ll. 43–60) the author makes frequent use of *ellipses. Rewrite this paragraph in a less journalistic manner, e.g. by employing linking words and drafting complete sentences. Then analyse the effect of these changes.

Beyond the text

► SF 35: Writing a letter to the editor

4 Intercultural communication Imagine being a journalist like Jessica Bruder. You have the chance to interview one of the nomadic workers in the U.S. Work on task **a** or **b**.

a Explore this different way of life and work routine by drafting 6–8 interesting interview questions.

b Challenge Explore this way of life and work routine by drafting 6–8 interview questions. Imagine the answers and write an article for the local newspaper based on your interview.

Text 11

Global job and migration effects on the world of work

*A defunct phone battery factory in Finland which closed in 2003 becomes the vehicle for exploring modern working conditions on a global scale. The film clip 'The Factory of the World' *juxtaposes compelling video images of factories in Finland and China and focuses on migrant workers.*

- Relate the photo to the globalization of the world economy and find a suitable title.

Comprehension

1 Watch the first two minutes of the film. Describe the atmosphere created by the nature scenes in 2–3 sentences. Include adjectives.

2 In the second part of the film typical work routines of migrant workers in China are talked about. Examine the difficulties faced by Xiao, Zhangli, Luo, and Meixiu. Note down at least two for each worker.

Analysis

3 Analyse the music, *tone, and long takes of the different scenes. Explain which effects on the audience can be observed.

► SF 39: Analysing films and videos

4 Explain how the *voice-over helps with understanding the film's messages. Say how difficult it was for you to follow it and give reasons.

Beyond the text

5 Writing Write a short review of this film and rate it by awarding 1–5 stars. Don't forget to draft an interesting title for your review.

► SF 28: Writing a review

► Check

6 Intercultural communication 'You can either manufacture in comfortable, worker-friendly factories, or you can reinvent the product every year [...]. Right now, customers care more about a new iPhone than working conditions in China.'
In groups of four, discuss different aspects of the global labour market. One group argues for the ongoing development of new (technical) products at any cost. The other group underlines the importance of human rights and good working conditions in all countries of the world.

Chapter task

Today's working population faces great challenges. There are many competing and conflicting interests to consider, and a great number of decision-makers are involved. Imagine the following situation:

► Getting started

Your school is organizing a **Career Day.** Form groups and collect ideas on what could be done on that day. Also think about a catchy slogan. Set an agenda and design a poster showing what's going to happen. The centre-piece of the day can, for example, be a **panel discussion** in which various people talk about their jobs and scientists present new ideas and findings on the challenges of the modern world of work.

Chapter 7
The Media – Tool, Drug, Manipulator, Friend?

1 Work in groups of five. Each of you chooses one of the pictures above and describes the advantages of the media shown in them.

2 a **Think** Make a table. List types of media for communication and types of media for information, beginning with the media you use most often, then second most often etc.
b **Pair** Talk to a partner about your lists. Together, agree on examples of each type of media that both of you consider relevant and helpful.
c **Share** Share your ideas with another pair of students.

► Getting started

3 Take a look at the Chapter map on the right and speculate about the content of this chapter. Which of these aspects help you to form a tentative answer to the guiding question?

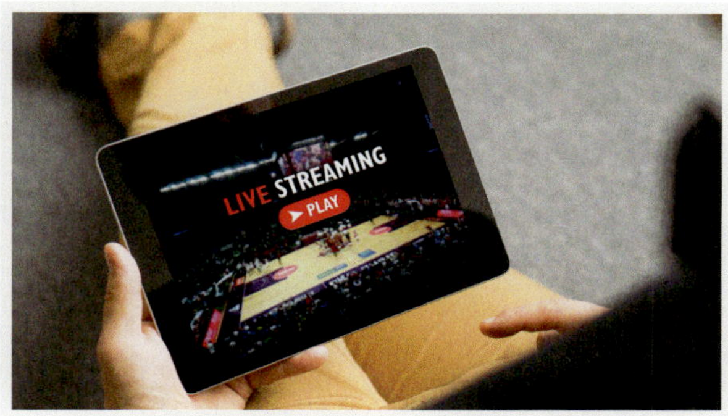

Chapter map

clicktivism

social media

news avoidance

knowledge

fake news

Chapter task: a podcast

The Media – window to the world or distorted picture of reality?

Speaking

reality TV

media diversity

media literacy

advertising

influencer

▶ More language

The multifaceted media

Engraving of Johannes Gutenberg's printing press that enabled mass printing

The development of the media

The media not only offers access to information, but also to different means of communication, and is constantly changing due to new inventions. The development of modern media as we know it gathered momentum with the advent of the printing press in the 15th century, eventually paving the way for the publication and distribution of newspapers: the first form of mass media. By the end of the 19th century, progress in electrical engineering enabled the invention of telegraphy and the telephone. Early in the 20th century, it was broadcast radio which provided news and entertainment with stunning immediacy, becoming the first electronic mass medium. Television followed suit in the second half of the century.

The digital revolution

The transition from analogue to digital technology, starting in the latter half of the 20th century, has deeply influenced all aspects of society. Not only has the digital revolution with its increase in computing and information technology induced technological improvements, it has also profoundly changed the ways we communicate, work, gain knowledge and even think. Social media can offer opportunities to find like-minded people; some online communities are even considered a safe space by their users. There are, however, some worries about the effects of digital media on one's mental and physical health, especially given how many people are inseparably connected to their electronic devices, especially their smartphones. Concerns have been raised around screen time, shortening attention span, cyberbullying and harmful content. Simultaneously, the rise of huge global tech and media companies has led some people to fear how our digital footprints – permanent traces we leave online – and 'big data' that is collected about us may be abused by private or even state organisations, e.g. for surveillance.

The digital divide

The digital revolution means computers and a home internet connection have become essential tools for students to access digital information. Families who are not well off cannot always afford the necessary technical equipment, putting their children at a possible disadvantage. The gap between those with easy access to the internet and those without it is called the digital divide.

The media and democracy

The media has always had a significant role in influencing public opinion and democratic participation. By exposing misdeeds by those in power, it can serve as a watchdog. In the form of public service broadcasting, the media enables the public to make informed choices and provides a platform for political debate. In recent years, however, trust in the democratizing effects of the media, and social media especially, has been severely damaged. The worrying growth in clickbait, bots, fake news, disinformation campaigns and hate speech seems to threaten democratic societies, and online users increasingly have to cope with privacy breaches and a full-blown economy of likes and followers. Journalistic ethics such as accuracy, fairness, respect, impartiality and truthfulness cannot be relied upon. Hence, users have to ask themselves whether the media is truly a clear window to the world, or if it offers a distorted picture of reality.

Words words words

1 Draw a mind map of the development, functions, opportunities and risks of the media. Use key concepts and highlighted phrases from the text.

Synonyms, antonyms and scales

2 **a** Take a look at the following words from the text: 'enable' (ll. 8, 37), 'provide' (ll. 10, 38), 'influence' (ll. 15, 35), 'improvement' (l. 17) and 'worries' (l. 21). Think of at least one synonym for each word.

▶ Check

b Now take a closer look at the ethics of the media as described in the text. Think of antonym for each characteristic: 'accuracy' (l. 43), 'fairness' (l. 43), 'respect' (l. 43), 'impartiality' and 'truthfulness' (l. 44).

c Explain why and when synonyms and antonyms are helpful in communication.

3 **a** Collect the effects that media usage can have according to the text.

b Copy the scale below and place the aspects you collected in **a** according to your personal evaluation: Put the dangers more to the left and the benefits more to the right. Use the words from tasks **a** and **b** and more words from the text.

– – – 0 + ++

Chunk it!

4 Search the text on the previous page for useful *chunks and add them to your mind map from **1**.

The media and you

5 You choose Work on either task **a** or **b**.

a Note down the three forms of media you use most in your everyday life. Based on this, decide whether your media consumption is balanced. Give reasons for your conclusion.

b List and explain situations in which media can cause unity or disunity among people.

Text 1

Social media – more than a means of communication?

Micha Frazer-Carroll

- Create a table with two columns, listing potential positive and negative aspects which you attribute to your personal use of media.
- Work with a partner. Compare your lists and agree on one positive and one negative aspect you find most relevant.

Micha Frazer-Carroll, a writer, former welfare officer for students' unions, and the founder of Blueprint *– a magazine on young people's mental health – addresses the risks and chances of social media in the following article.*

I remember my first phone. A sticky-buttoned Nokia, given to me by my mum when I was 11, to be used strictly for communication between myself and her (who else was I going to text?), on the way to and from school. I had to press '7' four times just to type the letter 's'.

I'm still in my early twenties, but in the intervening years the world of communication has changed dramatically for kids and teenagers. Almost all have smartphones, and many are so closely attached to them that they check them through the night.

A dossier of studies and news items have linked social media use by teenagers to mental health issues, including depression, anxiety, self-harm and suicide. Last week, an independent school made headlines for asking parents and pupils to sign a 'contract' that would ban phone use on their commute, at mealtimes and at night.

In adolescence, when status and popularity are given such importance, drawing comparisons with others' lives has frequently been linked to low mood. Meanwhile, the pressure to constantly be available, brought on by social media, has been blamed for making young people more anxious and sleep-deprived (even I sleep with Netflix or a podcast at the ready). And when a child falls victim to bullying at school, social media means that their harassment can continue long into the night.

Apps such as Instagram have increased anxieties over 'missing out' and body image. The list goes on. And last week the results of a new trial were announced, which is aimed at addressing the anxieties of schoolchildren by teaching life skills.

Yet despite these concerns, statistics around social media and mental health have never rung true for me. I and many young people I know believe that, overall, social media has been a positive force in our lives. Technology raises serious issues for today's young people – but it's not the only problem they face. In the period since social media use has soared, we've had years of austerity, increased poverty and a connected increase in adult mental health problems too.

A quarter of young people with emotional and behavioural difficulties have a parent with a mental health problem – so it's not a complete surprise that the statistics for teenagers would follow suit. And the marketisation of education also ploughs ahead, with increased exam pressures, exacerbated by school league tables, and the shadow of massive tuition fees – with suicides peaking around exam season. School days are not what they used to be, for far more reasons than social media.

Annotations

12 **commute** *(n)* way to school or work
16 **sleep-deprived** without enough sleep
18 **harassment** [həˈræsmənt] the act of annoying and/or tormenting sb.
26 **soar** increase quickly and significantly
26 **austerity** economy measures decided and enforced by the government to cut down on public spending
30 **plough ahead** *(v)* continue regardless of consequences
31 **exacerbate sth.** [ɪɡˈzæsəbeɪt] worsen sth.
32 **tuition fees** *Schulgeld*
32 **peak** *(v)* reach the highest level

Info

School league tables are rankings in the UK that compare the academic achievements of different schools. Listing the average number of A level qualifications per student, the average grades achieved by students or the rate of students accepted at universities.

The benefits of online platforms rarely receive as much airtime as the dangers. For teenagers, the internet can be a space to find like-minded people, especially for those who find it difficult to socialise.

I've worked in the field of student mental health and was often told that online communities provided spaces where they had found belonging. One autistic student I worked with described forums on Twitter and Tumblr as the places they best felt able to articulate themself and socialise. I also met students who found forums where they felt comfortable discussing their mental health, either due to the anonymity offered by the internet, or the fact that it allowed them to establish solidarity with others who were struggling. Personally, in terms of body image, I was able to find sources of diverse, less Eurocentric, more body-positive content.

The fact that smartphones and all that comes with them can be both enriching and detrimental to mental health is not a contradiction. But blanket bans [...] only serve to further demonise social media rather than opening up a conversation about how best to engage with it. Digital life, like mental health, is nuanced, and so our conversations around how they are linked should be accordingly sensitive, and balanced. And yes, open spaces like PSHE (personal, social and health education) classes in school might be a fitting arena to have this kind of open discussion. Wouldn't it be empowering to invite teenagers into a conversation about how they can have safe, productive and enjoyable digital lives?

Young people face myriad forces that can have significant impacts on their mental health, and it would be naive to deny that technology is one of them. But it's ultimately a tool that can be utilised in different ways. And the digital world won't be going away anytime soon – the days of greyscreen Nokias are gone and never coming back. For young people, the natural question shouldn't be 'social media: yay or nay', but rather how can we best help them navigate it?

From: 'Don't demonise social media, it can be a blessing for teens with problems', theguardian.com, *7 December 2018*

Annotations
46 **detrimental** harmful
46 **blanket** *(adj)* general

Comprehension

1 Outline the advantages and disadvantages of social media according to the text.

Analysis

2 Examine how the author conveys her attitude towards social media. Refer to both structure and language.

Language awareness

3 The text uses a number of passive constructions.
   a Identify the passive constructions in the text and re-write the complete sentences using the active voice.
   b Compare your sentences with a partner and discuss why the passive might have been preferred over the active voice.

▸ More language

Beyond the text

▶ SF 26: Argumentative writing

4 Writing Comment on the necessity of mobile phone bans at school.

▶ SF 42: Preparing and giving a speech
▶ SF 44: Having a discussion
▶ SF 45: Having a debate

5 You choose With a partner, do either task a or b.

a Speaking Prepare your arguments and debate whether social media is a gain or a pain. Following this, each one of you prepares and delivers a short keynote speech covering one perspective.

b Speaking Discuss and agree on measures intended to make the use of social media safer and as beneficial as possible for young people. Note down the aspects you agreed on.

Text 2

Development of new media

- Make notes on the following:
  - What social media platforms do you use, and how often do you use them?
  - Describe if and how your use of social media platforms has changed.

The following bar charts give insights into the use of new media by U.S adults.

Forms of new media used by U.S. adults

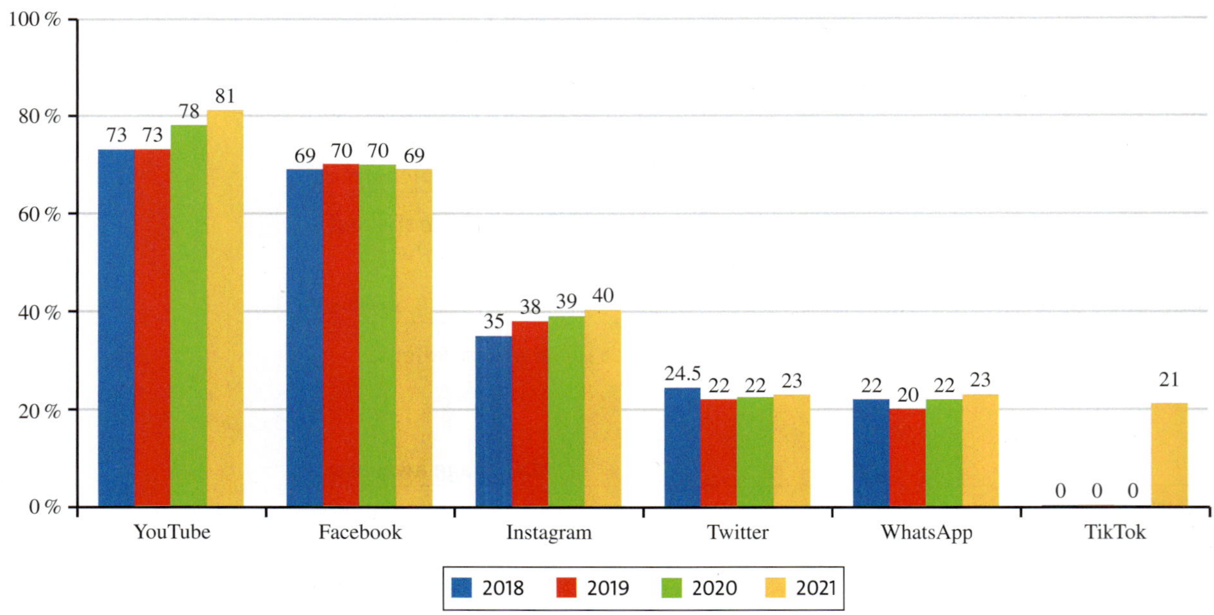

There is no availabe data for TikTok before 2021.

Source: www.pewresearch.org, *2021*

Comprehension

1 **a** Write three true and three false sentences about the data in the bar charts on six slips of paper. Mix them up.
b Exchange your sentences with a partner and decide which of your partner's sentences are true and which are false. Correct the false ones.
c Compare the results with your partner to check that you have both got your facts right.

Analysis

2 Analyse the development displayed in the statistic.

Beyond the text

3 You choose Work on either task **a** or **b**.
a Writing Discuss the following motion: social media platforms – the place to be?
b Note down ideas for a new social media platform. Be prepared to present your idea.

Text 3

Are we addicted to social media?

- List the three most common dangers and advantages of social media. Exchange your ideas in a group and agree on the top three numbers for each category.

In an episode of the BBC podcast Tricky*, Myles Bonnar, the podcast producer, discusses whether people today have become addicted to social media with his guests: Paul Black, writer, actor and comedian, Kumba Dauda, a social media consultant, Sean McDonald, a podcast maker, and Nova Scotia the Truth, a rapper.*

Comprehension

1 Listening Listen to a section from the podcast about social media use for the first time. Take notes on the following aspects:
- problems arising from social media
- measures to tackle these problems
- people's reactions to being unfollowed
- misrepresentation on social media

► SF 38: Listening/Viewing for gist

Analysis

2 Examine to what extent the use of social media discussed in the podcast describes addictive behaviour.

Language awareness

▶ Support p. 261

▶ More info

3 Listen to the podcast for a second time. Focus on the male speakers and pay attention to their Scottish accent. Describe how it differs from standard British pronunciation.

Beyond the text

▶ SF 21: Analysing diagrams

4 Writing Analyse the bar charts showing the screen time of U.S. teens. Then compare the opinions and attitudes expressed in the diagrams to the ideas articulated in the podcast.

U.S. teenagers' attitudes to time spent on social media

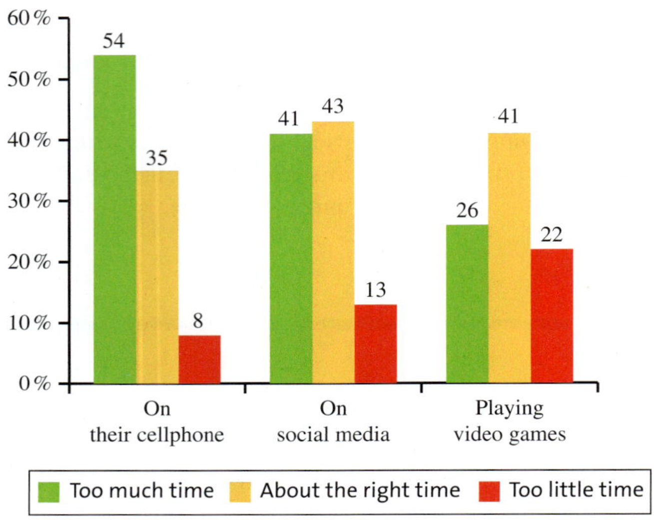

Percentage of U.S. teenagers that have ever reduced their use of different technologies

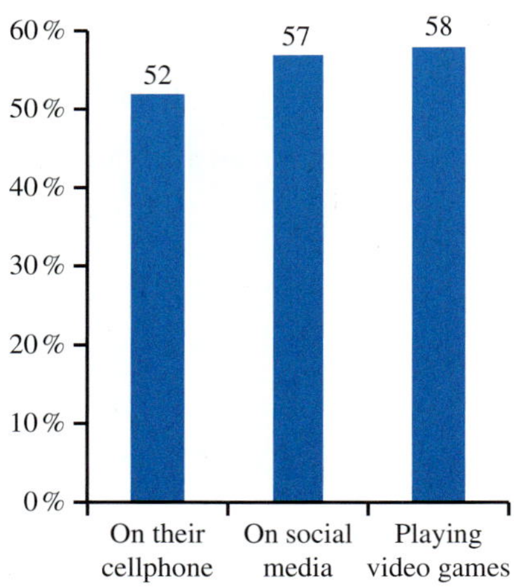

Data from: www.pewresearch.org, *20 December 2019*

Text Carol Ann Duffy

▸ More info

- *Quick write: You can only use one form of digital communication for the rest of your life. Which one would you choose and why?

Carol Ann Duffy explores texting as a form of communication in a relationship.

Annotations
10 **chord** [kɔːd] Akkord
12 **blurred** not clear visually, fuzzy

I tend the mobile now
like an injured bird

We text, text, text
our significant words.

I re-read your first,
your second, your third,

look for your small xx,
feeling absurd.
The codes we send
arrive with a broken chord.

I try to picture your hands,
their image is blurred.

Nothing my thumbs press
will ever be heard.

From: Rapture, *2010*

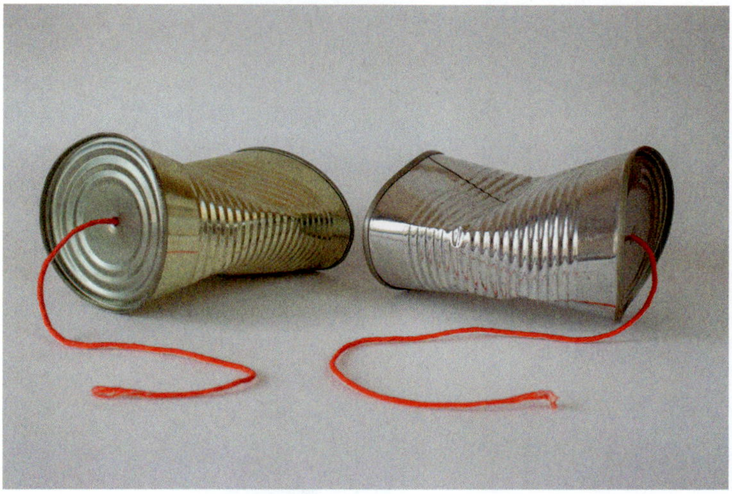

Comprehension

1 Describe the situation represented in the poem.

2 Explain the meaning of the 'small xx' (v. 7).

▸ SF 19: Reading and understanding poetry

Analysis

3 Analyse how language is used to express the shortcomings of texting. Examine how emotions are presented.

▸ Support p. 261

Language awareness

4 While in most of your writing tasks you will be asked to connect your sentences, this poem mainly consists of full sentences which do not contain any linking words. Discuss why the writer may have decided to write her poem in this way.

Beyond the text

5 Writing Imagine you are the addressee of the poem. Write a poem in response.

▸ SF 36: Creative writing

▶ SF 40: Essentials: speaking

Note

In an exam situation, a cartoon would be assigned to you and you would not be able to see your partner's material.

Focus on test formats

As a test format in your final years at school or as part of your school-leaving exam you may be required to participate in a speaking exam.
Read the following task:

Young people and the media
You are organizing a project day at your school on the use of media among young people.
With a partner decide which cartoon you will each work on. Then, working alone, examine your cartoon and prepare to describe it to your partner and to comment on it. Speak for about two minutes each.

Partner A:

CartoonStock.com

Partner B:

CartoonStock.com

Together with your partner, discuss different forms of media you want to address during the project day. Plan the day and outline at least four activities for different age groups. Agree on whether you would include one of the cartoons above on the leaflet advertising the project day. (8 to 10 minutes)

1 Understanding the task

Together with a partner, analyse the task answering the following questions:

a What parts does the task consist of?
b What do you have to do on your own, which parts need cooperation with your partner?
c What results are you expected to come up with?

Work it out

2 Preparing your monologue

► Check

a Decide which of the following aspects you have to include in your monologue:

1 assessing the quality of the cartoon
2 describing the layout and colouring
3 comparing it to the second cartoon
4 outlining the topic of the cartoon
5 assessing whether you consider it funny
6 naming the elements of cartoons in general
7 giving the sources
8 explaining what the criticism or humour is aimed at
9 talking about your own experiences with situations like the ones depicted in the cartoon
10 reading out the speech bubble or caption

b Put your answers from **a** in a logical order to form steps of your monologue.

c For each step, collect useful words and phrases.

3 Preparing a discussion: language and communication

a The following speech acts usually occur in discussions:

- starting the discussion
- stating your opinion
- involving a partner
- asking for clarification
- agreeing
- disagreeing/contradicting
- signalling that you would like to say something
- adding something
- buying time to think
- summarizing your point
- summarizing the results of the discussion.

Collect words and phrases you can use for these speech acts.

b Remember the feedback you may have got in discussions before and collect aspects you could improve on. You may think of:

- voice
- fluency
- pronunciation
- body language and gestures
- grammatical correctness
- politeness
- participation in the discussion
- the quality of arguments.

Choose three aspects and write down how you will improve on them during this discussion.

4 Preparing the content of your dialogue

a On your own, brainstorm ideas for your dialogue. Refer to the following aspects of the task:
- different forms of media
- age groups at your school
- arguments for and against using your cartoons from the monologue
- different activities for the project day
- other aspects necessary to plan and organize the day
- an opening and closing statement.

b Take notes and arrange them in a way so that they are helpful during the (mock) exam. Add discussion phrases from **3a** where necessary and possible.

5 Preparing to give feedback

a You will be listening to your partner's monologue and giving feedback on it afterwards. Prepare a table like the one below to structure your feedback:

Aspect	Student's performance	Tips for improvement
Grammar		
Vocabulary		
Completeness of description		
Analysis of the given cartoon		
Personal assessment of the cartoon		

b Collect words and phrases you can use to formulate your feedback in a polite manner.

Do it!

6 Participating in the speaking exam

You choose Work on either task **a** or **b**.

a After going through all the steps you actually do the mock exam with your partner. Keep track of the time. As it is only practice, you may interrupt the mock exam after the monologues and give direct feedback (cf. task **7**).

b Together with your teacher find a pair of volunteers to present their monologues and dialogues to the class. The class watches and makes notes on their performance. Be prepared to give detailed feedback (cf. task **7**).

Feedback

7 Giving feedback

a Task **6a:** Give feedback on your partner's monologue either directly after the monologue or at the end of your mock exam. Make sure to cover both content and form. Agree on at least two good aspects and two that need to be improved. Don't only criticize, but suggest concrete improvements, e.g. to the quality of arguments, the way contributions were phrased etc.
Listen carefully to your partner's feedback on your monologue and take notes.
Then self-assess your participation in the dialogue. Which points would you consider good and which less successful? Discuss your assessment with your partner.

b Task **6b:** Get together in a group of no more than 4 students and discuss your assessment of your classmates' mock exam. Make sure to cover both content and form. Agree on at least two good aspects and two that need to be improved. Don't only criticize, but suggest concrete improvements, e.g. to the quality of arguments, the way contributions were phrased etc.

Language help

you could/might have ... reacted to ... by saying ... • It would have been a good idea to ... • You forgot to ... • It might have been interesting to ... • use the following argument • refer to ... I really liked your point about ... because ... • What I thought was good about ... was ... • I thought you spoke clearly / in a lively way/... • You used lots of different/interesting/descriptive vocabulary ...

c Copy the *method card below and write down aspects you should work on yourself in order to improve your performance in a speaking exam.

Method card – speaking exam	
What I am good at	What I need to practise
...	...

Digital revolution and the availability of knowledge

In the history of mankind, important revolutions have shaped the world and brought about modern life as we know it. What impact has the so-called digital revolution had, and how has it affected our access to information and the availability of knowledge?

▶ Getting started

- **Think** about how digital technology has changed or is changing aspects of our daily lives. Make a list.
- **Pair** Work with a partner. Agree on one example from your lists where the benefits of digital technology are significant, then agree on one example where the benefits are outweighed by the risks or costs.
- **Share** Discuss your results with another pair of students.

Comprehension

▶ SF 23: Analysing cartoons

1 Work with a partner. **Partner B:** Go to p. 262.
Partner A: Describe the cartoon below.

"How should I know? All the information is stored in a cloud somewhere."

CartoonStock.com

Analysis

2 **a** Assess the irony of the cartoon, considering the critical questions about the effects of digitization that the cartoon raises.

b Present the cartoon and your findings to your partner. Discuss which cartoon is more convincing.

Beyond the text

3 You choose Work on either task **a** or **b**.

a Writing Douglas Engelbart, engineer and inventor of the computer mouse, claimed: 'The digital revolution is far more significant than the invention of writing or even of printing' (*Digital Sociologies*, 2017). Discuss if Engelbart's statement is valid.

b Draw or describe your own cartoon about digital technology and its consequences – positive or negative.

► SF 26: Argumentative writing: discussion and comment

Text 6

The subtle ways that clicktivism shapes the world

Richard Fisher

- How can you participate in online activism? Name methods and discuss their possibilities and limits.

Richard Fisher, a senior journalist for BBC Future, argues that online activism is far more effective than it first appears.

Often derided, online activism is far more effective than it first appears – but there are big differences between how the political left and right deploy it to spread ideas.

For some, it's the laziest form of activism. On social media, 'slacktivists' express their support for a cause by changing a profile image, retweeting a sentiment, or deploying a trending hashtag. The Urban Dictionary defines slacktivism as 'the self-deluded idea that by liking, sharing, or retweeting something you are helping out'.

But is such slacktivism – or 'clicktivism', as it's also known less pejoratively – really so useless? Accumulating evidence suggests that online activism is more effective than many people might assume. And recent research suggests it is deployed by the political right and left in different, often hidden, ways to spread beliefs and ideas.

Clicktivism has a bad reputation. As one commentator put it a decade ago: 'clicktivism is to activism as McDonalds is to a slow-cooked meal. It may look like food, but the life-giving nutrients are long gone.' And last year, former US president Barack Obama suggested that social media activism – particularly 'woke'

Annotations

1 **deride sth.** mock sth.
2 **deploy sth.** use sth.
3 **slacktivist** online supporter of a political cause etc.
6 **self-deluded** making yourself believe sth. that is not true
8 **pejorative** [pɪˈdʒɒrətɪv] disapproving, critical
9 **accumulate sth.** collect sth. in growing amount

Annotations
27 **in the aggregate** altogether
30 **disseminate sth.** spread information, news, etc.
33 **advocate** *(n) Fürsprecher*
33 **further sth.** promote sth., support sth.
36 **correlate with sth.** *mit etwas in Wechselbeziehung stehen*
39 **multi-pronged** having several points or elements
42 **dog whistle** a hidden political message aimed at and understood by a certain group of people
46 **hyperpartisan** extremely biased
55 **subtle** indirect

culture – was no substitute for community organising or protest in the physical world. 'There is this sense,' he said, that the way to provoke change 'is to be as judgmental as possible about other people, and that's enough. That's not activism. That's not bringing about change. If all you're doing is casting stones, you're probably not going to get that far.'

Perhaps. But as Deen Freelon and colleagues at the University of North Carolina, Chapel Hill, write in a new paper in the journal Science, many criticisms of clicktivism rest on two mistaken assumptions. 'One of the biggest misconceptions is that it doesn't do anything,' says Freelon. 'The second is that it somehow displaces or replaces offline activism. We know that both of these are not true.'

Evidence collected over the last decade suggests that clicktivism, in the aggregate, can be very effective in spreading little-known ideas and publicising non-mainstream notions. While one tweet or post won't change the world, thousands of them can disseminate beliefs that will. 'Clicktivism has a major effect in terms of offering movements an alternative pathway to the public,' says Freelon.

In the US and internationally, Occupy Wall Street, Black Lives Matter, #MeToo, far-right anti-immigration advocates, and the men's rights movement have all furthered their aims through clicktivism, according to research in recent years. Meanwhile, studies suggest that people who engage strongly with politics online also do so in their offline lives. Sharing and tweeting politics on social media correlates with attending political meetings, donating to campaigns and other forms of civic engagement.

'Most truly effective activist movements in the 21st Century are multi-pronged,' says Freelon.

Clicktivism has also propagated new vocabulary, both good and bad [...]. For example, a decade ago the term 'globalist' – an anti-semitic dog-whistle – was restricted to far-right corners of the internet. But as researchers have found through textual analysis, the online efforts of right-wing activists gradually introduced it to websites such as Breitbart, before it was eventually picked up by Fox News [...].

So-called hyperpartisan news sites such as Breitbart, the German Compact magazine and Swedish Nyheter Idag can act as 'bridges' for once-extreme views into mainstream right-wing outlets, researchers have found.

Intriguingly, the science suggests the right and left deploy different tactics in their clicktivism, at least in the US. While it risks some over-simplification, research to date suggests that a predominant way that left-wing activists aim to spread ideas is via hashtag activism, such as #TakeAKnee, #TimesUp, or other hashtags publicising an action or cause. Meanwhile, activists on the right – particularly the far right, which Freelon argues has grown on US social media in recent years – aim for subtler routes. It's known as 'trading up the chain' and goes like this: plant a story, opinion or idea in a small or obscure news site, or on social media, encourage followers to share it too, then hope a bigger outlet with a bigger audience picks it up, and another, all the way up to major publishers or TV networks.

Disinformation follows a similar path, according to Claire Wardle of First Draft News, a non-profit organisation set up to fight fake news. A false assertion starts on private channels like WhatsApp, before moving into online conspiracy content on

Info

Occupy Wall Street, Black Lives Matter and **#MeToo** are social movements protesting against economic inequality, racial injustice and police brutality and sexual harassment respectively.

Info

Breitbart is a news website which features right-wing political views and open opposition to liberal and left-wing groups, such as the Democratic Party.
Fox News is an American cable news television channel often associated with biased reporting in favour of the Republican Party and conservative causes.

Reddit or Youtube, then more open social media such as Twitter or Facebook, and then all it takes is for a credulous journalist for a major outlet to pick it up, and it reaches thousands or even millions of people.

Even if mainstream media is only shooting down the false story, the goal is achieved. For many campaigners, 'a debunk is better than nothing. It provides oxygen,' writes Wardle. After all, if more people are searching for the story that means more people discovering the campaigners' ideas, narratives or beliefs. The researcher Whitney Phillips of Syracuse University has called this 'the oxygen of amplification'.

Some activists deploy their messages hidden within viral content, easy to miss for even the most sophisticated internet user. For example, last month Marcia Allison of the University of Southern California published a paper describing how fascist campaigners have been using shareable faked animal pictures to spread their ideas. During the Covid-19 pandemic lockdowns, many false images appeared online of animals supposedly returning to uninhabited places, from Welsh sheep playing in a children's park to dolphins swimming through the canals of Venice.

One particular group of far-right activists, called ecofascists, who hold a white supremacist, pro-environmental ideology, latched on to these images, as a way to attach their racist ideology to potentially viral content.

It was a tactic they'd used before: in their social media posts, ecofascists use apparently benign emojis such as a pine tree, an Earth and a mountain accompanied by subtle far-right dog-whistle symbols such as Norse runes and ideological hashtags. This makes it easier for milder environmentalists to inadvertently share fascist accounts and hashtags, as well as allowing disparate ecofascists to find each other. (I am not unaware that by debunking this content I risk amplifying it, but would argue that the hidden agenda justifies doing so.)

So, those who dismiss online activism as the work of slacktivists fail to understand the subtlety and power of how messages and beliefs move through the modern digital ecosystem. And there is still much unknown about how clicktivism spreads ideas through society, says Freelon. There are whole areas of discourse that researchers cannot study because they are closed off and private, such as Whatsapp groups.

But what we do know is that clicktivism can and does work – and it's often far more sophisticated and hidden than many people realise.

From: www.bbc.com, *16 September 2020*

Participant of a #MeToo demonstration in Sweden, 2017

Annotations

- 63 **credulous** [ˈkredʒələs] *leichtgläubig*
- 63 **outlet** (here) a publishing or broadcasting organization
- 66 **debunk sth.** reveal that sth. is not true
- 70 **amplification** *Vergrößerung, Erweiterung*
- 78 **supremacist** [suˈpreməsɪst] a person who believes that they and the group they belong to are superior to other people
- 79 **latch on to sth.** *(infml)* grasp an idea, comprehend what sb. is saying
- 82 **benign** *(fml)* harmless

Comprehension

1 Outline the past assumptions and the new findings about 'clicktivism' according to the text.

2 Make an infographic that visualizes the distribution of disinformation.

Analysis

3 Analyse the author's message, examining how it is conveyed through his use of language.

Language awareness

► More language

Info

More examples for blended words are:
smog (smoke + fog)
Eurovision (European + television)
Oxbridge (Oxford + Cambridge)

4 The terms 'slacktivism' (l. 5) and 'clicktivism' are (l. 8) examples of *blending. Blending is a word formation process that creates new words by combining parts of already existing words.

- **a** Which words make up the two terms? Note them down and define the meaning of *slacktivism* and *clicktivism*. You may use a dictionary.
- **b** The use of blending has increased since the late 20th century. Try to find more examples and speculate on reasons for this development.

Beyond the text

► SF 27: Writing a blog post

5 You choose Work on either task **a** or **b**.

- **a** Writing You are a member of a political activist group and want to point out the dangers of disinformation. Write a blog post for the website in which you address the risks of fake news.
- **b** Speaking With a partner, discuss the question: clicktivism – a means of democratic discourse or antidemocratic manipulation? Present your conclusion.

Text 7

► More info

Digital billboard in Times Square, New York

Art in Context – the art in advertising

While art *refers to the use of creative skills and the imaginative mind for aesthetic and emotional ends,* advertising *implies the application of imagination and creativity in order to sell something. Despite their commercial function and the communicative tactics involved, print and film adverts may nevertheless be of considerable aesthetic value.*

- Work in groups of three. Take turns to either ...
  - hum the melody of a commercial jingle
  - quote a brand slogan in English
  - describe a print advert.

  The others have to guess what product, brand name or organization goes with the jingle, slogan or advert.
- Discuss how the adverts you referred to make a product or brand name recognizable and distinct.

Info

The **AIDA formula** is frequently used in advertising to make ads as appealing as possible to customers. Knowledge of this formula can also help to analyse an ad. *AIDA* stands for:

- **A**ttention
- **I**nterest
- **D**esire
- **A**ction

Every part has a specific aim. First of all, the ad has to attract the *attention* of the audience. Following this, *interest* in the product has to be raised and the customer's *desire* to have the product aroused. Lastly, the customer should take *action*, e.g. research the product or purchase it.

Comprehension

1 Describe the situation presented in the advert.

Analysis

► SF 22: Analysing visuals

► Support p. 262

2 **a** Analyse the visual presentation of the product and the language used.
b Explain how the product relates to the advert.
c Examine what sort of emotional response the advert attempts to achieve.

Beyond the text

3 Speaking Discuss to what extent adverts can be classified as art. Give examples

4 Research commercial clips, choose one and analyse it. Pay attention to the effects of soundtrack, camera movement and the actors' performance. If a slogan is used, analyse its wording and message. Present your findings in class.

► SF 39: Analysing films and videos

Language help

- The use of ... put sth. in ... / grab your attention / make sth. easy to remember / influence the perception / make sth. appear ... / draw attention to ...
- The plot/context/setting/situation/action/catchphrase ... associate the product with .../ reflect on .../ refer to ...
- The viewer's perception of / reaction to ... is influenced by ...
- The advert is aimed at ... / The advert's target audience is ...
- The use of bright colours / sharp contrasts / a busy background / well-defined details... leave the reader/audience ...
- The voice-over / The use of suspenseful/romantic/exciting music suggest/tell the audience ...

Info

The diversity of advertising

Print adverts have a long tradition, but many other forms of advertising have emerged with the advent of new forms of media. Today, people are exposed to advertising nearly everywhere they go: be it through printed advertising, audio advertising in podcasts/radio, TV commercials, product placement in movies, event sponsorship, outdoor advertising, promotional e-mails or online advertising on the internet. There are numerous ways to reach a potential customer.

In the last few years, advertising has changed immensely with the rising popularity of social media platforms. On these platforms, influencers often get paid by companies to promote their products. The companies benefit because they improve their reach and, hopefully, increase their sales. For them, this form of advertising is worthwhile, but it has its downsides for the costumer. Despite advertising rules, it is often difficult to know whether an influencer's post is their honest opinion of a product or whether they are being paid or receive free goods to say positive things.

Another method which is used by companies is targeted advertising. This is a form of online advertising intended to reach potential customers according to their specific individual interests. While traditional advertising strategies tend to focus on content and context (e.g. promoting a new record by placing an ad in a music magazine), targeted advertising exploits the personal data of internet users to find out who is most likely to be interested in a particular product. Depending on their age, location, purchases, and online habits, different people may be shown different ads, even if they are visiting the same website.

Although internet browsers and EU laws allow users to clear or even refuse the small text files that websites place on their devices, so-called 'cookies', questions remain as to how effective attempts at eliminating this practice really are. Fears remain that targeted advertising may result in a significant loss of privacy and an increase in digital surveillance and data mining which could eventually endanger democratic values and standards.

1 Name the different forms of advertising and briefly explain their characteristics.

2 Do you have any experience with influencer marketing? If so, share it and discuss with a partner the pros and cons of this form of advertising.

Making reality, faking reality

- Give examples of deepfakes and/or fake news. What dangers do they entail?

Viewing *Watch the video about the dangers deepfakes and fake news pose to democracy.*

> **Info**
> ***Deepfakes*** have attracted more and more attention in the media during the last years. The term *deep-fake* is used to describe videos that have been edited to make it seem as if a specific person, often someone famous, is participating in this video. In reality someone's appearance has been changed to look like a celebrity (or anyone else required) with the help of an algorithm. Such videos can seem very authentic and sometimes make it impossible to differentiate between reality and fiction. Therefore, they are also popular methods to spread fake news and disinformation.

Comprehension

1 Complete the following sentences:
1 For democracy to function, it is necessary that ...
2 The Spectre Project aims to find out how the use of personal data by companies affects people and ...
3 Bill distributed his deepfakes on a social media platform to ...
4 Mark Zuckerberg's company reacted to the deepfakes by ...
5 Technological companies and the government don't know ...
6 Joseph Stalin used visual manipulation to ...
7 Aviv Ovadya warns that deepfakes may help corrupt politicians ...
8 *Reality apathy* means that people give up when ...
9 The aim of Dr van der Linden's game is ...
10 Once people played van der Linden's game, they ...
11 People have to learn to ...

2 Visualize or describe the process of Bill's deepfake experiment.

Analysis

3 Watch the film again and take notes on cinematic devices used in the clip, focusing on how they attract the viewer's attention and add to the film's message.

► SF 39: Analysing films and videos

4 Say which of the interviews could have been a deepfake and why.

Beyond the text

5 Think back to the guiding question of the chapter. How would you answer it at this point? Take into consideration everything you have learned so far.

6 You choose With a partner, do either task **a** or **b**.

► SF 44: Having a discussion

a Speaking Discuss measures that can prevent the spread of deepfakes and strengthen people's media literacy. Present the three most convincing ideas.

b Speaking Discuss how the media can strengthen democracy. Take all forms of media into consideration. Present the three most convincing ideas.

> **Info**
> **Fact-checking – how to spot fake news**
> In order to verify whether a piece of information on the internet is trustworthy or not, you can apply the following questions to texts, pictures, videos and sources.
> - Check the headlines – do they describe content objectively? Be careful if they are overtly sensational, emotional or speculative.

- Examine the URL – does it belong to an established source you can trust (e.g. renowned news associations, quality papers, etc.)?
- Examine the sources the website uses – are they reliable and authentic, i.e. does it give precise details about authors, editors, donors, charities, enterprises, locations and addresses?
- Look critically at the quality and appearance of photos, layout and language – do they meet the standards of high quality journalism? Significant shortcomings such as low resolution, poor formatting or spelling and grammar mistakes may suggest an unreliable source.
- Check the dates and the timeline of events as well as numbers and statistics – are they coherent and are they supported by other sources? Don't trust the article if there are inaccuracies and contradictions.
- Examine if the article under scrutiny is supported by other evidence – are there more articles on other websites about the same story?
- Look at the context of the article – does it present original content, or was it shared/copied? Who is the intended audience? Was there a special occasion for the publication? If the article was shared, consider who shared it and what their motives were.

1 Spotting fake news is an important part of media literacy. Visualize the guidelines above in a form that suits you best (illustration, table, mind map ...).

Text 9

▸ More info

Info

Reality TV shows claim to broadcast how normal people manage their everyday lives. How these people are perceived by the public can be strongly influenced by those working behind the cameras as they decide which snippets are shown and how an episode is cut. It can also happen that specific situations are created to ensure that the protagonists behave in a particular way.

Annotations

2 **nose one's way** *(infml)* move slow-paced in a specific direction

Scripting reality

Ben Elton

- Play in groups. Every player holds up one hand with five fingers showing. Read out the confessions below. Every time a player has done what the confession says, they lower a finger.

I have ...

1. defended reality TV.
2. watched a reality show on TV.
3. disliked a contestant in a reality TV show.
4. voted on who stays in a reality TV show.
5. watched the live stream of a reality TV show.
6. auditioned for a reality TV show.
7. visited the website of a reality TV show.
8. had a crush on a contestant in a reality TV show.
9. felt sympathy for a contestant in a reality TV show.
10. followed a reality show contestant on social media.

In this extract from Ben Elton's novel Dead Famous, *Trisha, a detective constable, is interviewing Bob Fogarty, the editor-in-chief of the reality TV show* House Arrest, *to find out who murdered one of the house mates.*

DAY THIRTY. 9.15 p.m.

While Coleridge and Hooper nosed their way along the M25, Trisha was interviewing Bob Fogarty, the editor-in-chief of *House Arrest*. After Geri the Gaoler, Fogarty was the most senior figure in the Peeping Tom hierarchy. Trisha wanted to know more about how the people she had been watching came to be presented in the way they were.

'*House Arrest* is basically fiction,' said Fogarty, handing her a styrofoam cup of watery froth and nearly missing her hand in the darkness of the monitoring bunker. 'Like all TV and film. It's built in the edit.'

'You manipulate the housemates' images?'

'Well, obviously. We're not scientists, we make television programmes. People are basically dull. We have to make them interesting, turn them into heroes and villains.'

'I thought you were supposed to be observers, that the whole thing was an experiment in social interaction?'

'Look, constable,' Fogarty explained patiently, 'in order to create a nightly half-hour of broadcasting we have at our disposal the accumulated images of thirty television cameras running for twenty-four hours. That's seven hundred and twenty hours of footage to make one *half-hour* of television. We couldn't avoid making subjective decisions even if we wanted to. The thing that amazes us is that the nation *believes* what we show them. They actually accept that what they are watching is real.'

'I don't suppose they think about it much. I mean, why should they?'

'That's true enough. As long as it's good telly they don't care, which is why as far as possible we try to shoot the script.'

'Shoot the script?'

'It's a term they use in news and features.'

'And it means?'

'Well, say you're making a short insert for the news, investigating heroin addiction on housing estates. If you simply went out to some urban hellhole with a camera and started nosing around, you could be looking for the story you want till Christmas. So you *script* your investigation before you leave your office. You say ... all right, we need a couple of kids to say they can get smack at school, we need a girl to say she'd whore for a hit, we need a youth worker to say it's the government's fault ... You write the whole thing. Then you send out a researcher to round up a few show-offs and basically tell them what to say.'

'But how could you do that on *House Arrest*? I mean, you can't tell the housemates what to say, can you?

'No, but you can be pretty sure of the story you want to tell and then look for the shots that support it. It's the only way to avoid getting into a complete mess. Look at this, for instance ... This is Kelly's first trip to the confession box on the afternoon of day one.'

DAY ONE. 4.15 p.m.

'It's brilliant, wicked, outrageous. I feel just totally bigged-up and out there,' Kelly gushed breathlessly from the main monitor. She had come to the confession box to talk about how thrilling and exciting it all was.

'I mean, today has just been the wickedest day ever because I really, really love all these people and I just know we're all going to get along just brilliantly. I expect there'll be tension and I'll end up hating all of them for, like, just a moment at

Annotations

4 **Peeping Tom** (here) name of the production firm

9 **edit** *(n)* the act of altering films or texts, usually for length, correctness, etc.

33 **smack** *(n sl)* the drug heroin

some point. But you could say that about any mates, couldn't you? Basically I *love* these guys. They're my posse. My crew.'

Deep in the darkness of the editing suite Geraldine glared at Fogarty. 'And that's what you want her to say, is it?'

Bob cowered behind his styrofoam cup. 'Well, it's what she did say, Geraldine.'

Geraldine's eyes flashed, her nostrils flared and she bared her colossal overbite. It was as if the Alien had just burst out of John Hurt's stomach. [...]

'I could get a monkey to broadcast what she actually said! I could get a work-experience school-leaver pain-in-the-arse spotty fucking waste-of-space teenager to broadcast what she *actually* said! What I pay you to do is to *look* at what she *actually* said and *find* what we *want her to say*, you *cunt!*'

Fogarty threw a commiserating glance at the younger, more impressionable members of staff.

'Who is Kelly, Bob?' Geraldine continued, throwing an arm towards the frozen image of the pretty young brunette on the screen. 'Who is that girl?'

Fogarty stared at the television. A sweet smile beamed back at him, an open, honest, naïve countenance. 'Well ...'

'She's our bitch, Bob, she's our manipulator. She's one of our designated hate figures! Remember the audition interviews? All that pert ambition? All that artless knicker-flashing. All that *girl power bollocks*. Remember what I said, Bob?'

Fogarty did remember, but Geraldine told him anyway.

'I said, 'Right, you arrogant little slapper, we'll see how far you get towards presenting your own pop, style and fashion show once the whole nation has decided you're a back-biting [...] fucking *dog*,' didn't I?'

'Yes, Geraldine, but on the evidence of today she's turned out to be really quite nice. I mean, she's a bit of an airhead, and vain, certainly, but she's not really a bitch. I think we'll find it quite hard to make her look that nasty.'

'She'll *look* however we want her to look and *be* whatever we want her to be,' Geraldine sneered.

DAY THIRTY. 9.20 a.m.

'Does Geraldine normally talk to you like that?' Trisha asked.

'She talks to everybody like that.'

'So you get used to it, then?'

'It's not something you get used to, constable. I have an MSc in computing and media. I am *not* a stupid cunt.'

Trisha nodded. She had heard of Geraldine Hennessy before her *House Arrest* fame.

Most people had. Geraldine was a celebrity in her own right. A famously bold, provocative and controversial broadcaster, Trisha ventured.

'Rubbish!' said Bob Fogarty. 'She's a TV whore masquerading as an innovator and getting away with it because she knows a few popstars and wears Vivienne Westwood. What she does is steal tacky, dumbed-down tabloid telly ideas, usually from Europe or Japan, smear them with a bit of hip, clubby, druggy style, and flog them to the middle class as post-modern irony.'

'So you don't like her, then?'

Annotations

65 **commiserate** *mitfühlen*

71 **designate** officially assign a particular role to sb.

72 **pert** direct, without respect

79 **airhead** *(infml)* fool, not an intelligent person

87 **MSc** = Master of Science

▸ More info

'I loathe her, constable. People like Geraldine Hennessy have ruined television.
She's a cultural vandal. She's a nasty, stupid, dangerous bitch.'
In the gloom Trisha could see that Fogarty's cup was shaking in his hand. She was taken aback. 'Calm down, Mr Fogarty,' she said.
'I am calm.'
'Good.'
Then Fogarty played Kelly's confession as it had been broadcast.
'I'll end up hating all of them.'
Seven words were all she said.

From: Dead Famous, *2001*

Comprehension

1 Point out how the TV show is manipulated by the producers.

Analysis

2 Examine how the author is maintaining the reader's interest, considering the use of language and structure.

▶ Getting started

3 Analyse the way Kelly is characterized.

Language awareness

4 **a** In their dialogues, the characters make extensive use of *colloquial expressions, even of *slang words. Find examples from the text.
b Rewrite ll. 28–37 in a more formal *register.

Beyond the text

5 Intercultural communication A friend of yours in the UK has to prepare an article about the popularity of reality TV shows in different countries. Write a letter in which you name some German reality TV shows and explain why they are popular or unpopular.

6 You choose Do either task **a** or **b**.

a Writing Later in the book Bob Fogarty says: 'The public, they're worse than us! [...] They know they're watching ants getting burnt under a magnifying glass, but they don't care.' Comment on the viewers' responsibility for the quality and realism of reality shows, using this quotation as a starting point.

b Writing As one of Kelly's closer friends sees her appearance in the confession box, they join the show's chat room. Write their post, considering the circumstances of the show and either defend Kelly or express irritation.

▶ SF 26: Argumentative writing: discussion and comment

▶ SF 36: Creative writing

▶ Getting started

Words revisited

Collection of big data in Shanghai

1 Negative and positive meanings

Throughout this chapter you have come across words dealing with different aspects of the media. Some of them refer to its benefits, some to its flipsides – and some can do both, depending on the context they are used in. Here are some words from Words in Context, p. 214:

big data
bot
clickbait
cyberbullying
digital divide
digital revolution
disinformation
fake news
hate speech
information
technology
mass media
privacy
safe space
screen time
smartphone
social media
surveillance
digital footprint

► SF: 6: Essentials: language and study skills

a Copy the table below and write the words in the respective column.

Positive meaning	Negative meaning	Neutral meaning	Depending on context
...	...	...	...

b Add at least two more words dealing with media to each of the four columns. Look at the texts you've read for inspiration.

c For the words in the right column, choose three and use them in two different contexts, illustrating their positive and negative sides.

d Go back to the Chapter map on p. 213. Choose five words from the table and say which topic from the chapter map they might be connected to.

Language awareness

► More info

2 Communication problems and conflicts

Communication problems are a common experience in your first language and happen even more in a foreign language. Sometimes the choice of media can be part of the problem.

a Have a look at the following situations in which a problem or conflict occurs:

Situation 1: *You're an intern with a prestigious company. You're supposed to give a presentation together with another intern, who's from the USA. As you meet for the first time to develop some general ideas for the presentation, you've come prepared: read lots of articles, collected pictures and developed a structure for your presentation. The American intern comes empty-handed, however.*

Situation 2: *You interviewed a local politician for your school magazine on the topic of making cycling safer. At the end she said, 'Text me if you need more information'. Three weeks later you open your messenger service and write, 'Please send info on plans for bike lanes. Thx'. The politician doesn't reply.*

Situation 3: *You're an intern with a bank in London. On the first day one of the managers shows you around. She hands you a dossier and says, 'You might like to have a look at this'. You flip through it and toss it aside because you don't find it interesting. The next day, the manager asks you what you found most intriguing about the dossier.*

Work in three groups. Each group focuses on one of the situations and analyses the problem and its origins.

b Present your results to class. Discuss how convincing you found the explanations given for the problems.

Practice

3 a With a partner, choose one of the three situations and discuss how the problem could be resolved.

b Look at the phrases below for your chosen situation. Say which you consider useful and which counter-productive.

Situation 1:

a *Cool down, it's no big deal! We've plenty of time.*
b *You're not saying you haven't prepared anything, are you?*
c *We were meeting to brainstorm together – why should I prepare anything?*
d *I'm a little surprised you haven't brought anything for the meeting.*

Situation 2:

a *I texted you yesterday, still no reply. ???*
b *Who do you think you are?*
c *I don't think I find your tone appropriate in this situation.*
d *I didn't realize. I thought it was ok because we were texting.*

Situation 3:

a *I thought I asked you to read the dossier.*
b *I didn't find the dossier relevant for my work.*
c *Do you usually not do what you are asked?*
d *Oh, sorry I thought you meant it as a suggestion.*

c Prepare and carry out a role-play for your situation in front of the class. Use useful phrases from **b.**

Text 10

News avoidance in times of media fatigue

In a recent interview, German neuroscientist professor Maren Urner explains how news about terror, war or the climate crisis influences our view of the world.

- Do an *acrostic on the words *BAD NEWS*.

Frau Urner, Sie beschäftigen sich seit vielen Jahren damit, wie wir Informationen verarbeiten. Ein Instrument, was Sie dabei verwenden, sind Wissenstests. Im Ergebnis zeigt sich immer, dass die Befragten den Zustand der Welt meist negativer beurteilen, als er tatsächlich ist. Warum ist das so?

Tatsächlich können wir sagen, dass es nicht nur meistens so ist, sondern immer. [...] Mittlerweile habe ich den Test in sämtlichen gesellschaftlichen Gruppen, Kontexten und Settings benutzt und es war immer so, dass die Einschätzung des Publikums negativer ist, als die Realität tatsächlich ist.

Woran liegt das?
Zum Großteil daran, welche Informationen wir zur Verfügung gestellt bekommen. Die stammen vor allem aus medialen Kontexten, von den klassischen Medien, wie Zeitung, Radio, Fernsehen und natürlich auch, seit mittlerweile einigen Jahrzehnten, aus dem Internet und den eher noch neuen sozialen Medien. Generell haben wir da eine Überrepräsentanz, eine Fokussierung auf Negatives. Das ist gut untersucht, auch in den unterschiedlichen Formaten, sei es in der Zeitung oder eben generell in Online-Medien. Die Anschlussfrage ist natürlich: Woher kommt diese Fokussierung aufs Negative? [...]

Wir alle tragen den sogenannten „Negativity Bias“ in uns, also einen Fokus auf negative Inhalte. Wir speichern negative Informationen und potentielle Gefahren nicht nur besser ab und reagieren intensiver auf sie, sondern suchen auch mehr danach. Also ganz einfach runtergebrochen: Negatives verarbeiten wir besser, schneller und intensiver als Positives oder Neutrales. [...]

Was macht diese Fokussierung der Medien auf die negativen Nachrichten mit uns?
Zunächst sorgt es für das bereits erwähnte zu negative Weltbild. Manch Journalist argumentiert gern, dass das nicht weiter schlimm sei und die Menschen in der Folge besonders aktiv würden, um an den schlechten Zuständen etwas zu ändern. Doch sämtliche Forschungsergebnisse aus der Verhaltensforschung zu der Thematik zeigen ein anderes Bild. Sie zeigen, dass genau das Gegenteil der Fall ist.

Ein zu negatives Weltbild führt nicht dazu, dass wir besonders aktiv, hoffnungsvoll und mit möglichst guten Ideen auf diese Herausforderungen und Probleme reagieren, die ja offensichtlich unsere Zeit beeinflussen. Stattdessen sind wir gefühlt dauerhaft im Krisenmodus und das führt dazu, dass wir chronisch gestresst sind. Damit einher gehen häufig Gefühle von Hilflosigkeit und Hoffnungslosigkeit. Am Ende des Tages führt das dazu, dass sich immer mehr Menschen vom Weltgeschehen abwenden, weil es einfach zu viel erscheint. Dieses Phänomen ist mittlerweile sehr gut untersucht und wird als „News-Avoidance“ bezeichnet.

Außerdem kann der exzessive Konsum der negativen Nachrichtenflut uns tatsächlich gesundheitlichen Schaden zufügen. Denn chronischer Stress ist ein Risikofaktor für sämtliche Krankheiten, egal ob Herz-Kreislauf-Probleme oder psychische Leiden.

Schlussendlich sind wir gestresst und ängstlich nicht in der Lage, gute und langfristige Entscheidungen zu treffen. [...]

Führt die ständige Dauerberieselung an negativen Nachrichten auch zu Politik- und Medienverdrossenheit?
Genau richtig. Das Phänomen, was Sie jetzt gerade beschrieben haben, ist das Phänomen der sogenannten „erlernten Hilflosigkeit". Sehr anschaulich auf den Punkt gebracht durch die oft bemühte Aussage: „Die da oben machen sowieso, was sie wollen!" Gemeint ist der Punkt, an dem viele Menschen ankommen, wenn sie erfahren, dass sie nichts ändern können und die Welt nun mal schlecht und ein grausamer Platz ist, auf den sie wenig Einfluss haben. Gesamtgesellschaftlich und demokratisch gedacht, führt das dazu, dass sich Menschen nicht mehr an der Gesellschaft beteiligen. [...]

Was müssen Schülerinnen und Schüler erlernen, damit sie gesund Medien nutzen können? [...]
Ich bin wirklich fest davon überzeugt, dass die wichtigste Kompetenz das sogenannte „kritische Denken" ist. Das bedeutet, Informationen von außen, aber auch sich selbst und die eigene Wahrnehmung stets kritisch zu hinterfragen. [...] Der Bestätigungsfehler beispielsweise meint das Phänomen, dass wir Informationen eher glauben, wenn sie in unser bestehendes Weltbild passen. [...]

Medien schaffen mediale Wirklichkeiten. [...] Welche Kompetenzen müssen junge Menschen haben, um stärker zwischen medialer und tatsächlicher Wirklichkeit unterscheiden zu können?
Ich denke, dass das Stichwort Ehrlichkeit eine wichtige Rolle spielt. Das, was ich erlebe und was mir viele aus dem Bekannten- und Freundeskreis, die auf journalistischer Ebene tätig sind, zurückspielen, ist eine grundsätzliche Verwirrung über die Vorstellung vieler Menschen, wie Journalismus funktioniere. Mit Ehrlichkeit und Transparenz meine ich, einen größeren Austausch zu schaffen. [...]

Das Tolle am Internet ist doch, dass wir das klassische Sender-Empfänger-Modell hinter uns gelassen haben. Wir sollten diese Chance des Austauschs noch mehr nutzen und wahrnehmen. Wir können dabei nicht nur über Inhalte reden, sondern auch über Methoden. [...]

From: 'Negative Nachrichtflut führt dazu, dass sich Menschen nicht mehr beteiligen', SMK-Blog, *30 June 2021*

1 Mediating You started an initiative with your partner school in the UK that tackles the question of how media fatigue and news avoidance can be prevented. Write an article for your project website taking Maren Urner's explanation as a basis.

► SF 47: Mediating from German into English
► Support p. 263

Beyond the text

2 Writing Write a letter to the editor in which you comment on the fact that the newspaper he/she is responsible for contains almost exclusively bad news.

► Check

3 Reconsider the guiding question of the chapter. Has your opinion changed in the course of the chapter? If so, how and why?

Resignation or resistance? The power of the media

- Consider which type of media from the box on the right meet which criteria in the table below. Copy the table and enter the types of media in the respective column. Different types of media can be used more than once. Then give the media types numbers to rank them according to which type of media fulfils the criterion best. Compare and discuss your results.

Accessible	Influential	Reliable	Thorough	Up to date
...	...	...	...	...

- radio news
- newspapers
- news websites
- TV news programmes
- weekly magazines
- social media platforms

Worries about the effects that the media can have on people and society were articulated as early as in 1899 by the editors of the Post, *long before the arrival of electronic media.*

Annotations
1 **peril** danger
5 **accustomed to sth.** used to sth.
6 **suffering** pain
6 **evoke sth.** *etwas hervorrufen*
6 **indignation** *Empörung*
13 **deceive sb.** trick sb., make sb. believe that sth. false is true

The first peril of careless newspaper reading is that of being morally hardened by constant contact with the physical and spiritual evils of the world, without being called upon to any action with regard to them.

It requires a notable degree of moral culture to keep from becoming 'used to' such things; and there are few things worse for us than to grow accustomed to men's sufferings and their sins, so that these no longer evoke pity, or indignation, or any other emotion in us.

The great minds are those which show the least disposition to become familiar with wrong, so as not to feel indignation every time they see it. They have a moral freshness which is our right and normal condition. They never 'get used to' good or evil.

It is very hard for us to keep this freshness of moral impression in our daily contact with what the newspaper tells us of the world's evil. It is even harder not to be deceived as to the comparative weight of evil and goodness in the world. The news-gatherer is drawn naturally to the former.

From: Post, *March 1899*

Comprehension

1 Summarize the editorial in two to three sentences.

Analysis

2 Work on either task **a** or **b**.

a Assess which role newspapers play according to the author, considering their contribution to moral stability or decline.

b Challenge Assess which role newspapers play according to the author, considering their contribution to moral stability or decline. Consider the stylistic devices used to support the statements.

Language awareness

3 The editorial was written in 1899 and differs from texts written nowadays.
  a Find words and phrases that are no longer commonly used today.
  b Rewrite the last two paragraphs in modern English.

▶ Check

Beyond the text

4 Speaking With a partner, discuss to what extent the criticism expressed in the editorial is still representative for:
- television
- social media
- newspapers.

Present your findings in class.

Chapter task

After dealing with various aspects of the media, you will have the opportunity to put your argumentation and speaking skills to the test and show what you have learned about this topic by producing a podcast.

You and your partner are going to produce a podcast on 'The media as a window to the world' for senior students in the English classes at your school.

You should prepare your podcast before recording it:
- Which aspects do you want to cover? Collect them and write them down.
- Who will present which aspects? Distribute them evenly.

Now write a coherent script for your podcast, then record it (you may use your smartphone).

Present your podcast to your class.

▶ Getting started

Chapter 1 — Text 3

► p. 21

Not being normal

3 Support

Look for different elements that are used to characterize the two characters in the excerpt:

- examples of Marianne's and Connell's actions in the text. Example: 'Marianne had a row with the History teacher last year' (ll. 4f.).
- examples of what Marianne and Connell actually say / have said in the text. Example: 'Connell said ...' (l. 20)
- examples of Marianne's and Connell's thoughts in the text. Example: 'It seemed so obviously insane to her ...' (ll. 8ff.)

Now think of suitable adjectives and phrases to describe those actions, words and thoughts.

Now use these ideas to go back to your original task.

Text 8

► p. 38

A prank

8 Partner B

Study the infographic below. Tell your partner what it shows about people's perception of society and racism.

Racism in Germany – a problem in every area of life

Proportion of respondents who believe that racism is a (very) big problem in the following areas

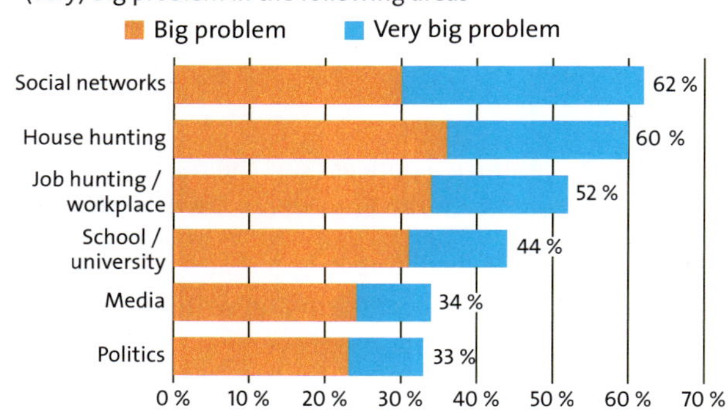

Sample: 2049 respondents older than 18, Germany June 2020
From: YouGov, June 2020

Text 10

Sonnet 130

► p. 40

4 Support

Poets and novelists often work with comparisons and contrasts if they want to question or criticize something. Think about the last two lines of the poem (the couplet) and their relationship to the rest of the sonnet.

Now go back to your original task.

Chapter 2 Text 3

Using DNA technology to combat disease

► p. 61

2 Support

Step 1: Find examples in the text of how the author describes

- Jennifer Doudna's work.
- how CRISPR has changed the world.
- the future impact of CRISPR.

Then think: Is CRISPR described in a positive or negative light?

Step 2: Find an example in the text of the author directly commenting on Jennifer Doudna's work. Then think: Does he agree or disagree with the scientist?

Step 3: Summarize your insights from 1 and 2 using the simple present. The following sentence beginnings can help you:

Language help

A close analysis of the text reveals that John Arlidge views CRISPR in a ... light. • In his view, CRISPR clearly has more ... than ... • His opinion shines through when ... • His choice of [word or phrase] signals that ...

Text 4

Neuroenhancement – boon or bane?

► p. 63

1 Mediation Support

When preparing your talk, follow the procedure below:

Step 1: Introduce your topic by defining the idea of 'neuroenhancement' and what 'neuroenhancers' are:

- 'Today I would like to give a short presentation on ... Neuroenhancement describes ...'
- 'A neuroenhancer is ...'

Step 2: Present your development:

- 'One development in this area I find very interesting and would like to have a closer look at now is ...'

Step 3: Present the information from Ms Tesch's book review:

- 'At this point let me give you some background information about the benefits and dangers of neuroenhancers and the ethical implications of this development. In fact, a German journalist ...'

Step 4: End your presentation in an interesting way:

- 'To conclude, I would like to emphasize that ...'
- 'Now think: Would you ...?'

Text 5

▸ p. 65

What is love? A clinical trial

4 Mediating **Support**

b Follow the tips below on how to prepare and conduct an interview:

- Prepare your interview carefully: Using your notes from **a**, compile a list of questions you would like to ask Helen Fisher. Keep the questions simple.
- Start your interview slowly and make your partner feel relaxed.
- Ask open-ended questions throughout the interview so your partner can act out his/her role comfortably and share with you what he/she found out about Helen Fisher and her work.

Text 7

▸ p. 71

Will AI outsmart humanity?

Partner B

1 Study the infographic on the right, then go back to task **1b**.

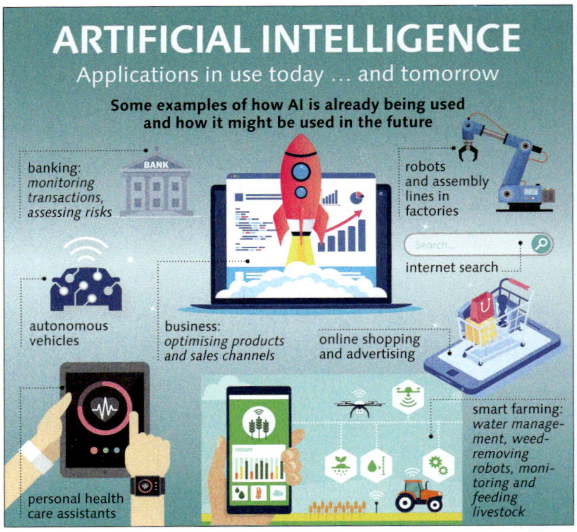

Text 8

R'ha

► p. 74

3 Support
The questions below may help you analyse your aspect of the film:

Animation techniques
- A *shot* is a single continuous motion captured by the (virtual) camera between two *cuts*. When does the film use many cuts, when only a few? Why?
- Can you find scenes in which the film uses (virtual) close-up/medium/long/ low-angle/high-angle shots? What are the intended effects?

Sound:
- Can you find scenes in which the film makes special use of music and sounds? What are the intended effects?
- What do you notice about the human voices used in the film?

Colour
- What colours are predominant in the short film? What mood or atmosphere is evoked?
- What do you notice about the use of brightness and darkness in the film? What purpose does it serve?

Text 9

The universe: a mystery

► p. 77

2 Support
Consider the following criteria for a good conclusion: A good conclusion ...
- suggests that the author has accomplished what they want to accomplish
- does not bring up any new ideas, but adds fresh and deeper understanding
- helps readers feel a sense of closure
- demonstrates the importance of the main ideas
- ends on a positive note
- offers a brief summary of the main points
- includes a provocative insight
- points to broader implications.

Chapter 3 Text 3

Playing by the rules: the WTO

► p. 89

2 Support Look at the verbs in ll. 26–35.

a Which tenses are used most often? How do you explain this? (Hint: pay attention to the adverbs of time.)

b Examine the meaning(s) of the verbs: are they mainly action verbs or mainly state verbs?

Text 5

▸ p. 96

Am I rootless, or am I free?

5b Support

Below you can find different forms of poems that could be used.
Haiku: consists of three short lines that do not rhyme
syllables are distributed between the three lines as following: 5–7–5.
Acrostic: The first letters of each line can be read downwards to form a word, phrase or name.
Shape poem: Its words form a shape or picture and the image usually reflects the content of the poem.
Cinquain: consists of eleven words, distributed over five lines:
- line 1: a noun
- line 2: two words, often adjectives, that explain the functions of the noun
- line 3: three words, more information about the noun
- line 4: four words, further explanations about the noun
- line 5: a one word synonym or any other reference for the noun.

Text 6

▸ p. 98

A stranger in Manila

2 Support

Put the headlines of the sections in the box below in the right order.

on arriving in Manila • on the job • on the flight to Manila • the traffic incident

Skills Lab

▸ p. 99

3a Support

Put the phrases in the box in the right order so that they correspond to the structure of the text:

final form of law • consequences for EU • the problem • original form of law • consequences for firms • the solution • (global exploitation of low-wage countries) • (German supply-chain law)

Swept up or left behind?

► p. 108

Partner B

While the general theme of decline was common across the two countries, an alternate narrative of being swept up by global currents of change also emerged. This sense was palpable across several focus groups in Seattle. All groups there agreed that local investments by multinational corporations like Amazon, Microsoft, Boeing and Starbucks had led to a major influx of people and money, which had put upward pressure on the cost of living in the city.

Across the Atlantic, the narrative of being swept up by globalization was most evident among focus groups in London. Participants noted how the city's position as an international hub, or 'magnet,' affects daily life for Londoners. Examples of negative impacts included increases in traffic, crime and housing costs, plus constant construction. Some mentioned that, paradoxically, all of this growth actually meant fewer employment and housing opportunities for local residents. One woman, for instance, faulted 'overseas investor' looking to profit off of the city's housing shortage with the construction of luxury flats that sit vacant when the city was in need of affordable housing.

Although they experienced globalization differently, groups who felt swept up pointed to some of the same outcomes as those left behind, such as the rising cost of housing, declining home ownership and the disintegration of social ties and community. Similar stories also surfaced with respect to increases in local homelessness, drug abuse and crime.

From: *'In U.S. and U.K, globalization leaves some feeling "left behind" or "swept up"'*, www.pewresearch.org, *5 October 2020*

Annotations
1 **decline** *(n)* decrease
2 **current** *(n)* *Strömung*
3 **palpable** [ˈpælpəbl] noticeable, easily noticed
5 **influx** arrival

Comprehension

1. Make notes on the following aspects of the Pew report: reasons for the survey, main themes of globalization, daily influence of globalization and perspectives on globalization. Compare results with your partner.
2. Explain to your partner what it means to feel *swept up*. Then listen to your partner's explanation of feeling left behind by globalization.

Now go back to task 3.

Text 12

▶ p. 111

Welcome to the pandemic era

3 Support
Look at the pronouns the writer uses in the last two paragraphs.

Chapter 4 Text 1

▶ p. 117

Taking stock: the mood in the UK

2 Support

- Emotions can be captured and conveyed with the right choice of words. Take a closer look at the *connotations of adjectives, nouns and verbs used in the text. It might help you to find *antonyms for some of the words to determine their connotation.
- Imagery is also often used to support the message of a text. The metaphor 'crumbs of comfort' (l. 30) suggests that there is very little comfort, as breadcrumbs are very small fragments of bread.

Text 2

▶ p. 118

A united kingdom or regional identities?

CartoonStock.com

Partner B

2 a Look at the cartoon on the left and analyse how it stresses British disunity. Prepare a 2-minute presentation for your partner that includes a detailed description of the cartoon. Then go back to task b.

3 Support
Look for examples of expressions like 'belying' (l. 1) or 'surprisingly little' (l. 2). Decide if these words and phrases have a positive or negative *connotation. Find more examples like the above mentioned. Then think about how this choice of words might influence the readers' perception of the topic.

Don't neglect the UK's indigenous languages

▶ p. 121

Partner B

Read the following text on a Welsh-only primary school in Carmarthenshire. Then do the tasks below.

A nation divided by languages? *Louise Tickle and Steven Morris*

With a third of schools in Wales teaching pupils primarily in Welsh, debate rages over the ethics of using the classroom to support a minority language.

'We've been told we are anti-Welsh bigots and even fascists,' says Alice Morgan in her soft Welsh accent. The comments she is talking about began when she and other parents raised objections to a plan to turn their primary school in the village of Llangennech into one that teaches only in Welsh. They are worried that some children used to being taught in English won't cope.

Feelings are running high. On one side are those who want to increase the number of Welsh speakers in the country. On the other are campaigners who say the evidence shows this method is futile and that children's education is being sacrificed for politics.

One mother said she was now too frightened to walk down to the Co-op in the village to buy a loaf of bread. 'It's got that bad. Perhaps I'm being paranoid but I'm really scared at the moment. I'm not sure it's good for the reputation of the Welsh language.'

While a Labour councillor described the move as a form of segregation or apartheid, some supporters of it have said that those who didn't want to live in a Welsh-speaking village could always move out. The decision, voted through in January by Carmarthenshire council, will mean Llangennech school will join 479 others – just under a third (31.9%) of all schools in Wales – that teach exclusively in Welsh.

The change will come into operation for reception pupils in September and has delighted those who believe it will help revive the declining fortunes of the Welsh language. But opponents say it could damage the education of children whose first language is English and will force some parents to send their children outside the village or county for their education.

Morgan – who asked that her real name not be used to protect her family – has three primary-age children. Until now, villagers have had a choice about whether their children go into the Welsh or the English stream in school. Her eldest son started at Llangennech in the Welsh stream, but had difficulties. 'He struggled tremendously for two years,' she says. 'He was depressed and unhappy, vomiting before school, and he fell behind. Although we speak Welsh at home I think it was the fact that no English was used whatsoever that made him feel overwhelmed.' Things improved when he was able to move into the English stream. 'He was a changed little boy.'

Her second son has special needs and a pre-school assessment judged that he would find it hard to learn more than one language, so he began in the English stream from the off. She is concerned for children like him in the future.

After an unpleasant meeting involving campaigners, councillors and those in charge of running the school, Morgan decided to remove her children to another primary where they can be educated in English. The eldest two have lost their friends and the new school is three miles from their home. But she now feels more optimistic about their future. 'We've found a new school that is absolutely wonderful, and my kids are valued for who they are.'

Another local parent, Michaela Beddows, says: 'We have English and Welsh both as official languages in Wales. I think all parents should have a choice.' Morgan agrees. 'It's become a political football. They're not taking account of the impact on children.' [...]

Ceri Owen, of the group Parents for Welsh Medium Education, says Carmarthenshire council's decision is about levelling the playing field. 'A lot of Welsh families are being denied education through the medium of Welsh,' she says. Parents who want their children educated in English 'won't be denied the English language. They will be able to travel [to schools that offer it].'

And that is what Morgan has felt forced to do. 'Our children feel they are no longer welcome. They've been ostracised from their peers. Their community is divided on the basis of language and they are now treated like second-class citizens. My neighbour actually said she wanted our children out of the school. The village is damaged.'

From: 'We're told we're anti-Welsh bigots and fascists'– the storm over Welsh-first schooling', www.theguardian.com, *20 June 2017*

Comprehension

1 Summarize the problem of having a Welsh-only primary school in Llangennech as presented in the article. Make notes only.

Analysis

2 Examine the effect the use of the personal example of the Morgan family has on the reader.

Language awareness

3 In their article the authors frequently use emotional language. Find examples and explain their effect.

Now go back to task **4**.

Text 6

► p. 126

British monarchy – unifying tradition or outdated anachronism?

3a Support

Below you can find a possible structure for the spidergram.

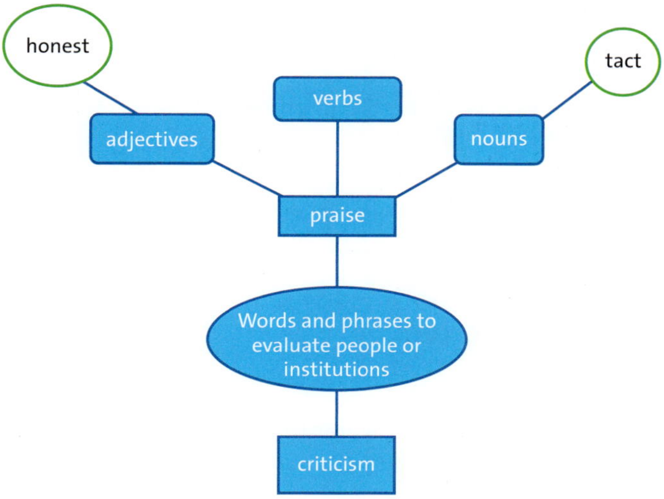

Skills Lab

► p. 129

2 Support

The *method card below already includes helpful information about argumentative writing. Keep adding relevant aspects.

Method card – argumentative writing	
Introduction	• starts with an introductory phrase • includes your own opinion on the matter • ...
Main part	• each paragraph develops one argument • ...
Conclusion	• refers back to the introduction • clearly states your point of view • ...
General characteristics	• ...

Text 7

► p. 132

Nobody is an island – the UK and Europe

2 Support

The following ideas can help you with your analysis:

- Check the text for exaggerations – which examples can you find? Which effect do they have on the reader?
- Find funny anecdotes or episodes the author uses to paint a picture of the British. Explain, how the reader perceives the British because of this.
- Find passages in which the author criticizes the British. Check how he does this and why this description is not hurtful or offensive.

Text 9

► p. 135

Brexit: A German perspective

1 Support

Step 1: Find ways to express the following words from the comment in English:

- 'Wirtschaftsstandort' (l. 18)
- 'Konkurrenz' (l. 18)
- 'Bürokratieabbau' (l. 24)
- 'uniforme EU' (l. 26).

Step 2: Bear in mind that Brexit is a controversial and highly emotional issue in the UK. Are there any parts of your presentation that might cause cultural clashes? If yes, find a diplomatic way to get those parts across.

Language Lab

► p. 136

2 Support

Adverbs of comment give information about the speaker's opinion or point of view. Comment adverbs usually go at the beginning of a sentence or clause. They are usually separated from the rest of the sentence by a comma.

Adverbs of degree can be used to intensify or tone down adjectives, verbs or other adverbs. They usually go in front of the adverb/adjective/verb they describe.

3 Support

Go back to the Skills Lab and read the written comment you find on p. 00 to see linking words used in the text.

5 Support

Possible arguments could be:

- English as lingua franca
- renowned universities like Oxford and Cambridge with a long tradition
- closeness to home country.

Text 12

Racism in Britain

► p. 142

Partner B

Comprehension

a Take a look at the bar chart below. Prepare a 2-minute presentation for your partner in which you tell her/him what your bar chart reveals about the different attitudes towards racism in Great Britain.

For more information on 'Black Lives Matter' have a look at the info box on p. 129.

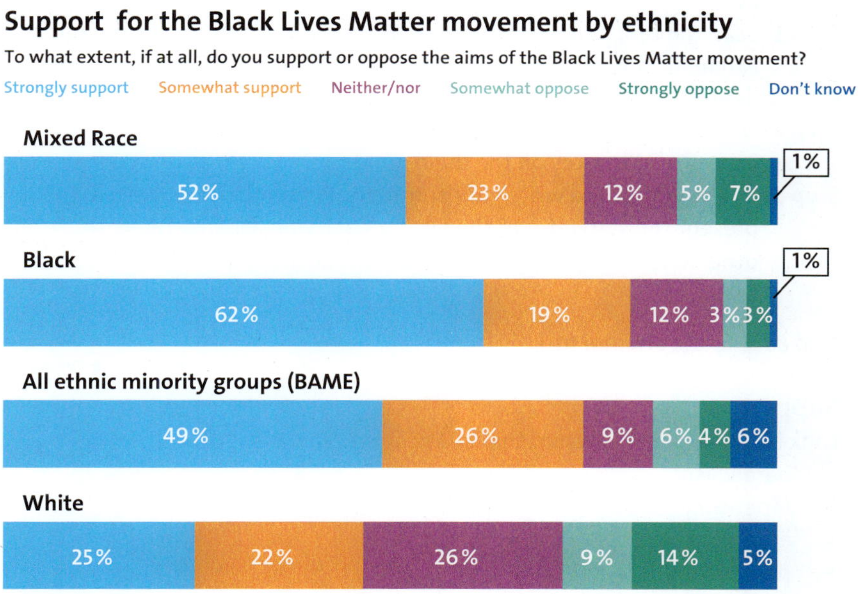

Source: © Ipsos

Now go back to task 2.

Text 13

► p. 143

New way, new life

2 Support

- Collect foreign-language expressions in the song. Which languages are used? What is the function of using these expressions and to what extent can they be regarded as a statement on Britain as a multicultural society?
- 'Inna' (l. 8), 'de' (l. 8), 'an' (l. 10), 'dis' (l. 24) und 'riddim' (l. 44) are all spellings that depict a Jamaican accent. Although none of the members of Asian Dub Foundation are of Caribbean descent they use this accent. What does this tell you about their view of the possibilities of language in a multicultural society?

Chapter 5 Text 1

► p. 151

At this moment in history

1 Support

Step 1: Scan the text to determine what aspects it deals with. The paragraphs can help you: good writers use a separate paragraph for each topic they deal with. But one aspect may extend to more than one paragraph.

Step 2: Use the aspects you have found to structure your summary. For each aspect, make notes on the main points.

Step 3: Use your notes to write your summary. Remember that we use the present tense to refer to the author's activity ('Obama refers to...'), but otherwise the same tenses as the original (i.e., past tense for action in the past).

Now go back to the original task.

4 Support

Look for examples of each of the following:

- *parallelism
- *repetition
- *enumeration
- *parenthesis
- *antithesis

Now go back to the original task.

A visit to Monticello

► p. 165

Partner B

Info

From Jim Crow to Black Lives Matter

The 'Jim Crow' South: After control was restored to local politicians, the white population of the South adopted measures to put Black Americans back in their former place. They were denied the right to vote, and an economic system called sharecropping was installed to ensure that Blacks continued to labor in the fields under a burden of debt they could never escape from. Segregation became the backbone of Southern life: separate schools for black and white, separate churches, separate toilets and drinking fountains. Lynch mobs dealt with those who dared to defy the unwritten rules of Southern life.

The Great Migration: Beginning around 1900, millions of Blacks left their traditional homelands in the South and migrated to the cities of the North looking for jobs and freedom from fear. The black quarters of Northern cities arose (e.g., Harlem or Chicago's South Side).

The Civil Rights Movement: Resistance to discriminatory practices in the South began in 1955 with the Montgomery bus boycott, a protest against a ruling in Alabama that forced Blacks to sit in the back of the bus. Organized by a young Baptist preacher, Martin Luther King, the movement was successful and led to a decade of similar protest movements, culminating in a mass demonstration in Washington in 1963, where King made his famous 'I have a dream' speech. Under President Johnson, a Southerner, Congress passed a number of laws guaranteeing equal rights and prohibiting discrimination.

'Black Lives Matter': In spite of considerable progress, Black Americans continue to suffer from the legacy of slavery. In particular, they are singled out for arrest and are sent to prison far more often than white Americans ('racial profiling'). Moreover, Black men are frequently victims of police brutality. In response to such incidents, a new protest movement emerged in 2013 under the hashtag #BlackLivesMatter. Repeated incidents of the (oftentimes deadly) use of force on the part of white police officers have kept the movement alive to the present day.

1 Make notes on the history of African Americans after the abolition of slavery, then explain to your partner how African Americans continued to be discriminated against despite the abolition of slavery.

Now go back to the original task.

Text 9

▸ p. 167

The health card

4 Support

Compare the examples in the box below. Pay special attention to:

- Mildred's pronunciation of certain endings and prefixes
- personal pronouns that refer to groups of people (both women)
- the use of adverbs without the *–ly* ending
- the complexity and completeness of sentences.

Mildred	Mrs. Jones
'Sure,' I said, 'indeed one must, and I am glad you are so understandin', 'cause I was just worryin' and studyin' on how I was goin' to ask you for yours [...].' 'On second thought, you folks look real clean, too, so ...'	'Do you live in Harlem, Mildred?' 'I don't mean any offense, but one must be careful, mustn't one?' 'Mildred, you don't have to bring a health card. I am sure it will be all right.'

From: Alice Childress, Like One of the Family*, 1956*

Chapter 6 Text 2

▸ p. 187

What's the next step for me?

Partner B

'School was very anti-apprenticeship'

When Matt Carpenter left school at 17, a lot of his classmates were aiming for university. He could have joined them.

'I was the only person in my class who didn't go,' he says.

Instead, he took up a three-year apprenticeship with the Merchant Navy, spending half his time at college and half his time at sea on oil and gas tankers, passenger ships and bulk carriers.

'School was very, very anti-apprenticeship - even when I had the place, they were very against it. Up until the last day, they were still asking, "Do you really want to do this?"'

For him, the choice was clear: no student debt and pay of £175 a week. Now, at 21, he's on an annual salary of £37,000 tax-free and qualified to drive the world's largest ships.

He admits the social life didn't compare to what his friends were up to, though. 'When you're at sea, you're quite cut off. There's no internet. You're working every day.'

'To learn about something I loved was brilliant'

Jenny Willbourn, 29, joined engineering firm Atkins after gaining undergraduate and post-graduate degrees in geography. The firm has a well-established apprenticeship programme, but she says that wouldn't have been the right route for her.

'I believe there's something valuable in academic study - the opportunity to understand a particular area of knowledge.'

'To push your communication skills is one thing, but to critically evaluate – that's a skill that university teaches. I value that as second to none.'

She works in a highly specialised team at Atkins looking at spatial data, including mapping the locations of badgers and bats as part of the HS2 planning process.

'I needed a degree to tell me what the options were and give me the skills I now have. For me, the ability to hone my skills at an academic level was very important.'

But above all, she enjoyed the experience: 'To learn about something I loved was brilliant.'

'I feel really proud of myself'

Joy Shepheard-Walwyn, 19, had a place at Durham University to study philosophy and Russian. She rejected it in favour of a management consultancy apprenticeship with accountancy firm PwC.

Moving to Leeds on her own just a few days after her 18th birthday was nerve-racking, she says. But PwC has helped provide a community for her in and out of work. She's joined the firm's netball team and teaches English to refugees. She loves the work, managing change in the public sector, adult social care, local government and schools. 'I feel really proud of myself in terms of what I've achieved.' She thinks university can be about putting off adult life a little longer. 'My friends are out partying a lot, but I'm earning a salary.'

'I don't feel I missed out. I just went about it a different way.'

From: www.bbc.com, 12 July 2019

Comprehension

1 Collect the information given about Matt, Jenny and Joy (name, age, career choice, arguments mentioned etc.).

Analysis

2 Examine how the text presents what Matt, Jenny and Joy are saying and the effect created by this.

Language awareness

3 a The text uses words and phrases that show that Matt, Jenny and Joy are happy with their decision, but also the concessions they are making. Collect them.

b Present your notes on tasks **1–3a** to your partner. Listen to your partner's findings on Amy and Nick.

Now go back to task ***3c****.*

Text 4

► p. 192

'So how's the PhD going?'

3 Support

Read the following quotes from the text. What emotions are being portrayed?

- 'Doro, alas, is also wearing terrible clothes, which is a shame [...].' (l. 9)
- 'And that green linen jacket might have been okay in its heyday, but that was some twenty years ago.' (l. 12)
- 'She has this embarrassing way of raising her voice in public.' (l. 51)
- Serge: 'If everyone was like you, Mum, the system would collapse.' (l. 54)
- Doro: 'So how's the PhD going? [...] Just remind me again, darling. What is it about?' (l. 58)
- 'God knows what she'll says when she finds out about his job [as a banker].' (l. 62)

Skills Lab

► p. 195

4b Support

Here is a selection of common interview questions. Go through them, adapt them to your needs and make your own questions:

- 'Tell me about yourself.'
- 'Why did you apply for this internship?'
- 'Why should we consider you for this internship? / What can you bring to our company?'
- 'Tell me/us about a time when you were part of a team.'
- 'What achievements are you proud of?'
- 'What are your strengths and weaknesses?'
- 'Which requirement do you think will be the most difficult for you to meet during the internship?'
- 'How would your friends/fellow pupils/co-workers describe you?'
- 'Where do you see yourself in five years?'
- 'What do you know about this industry/company?'

Text 6

'Money is just a social construct'

► p. 200

2 Support

Have a look at the following sentence and the position of the quotation marks:
'Did you hear that sound?' whispered Sally.
Now look at three parts from the text that include direct speech. Rewrite them by adding the missing quotation marks.

a	It's the time you'll never get back, Marianne adds. I mean, the time is real. The money is also real.
b	Do you think I judge you for being so idle? says Joanna.
c	Okay. You can call tomorrow after the thing if you feel like talking. Thanks, says Marianne. You're a good friend. Bye.

Chapter 7 Text 3

Are we addicted to social media?

► p. 220

3 Support

Listen closely to the way the following sounds are pronounced:

- the 'r' in *interesting, personal*
- the 't' in *it is*
- the vowels in words like *don't, down, thousand, life, personal.*

Also pay attention to intonation (i.e. sentence melody).

Text 4

Text

► p. 221

3 Support

- Analysing the language of a poem, it can be useful to start with the peculiarities of the text: note down the most important words, *stylistic devices such as *repetitions and *parallelism, *imagery etc.
- Don't analyse language for its own sake but relate form to content: explain how these linguistic peculiarities and stylistic devices add to the description of personal emotion by means of communication technology.
- Make conclusions about the deficiencies of texting: consider what is missing when two lovers cannot meet in person but have to rely on their mobile devices only. How is this expressed in the poem?

Text 5

▶ p. 226

Digital revolution and the availability of knowledge

Partner B

Comprehension

1 Describe the cartoon below.

"Wow!...Hold it up, and the app tells you what that is."

CartoonStock.com

Analysis

2 a Assess the irony of the cartoon, considering the critical questions about the effects of digitization that the cartoon raises.

Now go back to task ***2b****.*

Text 7

▶ p. 231

The art in advertisement

2 a Support

Take into account:

- graphic elements and characters
- spatial division (including background, foreground, perspective)
- light and colour
- mood and atmosphere
- typeface
- visual references.

2 c Support

Take into account:

- the way readers or viewers are addressed
- register and stylistic devices
- quotations and references.

Text 9

Scripting reality

► p. 237

6 a Support

- Explain the statement in the context of the story, pointing out what additional aspects are covered.
- Critically engage with the viewers' responsibilities.
- To round off your comment, come back to the quotation and compare the viewers' responsibility with that of the producers.

b Support

- Make sure you make your position clear.
- Use aspects of Kelly's original message in the confession box to describe her the way you used to know her.
- Choose a register that is appropriate for a post in the chat room, i.e. rather colloquial language, with features of spoken rather than written language.

Text 10

News avoidance in times of media fatigue

► p. 241

1 Support

- List the shortcomings of an uninvolved form of journalism according to the text. Find appropriate English expressions.
- Identify persons and institutions that relate to a German background. Make notes on how you can explain these aspects to a person with a different cultural background.

General exam skills

Language and study skills

Reading, text and media skills

Writing skills

Listening and viewing skills

Speaking skills

Mediating skills

General exam skills

SF 1 Essentials: exams

You will encounter many different English tests and exams at and after school. Before any exam, you should familiarize yourself with its specific format. However, there are some general tips that will help you to be successful. Most important: start early and organize your work.

Preparing for the exam

Step 1 Collecting information

- Find out where the exam will take place, how long it is and, especially for speaking exams, if you will be given preparation time.
- Look at past exam papers to see what they require.
- Make sure you understand what the different tasks require you to do.
- To get the maximum number of points in your exam, find out about the evaluation criteria to help you to focus on the relevant aspects.
- Make sure you know how to use aids that are allowed in the exam, e.g. dictionaries.

Step 2 Practising

- Go over past exam or homework tasks to identify any problem areas and learn from your mistakes.
- Focus on your weak areas. Don't practise what you already know.
- Practise the specific type of exam you will be doing.

Doing the exam

- Read the instructions carefully. They provide crucial information. Make sure you understand what you are supposed to do – it may help to highlight the exam tasks ('Operatoren') and content keywords.
- If you have to choose between tasks, read all the alternatives before deciding which one to do.
- If you notice that you are becoming nervous, take a quick break before continuing.
- Use your time efficiently and leave enough time to check your work.

SF 2 Working with closed test formats

During lessons and in written exams, you will come across test formats that do not require you to write complete texts or answers to questions. In **half-open** formats, you write keywords only, e.g. note-taking, completing tables or finishing sentences. In **closed** test formats, you only indicate which of the given solutions is correct or which items go together. The most common closed test formats are:

- **multiple-choice task** (choosing the correct answer from several options)
- **true/false statement** (classifying each statement as 'true' or 'false')
- **matching task** (matching items from two lists, e.g. paragraphs with headings)
- **gapped text** (identifying sentences or passages that have been omitted)

Closed test formats occur mostly in listening and reading comprehension tasks. In exams such as TOEFL, Cambridge Certificate and TELC, they may also be used for grammar or vocabulary.
The following strategies will help you deal with closed test formats.

Step 1 Reading the instructions
- Read the instructions carefully, work out which information is important, and underline keywords.
- Make predictions about the listening/reading text and the answers to the questions.

Step 2 Doing the closed test
- Focus on the information that is necessary to complete the task. Take notes.
- Read all the answers even if you are sure that you have found the correct one. The differences between the right and the wrong answers are often subtle or tricky.
- Fill in answers to questions that you are sure about straight away. If you are unsure, leave the question and come back to it later.
- Do not skip questions you cannot answer. Make educated guesses – for a multiple-choice question with four options, you have a 25% chance of success!
- Keep an eye on the time. Tasks that require you to read for gist only allow you a short time to skim the texts.
- In listening tasks, complete as much as possible during the first listening. Use the second listening to add any missing information or to correct your answers.

Tips

Working with closed test formats

Multiple-choice task
- Read the options carefully – they may contain traps. They may use keywords from the text, but say the exact opposite of what is said in the text.
- If you are unsure which of the options is correct, go through them one by one and ask yourself if you can exclude any answers.

True/False statements
- With false statements, you will often find the opposite information in the text.
- In a half-open version of this format, you may be asked to give evidence as to why you think an answer is right or wrong or to correct it.

Matching task
- Do not match items just because they contain words or phrases that are similar. Instead, paraphrase the items and match those with a similar meaning.

Gapped text
- Watch out for words that link sentences/ideas such as connectors (e.g. *therefore, moreover*), pronouns and adverbs (e.g. *she, this, there*) or connected vocabulary (e.g. *bird – eagle, sparrow*) and pay attention to the sequence of time in the text. They may all provide useful hints.
- After completing the text, make sure that the grammar is correct and the line of thought logical (e.g. cause and effect).

SF 3 Understanding text-based tasks ('Operatoren')

In general, when dealing with a text, you will be asked to consider the following three aspects:

'Anforderungsbereich I'	'Anforderungsbereich II'	'Anforderungsbereich III'
comprehension (focus on content)	analysis/interpretation (focus on form and function)	composition (focus on evaluation and re-creation)

In an exam (as well as for homework), you may be given tasks that clearly relate to one of these three aspects, or there might be complex tasks that combine two or all three of them.

Comprehension (understanding) ['Anforderungsbereich I']

This type of task focuses on the content of a text and is intended to check whether you have understood it. Comprehension tasks can be quite open, i.e. they require you to write a free text, as in summary writing ► SF 32: Writing a summary or an outline, or answer comprehension questions. They can also occur in the form of closed test formats, e.g. multiple choice or true/false exercises.

Below are some instructions that are frequently used for comprehension tasks. For the complete list of instructions, see ► pp. 000–000 ('Verbs for tasks').

Instruction ('Operator')	What you are expected to do	Example	Tips
outline ['− −] *umreißen, skizzieren*	Give the main features, structure or general principles of a topic, omitting minor details.	Outline the writer's views on genetic engineering.	Structure your answer using main and subordinate points.
state *darlegen*	Specify something clearly.	State the *author's opinion on the main character's decision.	Be precise and brief.
summarize (also: **give/write a summary of; sum up**) *zusammenfassen*	Give a concise account of the main points of something.	Summarize the incident in the church in no more than four sentences.	Be concise; leave out details and examples.

You may also get (half-)closed tasks to test your understanding.

complete *vervollständigen, ausfüllen*	Finish the sentence with a few words from the text.	Complete the sentences with words from the text.
tick *ankreuzen, abhaken*	Put a tick (✓) next to the right answer.	Tick which adjectives characterize the girl most appropriately.

Analysis/Interpretation ['Anforderungsbereich II']
This type of task requires you to 'read between the lines' of a text. You might have to examine why an author gives the text a certain form, why he/she characterizes the characters in a certain way, etc.

Below are some instructions that are frequently used for analysis tasks.

Instruction ('Operator')	What you are expected to do	Example	Tips
analyse *(BE)*, **analyze** *(AE)* ['ænəlaɪz] / **examine** [ɪg'zæmɪn] *analysieren, untersuchen*	Describe and explain certain aspects and/or features of the text in detail.	Analyse the main elements of the poster. Examine the writer's attitude towards the *protagonist.	Do not just list the *stylistic devices the author uses, but explain the effect they create.
explain *erklären*	Describe and define in detail.	Explain the main character's reaction to her mother in the first *scene.	Do not just describe something, but give reasons as to why it is the way it is.

Beyond the text (evaluation: comment and/or text production) ['Anforderungsbereich III']
This type of task goes beyond the text and requires you to give your opinion and/or evaluate a question or problem arising from the topic of the text or visuals. You may also be asked to be creative. The task may be called **comment, composition, re-creation of text, creative writing* or simply *writing*. Sometimes you will be asked to write a certain *text type, e.g. a *letter to the editor or an *interior monologue. The task may also give you aspects that need to or may be taken into consideration. If the text type is not specified, you may find one of the instructions listed below.

Instruction ('Operator')	What you are expected to do	Example	Tips
comment on ['kɒment] *kommentieren, Stellung nehmen zu*	State clearly your opinions on the topic in question and support your views with evidence.	Comment on the *speaker's belief that ...	Say exactly what you think and why.
discuss *diskutieren, erörtern*	Investigate or examine an issue; give reasons for and against your position.	Discuss how education influences attitudes towards immigration.	Structure your ideas clearly. Weigh up both sides of an issue and support your final position with arguments.
justify *begründen, rechtfertigen*	Show adequate grounds for decisions or conclusions.	Justify your answer.	If possible and appropriate, use statistics or research results as support.

SF 4 Writing a text analysis

Text analysis (of *fictional or *non-fictional texts) is an essential part of most written exams including the *Abitur*. The aspects you analyse will differ depending on the text type ► SF 16–24, but the process of analysing is usually the same.

Preparing the text analysis

Step 1 **Reading the task carefully**
Make sure you know exactly what you are asked to do. ► SF 3: Understanding text-based tasks
You may be given a specific aspect to analyse, or will be free to select aspects yourself.

Step 2 **Reading the text**
Make sure you understand the text properly. Use a dictionary where necessary. Here are some suggestions for questions you might ask yourself.
- Which stylistic devices and/or communicative strategies are used? To what effect?
- Which noteworthy words and phrases are used? To what effect?
- How does the structure of the text add to its general meaning / line of argument?
- How is the reader influenced by the text? To what effect?
- What information is being withheld? Why / To what effect?
- In what way does this text differ from other texts of the same type?

Step 3 **Making notes**
Make notes on features or aspects of the text that seem relevant for your analysis. Remember to note down references from the text that support your analysis.

Step 4 **Structuring your ideas**
Do not follow the text chronologically but structure your ideas according to the different aspects you are analysing.

Writing the text analysis

A text analysis is usually written in the present tense.

Step 1 **Introduction**
Write a short introductory paragraph that contains the following:
- the title, the author, the year of publication and the text type
- a first general idea (interpretive hypothesis) of the central message of the text.

Step 2 **Main part (body)**
Write the main part of your text.
- Present your findings to support the central message stated in the introduction.
- Use different paragraphs for different ideas and introduce each paragraph with a topic sentence to guide the reader. Structure your paragraphs coherently.
- Use linking words.
- Remember to provide evidence from the text, i.e. to use quotations with line references.
  ► SF 14: Quoting from texts

Step 3 Conclusion
Write a short conclusion.
- Refer back to your introduction and restate your first general idea in different words and based on your findings. Summarize the main points you have made.
- Do not add new aspects at this point.
- Do not give your personal opinion or an evaluation.

Step 4 Proofreading
Check your text for any spelling and or grammatical mistakes. Make sure that quotations from the text have been copied correctly.

SF 5 Doing a speaking exam

Many exams include a part in which you have to prove your speaking skills. ► SF 40–45 Preparing for and successfully passing a speaking exam is different from a written exam because of the different skills and strategies required. Speaking exams usually consist of two parts which are thematically linked, a *monologue and a *dialogue.

Monologue	Dialogue
In this part, you are asked to give a presentation based on, for example, a diagram, statistics, a picture, *cartoon, quote or short text.	In the second part, you are asked to interact with a partner or a group of students in a role-play or a discussion. It may be based on the material you have worked on for the monologue. Your fellow students have probably dealt with similar material.

Preparing for the speaking exam

Step 1 Finding out the conditions of the examination
Ask your teacher about the specific conditions of your exam, e.g.:
- What kind of prompts can you expect (i.e. cartoons, pictures, quotes, etc.)?
- Will you be given time to prepare only the monologue or both parts?
- If there is preparation time for the dialogue, will it be at the very beginning or shortly before the dialogue?
- How long will the preparation time be?
- How long will both parts of the exam be?
- How many people will take part in the dialogue?
- Will the participants in the dialogue be other students or teachers?

Step 2 Finding out the assessment criteria
To get the maximum number of points in your exam, find out which criteria your teacher will apply when assessing your exam:
- communicative strategies (structure, eye contact, interaction with partners, etc.)
- pronunciation (clarity, fluency, *intonation, accuracy)
- powers of expression (choice of words, ability to deal with unknown words / technical terms, flexibility, etc.)
- grammar: amount and types of mistakes
- content: quality and meaningfulness of statements/arguments, etc.

Step 3 Practising

- Practise monologues, e.g. by describing and explaining to a fellow student a picture or text that might appear in the exam.
- Practise dialogues, e.g. by discussing with a fellow student a picture or text that might appear in the exam.

Doing the speaking exam

- If there is preparation time, arrange your material so that you can use it effectively. Structure your ideas clearly. Use clear handwriting. Use abbreviations, keywords, etc.
- You may have to adopt a role or defend a position which you do not like. Try to disregard your personal opinion, stick to the facts and give evidence if possible.
- In the dialogue part, take your time to react but do not hesitate too long.
- Ask for clarification of crucial points. Be provocative and polite at the same time; avoid attacks or insults.
- Do not be too emotional.
- Use appropriate body language and facial expressions.
- Choose the right moment to sum up your points and introduce a new aspect.

Tips

Preparing for a speaking exam

- Learn phrases which you can use during presentations ► SF 41, *speeches ► SF 42 or discussions. ► SF 44
- Study your classroom material and look for controversial issues which could be discussed, then collect arguments for and against them.
- Watch (current) political debates online to get an idea of the culture of reflection and debate.

Language and study skills

SF 6 Essentials: language and study skills

You already use some of the skills and strategies presented in this Skills File. In the future, you will need to adapt them to support your language learning at school and beyond, for English or any other foreign language. There are three important questions you should ask yourself – and be honest with your answers!

Step 1 **Where am I?**
Take stock and review your language skills and learning strategies.
- Look at your results and achievements in English.
- Consider the results of self-assessment and peer assessment.
  ▶ SF 15: Assessing yourself and giving feedback
- Ask your teacher where you stand with learning English.
- Do you know how to actively learn more English to improve your results?

Step 2 **Where would I like to be?**
Set yourself achievable goals.
- Do you simply want to avoid some of your most frequent mistakes, or would you like to speak and write better English?
- Do you wish to be well prepared for your next exam?
- Do you need to write an application for a job, scholarship or an exchange year?

Step 3 **What are the next steps?**
Now you know where you are and what your aims are, you have to consider which methods and strategies you can use to achieve these goals.
- If your main aim is to expand your vocabulary, how can you best do this, for example by reading and writing more texts or by using a vocabulary app?
- If you have problems with mediation, is it because you have difficulties mediating ideas, concepts or arguments expressed in German into English? Should you practise explaining things in English?
- If you are not very good at giving presentations in English, do you need to improve your oral skills, or are you unsure about what to present? Should you practise how to identify relevant content or how to get your message across in front of an audience?

SF 7 Dealing with unknown words in a text

When you read or listen to texts, you don't usually understand every single word. Luckily, in many cases, you don't need to because you can understand texts without knowing each individual word. However, if the meaning of a word is essential to a sentence, there are some techniques that can help you work it out.

Look at the highlighted words in the text on the left, then at the strategies on the right to work out their meaning.

In order to remain competitive, industrial nations have to raise their productivity, encourage innovation and lower their production costs.
To reduce costs and to maximize profits, multinational companies often relocate facilities to other countries (= outsourcing) to profit from the lower wages they pay their workers and from less restrictive laws. The problem is that it diminishes work prospects for workers here.

- *competitive* Think of words from the same *word family that you know: *competition / (to) compete / competitor.*
- *encourage* Identify parts of the word that you know: *courage → give sb. courage.*
- *maximize* Think of similar words in other languages: German 'maximieren'.
- *multinational* Identify prefixes or suffixes, e.g. *multi* (= *many*): *multinational = belonging to many nations.*
- *wages* Use the context of the word: *they pay their workers.*
- *prospects* Watch out for false friends: *prospects* = 'Aussichten', not: 'Prospekte'.

Tips

Help with understanding new words
- Illustrations in the text (photos, charts, etc.) can help you to understand unfamiliar words.
- Sometimes there are annotations explaining the meaning of certain words.
- An e-book version of your text often gives you direct access to a dictionary.

SF 8 Working with dictionaries (print and online)

If you do not know the meaning or translation of a word, you can look it up in a bilingual or in a monolingual dictionary. The two types of dictionaries are useful in different situations. Practise using them before the exams.

Using a bilingual dictionary

A bilingual (English-German, German-English) dictionary is useful for finding translations and checking the meaning of individual words, e.g. the English word for 'Ruf' or the German translation of *reputation*. Familiarize yourself with the form of the entries in your dictionary.

- The running heads at the top of each page help you find the right page quickly (top left-hand corner: first entry on page, top right-hand corner: last entry at bottom of page).
- In the example on the right, 'Ruf' is the headword: the different translations are listed; numbers or letters in boxes indicate the different meanings.
- The notes in *italics* (e.g. *'auch übertragen'*) help you to find the particular meaning you are looking for.
- Examples and *collocations *('der **Ruf nach** ...')* are found below the headword.

Ruf
1 *auch übertragen* call /kɔːl/; *lauter* shout /ʃaʊt/:
der Ruf nach *schärferen Gesetzen* the **call for** tougher laws
2 ≈ *Ansehen* reputation /ˌrepjuˈteɪʃn/

From: *Schulwörterbuch English G 21*

If you are writing on a laptop or PC, it is convenient to use an online dictionary. *Linguee*, for example, is a useful and reliable website (and dictionary app) for translating individual words. Here too you can hear the correct pronunciation. Under each main entry, you will find example sentences from various sources on the internet, together with the corresponding translations. But be careful: the translations are marked as 'not reviewed', i.e. there is no guarantee that the text on the left has been translated correctly.

Using a monolingual dictionary

If you know the English word you need, but are not sure how to use it, then a monolingual dictionary is the right choice. It contains definitions and example sentences that help you to find the words that express exactly what you want to say. In order to choose the right meaning, always read the whole entry.

grim /grɪm/ *adj.* (**grim•mer**, **grim•mest**) **1** looking or sounding very serious: a ***grim face/look/smile*** ◇ *She looked grim.* ◇ *with a look of **grim determination** on his face* ◇ ***grim-faced** policemen* **2** unpleasant and depressing: *grim news* ◇ *We face the grim prospect of still higher unemployment.* ◇ *The outlook is pretty grim.* ◇ *Things are **looking grim** for workers in the building industry.* **3** (of a place or building) not attractive; depressing: *The house looked grim and dreary in the rain.* ◇ *the grim walls of the prison* **4** [not before noun] *(BrE, informal)* ill/sick: *I feel grim this morning.* **5** [not usually before noun] *(BrE, informal)* of very low quality: *Their performance was fairly grim, I'm afraid!* ► **grim•ly** *adv.: 'It won't be easy,' he said grimly.* ◇ *grimly determined* **grim•ness** *noun* [U]

From: *Oxford Advanced Learner's Dictionary*

Monolingual dictionaries contain useful supplementary information:
- information on spelling and grammar
- examples of common collocations and idioms
- information on usage and *style
- typical sources of error.

Monolingual dictionaries such as the *Oxford Advanced Learner's Dictionary* are usually also (easily) accessible online. The online versions provide the same (often more clearly arranged) information as the printed versions and sometimes even more. Usually, you can hear the words spoken (BE and AE). Most online dictionaries are regularly updated and supplemented.

grim *adjective*
/grɪm/
/grɪm/
(comparative **grimmer**, superlative **grimmest**)

Idioms

1 ★ looking or sounding very serious
- *a **grim face/look/smile***
- *She looked grim.*
- *with a look of **grim determination** on his face*
- *He set about the task with grim concentration.*
- ***grim-faced** policemen*

From: *www.oxfordlearnersdictionaries.com*

SF 9 Learning new words

Learning vocabulary is a lifelong activity – even in your own language. There are different methods for expanding your vocabulary. Try out various ways until you find the one that works best for you.

Step 1 Identifying useful words

Identify words that could be useful to you. These might be:

- words that are related to the topic you are dealing with (e.g. Shakespeare's plays)
- words that help you talk or write about texts or topics in class
- words that go together with other words (collocations) or that belong to a word family that you already know
- words that belong to a *neutral register (very formal or very informal words can only be used in limited situations).

Step 2 Arranging the words

Arrange your words in a suitable form. This could be on index cards, using a list or any form of *clustering as in mind maps, topic webs and flow charts.Indicate the meaning of your words by:

- giving *synonyms (e.g. *dogma* = *belief/principle*) or antonyms (e.g. *upheaval* ≠ *stability*)
- establishing word families
- making sketches/drawings
- giving examples (e.g. *the arts* = *art, music, literature, etc.*)
- giving the German equivalent (e.g. *achievement* = 'Errungenschaft', 'Leistung').

If possible, write down words in contexts or collocations. This will help you to use them in a sentence (e.g. *be torn between, remember sth. as sth.*).

> The Elizabethan Age is often remembered as a Golden Age for its many achievements in the arts. However, England was struggling for peace and stability at home – religious, social, political and economic developments challenged society. People were torn between a traditional world view and a more modern one; they generally accepted the Earth as the centre of the cosmos and the Church as the centre of life on Earth, but were keen to discover new truths beyond the old dogmas. Shakespeare's drama reflects this upheaval.

Step 3 Using new vocabulary

Use new vocabulary as often as possible: include it in a short text, study your index cards, etc.

Step 4 Revision

Revise your vocabulary regularly; first in short intervals, then in longer ones.

Tips

Being active when learning new words

- Do not just write new words down, say them out loud as well.
- Walking around while learning new words can be helpful.
- Giving new words a *rhythm or tune can be helpful.

SF 10 Learning languages through digital media

Here are some suggestions on how to use digital media to help you improve your English.

Help with your writing skills

Electronic (rather than handwritten) versions of texts are easier to change and correct. Rewriting and editing longer texts will help improve them – and your English! Giving a text a clear *layout helps the reader to follow your line of thought.

Help with your reading skills

Online dictionaries are a quick way to check the meaning of a word – if you are careful to check a word in its context. You can also listen to the pronunciation. ► SF 8: Working with dictionaries

Help with your listening and viewing skills

Watching films and videos in English is a good way to internalize sounds and speech patterns. Try to get as much language input as you can, whenever you can.

Help with your speaking and presentation skills

- Digital presentations are the best way to combine text, images and sound. There are lots of fun things that you can do with digital media to make your presentation more interesting. But remember: your message is the most important thing – and YOU are the most important medium!
- Record yourself to check how your ideas come across. Ask others for feedback.

Help with your language and study skills

- Both vocabulary apps and grammar apps help you to keep track of what you want or need to learn. They also keep track of your progress. Use them as your personal coach.
- It is becoming more and more important to work in a team even when you cannot meet in person. Video conference tools make it easy to work together online. Chats and shared documents saved in the cloud allow all the team members to make their own contributions at any time – no matter where they are.

Tips

Blended learning – the best of both worlds

- Your English book has gone digital too. Make sure you are familiar with the digital extensions your book or e-book offers. Use them when you need language help or online practice, background information or a kickstart with an assignment.
- Books are not everything – neither are digital media. Learning and working in a hybrid world means that you decide what is best for you and your language learning in any given situation.

SF 11 Building language awareness

To improve your language skills, it is not enough to write and speak English fluently. You also need to be aware of the following aspects of language and language use:

- How is language structured as a system?
- How does it work in different contexts?
- How can it have a certain effect on other people?

For different usages of English, you must therefore develop a sensitivity to language (called language awareness) that goes beyond the rules of grammar and how verbal communication works. The following steps will help you to develop/improve your language awareness.

Step 1 **Focusing on a language phenomenon**

When reading, writing, listening to or speaking English, you may encounter and should focus on linguistic phenomena or obstacles such as the following:

- a special accent
- a grammatical form that is different from your mother tongue, e.g. the progressive forms in English

- the fact that in English commands are often given in the form of a polite question
- a communication problem that involves explaining something in a different way, using different words and structures so that another person can understand it
- so-called false friends (e.g. English *sensible* and German 'sensibel')
- different stylistic levels that English speakers use when communicating with different audiences
- how the use of certain words with specific *connotations affects the reading or understanding of a text.

Step 2 **Analysing form**

Analyse the linguistic form of specific uses of English very carefully to understand how they work or why they did not work in case of misunderstanding.

- Try to identify the structure or phenomenon.
- Consider what (grammar) rules might apply.
- Consider how you can explain this specific form of English or why there was a misunderstanding.

Step 3 **Analysing function and meaning**

To be fluent in English, you need to know and understand not only the form of such (specific) language uses, but also what they express, i.e. when and with what intention they are used.

- Find out the function and meaning of the uses of language.
- Find out how they influence communication. For example, if somebody uses very formal English in communication, this might be due to the fact that there is a difference in authority between the communication partners. The speaker either wants to demonstrate power or, by adding politeness to formal English, addresses the other person in a way that achieves a certain goal, such as in a job interview.

Step 4 **Building language awareness and making use of it**

Once you have analysed a language phenomenon and recognized its form, function and meaning, you will be able to:

- use it in your own communication
- analyse the language use of others
- address different target audiences and use the appropriate language for the situation
- convince other people of your ideas because you are aware of how to use language correctly, appropriately and understandably.

SF 12 Communicating across cultures

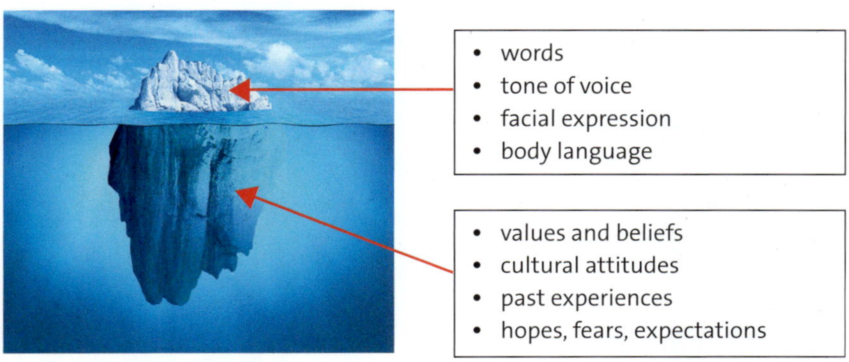

Looking below the surface

When we communicate with other people, what we see and hear is only part of the story – sometimes the smaller part, as illustrated in the photo above. The image of the iceberg shows that most of the meaning of language is determined by factors beyond words written, read and heard. This is especially true when communicating with people from a different culture. Not only language itself, but also the way we use it can vary. It is important to be aware that each culture may have different social conventions, e.g. regarding directness or sincerity.

- In some societies, you must say what you want directly if you wish to be taken seriously, e.g. *I want to speak to the manager – now.* In other parts of the world, it is good manners to express yourself as indirectly as possible, e.g. *I was wondering if it might be possible to speak to the manager.*
- People in the UK are generally far more indirect in their speech than Americans or Germans.
- In some cultures, it is considered impolite to express your opinion openly, especially if it is negative. The use of adjectives that are not very meaningful, such as *interesting* or *remarkable* is a polite way of expressing disapproval. In other cultures (e.g. American), people are extremely generous with praise and with vague, non-committal promises that are not necessarily to be taken literally, e.g. *You must come for dinner some time.*

Tips

Getting by in an unfamiliar culture

- Observe other people and behave accordingly, for example if they all queue up, then get in line too; if they all rush to the front, then do the same.
- Never take for granted that the person you are talking to understands what you mean just because they smile, nod or say *yes.*
- Be as polite as possible.
- If you do become involved in a misunderstanding, it is often best to apologize, even if you are convinced you are right. An unexpected apology will generally defuse the situation and motivate the other side to seek an agreement.

Language help

Being polite

Asking for confirmation

- So, you mean/think/believe that ...?
- Let me see if I've understood you correctly. You ...

Expressing wishes as questions

- Do you think it would be possible to ...?
- Would anyone mind if I ...?

Avoiding imperatives

- Would you mind taking your bags off my seat?
- Could I ask you to take your bags off my seat?

Apologizing

- I'm very sorry – it was probably my mistake.

SF 13 Doing research

For projects, presentations or other schoolwork, you usually have to research for specific information. To do so, you can use the internet or other sources of information. Here are some ways to make your research more effective.

Step 1 **Clarifying the topic**

- Make sure you understand exactly what the topic is, then brainstorm it. Decide what information you need so that you can structure your research accordingly.
- Make a list of keywords that you want to check.

Step 2 **Choosing sources**

- Decide which sources will be most helpful for your research: the internet, textbooks, encyclopaedias, newspapers or magazines, experts or contemporary witnesses.
- Concentrate on English language sources. Using information in German and translating it into English will take a long time and often leads to unidiomatic English.

Step 3 **Checking source quality and reliability**

- Older publications may contain outdated information – make sure you have the most up-to-date facts.
- Information published by individuals, interest groups or companies may be biased (i.e. in favour of this group or company). Check and do not rely on just one source.

Step 4 **Making notes on the information found**

- Use index cards to make it easier to organize your information later.
- Copy the exact wording and note down the source, as it normally needs to be given in a bibliography (an alphabetical list of sources used) at the end of your project work.

Tips

Finding the most useful information on the internet

Determine whether a website provides reliable information.

- Domain names ending with *.gov* or *.edu* indicate that the information is likely to be accurate, as it is usually an official website. Sites of scientific institutions are also usually reliable.
- Personal *blogs or home pages often just give statements by individuals – they tend to be biased.

Limit the number of hits so that you will find useful information more quickly.

- Brainstorm which keywords will most likely appear in an *article or a text which answers your search question.
- Combine them to get the most exact results. Typing in five or six keywords is better than just two or three.
- The more specific the words, the better.

Find the original source of a quote.

- Enter the full quote or parts of it, using quotation marks to find websites with this exact quote and thus normally the original source of the quote.

SF 14 Quoting from texts

Quoting is used when you want to support your own statements (e.g. in an analysis) by giving evidence from other texts or the text you are working on. You can either use a **direct quote** (i.e. use the exact words of the text) or **paraphrase / quote indirectly** (i.e. use your own words to express ideas from a text).

► SF 48: Paraphrasing

Here are some rules for quoting properly:

- Always give the exact **source** of your quotation: *line or *verse numbers and – when dealing with longer texts – page numbers. If you are quoting from more than one text, indicate the *author and year of publication.

- Remember these **abbreviations:**
  - *p./l.* is used for one page/line, e.g. *p. 4*
  - *pp./ll.* is used for more than one page/line, e.g. *pp. 11–14*
  - *f./ff.* is used after the number of a page/line and means 'and the following page(s)/line(s)', e.g. *p. 4ff.*
- When working on projects, you may have to quote from more than one source. In this case, you need to indicate in a **bibliography** which texts you have used. For each text, provide the author, title, place and date of publication, publisher or URL.

Indirect quotes

- If you use an indirect quote, you do not use quotation marks.
- Indirect quotes are often, but not always, preceded by *that* or *if*.
- Indicate that you are referring to somebody else's ideas by using *cf.* (German 'vgl.') and the page number and/or line.

Example
Franklin D. Roosevelt suggests in his speech that people who are threatened by poverty are easy prey for dictators (cf. p. 212, ll. 2f.).

Direct quotes

- In a direct quote, repeat exactly what the author wrote – this also applies to spelling, punctuation, etc.
- Use quotation marks to show where the direct quote begins and ends. A direct quote must be clearly indicated as someone else's thoughts to avoid plagiarism. Remember that in English, quotation marks start and end above the line ('...' or "...").
- When quoting complete sentences, make sure that you explain them, refer to or comment on them to avoid disconnected quotations.
- If you want to refer to individual words or phrases from the text (e.g. in an analysis), you can 'build' them into your own sentence. Be careful: work the quotations into your sentences as smoothly as possible so that they fit syntactically.

Example
'We must act now to save our planet and our future', writes a young climate activist in a letter to the editor of the *Guardian*.

Quoting poems or plays in verse

With texts written in verse, indicate the end of lines with a slash (/). When quoting from *plays, provide the *act, *scene and verse, e.g. *II/2/6 = act II, scene 2, verse 6.*

Example
The first two lines of the poem 'The Road Not Taken' by Robert Frost introduce the dilemma of choice that every human faces: 'Two roads diverged in a yellow wood, / And sorry I could not travel both' (ll. 1–2).

Deleting from or adding to a direct quote

- If you want to leave out part of a quote, indicate this by using square brackets [...].
- If you need to add to a quote, e.g. to make it fit into your sentence syntactically or logically, indicate this by adding words in square brackets too. Make sure that you don't change the meaning of the quote and that it is still syntactically correct.

Example
The author says that '[l]ove has made [her] a new [...] person'.
Cf. the original:
Love has made me a new, much more optimistic and likeable person.

Quoting texts containing quotation marks

When quoting a passage that includes quotation marks (e.g. in direct speech), use two different kinds of quotation marks, i.e. '...' and "...".

Example
In Genesis, the first book of the Bible, it says:
'And God said, "Let there be light" and there was light' (Genesis 1.6).
OR
"And God said, 'Let there be light' and there was light" (Genesis 1.6).

Tip

When not to use quotes

Check the assignment carefully before using quotes. For example, in comprehension tasks you are asked to express ideas from the text in your own words and are therefore not supposed to quote.
► SF 3: Understanding text-based tasks

Language help

Quoting

Indirect quotes

- The author says/claims/states/argues/believes that ... (cf. ll. 00–00).
- He/She draws attention to the fact that ... (ll. 00f.) and asks if ... (l. 00).
- Franklin D. Roosevelt suggests in his *speech that ... (cf. p. 00, l. 00f.).
- The work of ... shows/indicates that ...
- According to Albert Einstein, ...

Direct quotes

- Biden is convinced that immigration has benefitted the USA: '...' (p. 00. ll. 00–00).
- In her *essay ..., the author says, 'The world needs to wake up' (p. 00, l. 00).
- According to the author, 'British girls are among the most stressed at school' (p. 00, l. 00).
- The article goes on to say that more and more boys 'were also found to be ...' (p. 00, l. 00).
- 'It is disappointing', a teacher is quoted as saying, 'that you haven't learned from your mistakes' (p. 00, l. 00).
- In the *prologue to *Romeo and Juliet*, the unhappy ending of the play is already *foreshadowed by the phrase 'starcrossed lovers' (Prologue, v. 6).

SF 15 Assessing yourself and giving feedback

Self-assessment

Assessing yourself is an important part of learning. It helps you to learn by making you aware of your strengths and weaknesses. However, to assess your own performance, you must find and apply an objective benchmark.

- Try and compare your results, texts, presentations, etc. with a set of rules, a good example text or another model or pattern that helps you to identify your strengths, but also your weaknesses or mistakes.

- Ask your teacher for self-assessment sheets with criteria to help you analyse and evaluate your own performance. The Common European Framework of Reference for Languages or the marking schemes your teacher uses may also be helpful.
- Make a list of your 'favourite' mistakes. Or decide on a particular aspect of the task in question that you want to review and improve on.

Peer assessment: giving and receiving feedback

Giving others feedback not only improves your evaluation skills – something that you will find useful in other fields of life too – but also teaches you alternative ways of dealing with and solving a task.

- Before you give feedback, ask if there are any aspects you should pay particular attention to.
- Do not just point out mistakes, also highlight positive aspects.
- Always start with the positive feedback.
- Do not only criticize, but also suggest how to correct a mistake or improve a weakness.
- Focus on the work and performance, not on the person.

It is always easier to assess somebody else's work than your own. But getting feedback from others helps you to evaluate your own skills and products more objectively.

Tips

Giving and receiving feedback

- Make your feedback as specific as possible and refer to aspects such as:
  - the given topic
  - the quality and meaningfulness of content
  - language (correct structures and vocabulary)
  - pronunciation (e.g. in presentations)
  - clarity and readability
  - the needs of the target audience
  - the use of effective strategies for written, oral or visual communication
- A feedback sheet or checklist is helpful when giving and receiving feedback.
- Note down useful strategies and methods to help you with specific activities and for self-assessment (= to be aware of your frequent mistakes and/or see how things have improved).
- Do not feel attacked by critical feedback. Peer assessment is about supporting each other.

Language help

Giving feedback

- You did a good / an excellent job. What I really like about your work/text is ...
- Your text contains quite a few / a lot of good elements; however, ...
- Your text meets many of the relevant criteria such as ...
- You might want to focus more on ...
- Why not try to ... instead of ...?
- If you changed/rewrote the beginning/conclusion / the passage where you ..., your text would sound even more convincing/professional/emotional/...
- I think it would be a good idea to ... Maybe you could ... in order to ...

Reading, text and media skills

SF 16 Essentials: reading strategies and text types

When working with longer texts, there are different ways of reading. Which strategy you apply depends on what you want to do with your text: look for the main ideas or specific information, read for pleasure or analyse it. You also need a strategy to deal with unknown words.

► SF 7: Dealing with unknown words in a text

Skimming

Skimming (or reading for gist) means going through a text or material quickly to identify the main ideas. This technique is helpful when you are researching a certain topic and have to find relevant texts quickly.

Step 1 **Getting the gist**
Look at the title, (sub)headings, pictures, diagrams or keywords to get an idea of the content.

Step 2 **Going through the text quickly**
- Don't read every sentence.
- Read the beginning and end of each paragraph – the first sentence usually states the main idea and the last often contains a summary of the paragraph.

Step 3 **Summarizing**
Summarize the text. If you are able to do this, your skimming was probably successful.

Scanning

Scanning means looking out for specific information. This technique is helpful when you want to find answers to a particular question or to compare particular aspects in different texts.

Step 1 **Looking for particular keywords or details**
Think of useful keywords or phrases before looking for the information you need.

Step 2 **Reading the information around the keywords**
Move your eyes quickly down the page. Stop when you find a keyword or phrase and read the part where you found it. Then continue scanning the text.

Extensive reading

This means reading as much as possible, usually for pleasure, e.g. reading a *novel. You read at your own speed and concentrate on what is happening without looking up unknown words.

Close reading

Close reading is necessary when analysing a text in detail. ► SF 17–20 To do so, you will have to read the text more than once and make sure you understand every word. You will also have to **read between the lines** to understand what is implied rather than stated explicitly.

Tips

Reading strategies

Before you read
- Activate your **prior knowledge** by making a list of what you already know about the topic.
- Make **predictions**. Use the title, (sub)headings, pictures and diagrams as well as your own experience to speculate about the topic and the central message of the text.

While you read
- Ask and answer **questions** to clarify that you really understand the text.
- Think of **headings** for the paragraphs as a way of understanding the main message of each.
- Analyse the text **structure** (e.g. introduction/main part/conclusion, paragraphs).

Text types

Texts can be classified into two main categories.

Non-fictional texts ► SF 17	Fictional texts ► SF 18–20
• A *non-fictional text deals with factual events, people and places which are described precisely and are thus verifiable. • It was written to convey information, convince the reader, criticize something or to entertain (while informing about factual events or information). • Non-fictional texts come in many types, e.g. *newspaper/magazine article, *essay, feature article, information leaflet, *advertisement, questionnaire, *letter, review, *biography, political *speech, travel writing.	• A *fictional text describes a world created by its *narrator. It is based on imagination. • The *setting, *characters and events are invented by the *author. • The main types of fiction are: – ***narrative prose**, e.g. novel, *short story – ***poetry**, e.g. ballad, *sonnet – ***drama**, e.g. *comedy, *tragedy • Fictional texts tend to use *stylistic devices. • Within each type of fiction, there are different *genres, e.g. science fiction (or sci-fi), historical fiction, romance fiction.

Tips

Non-fiction and fiction

- Sometimes it is difficult to distinguish between non-fiction and fiction, as the boundaries between these two genres can be blurred, e.g. in the case of diaries, *autobiographies or historical novels.
- Writers of non-fiction often use the techniques of fiction as well as stylistic devices to make their texts more appealing.

SF 17 Reading and understanding non-fictional texts

When analysing a non-fictional text, you have to say more than just what it is about. You have to find out what type of text it is, e.g. a *feature story, an *editorial or a *comment. By looking at how the content, structure and language of the text interact, you can find out what its function and message might be. Follow the steps below.

Step 1 Skimming the text

- Try to get a general idea of the topic and main arguments of the text.
- Sum up briefly what the text is about.
- If possible, find out when and where it was published (newspaper, book, journal, internet).

Step 2 Identifying the text type

Knowing the text type and its characteristic features will help you to anticipate what kind of information might be given and how it might be presented. The info box lists some of the most common text types you will encounter.

Info

Text types

Expository texts (e.g. feature story, *news story, scientific paper)

- contain comprehensive and detailed information
- are intended to be objective and factual
- give no personal opinion
- describe a situation, scientific findings, historic events

Descriptive texts (e.g. travel book, biography)

- describe actual places, objects, events or people based on the author's observations
- are intended to create a vivid picture in the reader's mind
- tend to give a lot of detail

Argumentative texts (e.g. [written] discussion, comment, editorial, *column, *letter to the editor, review, speech)

- discuss problems and controversial ideas
- evaluate a topic by giving reasons and stating the pros and cons of an issue
- arrange arguments in a clear and logical order
- tend to use expert opinions, statistics, quotations and technical/scientific language
- aim to convince the reader/listener
- often use stylistic devices

Persuasive texts (e.g. speech, advertisement)

- often use imperatives as an appeal to take specific action
- try to persuade or convince the reader/listener
- use stylistic devices

Instructive texts (e.g. manual, brochure, recipe)

- tell the reader what to do and how to do it
- use imperatives and passive constructions

Step 3 **Examining the text more closely**
- Focus on the content and purpose of the text: is it meant to inform, persuade, entertain, ...?
- Look at the structure of the text (heading or headline, introduction, main part, conclusion, argumentation / line of argument)
- Analyse the language, *style, *tone and *register of the text: is it *formal/*informal, simple/complex, objective/*neutral/biased, *emotive, ...?
- Establish the author's reason for writing and what the reader is expected to do with the text.

Step 4 **Answering questions on the text**
- Always read the questions very carefully so that you know what to do or look for.
- Read the text or parts of it again before you answer.
- You may quote key words or (parts of) individual sentences to support your answer.

Language help

Analysing non-fictional texts
- The author uses vivid/informal/objective/emotive language.
- The sentences are long-winded/complex/simple.
- The author's tone is friendly/humorous/critical/optimistic/sarcastic.
- The author's choice of words underlines ...
- The stylistic devices used support/emphasize/underline ...
- The reader can easily picture the situation / follow the author's train of thought / line of argument.

SF 18 Reading and understanding narrative texts

When you have to analyse a short story, a novel or any other narrative text, you are usually asked to pay attention to one or two specific aspects. The most common aspects are:

Characters, character constellations and character relationships

► SF 29: Writing a character profile

Which characters in the story are the most relevant?
- How do the narrator and/or other characters characterize them, directly or indirectly?
- What relationships do the characters have to each other? Are they dependent on each other or equals, etc.? Do they like or dislike each other?
- Do they belong to similar/different groups (social/ethnic, etc.)?
- Do they serve as foils for each other, i.e. do they contrast with another character to highlight particular qualities of that character?
- How do the characters develop? Are they *'round characters' (complex and undergoing development) or *'flat characters' (not very complex and not changing over the course of the *plot)?

Narrator and narrative perspective
- From which *point of view (perspective) is the story told?
  - Is the narrator a *first-person or a *third-person narrator?
- How much does the narrator know or not know? What are the limiting factors?
  - Does the narrator have a *limited point of view – a limited third-person narrator?
  - Does the narrator have an *unlimited point of view – an *omniscient third-person narrator?
  - Does the narrator slip into one character and tell the story from that person's perspective (but still in the third person)? Is it the point of view of one character in the story? In this 'figural narrative situation', the narrator sees the world only through the eyes of the chosen character.
- What effect does the *narrative perspective have on the reader and the reading process?

Tip

The narrative perspective can change in the course of a story.

Plot

- How are the events connected by cause and effect to form a plot?
- How does the narrator attract or keep the reader's attention by creating *tension or *suspense?
- Is there a *climax and/or a *turning point? If so, what effect does it have?
- Does the story have an ending or a conclusion? Or is there an *open ending / a *denouement? What is the effect/consequence of the type of ending?

Setting and atmosphere

- Where and when does the *action take place?
- How do the characters react to the setting?
- How are the *atmosphere and mood created? The four most common ways of establishing atmosphere are setting, tone, the choice of words or the *theme (subject matter) the narrator uses, e.g. sunny spring days usually create an optimistic atmosphere, a crowded place may create a tense or an exciting atmosphere, etc.
- Is the atmosphere described directly, or does the reader have to draw conclusions?

Language help

Analysing narrative texts

- The relationship between the characters is strongly influenced by ...
- The power struggle between the characters reveals itself when ...
- The characters' lack of communication shows ...
- X's behaviour when ... reveals that ...
- The description underlines/emphasizes ... / conveys the impression that ...
- The *image suggests ...
- By using words like ..., the narrator stresses ...
- The overall effect is / can be portrayed as ...
- The perspective is biased/one-sided ...
- As the first-person narrator has a limited perspective, the reader must ...
- The author has chosen an omniscient narrator because ...
- The story has an open ending, so ...
- In the end, the *conflict is solved when ...

SF 19 Reading and understanding poetry

When you analyse a *poem, you should look at its poetic features (e.g. *rhythm or language) as well as at the content, and then link this to the structure and form of the poem. Only then will you be able to fully understand the message the poem is trying to convey.

Step 1 **Reading the poem**

Read the poem two or three times, then summarize it as briefly as possible. Consider:

- the title, setting and theme
- the *'speaker' and the addressee
- the link between the title and the content of the poem.

Step 2 Analysing structure and form

Look at the structure and form of the poem (*stanzas, *rhyme scheme, rhythm and *metre). It may help to read the poem out loud to get a feeling for the way it sounds.

- Is the rhythm or rhyme scheme regular or not? Are there interruptions?
- Is there a *refrain?
- How do structure and form contribute to the understanding/meaning of the poem?
- What type of poem is it? (e.g. sonnet, acrostic, limerick, ballad, *free verse)

Step 3 Analysing the language

Examine the language of the poem more closely. Look for:

- the poet's choice of words: how do they contribute to the meaning of the poem?
- *imagery, e.g. *simile, *metaphor, *analogy, *personification
- sound effects, e.g. *alliteration, *assonance, *onomatopoeia
- *contrasts, *repetitions and specific sentence structures (simple/complex sentences, *enjambement)
- mythological/literary/social/historical references
- *symbols and their meaning or function.

Step 4 Understanding the message

- Try to figure out the meaning of the poem. Ask yourself what the poet is trying to say.
- Connect your findings on the form, structure and language of the poem to its content. Describe how they link to the meaning and effects of the poem.

Language help

Analysing poems

- The poem '...' by ... deals with / is about ...
- In the poem, ... describes / reflects on ...
- The poet or speaker addresses ...
- The title reminds the reader of ... / refers to ...
- The poem is made up of ... / consists of ... verses/stanzas.
- The rhyme scheme is ... / There is no consistent rhyme scheme. / The word ... rhymes with ... / The use of ... creates rhythm.
- Line ... runs into *line ..., which emphasizes ...
- The poet employs specific images, such as metaphors or similes, in order to ...
- The *diction/register is simple/*colloquial/formal, which intensifies the feeling of ...
- The most prominent stylistic device used in the poem is ..., which serves to ...
- All in all, ... / The overall effect is ... / The overall message of the poem is ...
- The poem aims to show/illustrate/convey/express the idea that ...

SF 20 Reading, watching and understanding drama

A drama or *play is a *script in which a *playwright presents what characters say and do. Usually, a drama is written to be performed on stage. When analysing drama, the following aspects should be considered.

Dramatic structure

- Is the structure of the play linear, with events occurring chronologically? This could include *exposition, *rising action, *climax, *falling action, *resolution.
- Is the structure of the play non-linear, with the action of the play moving backwards or forwards in time?

- Does the play include subplots? What is their function?
- Is the play divided up into *acts and *scenes, or is there a different structure?
- What function do these divisions have in the play?
- Do they correspond to action, time, place?
- To what extent do they correspond to the line/arc of suspense?

The construction of action
- How does the action unfold through the *dialogues?
- Are there *monologues? What function do they have?
- What kind of language is used?

Setting
- Do we know when (year, season, time of day) and where (location) the play takes place?
- What sights, sounds, smells and tastes are described?
- Does the script contain *stage directions? If so, what information do they provide?

Characters, character constellations and character relationships ► SF 29: Writing a character profile
- Which characters in the play are the most relevant?
- Is one of the characters the *protagonist / the main character / the hero or heroine who fights against another character who is his/her *antagonist? Or are there only anti-heroes/anti-heroines?
- What relationships do the characters have to each other? Are they dependent on each other or equals, etc.? Do they like or dislike each other?
- Do they belong to similar/different groups (social/ethnic, etc.)?
- What issues do they have to deal with in the play?
- How do the characters develop? Are they 'round characters' (complex and undergoing development) or 'flat characters' (not very complex and not changing over the course of the plot)?
- Where do we get the information about the characters from (the stage directions, the characters themselves, other characters)?

Audience
- Does the audience know/see something that the characters do not know/see (*dramatic irony)?
- What is left to the audience's imagination?

Tips

Analysing plays
- Analysing a play is similar to analysing narrative fiction. The basic elements are the same: characters, a plot and a theme.
- When you read a play, imagine how it would look and sound on stage. This way you will understand it better and enjoy it more.

Language help

Analysing plays
- The play is divided into ... acts and ... scenes.
- The overall theme of the play is ...
- In the play, conflicts develop between ...
- The audience is drawn into the plot by ... / The action is supposed to please/shock/enrage/fascinate the audience.

- The ... act ends in a *cliffhanger, which causes the audience to ...
- At the end, the conflict is solved by ...
- The stage directions draw a concise picture of the scenery. / There are almost no stage directions, so ...
- The play works with almost no *props / a bare stage ...
- Even though X appears as a friendly character at first, later he/she demonstrates / stands for / represents ...
- The social differences between the characters can be seen in the language they use ...
- The characters speak in blank verse, which suggests ...

SF 21 Analysing diagrams

Charts and graphs present complex information visually. There are different types:

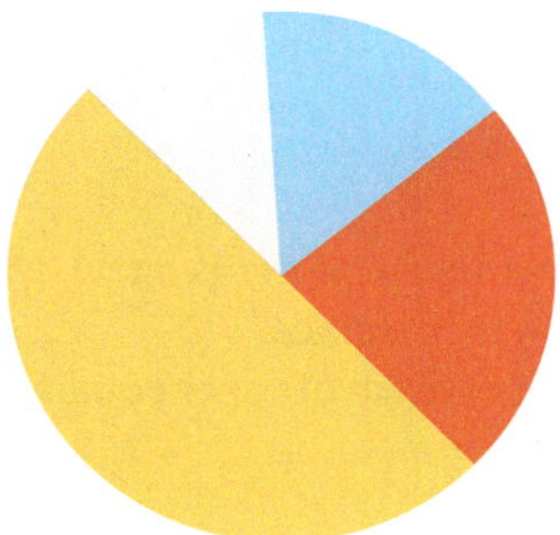

pie chart ('Tortendiagramm', 'Kreisdiagramm')

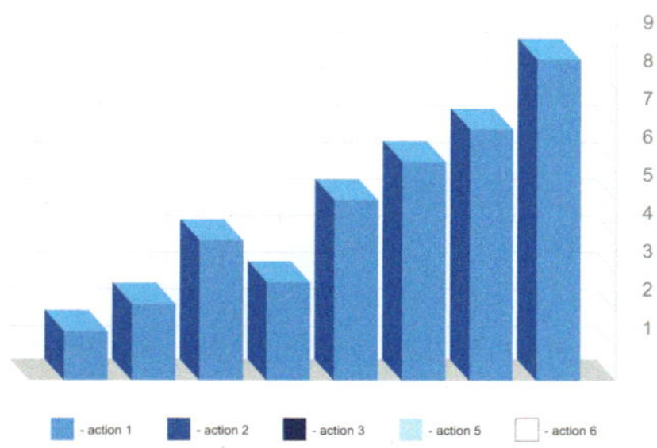

bar chart ('Balkendiagramm', 'Säulendiagramm')

line graph / line chart ('Liniendiagramm', 'Kurvendiagramm')

infographic ('Infografik', 'Piktogramm')

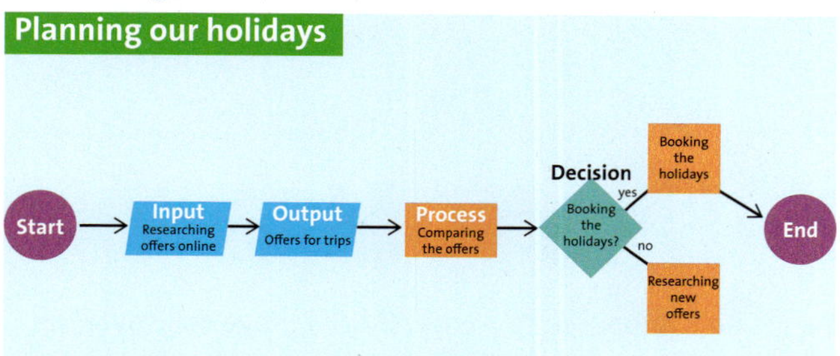

flow chart ('Flussdiagramm', 'Ablaufdiagramm')

Venn diagram ('Venndiagramm', 'Mengendiagramm')

Plans of graduate students after finishing school

	Percentage of students (in one class)
Gap year	20 %
Apprenticeship	15 %
Enroll *(study)* **at university**	40 %
Internship	15 %
Voluntary work	5 %
Other	5 %

chart/table ('Tabelle')

When analysing diagrams, follow these three steps:

Step 1 Identifying the type of diagram
- Identify the type of chart or graph you are dealing with.
- Try to determine whether the source is reliable. ► SF 13: Doing research
- Check if the data is up to date.

Step 2 Describing the diagram
- What is it about and what information does it give?
- What period of time is covered?
- Does it show a development, or does it compare different items at one point in time?
- Does it use absolute figures or percentages?
- Which developments can be observed (e.g. where are peaks and low points)?
- Can the diagram be divided into periods which show contrasting or similar developments?

Step 3 Analysing the diagram
- What conclusions can you draw from the chart/graph?
- Can you think of historical, social, political, economic developments which could help to explain the chart?
- Is the chart designed to give a brief factual overview or to influence or even manipulate the reader, e.g. by using differing intervals on the x-axis differ from those on the y-axis?

Language help

Analysing diagrams
- The bar chart / pie chart / line graph / table ... shows the different ...
- It compares the size/number of ... / deals with / is about ... / contrasts ... with ...
- It shows ... in contrast to ...
- It is taken from / It contains data from ... / It was published in ...

Pie chart
- The chart is divided into ... segments which show/represent ...
- The smallest/biggest segment represents ...
- The segments representing ... and ... constitute the majority ...
- A huge majority/minority is ...

Bar chart
- The bars are arranged horizontally/vertically.
- There are big/vast/surprising differences between ...
- At the top/bottom of the ranking comes ...
- ... is first/last in rank.
- ... has the largest / second largest ...

Line graph
- The graph shows the relationship between ... and ...
- ... is twice / three times as high as ...
- There are more than / nearly twice as many ... as there are ...
- ... increase/decrease / reach a high point / rise/fall/drop / grow steadily.

SF 22 Analysing visuals

There are different types of visuals: photos, posters, paintings, drawings or sketches. Often they are combined with a written text, either as a title or a caption.

Step 1 **Basic information / Introduction**
- What is your first impression of the visual?
- Read the title or caption. What is the general topic?
- When and where was the visual created or published?

Step 2 **Description**
Choose one of these approaches.
- Start with the main subject, i.e. a dominant object, describe it in detail, then describe the background (useful for a visual with one dominant image).
or
- Start at the left of the visual and work across to the right or vice versa (useful for pictures with a lot of activity).
or
- Start at the top of the visual and work down to the bottom or vice versa (useful for visuals where the interest tails off towards the top or bottom).

Step 3 **Analysis / Interpretation**
Draw conclusions about what the visual is meant to convey and how it achieves its effect. You might consider:
- the technique, colours
- the effect on the viewer
- who is addressed and why
- the artist's/photographer's message.

Step 4 **Evaluation**
Evaluate the image by thinking about the following questions:
- How effective is the image as a visual message?
- Can the visual be looked at in different ways?
- How does it compare/contrast to other examples that you know?
- If the image illustrates a text, to what extent does the image support, complement or contradict the text?
- If you are asked, say whether you like the image or not and why.

Language help

Analysing visuals

Basic information / introduction

- This picture/painting/photo/poster/drawing/sketch was created by ...
- It was published in ...
- It shows/depicts/portrays/illustrates ...
- It provides proof of / gives information on / introduces the topic of / conveys the impression that / is about ...
- In the picture, you/we can see ... / In the picture, ... can be seen.

Description

in the background

in the top right-hand corner

in the centre

in the bottom left-hand corner

in the foreground

Analysis and interpretation

- The artist's/photographer's use of ... creates ... / conveys the impression of ...
- The dominance of ... / The way the light/shadow ... directs the viewer's attention to ...
- As the foreground/ background is ..., the impression given is that ...
- ... is a symbol of ...
- ... helps to create an atmosphere of / which ...
- This has the effect that ...

SF 23 Analysing cartoons

The following steps will help you to describe and analyse a *cartoon systematically.

Step 1 Basic information / Introduction

- What is your first impression of the cartoon?
- What is the cartoon about? What is its topic / central idea?
- Is the cartoon black and white or in colour?
- What is the name of the cartoonist?
- Where and when was the cartoon published?

Step 2 Description

- Describe the cartoon systematically.
- Describe the choice of colours and the drawing style.
- Name any labels, speech bubbles or captions.
- What people, events or trends does the cartoon refer to?

Info

Cartoon – caricature

A **cartoon** is an amusing drawing in a newspaper or magazine that deals with human nature or a current political or social issue. Complex issues are reduced to memorable pictures. Cartoons often include captions or speech bubbles. Techniques employed by cartoonists include ***caricature,** *exaggeration, *wordplay and the use of symbols.

Step 3 Analysis

The following questions will help you when analysing a cartoon:

- Are the figures or issues presented in a positive or negative light? How is this achieved?
- What techniques are used to convey the message (symbols, *irony, exaggeration, caricature)? What is the effect?
- How do the drawing style and colour scheme contribute to the overall image of the cartoon?
- Does the cartoon express criticism of certain people, current events or trends? If so, what is criticized and how is this conveyed?
- What point is the cartoonist trying to make? What means are used to get the message across?

Step 4 Evaluation

The following questions will help you when commenting on a cartoon:

- How effective is the cartoon as a visual message? Give reasons, using your background knowledge of the topic.
- Do you agree or disagree with the message of the cartoon? Why / Why not?
- Do you find the cartoon convincing? Why / Why not?
- (if asked to compare the message of a text and a cartoon:) To what extent does the cartoon support, complement or contradict the text?

Language help

Analysing cartoons

Description

- The cartoon is (in) black and white / coloured / in colour.
- The cartoonist uses thick outlines, geometric shapes and colourful colours.
- In the centre/foreground/background, ...
- At the top/bottom, ...
- On the left/right-hand side of the cartoon, ...
- There is a caption underneath. It says ...

Analysis

- The characteristics of the illustrated person are simplified/exaggerated through sketching / pencil strokes / artistic drawings.
- The cartoon may be meant to show ...
- The cartoon is very eye-catching because of its use of ...
- The cartoon speaks to the viewer directly by ...
- The layout / use of colour / ... criticizes / makes fun of ...
- The cartoon conveys its message through ...
- The cartoon gets its message across by ...

SF 24 Working with multimodal texts

What is a text? According to dictionaries, a 'text' is any form of written material. Traditionally, texts were seen primarily as collections of words. But all texts are 'multimodal' because they use not only words but also other forms ('modes') of communication (e.g. *layout, images or sounds) to convey meaning.

Step 1 Identifying the type of multimodal text

Multimodal texts can be print, digital or 'live'.

- **Print** ('paper-based') multimodal texts include textbooks, graphic novels, posters and comics.
- **Digital** multimodal texts include films, podcasts, social media or computer games.
- **Live** multimodal texts include dance, theatre performance and oral storytelling.

Step 2 **Identifying the modes of communication used in the text**

When dealing with (multimodal) texts, it is useful to look at **all** the modes involved. This will deepen your understanding of the text and help you analyse it. In general, five different modes can be distinguished:

- the **linguistic** [lɪŋˈgwɪstɪk] mode (spoken or written words)
- the **visual** [ˈvɪʒuəl] mode (visuals such as photos, but also typography)
- the **spatial** [ˈspeɪʃl] mode (arrangement of objects in space, layout)
- the **gestural** [ˈdʒestʃərəl] mode (body language)
- the **auditory** (BE: [ˈɔːdətri], AE: [ˈɔːdətɔːri]) mode (sounds).

Step 3 **Exploring the functions of multimodality**

- Analyse how each mode contributes to the overall meaning of the text.
- Analyse how the different modes interact with each other to convey the message of the text.

Example:

The poster on the right uses four different modes of communication:

- linguistic mode: caption
- visual mode: picture of Uncle Sam, colours, capital letters
- spatial mode: layout (Uncle Sam in the centre, caption overlaps with the picture)
- gestural mode: fixed eyes, finger pointing.

A US Army recruiting poster (ca. 1917)

The combination of the four modes strongly communicates the recruitment efforts of the US military during World War I.

- The man in the centre immediately draws viewers in. Dressed in red, white and blue, he can be identified as Uncle Sam, a traditional personification of the US government or the nation in general. By looking the viewer straight in the eye and pointing at him/her, the impression of immediacy is created, as if Uncle Sam were addressing the viewer directly.
- The fact that the caption partly overlaps with the image suggests that the caption echoes Uncle Sam's own words. The use of capital letters in the caption adds emphasis and determination to the message. Significantly, the pronoun *YOU*, which is slightly bigger than the rest of the caption, has been highlighted in red to attract the viewer's special attention.

The message is very clear. Anyone who sees and reads this poster should immediately join the army.

Writing skills

SF 25 Essentials: the stages of writing

A well-structured text makes it easy for your reader to follow your line of thought and to understand your text. The structure you use will depend on the kind of text you are writing. There are some rules which apply to all kinds of texts.

Planning stage

Step 1 **Collecting information and ideas**

- Look at the task and make sure the topic you have to write about is clear.
- Collect ideas by brainstorming and going through class work you have done on the topic.

Step 2 **Deciding on the structure of your text**

- Most texts you produce will follow this general structure:
  1. Introduction – 2. Main part (body) – 3. Conclusion.
- Decide on the order in which to present your ideas in the main part. Often the text type you have to produce will require a specific structure. For example, if you are asked to discuss a statement, you will probably divide up your ideas into pro and con arguments. ► SF 26: Argumentative writing Other possibilities are a chronological order or *problem → cause → solution*. A flow chart may be helpful at this stage.

Step 3 **Outlining your text / Structuring your ideas**

- Make an outline of your text (cf. the box on the right). All the 'main ideas' are of equal importance, as are the 'important facts', etc.
- Add the ideas you have collected to your outline. Use keywords.
- Before you start writing notes or the final text, review your outline. Make sure that your main part follows a logical structure.

OUTLINE

1. Introduction
2. Main part (body)
   I. Main idea 1
      A. Important fact
         1. Supporting fact
         2. Supporting fact
            a. Example or detail
            b. Example or detail
      B. Important fact
   ...
   II. Main idea 2
   ...
3. Conclusion

Info

Outline

The term *outline* is used in two slightly different senses. Here it refers to the structure of a piece of writing in which each new thought or fact is separately written down (German: 'Gliederung', 'Entwurf', 'Konzept'). But it can also be used to mean a kind of summary of the main ideas or facts, without the details (German: 'Kurzfassung', 'Zusammenfassung').

Writing stage

Write out your text.

- Begin a new paragraph for each new event, point, argument or idea.
- Structure your text visually, for example by leaving spaces between your paragraphs.
- Each paragraph should start with a topic sentence stating what the paragraph will be about.
- Use linking words to make the connections between individual ideas clear.

Revision and proofreading stage

Step 1 Checking structure

- Have you included an introduction and a conclusion?
- Have you followed all the rules for a clear text structure? Do the ideas in your text develop from paragraph to paragraph?
- Are your paragraphs organized coherently? Do they include more than one sentence but still focus on one basic thought, argument or idea?

Step 2 Checking style

- Consider whether the sentence structure is clear and simple. If your text consists of a lot of unconnected main clauses only, make it more readable by adding linking words to express logical connections between your ideas.
- Decide if you can cut out any wordiness.
- Make sure you used the right *collocations. If in doubt, look them up in a dictionary.
  ► SF 8: Working with dictionaries
- Check for *repetitions. Substitute words you have used repeatedly with *synonyms. Again, check your dictionary for help.

Step 3 Checking correctness

- Check the content.
- Check the grammar. Use a grammar book if possible.
- Check spelling and punctuation. If you type your text on a computer, you can use the spellchecker. But always double-check its suggestions (with the help of a dictionary) rather than accepting them blindly.
- If you have inserted quotations from other texts, check you have followed the citation rules and quoted correctly. ► SF 14: Quoting from texts

Step 4 Rewriting your text

- If possible, give your text to a classmate to check for mistakes ('peer assessment'). Also ask them to tell you if your ideas are well organized and presented.
  ► SF 15: Assessing yourself and giving feedback
- Based on the Steps 1–3, rewrite your text. Make a clean copy of your work.

Tip

When checking correctness, make sure you check your 'favourite' mistakes first.

Language help

Linking words

Enumeration/Structure
first(ly)/second(ly)/third(ly) • to begin with • to start with • in the first place • next • then • finally • last (but not least) • lastly • to conclude

Addition
furthermore • moreover • in addition (to that) • above all • what is more

Comparison
equally • likewise • similarly • in the same way

Summary/Conclusion
then • all in all • to conclude • to sum up • in summary • in conclusion

Exemplification
namely • for example (e.g.) • for instance • that is to say (i.e.)

Reasoning
that is why • because • one reason for this is that ...

Result
consequently • as a consequence • therefore • thus • after all • as a result • this leads to ... • this results in ...

Reformulation
or rather • to put it another way • in other words

Alternatively
on the one hand, ... on the other hand, ... • either ... or ... • neither ... nor ...

Contrast
on the contrary • in contrast to ... • unlike ...

Concession
however • nevertheless • still • though • in spite of that • despite that

SF 26 Argumentative writing: discussion and comment

The main purpose of an *argumentative text is to get a certain perspective of an issue across, i.e. the writer tries to convince the reader of his or her opinion on a topic with the help of arguments. He or she uses quotations from experts as well as figures and statistics to support his or her view. Usually argumentative texts are divided into three parts: an introduction, the middle part with the development of the writer's arguments and a conclusion which again states the central arguments for the writer's opinion.

When writing an argumentative text, you need to structure your text clearly and argue logically to get your message across. The starting point for an argumentative text can be a statement, a text you have read or a *thesis you have been given.

- In a written **discussion** ('Operator': *discuss*), you give arguments for and against something, weigh them up and come to a well-argued conclusion.
- In a ***comment** ('Operator': *comment on / write a comment*), you want to convince the reader of your own opinion on an issue. You have to give arguments to support it and may even introduce counterarguments which you refute to make your own arguments even stronger.

Planning stage

Step 1 Understanding the task and brainstorming

- Make sure you understand the task.
- Are you supposed to
  - weigh up arguments (i.e. write a discussion)?
  - defend your own position (i.e. write a comment)?
- Brainstorm your topic and take notes of your first ideas.

Step 2 Collecting arguments

- [For a written discussion:] Collect arguments both in favour and against the thesis and note them down. Consider: What is your position on the topic/thesis?
- [For a comment:] Collect arguments in favour of your position and counterarguments you want to refute.

Step 3 Deciding on your line of argument and arranging arguments

- Decide if you are in favour of the thesis or against it.
- Then arrange your arguments in a way that will support your point of view. It is useful to follow one of these two patterns:

Pattern A	Pattern B
Present the arguments for and against in separate paragraphs: 1 Introduction 2 Arguments pro 3 Arguments con 4 Conclusion	Answer each argument immediately with its counterargument: 1 Introduction 2 Argument 1 > counterargument 1 3 Argument 2 > counterargument 2 4 Argument 3 > counterargument 3 5 Conclusion

Writing stage

Step 1 Introduction

- Write your introduction.
- Refer to the topic or thesis given. Introduce the topic in general and then narrow it down to the thesis to be discussed or commented on.
- Do **not** write 'In the following I am going to comment on ...'.

Step 2 Main part (arguments)

- Present your line of argument, following either pattern A or B (see above).
- Present your arguments in separate paragraphs (one argument = one paragraph).
- Structure your paragraphs clearly to guide the reader through your text.
- Connect the arguments coherently with linking words.

Step 3 Conclusion

- Round off your text with a conclusion in which you state your thesis once again.
- Do not give new information, and do not use the same phrases as in the introduction.
- If appropriate, outline consequences or future outlooks concerning the topic.

Tips

Arranging arguments

- It is usually a good idea to finish with the argument that supports your position most strongly because this is the one the reader will remember most.
- Sometimes, however, it may be helpful not to postpone your strongest argument until the very end, because you want to catch the reader's attention immediately.

Making your arguments more convincing

- Quote authorities, experts or statistics.
- Present facts.
- Refer to your personal experience whenever possible.

Language help

Argumentative writing

Presenting arguments

- One of the main reasons why ...
- It is often said that ...
- Some people think ...
- In addition to these points, ...

Ordering arguments

- To start with, ...
- First of all, ...
- Firstly/Secondly/Thirdly, ...
- Finally, ...

Contrasting arguments

- On the one hand, ... on the other hand, ...
- Contrary to what most people believe, ...
- ... while/although ...
- However, ...
- But it cannot be overlooked that ...

Giving examples

- This becomes clear when you look at ...
- For example, / For instance, ...
- ... can serve as an example ... / ... is an example of ...
- A good example to illustrate/prove this is ...

Summing up arguments:

- In conclusion, ...
- All in all, ...
- To sum up, ...
- Looking at the given arguments, ...

Explaining your conclusion

- [comment:] After looking into the matter in detail, ...
- [discussion:] After looking at both sides of the matter, ...
- Personally, I believe that ...
- It has been shown that ...

SF 27 Writing a blog post

Writing or mediation tasks often ask you to write a blog post, or blog entry. This is an online diary or informational website to showcase aspects of the blogger's life and/or attitudes.

Blog posts have a range of formats and may resemble an *article ► SF 30, a review ► SF 28 or a short, direct and conversational response to a point of view or an event. ► SF 35 They are always written with a specific audience in mind, normally in an *informal style unless the expected readership is more intellectual. Even if the post is informal, it must not contain *slang, offensive terms or incorrect information.

A typical blog post consists of:
- a catchy headline
- an introduction ('lead') which captivates the reader and explains why he/she should read on
- a main part divided into short paragraphs, ideally with subheadings
- a conclusion which relates to the headline and includes a call to action or invites a response to the points the blogger made
- a timestamp/date indicating when the blog post was published.

Additionally, it could include:
- pictures and illustrations that catch the reader's attention
- tags or hashtags which cross-reference other content that addresses the topic of the post.

Planning stage

Read the task carefully.
- Who is the blog post aimed at? The target group determines the *style and structure of the blog entry.
- What are you going to write about?
- Do you want to post an idea or a topic, start a discussion or contradict somebody else's viewpoint?
- Is it a 'How to ...' guide?

Writing stage

Step 1 Headline

- The headline should not be too long (as with real blog posts, it must fit on the screen).
- It should relate to the main topic of your post.
- It should attract the reader's attention, e.g.:
  - by giving numbers or lists *(Four ways to ..., The ten most important reasons for ...)*
  - by asking a provocative question *(Do you really believe in ...?)*
  - by giving good advice *(How to ...)*

Tip

Some *authors recommend writing the headline last in any kind of text because then they can best assess how to appeal to their readers.

Step 2 Introduction

- Write a captivating introduction.
- Mention the most important, attention-grabbing elements of your post in the first paragraph, e.g.:
  - how you came across the topic of your blog post
  - why it is so important
  - answers to the five *wh*-questions of a story you are going to tell.

Step 3 Main part (body)

- Divide your main part into paragraphs.
- Introduce each paragraph with a topic sentence or highlight the main points of your topic.
- Use subheadings to add structure to your blog post.
- You may add pictures/illustrations, but remember to name your sources.

Step 4 **Conclusion**

- Do not repeat everything you mentioned in the main part.
- Try to make a connection to the question or thesis you stated in the headline or introduction.
- Bloggers often include a call to action (e.g. *Why don't you …?, For more information, go to the LINK!*) or invite further comments or responses from their readers.

SF 28 Writing a review

When writing a review, you provide information on a book, film or *play you have read or watched, as well as expressing your opinion about it. Reviews are intended either to recommend the work in question or to discourage people from reading or watching it.

Planning stage

Step 1 **Reading, watching or listening to the work**
Read the book (*novel, *biography, travel book, etc.) or watch the film/play you want to write about more than once.

Step 2 **Making notes of relevant aspects**

- Outline the *plot.
- Make notes of interesting, very good or very bad aspects.
- Consider typical elements of the *text type in question.

Step 3 **Noting down basic information**
Write down important information about the book or film, e.g.:

- title of book/film/play that is being reviewed
- number of pages / running time
- your rating
- year of publication / release date
- author's / director's name.

Writing stage

Step 1 **Introduction**

- Give your review a catchy title which contains basic facts.
- Start with an introductory paragraph with basic information:
  - type of book/film/play
  - *characters
  - your first reaction.

Step 2 **Main part (body)**

- First give a short summary of the plot. Be careful not to give away the ending. It could spoil somebody else's pleasure in reading or watching it.
- Comment on the cast/characters.
- Then give your opinion on positive or negative aspects of the book/film/play, e.g. on the plot, characters, *actors, *dialogues, special effects, the 'message'.

Step 3 **Conclusion**

- Finish your review by summarizing the main aspects.
- Give a recommendation as to whether or not the book/film/play is worth reading/watching.
- Say for which target group you would recommend the book/film/play.

Tips

Writing a review
- Use the present tense.
- Avoid imprecise words like *good, really bad,* etc.

SF 29 Writing a character profile

Characters in *fictional texts are presented through descriptions by the *narrator or other characters (*direct characterization) and through their appearance, language, attitude, behaviour, relationships to other characters, and by their thoughts and actions (*indirect characterization).

Planning stage

Step 1 Collecting information about the character and their role in the story
Collect relevant passages in the text and make notes on the following aspects:
- What general information do we get about the character you are dealing with (name, outward appearance, social background, etc.)?
- What role does the character play in the story?
- What does the character say and do?
- What do other characters or the narrator say about the character?
- What does the character say about him/herself?
- Give details about the character, e.g. character traits, ambitions, aims, problems, inner *conflicts, etc.

Step 2 Analysing the character
- From your notes, draw conclusions about the character.
- Explain what the character's behaviour, thoughts and actions reveal about him/her. Why does the character act/react in this way?
- Always note down examples from the text (with line references) to give evidence on what you have concluded. ► SF 14: Quoting from texts

Writing stage

Step 1 Introduction
The introduction should include names, general information, the role the character plays in the story, etc.

Step 2 Main part (body)
The main part should include details about the character, e.g. character traits, ambitions, aims, problems, inner conflicts, etc.

Step 3 Conclusion
The conclusion (should summarize why the character acts/reacts the way he/she does).

Tips

Giving a characterization
- Do not describe what the character does, but explain why he/she says or does.
- Use the present tense.
- Support your findings using quotes from the text. ► SF 14: Quoting from texts

Language help

Giving a characterization
- X appears to be ... is portrayed as ...
- This behaviour shows/indicates ...
- Evidence for this can be found in *lines ...
- The way he/she talks implies that ...
- His/Her ... shows ...
- This proves that ... is someone who can be considered courageous/optimistic/trustworthy/unreliable/disloyal/...

SF 30 Writing an (online) article

An article is a text about current events or about a specific topic of general interest published in print (in a newspaper or magazine) or online (e.g. in an online paper or magazine or a blog). There are three types of articles: *news reports ► SF 31: Writing a report, feature articles and *leading articles (also called editorials).
► SF 26: Argumentative writing

- **News articles/reports** should be objective and unbiased and answer the five *wh*-questions (Who? What? When? Where? Why? And, if possible, How did it happen? What are the consequences?). Sources or people are often quoted.
- **Feature articles** put special emphasis on background information and try to give more (emotional) depth to topical events, people or issues. They are often written in a more narrative style and can also be human-interest stories.
- **Leading articles or editorials** (comparable to comments) express the writer's opinion on a particular topic.

Planning stage

Step 1 Identifying your readership and the kind of article you need to write
- Who is your target audience (e.g. schoolmates in a school magazine, young people in an online blog, people from your area in your regional newspaper)?
- What style/*register is appropriate for your target audience?
- What type of article should you write (e.g. are you reporting on an event, should you write a lively *feature story, or are you asked and allowed to express your opinion in an editorial)?
- Is there a word limit?

Step 2 Researching your topic
- Make sure you can answer all the *wh*-questions.
- Try to find examples, good quotes and anecdotes about the event or people you want to write about that will help you make your point more clearly.
- You could also look for extras such as illustrations, statistics or photos and add them if possible and appropriate.

Writing stage

Step 1 Headline
- A good headline should be short, but not too general. It does not have to be a full sentence.
- Often a question is more provocative because the reader then wants to know the answer.
- You can also add a subheading with additional information.

Step 2 **Introduction and main part (body)**

- It can be helpful to arrange your ideas in an outline.
- The first sentence or paragraph ('the lead') of a news article gives an overview of the event or story. In the introduction, you need to keep the reader's attention by presenting the most important or most exciting facts so that he/she wants to know and read more.
- After the introductory paragraph, the body of the news article usually gives the most important information first, followed by more minor facts and details. This structure is called the inverted pyramid.
- For each new idea or argument (but not for each sentence) start a new paragraph. Present your ideas/arguments in a coherent order.

Step 3 **Conclusion**

A good article stays in the reader's mind and makes him/her think.

- The last paragraph should therefore contain something that the reader will remember.
- If you asked a question at the beginning, you could come back to it.
- If you want to appeal to your readership, you could end your leading article with a call to action, a *rhetorical question or a quote.

Tip

Byline

Don't forget to include a *byline with the author's name at the beginning or end of the article.

SF 31 Writing a report

Reports offer factual information about a recent event. The information is given in chronological order and the language used is objective and *formal.

The following instructions will guide you through the steps of writing a report.

Planning stage

Step 1 **Gathering information**

- Gather as much information about the event as possible.
- Try to answer the five *wh*-questions:
  - Who [was involved]?
  - What [happened]?
  - When [did it happen]?
  - Where [did it happen]?
  - Why [did it happen]?

  and sometimes also:
  - How [did it happen]?
  - What is the consequence?
- If your report is based on a fictitious event (e.g. from a novel or play), you might need to add missing details such as last names, place names or dates.

Step 2 **Ordering the information**

Put the information in chronological order. If necessary, add further details.

Writing stage

- Start off with a summarizing sentence.
- Divide your report into paragraphs.
- Use the past tense.
- Use linking words to connect your ideas.
- Make your report sound formal and matter-of-fact by using objective language and the passive voice where possible.
- Do not state personal thoughts, feelings or opinions. Focus on the facts.
- Include quotes or witness statements as evidence. ▸ SF 14: Quoting from texts
- If possible, add a picture/photo with a caption so that the reader can visualize what happened and who was involved.

Language help

Writing a report

- On ..., an incident was reported to the police.
- It is believed/assumed that ...
- ... confirmed/claimed/revealed that ...
- People are concerned about ... / that ...

SF 32 Writing a summary or an outline

When you work with a written or spoken text, you are often asked to write a summary or an outline of the text. While a summary presents (all) the main information from the text in a condensed form, an outline includes only specific information or certain aspects, usually from a complex text. For example, you might be given one of these two tasks on a newspaper article about climate change:

- **Summarize** the article.
  OR
- **Outline** the effects of climate change on biodiversity in Northern Europe as described in the article.

To write a summary or to outline information, you need a good overview of the original text, its content and message. Then you have to decide what to include and what to leave out. The following steps can guide you.

Planning stage

Step 1 Skimming or scanning

Read the task carefully so that you know what is expected of you. Then read or listen to the complete text.

- For a **summary:** Take notes or mark the most important words and phrases or sections of the text. Find out which text type you are dealing with, e.g. a *non-fictional text or a fictional text. ▸ SF 17–20
- For an **outline:** Scan the text (or listen out) for the aspect(s) you are asked to include. Mark this information in the text or take notes.

If you have to write a summary, read or listen to the text again and continue with these steps:

Step 2 Answering the five *wh*-questions

- Try to answer the five *wh*-questions (Who? What? When? Where? Why? And, if possible, How did it happen? What are the consequences?).

Step 3 **Distinguishing essential and non-essential information**
- Decide which passages of the text contain essential information that needs to be part of your summary and which passages can be left out.
- Do not include examples, numbers, comparisons, quotes, *imagery, *direct speech, etc. in a summary.

Writing stage

Step 1 **Putting the key points in your own words**
- Write an introductory phrase, mentioning the title, author, source of the text as well as the topic and (for a summary) the main message.
- Do not copy from the original text. Remember to use your own words.
- Do not state your own opinion on the matter.
- Use the present tense.
- Use linking words to connect your ideas.

Step 2 **Checking your summary or outline**
- Does your summary contain the most important facts and ideas from the original text?
- Does your outline focus on the aspects in the text as specified in the task?
- Have you left out examples, unnecessary details, etc.?

Tips

Writing a summary or an outline
- Your summary should be (much) shorter than the original text. Sometimes a maximum number of words is given in the task.
- You do not have to follow exactly the same order as in the original text. Rearrange your points so that your summary is logical.
- As an outline only focuses on certain aspects of the text, it is usually shorter than a summary.

Language help

Summing up
- The story/article is about ...
- The story takes place in ... (**Not:** The story ~~plays in~~ ...)
- The film deals with ...
- In the podcast the reader gets to know ...
- The topic of the *essay is ...
- The article shows ...
- The author writes/says/states/argues that ...

SF 33 Writing a formal letter or email

When applying for a place at university, asking for information from a company or organization, etc., your *letter or email should follow certain formal rules.

Writing a formal letter

Mecklenburgische Str. 53 14197 Berlin Germany Tel +491234567890 lea.sindern@xxxx.com	Write your contact information – your address (without your name), your phone number and your email address – in the top right corner of your letter. Do not use typical German letters like *ä, ö, ü* or *ß*.
Joanne Sutton 14 Springfield Place Chelmsford CM2 7ZA United Kingdom Ref. No.: 315/14	Write the address of the person or company you are writing to on the left. If you have a reference number, write it below the recipient's address.
3 February 2022	Write the date on the right.
Application for an internship	State the subject of the letter.
Dear Mrs Sutton	Start your letter with *Dear Mr/Mrs/Ms ...* (Remember to use dots after Mr./Mrs./Ms. in American English). *Dear* is used for both German 'Liebe(r)' and 'Sehr geehrte(r)'. If you do not know the recipient's name, write *Dear Sir or Madam* or *Dear Sir/Madam*. In British English, there is usually no comma after the greeting; in American English a colon after the greeting is used in formal letters.
I am writing to apply for an internship at the National Gallery. I will be finishing school in July 2022, with A-levels in English, Art, History and Maths. As I have always had a particular interest in art and history, I would like to get a deeper insight into work in this field before I start my university course in art history at the University of Cologne in October 2022. As your website specifies that short-term internships are possible, I would be delighted to be given a chance to work at the National Gallery.	Always start with a capital letter (e.g. *With great interest, I read ...*). State the reason you are writing in the opening paragraph.
I enclose a copy of my CV, which shows that I have some experience of running educational classes and of working as a tour guide at a local museum in Berlin. I have also had the opportunity to take part in several art classes. As I speak English and German, I would also be able to deal with international visitors.	Add more detailed information in the following paragraphs (reasons for applying, qualifications, why you are the right person for the position, etc.).
I would welcome the opportunity of enhancing my experience. As I am reliable, willing to learn and enthusiastic, I would certainly be a helpful addition to the National Gallery.	Use long forms (*I am / We are / I would*) rather than short forms (*I'm / We're / I'd*) and abbreviations.
Thank you for considering my application. I look forward to hearing from you soon.	If you are asking for information or a favour, thank the recipient in advance.
Yours sincerely	Finish your letter with *Yours sincerely* (AE: *Sincerely, Sincerely yours* or *Yours truly*). If you do not know the recipient's name, write *Yours faithfully*.
Lea Sindern Lea Sindern	Type your name at the end of the letter, leaving space for a handwritten signature.

Writing a formal email

- You do not need to include the recipient's address or the date in the main part of your email, as they appear automatically in the header.
- Open and close your mail the same way you would when writing a formal letter.
- Do not use emoticons, smileys, etc.
- Type your name and contact details (the email signature) at the bottom.

SF 34 Writing an application: cover letter and CV

If you want to apply for a holiday job or a position in a company (e.g. an internship), you should send a cover letter and a CV (curriculum vitae).

The cover letter

The cover letter for an application follows the rules of a formal letter. ► SF 33: Writing a formal letter or email
Since you are presenting yourself, it is important to avoid mistakes and to use formal language. State in what ways you are suited for the position you are applying for. Show that you have collected information about the company you are applying to and that you have a real interest in the position advertised. Mention what documents you are enclosing. At the end of the letter, express hope for a reply or an invitation to an interview.

The CV (American English: **résumé** ['rezəmeɪ])

Your CV gives information about you, about your education, qualifications, etc. to the person you are applying to. A CV should be clear and effective – remember the KISS rule ('Keep it short and simple'). Use a clear and easy-to-read font, highlight particularly relevant information, and do not forget to check your CV for spelling mistakes.

CURRICULUM VITAE
Lukas Meister

Mecklenburgische Str. 53, 14197 Berlin, Germany
Telephone: +491234567890 Mobile: +491234567890
Email: Lukasmeister@mail.de

→ Give your personal details: name, contact details, nationality, etc.

Personal statement
I have always enjoyed working with visual media and with computers. Being creative, I enjoy developing ideas to solve problems. English is my favourite subject at school, and I expect to improve my language skills further and to become a more independent person by spending time in the UK.

→ Add a personal statement explaining why you are suitable for the specific place or job.

Work experience
May 2020 Placement: two weeks at local IT company

→ Give information on any work experience.

Education		Show the stages of your education so far (schools, exams, etc.).
2016–date	Secondary/High School: Alfred-Krupp-Schule, Berlin	
2012–2016	Primary/Elementary School Gartenstrasse, Essen	
Qualifications/skills		List your qualifications and present your key skills, especially those the employer is looking for.
IT skills	Excellent knowledge of MS Word, PowerPoint, Excel, web design, Photoshop	
Language skills	German native speaker; good written and spoken English, basic French	
Technology	Winner of the gold medal 2019 for 'school inventors' in the 'Junior Ingenieur Akademie' (school engineering course)	
Hobbies and interests		Write something about your hobbies or interests.
Member of school drama club, member of school computer club, member of after-school basketball club. I enjoy listening to and playing music and making films.		
References		Add that references are available on request.
Available on request		

SF 35 Writing a letter to the editor

Newspapers often have a special section for *letters to the editor ('Leserbriefe'). Those on particularly interesting and controversial topics are printed there.

In a letter to the editor, a reader reacts to a *newspaper article and expresses his or her own opinion about it. The reader may agree with the author's opinion or hold a different opinion. He or she can therefore criticize, praise, comment on, add to or correct aspects with which he or she agrees or disagrees. Letters to the editor have a similar structure to other persuasive forms of writing, like written comments. The intention of the writer of a letter to the editor is that it should be published in the newspaper.

Info

Editor

The editor is a person in charge of a newspaper (department) who decides what should be published. Editors also write articles, but usually articles are written by authors and edited by editors.

Writing stage

A letter to the editor follows most of the conventions of a formal letter or email. ► SF 33: Writing a formal letter or email

Note the following, however:
- Nowadays, letters to the editor are very often sent by email. Watch out for contact information on the magazine's or newspaper's website.
- Your letter should be brief and to the point.
- Start like this: *Sir or Madam* (leave out *Dear*).
- Refer to the article (give title, date and main topic).
- Omit the closing remarks *(Yours faithfully/sincerely)*.
- End with your name and (postal or email) address.

The main part of a letter to the editor is structured like a comment. ► SF 26: Argumentative writing
However, in a letter to the editor, you limit yourself to the arguments that support your point of view.

Language help

Writing a letter to the editor
- I refer to your article '...' about ... published on ... 2022.
- I am writing to you after reading the article '...' about ...
- I am writing to you in response to the article '...' about ...
- I support / agree with / disagree with the author's opinion on ...
- I disagree with this idea / the idea of ...
- I approve the author's belief in ...
- I do not think that the author understands ...
- In my opinion, it is essential to consider/include the perspective of ...

SF 36 Creative writing

Most creative writing tasks ask you to write ('create') a text based on an existing piece of writing ('material-based writing'). You may have to rewrite part of a story (possibly from a different perspective) or create something new, such as a letter, that is only mentioned in the original text.

Type 1 Continuation of a story

When dealing with fictional texts, a common creative task might be to write an ending to a story.

Planning stage

Step 1 **Reread the original text**
Look at the *setting, events, dates, characters and their relationships in the original text and watch out for hints as to how the story might continue. Make notes.

Step 2 **Check your ideas against the original text**
Brainstorm ideas for a continuation and compare them to the original extract to make sure they do not contradict the reality depicted in the story.

Step 3 **Analyse the narrative perspective of the original text**
Identify the *narrative perspective of the original text (e.g. *first-person narrator) and consider what limitations that specific perspective might have or not have.

Writing stage
Create a new text that corresponds to the original. Try to imitate the style and language used in the original.

Type 2 Change of perspective

A change of perspective means that you take over the view of one of the characters in the story from whose perspective the story is not told. You retell and evaluate ('re-create') the events from this person's point of view, e.g. in a diary entry, a letter or an *interior monologue.

In the case of a non-fictional text (e.g. a *speech or newspaper article), you usually have to evaluate a situation through the eyes of a fictitious character. You might, for example, be asked to read a text on a climate conference and then write an article from the perspective of a reporter who attended the conference.

Example: Writing a diary entry
You may be asked to write a diary entry from the perspective of a literary character.

Planning stage
- Look at the original text and ask yourself what this character thinks, feels, hopes, expects and/or fears in various situations and also what your character knows and does not know.
- Think about a *theme or question that is important to this character. The diary entry should focus on the character's experiences as described in the text.
- Think about what might have led to your character's current situation and/or what you expect to happen next.

Writing stage
- The style of a diary entry is usually informal and it is arranged in chronological order.
- Make it clear at what time, where, in what situation and why you are writing.
- A diary entry usually contains opinions and chit-chat as well as facts. It must not only refer to events but also comment on and evaluate them.
- The diary entry should be written to match the character's personality and language. Age, social status and other features usually determine how someone speaks or writes.

Tips

The difference between a diary entry and an interior monologue
- An evaluation in a diary entry looks back on events and is made in retrospect.
- An interior monologue represents the thoughts and feelings going through a character's mind. It should therefore be conceived as an immediate reaction to the events in the text extract.
- Interior monologues are normally narrated in the present tense.

Type 3 Writing a film script (screenplay)

You may be asked to write the text for a film, including instructions for the actors and directions for filming. A film script has a standard format that is functional rather than attractive to read.

Step 1 **Slug line**

At the start of each *scene there is a line of text (the so-called slug line) that indicates:
- whether the scene takes place inside or outside (INT. = interior / EXT. = exterior, outside)
- the exact location
- the time of day
- the type of camera shot.

Step 2 **Screen directions and dialogue**

The slug line is followed by:
- the screen directions (describing the *action, location and objects in the scene as well as the characters)
- the dialogue, i.e. the words the characters speak.

As a rule, the present tense is used for the screen directions, similar to a picture description. The dialogue is usually written in a centre column.

Example:

INT. ARYANE'S FLAT – MIDNIGHT – CLOSE-UP
The two large profiles fill the screen. Aryane kisses the boy firmly, but not passionately. Then her phone rings ...

ARYANE (softly)
Are you feeling better?

GREG (seen from the back, barely audible)
Hmmm ... a little.

You may also be asked to turn a *short story or a key scene from a novel into a film script. In this case, you need to consider which aspects of the original text can be represented in the film and how, and which details can be omitted without changing the message of the text.

Tips

Creative writing

- In a material-based creative writing task, you have to work on and with the original text. Do not move too far away from it, or your own text may become illogical or contradict the events of the original story.
- Think of your task as 'reading between the lines' rather than inventing completely new scenes, etc.
- Pay attention to the text type you are using. If you write a diary entry, you should focus on thoughts and feelings. If you write a letter, you must address the addressee and sign it. ► SF 33: Writing a formal letter or email If you write dialogues, you should use typical elements of spoken language.

Listening and viewing skills

SF 37 Essentials: listening and viewing

The ability to understand spoken English is key to speaking it. Below are some of the challenges of listening and viewing.

- In real-life situations, e.g. in conversations, you can usually listen to or look at what you hear or see only once. This is fundamentally different from reading where you can reread the words as many times as you like or feel necessary, e.g. when you get distracted or interrupted.
- When listening or watching, you need to decode both verbal and non-verbal messages, such as *intonation, tone of voice, *pitch, tempo, volume, facial expression and posture. These help you to identify the *speaker's attitude or intentions.
- People speak differently than they write. Many have accents and/or speak too fast, loudly, softly or even very informally. There may also be background noise that makes listening difficult.

There are different listening and viewing skills to be applied depending on the situation or task.

- **Listening/Viewing for gist** enables you to get a general idea of the content or main topic.
- **Listening/Viewing for detail** is necessary if you need to collect information about certain aspects of a spoken text. In exams, you may have to listen/view for specific information.
- **Listening/Viewing and making deductions** is drawing conclusions about the meaning or the speaker's intentions based on the information you hear or see.

A listening or viewing task may be based on a short audio (e.g. an interview, a *speech) or video (e.g. an interview, a documentary, a film clip). Listening tasks often focus on 'Anforderungsbereich I', i.e. text comprehension, and use closed test formats such as multiple choice. Viewing tasks, but also some listening tasks, go beyond simple comprehension and require you to analyse the video or audio more fully. Therefore, make sure you are familiar with the aspects to be tested. ▶ SF 2–3

Tips

Listening and viewing strategies

Pre-listening/Pre-viewing

- Read the instructions carefully and make sure you know what to focus on.
- Examine the background information.
- Make predictions about the audio/video and the answers to the questions.

While-listening/While-viewing

- Read all the answers, even if you are sure that you have found the correct one. The differences between the right and the wrong answers are often subtle or tricky.
- If you take notes, only jot down keywords or short phrases.
- If the task is to write a text, note down phrases from the audio/video to use as quotes.
- For viewing tasks, it may be helpful to work with a film diary (viewing log) in which you record the action or individual important scenes as well as your reaction to them.

SF 38 Listening/Viewing for gist and detail

Listening or viewing for gist is when you try to understand what is happening, even if you do not (need to) understand every phrase or sentence. Instead, you try to pick up keywords, intonation and other clues that help you to work out the general meaning.

Listening or viewing for detail is when you listen/watch out for specific aspects or pieces of information to complete a task.

Listening/Viewing for gist

Step 1 **Pre-listening/Pre-Viewing**
Read the task(s) carefully. If possible, collect information on the following:
- the *text type (e.g. podcast, panel discussion, interview, webinar, *feature film) and its addressee(s)
- the situation and *setting
- the number of speakers and their role, e.g. will there be conflicting points of view?
- the topic dealt with and what *points of view or concepts you are likely to encounter.

Try to predict what the listening/viewing will be about and what the speaker(s) might say.

Step 2 **While-listening/While-viewing**
- Identify the topic / main idea / main point of the text. Ask yourself: What do the speakers talk/think about ...?
- Do not try to understand every detail that is said or shown.
- Listen out for 'signpost expressions' that show somebody's train of thought, e.g. *the biggest issue is ..., the most important argument is ..., on the one hand ...*
- Remember to take notes on key points.

Listening/Viewing for detail

Step 1 **Pre-listening/Pre-viewing**
- Examine what you know about the audio/video (its speaker(s), addressee(s), situation, setting and/or topic).
- Try to anticipate what might be said/shown in the audio/video.
- Collect keywords that are relevant to your task, e.g. names, dates or numbers.
- Prepare so that you can take notes quickly.

Step 2 **While-listening/While-viewing**
- Listen/Watch out for the aspects you collected.
- Take notes, using abbreviations and symbols.

Tip

Using the breaks between listening/viewing times
- After the first (or second) listening/viewing, look at your notes and work on the task(s).
- After the second (and/or third) listening/viewing, complete your task(s) and check your answers.

SF 39 Analysing films and videos

Watching a film or video can make you laugh or cry, feel angry or scared. Such reactions are not only caused by the story itself but also by the way the film tells it. Just as written texts can provoke a reaction in their readers through the choice of words and *stylistic devices, films can achieve similar responses in their viewers through, for example, the camera work, lighting, sound and editing.

Step 1 **Pre-viewing**
- Find out what film or video you are going to watch and get an idea of what to expect by looking at any available information, e.g. film posters, reviews, Blu-ray covers, magazine information.
- Identify the genre: Is it a documentary, a feature film such as a thriller, a science-fiction/sci-fi movie, a *comedy or a drama? Is it a news clip, a music video or a *commercial?

Step 2 **While-viewing**
Make notes on the story (setting, location, *plot) and the cast (*actors).

Step 3 **Analysing cinematic devices and their effect**
Watch once more and have a closer look at the cinematic devices used (such as camera work, lighting and sound) and the effect they achieve. You will find details and useful terms below.

Camera range ('Einstellungsgröße')

long shot ('Totale', 'Gesamtaufnahme')
a view of a situation from a distance
establishing shot ('Eröffnungsszene')
a long shot at the beginning of a *scene (or a sequence), often an **aerial shot** ('Luftaufnahme')
Long shots give an overall impression of the setting.

medium shot ('Halbnahe', 'Halbnahaufnahme')
a shot which shows one or two people from the waist up
This allows the viewer to get an idea of the interaction between the *characters.

close-up ('Nahaufnahme', 'Großaufnahme')
a full screen shot of one person's face or one object
This allows the viewer to see clearly the emotions a character is experiencing or to consider the role of the object that is shown.

Camera angle ('Kameraperspektive)

low-angle shot ('Froschperspektive')
a shot which looks up at the subject (a person, a building, etc.) from below eye level
The character appears to be bigger than others in the scene, thus seeming powerful, dominant or dangerous.

high-angle shot ('Vogelperspektive')
a shot which looks down on the subject (a person, a building, etc.) from above eye level
The character appears to be smaller than others in the scene, thus seeming vulnerable, inferior or frightened.

eye-level shot ('Normalsicht')
a shot which is taken with the camera approximately at human eye level
This has a 'neutral' effect and gives the viewer the feeling of actually being in the scene.

over-the-shoulder shot ('Über-die-Schulter')
a shot of one character over the shoulder of another
In this shot, the viewer sees a character's point of view. It is useful for showing reactions during conversations.

Camera movement ('Kamerabewegung')

pan shot ('Schwenk')
a shot where the camera moves horizontally (pans) – left to right or right to left – from a static position

tilt shot ('vertikaler Schwenk')
a shot where the camera moves up or down (tilts) from a static position

tracking shot ('Kamerafahrt', 'Mitschwenk')
a shot where the camera moves along tracks beside, behind or in front of a moving person or object

zoom ('Zoom')
a shot from a stationary camera in which the lens achieves the effect of moving towards the subject (zoom-in, 'Ranfahrt') or away from the subject (zoom-out, 'Wegfahrt')

Editing ('Filmschnitt')
Film editing is the technique, practice and art of assembling shots into a coherent sequence.

cut ('Schnitt')
the point at which one shot changes (cuts) directly to another

cross-cutting ('Kreuzschnitt', 'Parallelmontage')
cutting separate actions together to illustrate moments that take place simultaneously

jump cut ('harter Schnitt', 'diskontinuierlicher Schnitt')
an abrupt and unexpected cut from one shot to another where, for example, an element of time or space has been left out

fade-in/fade-out ('Aufblende'/'Abblende', 'Ausblende')
the gradual appearance or disappearance of a shot – usually at the beginning or end of a scene

(cross-)fading ('Überblendung')
fading in (one sound or picture source) as another is being faded out

Lighting ('Beleuchtung[sstil]', 'Lichtgestaltung')

high-key lighting ('High-Key-Beleuchtung[sstil]')
a style of lighting that emphasizes bright and soft lighting with few shadows to create a friendly atmosphere

low-key lighting ('Low-Key-Beleuchtung[sstil]')
a style of lighting where a scene is dominated by shadow, and light is used without producing great contrast

high-contrast lighting ('kontrastreiche Beleuchtung', 'starkes Kontrastlicht')
a style of lighting that results in dark shadows and bright highlights to create eye-catching shots

Sound ('Ton')

soundtrack ('Ton[spur]', 'Filmmusik')
all the sounds, speech and music recorded for a film

on-screen sound ('On-Ton')
sounds, speech or music whose source can be seen in the shot

off-screen sound ('Off-Ton')
sounds, speech or music whose source is not visible in the shot and only the viewers can hear it

voice-over ['– –] ('Begleitkommentar', 'Offkommentar')
a spoken commentary while other sounds including voices of the characters continue, often used to convey a character's thoughts or memories

Tip

Viewing log

A viewing log can help you structure your notes. Here is one example. You may choose other categories (e.g. *images, *dialogue, costumes, mood, *characterization, plot) to serve your own purposes.

Scene (What? Where? Who?)	Camera work + its effect	Lighting + its effect	Sound + its effect	Your reaction
...	...	...	...	...

Language help

Film analysis / Describing cinematic devices

Camera work – static shots

- The director uses a long shot of the scene so the viewer can see the group and the setting ...
- There is a medium shot of the two characters so the viewer can see ...
- The viewer sees the character in close-up / There is a close-up of the character ...
- The establishing shot of the film shows ...
- This scene is shot from X's point of view.
- The director uses a high-angle shot of ... in order to ...
- The camera takes a steady position. As a consequence, the action appears slower.

Camera work – moving shots

- The camera pans from left to right / tilts up/down ...
- We first see X as the camera tilts from ... to ...
- There is a tracking shot in this scene as the camera follows ...
- The camera zooms in on ... in order to show ...
- The camera zooms out to reveal ...

Editing

- The director uses a lot of cuts in this scene ...
- There are short shots and a quick succession of cuts to increase the pace of the action and make it more exciting.
- Cross-cutting is used to show X approaching the house, while Y is still asleep.
- *Flashbacks (showing past events) and flash-forwards (showing future events) are used.
- The scene gradually fades in to show ...
- The director uses a fade-in in order to ...
- The use of cross-fading between these two scenes makes the connection stronger / produces a/an ... effect.

Sound and lighting

- The music intensifies/fades as ... / creates/builds tension/suspense/joy/...
- In this scene, the music and lyrics support the plot / underline the feeling of ...
- The soundtrack is eerie and moves towards a *climax.
- The soundtrack helps to ... / underlines/emphasizes ...
- The soundtrack/lighting/editing establishes/reinforces the mood of the scene.

Speaking skills

SF 40 Essentials: speaking

Speaking is a special skill that is determined by the following factors.

- Speaking occurs 'in real time'. This means you have to react quickly in conversations, discussions or even presentations, especially in the case of mistakes or misunderstandings, but also to make your point.
- Speaking takes place in a particular environment, situation or context, i.e. under varying conditions. You react differently to different partners, you deliver a *speech to a certain target audience, you are emotionally involved in a heated argument, etc.
- Speaking tends to be *informal and conversational in *tone and *style, but may also be *formal, e.g. public speeches or academic presentations. ► SF 41-42
- Speaking also involves non-verbal forms of communication, and good speakers use them effectively to get their point across.
- Every communicative situation consists of different stages, also called speech acts (e.g. starting it, adding to it, interrupting, contradicting, etc.). Being aware of these stages enables you to keep a conversation going and make it more successful.

Step 1 Preparing for a speaking task

- Analyse the situation:
  - Are you talking to your teacher, classmates, a friend, an interviewer, etc.?
  - Are you taking part in a conversation, discussion, an argument, an interview, etc.?

This will help you to adapt your message to your own needs, those of your communication partner(s) or to your target audience.

- Analyse the task:
  - Is it a *monologue or a *dialogue – with one person or more?
  - Do you have to contribute to a discussion, present an idea, describe a photo or a *cartoon, give an oral presentation, etc.?
- Check you have relevant information/arguments/facts about the topic.
- Collect useful words and phrases for the topic and communicative situation in question.

Step 2 Speaking

Successful speaking involves various expressive and receptive skills, often performed spontaneously or simultaneously. To be effective, it requires paying attention to:

- fluency
- vocabulary (including specialist vocabulary for your topic)
- rules of pronunciation
- rules of grammar
- non-verbal communication, e.g. body language, gestures and facial expression
- in some cases: intercultural communication – to avoid (cultural) misunderstandings.

► SF 12: Communicating across cultures

As you speak, react to mistakes or misunderstandings by trying to correct them or by rephrasing what you want to say.

Step 3 **Receiving feedback and acting on it**
Sometimes you will receive feedback from your communication partner(s) or audience on the content of your speech or on your performance. This may be questions, applause, expressions of boredom, etc. Use this feedback to improve your speaking skills.

Tips

Improving your speaking skills
- Study communicative strategies, e.g. how to respond to questions, how to introduce new ideas, how to be persuasive, how to disagree, etc.
- Learn and practise words, phrases and parts of sentences so that you can use them automatically and without thinking when you speak
- Observe other people speaking to learn from their examples.

SF 41 Giving a presentation

Informing an audience about a topic is an important skill to master and one that is useful at school and in later life. To give a successful presentation, these steps can be a helpful guide.

Preparing a presentation

Step 1 **The general framework for your talk**
Find out about:
- the topic of your talk
- the time limit for your presentation
- your audience and their background knowledge of the topic
- the equipment available (smartboard, blackboard, flip chart, digital/video projector, laptop).

Step 2 **Researching your subject** ► SF 13: Doing research
- Collect information from different, reliable sources to ensure you cover all the relevant aspects.
- Decide which information is relevant for your presentation.
- Take notes, preferably in English.
- If you are working in a team, decide who is going to work on which aspect.

Step 3 **Structuring your presentation**
- Work out an outline for your presentation.
- Make notes to guide you through your presentation and help you to speak freely.

For team presentations:
- Decide who is going to present which parts.
- Check that the different parts create a coherent presentation.
- Make sure that everybody takes part in the presentation.

Step 4 **Making your presentation interesting, effective and easy to understand**
- Get off to a good start: refer to interesting facts or tell an anecdote to introduce the topic of your presentation.
- Remember the KISS-rule: **K**eep **i**t **s**hort and **s**imple!

- Keep your audience's attention by giving interesting or funny details or examples.
- Explain any difficult or specialist terms so the audience can follow your presentation.
- Avoid extremely long sentences and too many figures or new words. Remember that your audience can only listen to your presentation once.
- If appropriate, prepare charts, visuals, diagrams, etc. to present facts and figures visually.

Step 5 **Using presentation tools**
- Prepare a handout or poster or use presentation software to accompany your presentation.
- Design such material in a way that helps your audience to follow your presentation.
- Proofread your material.

Step 6 **Practising your presentation**
- Check the pronunciation of difficult words in a print or an online dictionary.
  ► SF 8: Working with dictionaries
- Practise your presentation in front of friends or record it. If you are doing a team presentation, practise as a team.
- Rehearse with any technology you plan to use. Make sure it is working.
- Do not exceed your time limit.

Doing the presentation

Step 1 **Introducing your presentation**
- Wait until the audience is quiet.
- Then greet them and give an overview of your presentation.
- Say that you will take any questions at the end of the presentation.

Step 2 **Giving your presentation**
- Speak clearly, loudly and not too fast. Make suitable pauses.
- Speak freely and do not read out complete sentences.
- Use 'signposting language' so your listeners can follow what you are saying.
- Refer to your handout, poster or slides without reading from them word for word.
- Maintain eye-contact with your audience.
- Write any new or difficult words on the board and explain them to help your audience.

Step 3 **Rounding off your presentation**
- Summarize the most important aspects.
- Thank your audience for their attention.
- Ask them if they have any questions.

Tips

Making and using effective presentation tools

Handout
- Decide if you should distribute it before the presentation so your audience can follow your talk or afterwards as a reminder of the main points.
- Give it a clear structure. A handout should only contain the most relevant points of your presentation. Usually it should not be more than one page.
- Present the most important information, key quotations, diagrams and/or charts on it.
- Use bullet points, short sentences or keywords and try to avoid any redundancies.
- Indicate the sources you used.

Poster

- Give it a clear structure to guide the reader through the various sections.
- Make it visually attractive and informative.
- Present complex information visually, e.g. with diagrams.
- Keep a good balance between visuals and written information.
- Make sure that the writing can be read from the back of the room.
- Use bullet points, short sentences or key words and avoid redundancies.
- Indicate the sources you used.

Presentation software

- Choose the right font and size.
- Use good-quality images.
- Avoid too many special effects.
- Limit the number of slides.
- Limit each slide to one idea and keep text to a minimum (6–8 lines per slide).
- Do not read from your slides and do not 'speak to them'.

Speaking notes

- Do not learn a full script by heart or read from it.
- Write keywords or notes on index cards.
- Number the cards and use them during your presentation.

Language help

Giving a presentation

Introduction

- Hello everybody. My/Our talk today is going to be on ...
- Today I'm going to talk about ...
- The topic/subject of my presentation is ...
- Today I'll be talking about / discussing ...
- First, I will give you a general idea of ... Then I'll go on to ... After that I'll tell you more about ... And, finally, I'll...
- At the end of my talk, I will explain why ... and give you some examples.
- I'll be happy to take any questions at the end of my presentation.

Starting a new section

- Now, let's turn to ...
- I'd now like to talk about ... / to discuss ...
- The next/second ...
- The next issue/topic/area I'd like to focus on is ...

Conclusion

- So, as I have pointed out, ...
- It's important to keep in mind that ...
- That was my presentation on ...
- Thank you for listening. I hope you enjoyed my/our presentation.
- Do you have any questions? / Are there any questions?

SF 42 Preparing and giving a speech

When you give a speech, you want to get and keep your audience's attention as well as convince them of your point of view on a topic. To do so, plan your speech carefully and deliver it effectively.

Preparing a speech

Step 1 Establishing the general framework for your speech
- Determine the topic of your speech.
- Check the time available.
- Be clear on the purpose of your speech, e.g. to inspire people / lead to a specific action / ...
- Find out about your audience and their background knowledge / attitudes.

Step 2 Brainstorming and/or researching your topic
- Collect any ideas, stories or arguments that fit your topic.
- Form your own opinion on it.
- Make notes.

Step 3 Structuring your speech
- Select the ideas that are the most relevant to the topic and message you wish to get across to your audience.
- Take notes and structure them into introduction / main part / conclusion.
- Put the ideas for the main part of your speech in a coherent order.

Step 4 Preparing the presentation of your speech
- Decide whether you want to prepare a speech script. If so, print out your speech in a format that is easy to read (fonts and margins not too small).
- Write keywords or notes on index cards if you plan to speak freely. Number the cards and use them during your speech.
- Mark passages and words that you want to emphasize.

Step 5 Practising your speech
- Read it out loud to check the pronunciation of difficult words.
- Make your speech sound as if you are speaking freely even if you are using a script.
- Practise it in front of friends or record it.
- Make sure you do not exceed the time limit.

Giving the speech

Remember: Giving a speech is not like reading something out (even if you have written it down).
- Wait until the audience are quiet, then greet them and state your topic.
- Develop your ideas step by step.
- Speak as freely as possible and keep your listeners' attention.
- Speak clearly, loudly and not too fast. Pause in suitable places.
- Try to maintain eye-contact with your listeners. Use facial expressions and gestures to emphasize important points.
- Thank your audience for their attention.

Writing a speech script

If you are not a very experienced speaker, it can be helpful to write down your complete speech. Writing a speech script is also a task you might be asked to do in an exam. A speech script is a type of argumentative text that should have an introduction, a main part and a conclusion. ► SF 26: Argumentative writing

Step 1 **Writing out your speech**
- Choose the correct *register for your specific audience, e.g. scientific, informal.
- Use clear and short sentences. Make logical connections clear by using linking words.
- Be persuasive: use *stylistic devices to convince your audience, e.g. *contrasts, *rhetorical questions, *enumerations, *alliterations, *direct address.

Step 2 **Writing the introduction and conclusion**
- Write a conclusion: sum up the main points, give a final effective example supporting your message, further food for thought or an appeal for action.
- When you have prepared most of your speech, think of a good introduction, e.g. a true story, a quotation, a rhetorical question, an interesting statistic or a joke.

SF 43 Taking part in an interview

At school or when applying for a job, you may be asked to take part in interviews, either asking or answering questions. It is essential to prepare for an interview and to follow some general guidelines.

Preparing for an interview
- On the basis of your role card or the task given, prepare questions to ask (as the interviewer) or think of possible answers to questions you might be asked (as the interviewee).
- For job interviews, you need to be prepared to explain why you are suitable for the position. Research the company you are applying to and prepare some relevant questions. It might be useful to rehearse a job interview with a friend or parent.

Mastering the interview
- Smile when saying hello or thanking your interviewer/interviewee at the end.
- Introduce yourselves and the situation.
- Speak loud enough and clearly.
- Be aware of your non-verbal communication. Maintain eye-contact with the interviewer/interviewee.
- Use a *neutral or formal register.

As an **interviewer:**
- Start off by using your prepared questions but be flexible.
- If an interesting aspect comes up, ask new questions.
- If you feel that your question was not answered fully, ask again in other words.

As an **interviewee:**
- Take time to think about your answers so your reply does not show you in a bad light.
- Do not simply answer questions with *yes* or *no,* but use your answers to show your qualifications or to express your thoughts.
- If you have not understood a question fully, ask the interviewer to clarify it.
- Always be polite.

Language help

Interviewing

Interviewer
- Nice to meet you. / Thank you for coming.
- To start off, would you like to say something about ...? / First, let me ask you ...
- My next question would be ...
- If you think so, then why didn't you ...?

- Let's get back to my original question ...
- You just said ..., how does that relate to ...?
- Thank you very much for taking part in this interview.

Interviewee
- Nice to meet you too. / Thank you for inviting me today. / I am fine, thank you.
- I am not sure I have understood your question correctly. / Sorry, could you rephrase that?
- I'm glad you asked that question because ... / ... is very important to me, as ...
- A good example of the aspect you mentioned is ...
- Let me explain that in some more detail.
- Thank you for the chance to speak to you.

SF 44 Having a discussion

In a (classroom) discussion you exchange ideas and opinions with others. Discussions may be spontaneous or more formal, e.g. in panel discussions or debates. ▸ SF 45: Having a debate If possible, you should prepare so that you have your arguments and useful words and phrases ready.

Preparing a discussion

Step 1 Researching the topic and making notes
- Form an opinion on the topic and note down arguments.
- In a role-play, you may have to take a position which is not really your own, so make sure that your arguments are in line with *your role*.
- Think of counterarguments and of ways to refute them.
- Arrange your notes so that you have the relevant facts ready during the discussion.

Step 2 Preparing an initial statement
- A prepared opening statement on the topic will ease your way into the discussion.
- If you are assigned a specific role, be prepared to introduce yourself.

Step 3 Choosing a chairperson

It is advisable to choose a chair(person) to lead the discussion. He or she:
- moderates the discussion without taking sides
- steers the flow of the discussion
- is responsible for getting the discussion going and keeping it going.
- must be well informed about the various aspects of the discussion topic.

Holding the discussion

Step 1 Stating your point of view on the topic

For example, give your prepared statement.

Step 2 Listening to what others say and referring back to their statements
- Say which of the arguments do not convince you and why.
- You might counter an argument by asking a provocative question.
- Remember to bring in the facts you collected to support your view.

Step 3 Summarizing

At the end of the discussion, summarize your point of view or your main arguments.

Step 4 (optional) **Chairperson's summary**

If a chairperson has moderated the discussion, he/she may summarize the main line of the discussion and round it off.

Language help

Taking part in a discussion

Stating/Expressing your opinion

- In my opinion/view, ...
- As far as I'm concerned, ...
- The way I see it, ...
- If you ask me, ...
- It seems to me that ...
- I (personally) think/feel/reckon/believe ...
- First of all, / To start with, I'd like to point out that ...
- There can be no doubt that ...
- I'm (absolutely) convinced that ...

Involving a partner

- What do you think about ...?
- Is there anything you'd like to add?
- Would you agree with that?

Agreeing

- I quite agree.
- I couldn't agree with you more.
- Quite!/Exactly!/Precisely!/Certainly!/Definitely!
- You're quite right.
- I agree entirely/completely.
- That's just/exactly how I see it / how I feel about it.
- You've got a good point there.

Disagreeing politely / Contradicting

- I'm afraid I don't quite/really agree there.
- Well, that's one way of looking at it, but ...
- I'm not convinced that ...
- Well, I have my doubts about that.
- This is true to a certain extent, but ...

Disagreeing strongly

- I doubt that very much.
- That doesn't convince me at all.
- I don't agree with you at all.
- I disagree entirely.
- It's not as simple as that.

Asking for clarification

- Excuse me, I didn't quite catch your point about ...
- Do you mean ...?
- I'm sorry, but I don't understand/know what you mean by ...
- Sorry, could you say that again, please?
- Could you give an example / explain that, please?

Interrupting / Signalling that you would like to say something
- May I interrupt? / May I interrupt you for a moment, please?
- Sorry to interrupt you but ...
- Excuse me, I would like to add to that.
- That illustrates perfectly what ...
- Can I just say/explain that ...?
- I would just like to jump in here, to clarify that ...

Adding a point
- Another thing is ...
- We must also consider ...
- I would like to add to that ...
- Have you ever considered / thought about ...?

Buying time / Gaining time to think
- Well, I would say ...
- It's difficult to say exactly, but ...
- If I understood the question correctly, ...
- Well, that's an interesting point.
- I see what you mean.
- Why don't we see what X has to say about that?

Summarizing your point of view
- I have shown that ...
- It has become clear that ...
- Let me just state again that it is vital to ...
- If we don't ..., then ... / In spite of everything we have heard from the other side, ...

Summarizing the course and results of the discussion
- So, to sum up ...
- In brief, ...
- We have seen/heard that ...
- Some are in favour of ..., others against it, but in general you can say that ...
- The general trend seems to be ...
- On the one hand, ... On the other hand, ...
- All in all, this discussion has shown ...

SF 45 Having a debate

A debate is a formal discussion of a 'motion' (proposal) that ends in a vote. Similar to a discussion, the aim of a debate is to present arguments as convincingly as possible. Participants therefore need well-prepared arguments as well as rhetorical skills. There is often a set of rules that the participants have to agree on before the debate.

The starting point for the debate, the 'motion' (i.e. a controversial topic), is normally phrased as a statement starting 'This house ...'.
- 'This house proposes that ... (students should be allowed to use phones during lessons).'
- 'This house believes that ... (minimum wages are a threat to the German economy).'
- 'This house would ... (abolish the death penalty worldwide).'

Step 1 **Preparing the debate**

- Divide the class into two groups: one <u>for</u> the motion (the proposition or 'prop' team) and one <u>against</u> the motion (the opposition or 'opp' team).
- Choose a chair(person), judges (so-called adjudicators [əˈdʒuːdɪkeɪtəz]) and a timekeeper. Then specify a time limit for each speaker (often 3–6 minutes per speaker).
- In your team (either proposition or opposition), research the topic and collect and note down arguments for your side. Your personal opinion on the motion is not relevant here – you must argue for your team. List and rank your team's arguments in order of importance.
- Write your arguments on index cards so that you have them ready during the debate.
- Think of arguments for the opposing view and ways to refute them.
- Choose speakers for your side.
- Remaining group members are the audience, called the 'floor'.

Step 2 **Holding the debate**

A debate follows a clear structure:

- **1st proposal** from the team in favour of the motion
  The first speaker proposes the motion (= argues in favour of the motion) and gives some main arguments.
- **1st opposition** from the team opposing the motion
  The first speaker of this team opposes the motion (= argues against the motion).
- **2nd proposal** from the team in favour of the motion
  The second speaker of the affirmative team presents further arguments in favour of the motion. He/She also responds to the aspects mentioned by the first speaker of the opposing team, outlining where the positions *conflict.
- **2nd opposition** from the team opposing the motion
  The second speaker of the opposing team presents further arguments against the motion and/or restates the position of his/her team. The main task here is to defeat the arguments presented by the team in favour of the motion.

[A short recess may be taken here to prepare for the following 'rebuttals'.]

- **1st rebuttal** from the team opposing the motion
  The team against the motion defends their arguments and tries to rebut the arguments of the affirmative team.
- **2nd rebuttal** from the team in favour of the motion
  The affirmative team supports their point of view and tries to rebut the arguments of the opposing team.
- **3rd rebuttal** from the team opposing the motion
  The opposing team gives their closing statements.
- **4th rebuttal** from the team in favour of the motion
  The affirmative team gives their closing statements.

Info

Rules for the debate

- The chair(person) controls the debate and makes sure that the rules are followed and that time limits are respected. He or she introduces the topic, the judges and speakers and calls on them to deliver their speeches.
- The judges will watch the entire debate and decide at the end which team won.

- Speakers may not interrupt each other at any point. They must wait their turn. However, in competitive debates, a member of the team opposing that of the current speaker may briefly interrupt, offering a POI (point of information) in the form of a short question or a statement (10 seconds or less).
- The time limits as given by the chair must be respected.
- Speakers must remain polite and respectful of the other team.
- Statements must be backed up by examples or proof, by referring to research, experience, etc.

Step 3 Concluding the debate

- The 'floor' (i.e. the audience) may ask questions and/or present their ideas on the topic.
- The 'house' (i.e. everyone present) may take a vote on the motion by a show of hands, not based on what they personally agree or disagree with, but on who made the better case by presenting the better arguments and speaking more convincingly.
- Members of the two debating teams may get some feedback from the audience.
- The judges mark each team on their style, content and strategy, comment on their performance and finally decide who is the winner of the debate.

Language help

Debating

1st proposal
- This house firmly believes that ...
- Not only is ... but also ...

1st opposition
- We strongly advise against following the proposed motion because ...
- The most obvious reason for this is that ...

2nd proposal
- The opposing team has tried to create the impression that ...
- However, we can prove that ...
- It is therefore evident that ...

2nd opposition
- Again, it needs to be stated that by following the arguments, ...
- ... would lead to / cause ...

Mediating skills

SF 46 Essentials: mediation

What is mediation?

Mediating basically means transferring written or spoken information in one language to another language. The main objective is 'to get the message across'. You may also use mediation skills in real-life situations where – as a mediator – you help speakers of English and your own language to understand each other or to understand a text in the other language.

How to do a mediation task

In a mediation task, you should not translate word for word. You should select and pass on only the information that is relevant to another person, the addressee. Usually, the original text is in your native language and the text you need to produce (your mediation text) is in the second language, i.e. English. Pay attention to the following steps when working on a mediation task.

Step 1 Analysing the communicative situation

- Read the task carefully.
- Who is the addressee?
- Will you be writing or speaking? (Speaking allows you to use gestures and other non-verbal means of communication.)
- What *text type are you expected to produce? A (personal or formal) *letter, a (personal or formal) email, a *newspaper article, a school magazine, an internet article, e.g. a blog entry? ► SF 26-36

Step 2 Selecting the relevant information

- Select the aspects of the text that are relevant to the given task or situation.
- Answer all of the addressee's questions, but do not give any unnecessary details.
- Decide what ideas, names or technical terms you need to explain.
- Decide which (cultural) aspects or concepts that might not be familiar to the addressee you need to explain. Watch out for possible (cultural) misunderstandings.

Tips

Mediating

- Do not summarize the whole text and do not translate every sentence.
- Use an appropriate *style and *register for the given situation and the text type you are expected to produce.
- Paraphrase words you do not know as well as technical terms. ► SF 48: Paraphrasing
- Avoid German-sounding sentence patterns and 'false friends' such as 'spenden'/*spend*.

SF 47 Mediating from German into English

Usually in a mediation task, you are expected to inform your (English-speaking) reader(s) about ideas which you have found in a German text.

Preparing a German-English mediation

- Read the task carefully.
- Check what text type you are expected to produce.
- Make sure you understand the content of the original German text perfectly.
- Bear in mind what specific information the English-speaking addressee needs. Highlight key words and sentences in the German text.
- Take notes on the relevant information you need, then structure it and phrase it in English. Use a dictionary if necessary. ► SF 8: Working with dictionaries

Doing a German-English mediation

- Make sure you use the correct text type.
- Sum up the information relevant for the addressee.
- Name the source.
- Include all the necessary explanations.
- Watch out for aspects that are specific to one culture (here: German) and explain them in more detail.
- Paraphrase any words you do not know in English. ► SF 48: Paraphrasing
- Structure your text as clearly as possible.
- Remember: the mediated English text will usually be shorter than the original German text because you select only the information that is relevant.

Tips

Mediating information from German into English

- If the original text is German, and the text you need to write is English, you can take notes on the text in either German or English.
- As you are working with a German text, you may find it easier to take notes in German. On the other hand, if your notes are in English, it will be easier for you later to write your own text in English from your notes.
- Find out on your own which method works better for you and use it in all your exams.

SF 48 Paraphrasing

If you paraphrase a text or *speech, you rephrase it in different words, without changing the meaning. Paraphrasing is useful

- for summaries or outlines, i.e. to avoid copying from the original text and to show that you have really understood it
- when you do not know the exact English word or expression, e.g. when mediating into English, when writing a text or in conversation.

There are different paraphrasing techniques.

Using antonyms ['æntənɪmz]

*Antonyms denote the opposite of the original word.

Examples:
- 'Reichtum' → *the opposite of poverty*
- 'stumpf' → *the opposite of sharp*

Using comparisons

Comparisons help you illustrate what you mean by creating *images.

Examples:
- 'Handschuh' → *like a shoe for your hand*
- 'Wendeltreppe' → *a set of stairs shaped like a spiral*

Definition or explanation (often using relative clauses)

With definitions or explanations, relative clauses help you add details to general terms such as *person, thing, machine, activity.*

Examples:
- 'Freiwillige/r' → a person who offers to do something but doesn't ask for money in return
- 'Wahl-O-Mat' → an internet website that is designed to help people decide which party to vote for in an election
- 'Apotheke' → a place where you can get something for headaches or other illnesses

Language help

Paraphrasing
- It's the opposite of ...
- It's the same as ...
- It's like ...
- It's similar to ...
- It's somebody / a person who ...
- It's something / a machine / a tool that you use to ...
- It's an animal / a plant / a building / a custom that ...
- It's a place that/where ...

Glossary

An asterisk (*) or an arrow (►) before a term indicates that it can be found as a separate entry in the Glossary.

accumulation [əˌkjuːmjəˈleɪʃn] *Akkumulation, gehäufte Aneinanderreihung*	using a lot of similar words or phrases within a few lines in order to emphasize a description or impression **Example:** *Motorcycles, busses, cars, coaches, bicycles, lorries, vans* were passing by – there was no way to cross the road.
acronym *Akronym, Kurzwort*	a term formed from the first letters of several words **Example:** *NASA* is an acronym for **N**ational **A**eronautics and **S**pace **A**dministration.
act *Akt*	a major division in a *drama Each act is usually subdivided into *scenes.
action *Handlung*	in *fictional texts, everything that happens in the story ► external action, internal action
actor/actress *Schauspieler/-in*	a person who performs in a theatre, in a film, on TV or on the radio, especially as a profession The actors express themselves in the form of *dialogues, *monologues or *soliloquies.
advertisement (infml also: **advert/ad**) [ədˈvɜːtɪsmənt] *Werbung, Anzeige, Annonce*	a text which attempts to persuade people to do something (e.g. buy a particular product or contribute money to a cause) An advertisement normally consists of pictures and text (called *copy)* and is designed to catch the attention of the reader through its *layout.
alliteration [əˌlɪtəˈreɪʃn] *Alliteration, Stabreim*	the repetition of a consonant at the beginning of neighbouring words, or of stressed syllables within such words to produce a rhythmic effect **Example:** **A**round the **r**ugged **r**ock the **r**agged **r**ascal **r**an. ► assonance
allusion [əˈluːʒn] *Anspielung, indirekte Bezugnahme*	an indirect reference to something or somebody the reader or listener is supposed to recognize and respond to An allusion may be to a work of literature, a historical event, a well-known person, etc.
alternate rhyme *Kreuzreim, alternierender Reim*	an **a b a b** *rhyme scheme where every other *line rhymes with each other
analogy [əˈnælədʒi] *Analogie, Ähnlichkeit, Vergleich*	the comparison of two things which are similar in several aspects By comparing an object, situation or person to something familiar, the explanation becomes easier to understand. **Example:** What's in a name? That which we call a rose. / By any other word would smell as sweet. / So Romeo would, were he not Romeo called. (William Shakespeare, *Romeo and Juliet)*

anaphora [əˈnæfərə] *Anapher*	the repetition of the same words or group of words in neighbouring sentences, *lines, *stanzas, etc. usually at the beginning of the clause **Example:** **In every** cry of every man, **In every** infant's cry of fear, **In every** voice, **in every** ban (William Blake, 'London', 1794)
antagonist *Antagonist/-in, Gegner/-in, Widersacher/-in*	in *fictional text, the person who opposes the *protagonist
anticipation *Vorwegnahme*	the technique of hinting at later events in a *fictional text so that the reader or audience is prepared for them or can anticipate them
antithesis [ænˈtɪθəsɪs] *Antithese, genaues Gegenteil, Gegensatz*	an idea that is the opposite of an idea (*thesis) already put forward by a writer Often the writer will put forward the antithesis in order to stress his or her own thesis.
antonym *Gegenbegriff, Antonym*	a word meaning the opposite of another word **Example:** *Sweet* is the antonym of *sour* or *savoury*. <> synonym
argumentative text *argumentativer Text*	a text that presents arguments about both sides of an issue The main purpose of an argumentative text is to get a certain perspective of an issue across, i.e. the writer tries to convince the reader of his or her opinion on a topic with the help of arguments. Typical examples are *columns, *editorials, *letters to the editor, *speeches, and *essays. ► text type
article *Artikel, Aufsatz*	a story or report in a newspaper or magazine
assonance *Assonanz, vokalischer Gleichklang*	the repetition of the same or similar vowel sounds within stressed syllables of neighbouring words **Example:** the p**o**ppies bl**o**w / Between the cr**o**sses, r**o**w on r**o**w. (John McCrae, 'In Flanders Fields', 1915) ► alliteration
atmosphere [ˈætməsfɪə] *Atmosphäre, Stimmung*	the feeling or mood created by a *narrator in his/her story The *setting, the use of language (i.e. adjectives, adverbs, choice of words, length of sentences, etc.) and *characterization all contribute to the atmosphere.
author *Autor/-in, Verfasser/-in*	a person who writes books, *articles, *essays, etc.
autobiography [ˌɔːtəbaɪˈɒgrəfi] *Autobiografie*	a book written by a person about his/her own life

biography [baɪˈɒgrəfi] *Biografie*	a book written by a person about the life of another person
blog *Blog*	a regularly updated website containing blog posts or blog entries that publish information or discussions on current issues or topics
blurb *Umschlagtext, Klappentext*	the short promotional text on the back cover of a book or a Blu-ray case
byline *Zeile mit dem Namen des Verfassers oder der Verfasserin*	a line at the beginning or end of a piece of writing in a newspaper or magazine that gives the writer's name
caricature [ˈkærɪkətʃʊə] *Karikatur, Karikierung*	a crude representation of a *character which is meant to be laughed at
cartoon *Cartoon, Karikatur*	an amusing drawing in a newspaper or magazine that deals with human nature or a current political or social issue Complex issues are reduced to memorable pictures. Cartoons often include *captions or speech bubbles. Techniques employed by cartoonists include *caricature, *exaggeration, *wordplay and the use of *symbols.
character *Charakter, Figur, handelnde Person*	a person in a *fictional text Characters can be presented through their actions, speech and thoughts as well as through description. Characters can be classified according to their importance as main characters or minor characters and according to their type as *round characters or *flat characters. ► antagonist, characterization, protagonist
characterization [ˌkærəktəraɪˈzeɪʃn] *Charakterisierung, Kennzeichnung*	the way in which the *author of a *fictional text presents his or her *characters to the reader or, in the case of a *drama, to the audience We usually distinguish between two ways of presenting a character: ***direct/*explicit characterization** (*'telling') – somebody tells the reader what sort of person a character is. When the reader has to draw conclusions about a character on the basis of his or her actions and words, we speak of ***indirect/*implicit characterization** (*'showing'). This kind of characterization is predominant in *plays.
chunk *Wortkombination*	words that are commonly placed together, e.g. *collocations or fixed phrases **Examples:** give a presentation, a lame excuse, by the way, a long way off, out of my mind
classified ads / small ads (pl) *Kleinanzeigen*	newspaper or magazine advertisements dealing with job offers, buying, selling or renting something, etc.
cliché [ˈkliːʃeɪ] *Klischee, Gemeinplatz, abgedroschene Phrase*	an expression which has been overused and no longer has any effect
cliffhanger *offenes Ende*	an exciting situation that makes you want to know what will happen next
climax *Höhepunkt, Klimax*	the part of the *plot where the *suspense reaches its highest point ► anti-climax

cluster *Cluster*	spontaneous association of a group of words based around a concept
collocation *Zusammenstellung, Anordnung*	words that are are commonly placed together **Example**: strongly suggest, go crazy, economic growth, big decision
colloquial [kə'ləʊkwiəl] *umgangssprachlich*	*informal words and phrases, used in conversation rather than in writing
column *Kolumne; kurzer, regelmäßig erscheinender Zeitungsartikel*	an *article that appears regularly in a newspaper or magazine Columns can be *humorous or serious, and they can deal with any subject, e.g. lifestyle, gossip, personal problems, finances or politics. Any opinion expressed in a column is the opinion of the writer, or 'columnist', and not of the newspaper or magazine it appears in. Thus a column is often an *argumentative text.
comedy *Komödie, Lustspiel*	a type of *drama which deals with a light topic or a serious topic in an amusing way A comedy always has a happy ending.
coming-of-age story / story of initiation *Entwicklungsroman, Initiationsgeschichte*	a *short story or *novel in which the process of growing up is portrayed Usually the *protagonist is a child or an adolescent undergoing an experience which changes his/her outlook on life and marks an important stage in his/her development towards adulthood.
comment *Kommentar, Stellungnahme*	an *argumentative text in which the writer tries to convince the reader of his or her opinion on a topic
commercial (n) [kə'mɜːʃl] *Werbespot, Werbung*	an *advertisement on television, on the radio or on a website
compound *Kompositum*	Combination of two words to make a new word **Example:** afterlife, daydream, lifestyle, cheesecake
concrete poetry / shape poetry *konkrete Poesie*	*poems in which the printed words form a shape or picture The shape usually reflects the *theme or contents of the poem.
conflict *Konflikt, Kontroverse, Streit*	a struggle or opposition between different forces which produces tension
connotation *Konnotation, Nebenbedeutung, Beiklang*	the additional meaning and association(s) a word has beyond its literal or dictionary meaning
contrast *Kontrast, Gegensatz*	the bringing together of opposing views, words or *characters to emphasize their difference and usually to highlight one of the opposing elements ► juxtaposition
couplet *Reimpaar, Verspaar*	two successive *lines which *rhyme
denotation [ˌdiːnəʊ'teɪʃn] *Denotation, (Haupt-) Bedeutung, Begriffsumfang*	the literal and limited meaning of a word, regardless of the ideas and emotions it might connote

denouement [ˌdeɪˈnuːmɒ̃] *Auflösung, Lösung des Knotens, Ausgang*	the *resolution of the *conflict in a story that is achieved at the end of a play, book, etc.
descriptive text *deskriptiver Text, beschreibender Text*	a text that presents the physical characteristics of living things or objects ► text type
dialogue [ˈdaɪəlɒg] *Dialog, Gespräch*	a conversation in a book, play or film that involves at least two *actors
diction *Diktion, Ausdruck, Wortwahl*	the words a writer chooses for his or her text In many argumentative texts, for example, the writer will use words that have a positive *connotation to support his or her arguments, or words with negative connotations to attack those he or she opposes. The choice of words often reveals the writer's attitudes. A writer can also use *emotive language and so influence the reader to react in a particular way.
direct address *direkte Anrede*	a way of addressing the audience directly in order to establish contact with them
direct/explicit characterization *direkte/explizite Charakterisierung*	a way of presenting a *character directly The *author may provide a description of a character through the words of the *narrator (especially an *omniscient narrator), or another character in the text may comment on the character, or the character may describe him- or herself.
drama / dramatic text *Schauspiel, Drama / dramatischer Text*	a text written to be performed by *actors in a theatre or in a film A drama is usually divided into several *acts. *Tragedies and *comedies are types of drama.
dramatic irony *dramatische Ironie, dramaturgische Ironie*	a situation in a *play when the audience has more knowledge of events or individuals than the other *characters and *actions can take on different meanings for the audience than for the other characters of the play
dramatist/playwright *Bühnendichter/-in, Dramatiker/-in*	the *author of a *play
editorial/leader *Leitartikel*	an *article that expresses the opinion of the newspaper's editor or another member of the editorial staff about an item of news or a political or social issue of topical interest ► argumentative text
ellipsis *Auslassung, Ellipse*	the shortening of sentences by dropping a word or several words which can be understood from the context **Example:** *Coming?* (= *Are you coming?*)
emotive language *gefühlsbetonte Sprache*	words and expressions with particular *connotations that appeal to the reader's or listener's emotions
emphasis [ˈemfəsɪs] *Betonung, Nachdruck, Emphase*	special importance that is given to a word or phrase

enjambement / run-on line [ɪnˈdʒæmbmənt] *Enjambement*	incomplete syntax at the end of the *line where the meaning runs over to the next line without any punctuation at the end
enumeration [ɪˌnjuːməˈreɪʃn] *Aufzählung*	the listing of words, phrases or ideas In *instructive or *argumentative texts, the list of enumerated elements can be given numbers or dashes ('Gedankenstriche') so the reader can see each new element clearly.
epilogue *Epilog, Nachwort*	speech, etc. at the end of a *play, book or film/movie that comments on or acts as a conclusion to what has happened ► prologue
essay *Essay, Aufsatz*	a text form in which a writer expresses his or her personal views on some topic Essays can vary widely in length, subject matter and *tone. Some are serious, others are light-hearted and entertaining.
euphemism [ˈjuːfəmɪzm] *Euphemismus*	a *stylistic device used to hide the true nature of something unpleasant by expressing it in a more pleasant, less direct way **Example:** He passed away. (= He died.)
exaggeration [ɪɡˌzædʒəˈreɪʃn] *Übertreibung*	a strong overstatement Exaggeration may be used to create either a serious or comic effect. **Example:** There were thousands of guests at Tom's party. <> understatement
explicit characterization *explizite/direkte Charakterisierung*	► direct characterization
exposition *Exposition, vorbereitender Teil eines Dramas*	the first part of the *plot, in which the *characters and *setting are introduced The exposition is also the beginning of the *action.
expository text/writing *expositorischer Text*	a *text type in which the writer analyses and explains some relatively complex matter in an objective and precise way
external action *äußere Handlung*	what the *characters do in the 'real', physical world ► internal action
fable *Fabel*	a short *narrative text in which animals represent human types or act like human beings Fables are usually didactic since they intend to teach a moral lesson, make a satirical comment or illustrate some general truth.
falling action *fallende Handlung*	a structural element of a *fictional text, marked by a reduction in the *suspense of the *plot, normally following the *turning point or *climax
feature film *Spielfilm*	a full-length film that has a story and *characters, who are played by *actors A feature film is based on a film script, which the director then turns into a film. Important elements in a film are the *dialogue, the use of camera techniques and the acting.

feature story *Zeitungsreportage*	a piece of *non-fiction news writing that deals with a topic by concentrating on a particular person or on particular people A feature story often takes an individual case as its starting point to discuss the different aspects of the topic on a personal level and leaves the reader to draw more general conclusions from this individual case. The writer of a feature story makes use of direct quotes from the people involved in the story thus relying on first-hand reporting.
fictional text / fiction *fiktionaler Text / Prosaliteratur, Dichtung*	a text or type of literature that does not deal with facts of the real world but creates its own world or reality A piece of fiction can take different forms. The main types are *narrative prose like *short stories or *novels and *drama.
figurative language [ˈfɪɡərətɪv] *bildhafte Sprache, Bildsprache*	► imagery
first-person narrator *Ich-Erzähler/-in*	a *character in the story who refers to him- or herself as 'I' The *first-person narrator tells the *action from his/her perspective so he/she only has a *limited point of view.
flashback *Rückblende*	a part of a film, *play, etc. that goes back into the past to describe or show a *scene that happened earlier in time than the main story but is essential for the *plot
flat character *typisierte Figur („flacher Charakter")*	a *character who only has a limited number of traits and may even just represent a single quality Flat characters are usually minor characters in a *fictional work. ► round character
foot *Versfuß*	a unit of *rhythm in a *line of a *poem consisting of an unstressed syllable followed by a stressed syllable
foreshadowing [fɔːˈʃædəʊɪŋ] *Vorwegnahme*	► anticipation
formal style *formaler (Sprach-)Stil*	a *style that consists of difficult vocabulary, often of Latin origin, and complex sentence structure Formal style is usually only used for serious purposes, e.g. *essays or academic publications, or in official situations, and would not be appropriate in normal everyday conversation.
frame story / frame narrative *Rahmenhandlung*	a *novel or *short story which contains one or more quite independent stories within it (also called 'a story-in-a-story') The main story provides the frame for the other stories. Often the main story consists of a *character in one *setting telling another story in another setting.
free verse *freier Vers, freie Verse*	a literary device that makes little use of *rhyme
genre [ˈʒɒ̃rə, ˈʒɒnrə] *Gattung, Genre*	a type or style of literature, e.g. science fiction

humour (BE), **humor** (AE) ['hjuːmə] *Humor*	a quality in something that makes you laugh, e.g. at the strangeness of a *character, an *action or comment, etc. because it is unexpected or unsuitable in a particular situation
hyperbole [haɪ'pɜːbəli] *Übertreibung, Hyperbel*	a deliberate *exaggeration The purpose of hyperbole is to emphasize something or to produce a humorous effect. **Example:** I'm so hungry I could eat a horse.
iambic pentameter [aɪˌæmbɪk pen'tæmɪtə] *fünfhebiger Jambus*	the most common *metre in English, which consists of a *line of five feet (each *foot consists of an unstressed syllable followed by a stressed syllable) **Example:** This **ró** / yal **thróne** / of **kíngs** / this **scépt** / red isle. (William Shakespeare, *Richard II)*
image/imagery *Bild/ Bildsprache*	the use of language beyond its normal dictionary definition and meaning All non-literal (i.e. *figurative) use of language falls into the category of imagery, e.g. *metaphors, *similes and *symbols.
implicit/indirect characterization *implizite/indirekte Charakterisierung*	a way of presenting a *character indirectly The reader or audience learns of the character through *dialogue and *action, rather than through description. ► explicit characterization
informal style *informeller (Sprach-)Stil, umgangssprachlicher (Sprach-)Stil*	a *style characterized by fairly simple, often incomplete sentences, short forms (e.g. *can't, you'll*), phrasal verbs and *colloquial words Informal style is used between friends or in a relaxed or informal situation. It may include the use of *slang and/or *taboo words.
instructive text / instruction *instruktiver Text / (Gebrauchs-) Anweisung*	a text that tells the reader what to do in order to achieve a certain goal Typical examples of instructive texts are travel guides, how-to books or user's manuals. Typical features are the use of imperatives, the use of the passive voice, graphics and illustrations and printing techniques like **bold** or *italic* print, dashes, etc. ► text type
interior monologue [ɪnˌtɪəriə 'mɒnəlɒg] *innerer Monolog*	a particular kind of *scenic presentation in which the *author depicts the thoughts and feelings passing through a *character's mind Often an interior monologue does not follow a chronological order because when people think, their thoughts jump from one subject to another. The more common way of portraying thought is through *'reported thought', in which the thoughts are presented as reported speech, introduced by reporting verbs like *think.* ► soliloquy
internal action *innere Handlung*	what takes place in a *character's mind, i.e. his or her thoughts, feelings, memories, associations, etc. ► external action
intonation *Betonung*	(effect created by) the tone of a person's voice as they speak
ironic / irony [aɪ'rɒnɪk / 'aɪrəni] *ironisch / Ironie*	saying the opposite of what you actually mean **Example:** Oh, what a nice present! (when you actually mean 'It is rather ugly').

juxtaposition [ˌdʒʌkstəpəˈzɪʃn] *Gegenüberstellung, Nebeneinanderstellung*	a very strong *contrast of opposing ideas, arguments, views, mostly introduced by words like for example *but, however, nevertheless*
layout *Layout, Aufbau, Anordnung, Gestaltung*	the way elements are arranged on a printed page The layout includes elements such as the type and size of letters, the use of **bold** or *italic* typeface, underlining, headings and sub-headings, bullets (i.e. dots or other symbols used at the beginning of a text passage), the size and number of *columns, the length of paragraphs, the colour and the placement of illustrations. The layout determines whether a text attracts the attention of the reader and is pleasant to read, and it helps writers to structure their texts and to emphasize certain words, phrases or passages. The layout is particularly important when considering *newspaper articles, *advertisements and brochures.
leader / leading article *Leitartikel*	► editorial
letter *Brief*	a handwritten, typed or printed message that is put in an envelope and sent to somebody A letter can be personal or business-oriented, depending on the relationship between the sender and receiver, the occasion and the purpose of the letter. Letters are a very flexible text form and comprise thank-you notes, emails, covering letters (*AE* cover letters), letters of complaint, *letters to the editor, etc. The beginnings and endings of letters follow certain conventions.
letter to the editor *Leserbrief, Leserinnenbrief*	a *letter in which a reader expresses his or her opinion concerning an *article in a newspaper or magazine or a problem which is of public interest A letter to the editor may criticize or support an *article, or state a personal opinion concerning a topic of current interest. ► argumentative text
limited point of view *eingeschränkte Erzählperspektive*	a method of storytelling in which the *narrator sees only what's in front of him/her but does not know everything that occurs, therefore imposing his or her understanding and interpretation on the *action A *third-person narrator can have a limited point of view: the narrator looks at the events and *characters from the perspective of one of the characters or from the outside (as an observer narrator) and so does not have access to the thoughts and feelings of all the characters.
line *Zeile, Vers*	the row of words of a song or poem A *sonnet, for example, always has 14 lines.
literary text *literarischer Text*	a piece of writing that is valued as a work of art, e.g. a *novel, *play or *poem (in contrast to *non-fiction texts) A literary text is often structured and held together by a specific *theme or a so-called *motif, which may be a recurring image or a specific phrase or sentence.

metaphor ['metəfə] *Metapher*	a comparison between two things which are basically quite unlike one another without using the words *as* or *like* The things are meant to create a picture (image) in your mind that sheds more light on a topic. **Example:** There's daggers in men's smiles. (William Shakespeare, *Macbeth)* ► simile
method card	an individual compilation of strategies to help you with skills, language learning or exam preparation
metre (BE), **meter** (AE) ['mi:tə] *Metrum, Versmaß*	the regular *rhythm of words in a *poem The most common metre in English is the *iambic pentameter.
mode of presentation *Erzählweise*	the way a writer narrates events There are two modes of presentation, and usually a combination of both is used in a *narrative text: *scenic presentation and *panoramic presentation.
monologue ['mɒnəlɒg] *Monolog, Selbstgespräch*	a lengthy speech by just one character in the company of others ► dialogue
motif *Motiv, Leitmotiv, Leitgedanke*	a dominant idea in a *fictional text that is often part of the main *theme If the motif is an *image or *metaphor and is repeated often, it may be called a 'leitmotif'.
narrative perspective *Erzählperspektive*	*narrator, *point of view from which a story is told ► narrator
narrative prose *Erzähl-/Prosatext*	a *fictional story told by a *narrator and written in a continuous flow of sentences, not as a *poem or *drama Typical examples of narrative prose are *novels and *short stories.
narrator BE: [nə'reɪtə], AE: ['næreɪtər] *Erzähler/-in*	the person who tells the story in *narrative prose There are two main types of narrator: the *first-person narrator and the *third-person narrator. The third-person narrator with an *unlimited point of view is also known as an *omniscient narrator. The narrator is not the same as the *author of a story.
neutral style *neutraler (Sprach)Stil*	the style generally used by educated people Neutral style falls between *formal and *informal style. It is used in *feature stories, *news stories, etc.
news item *Nachricht*	a single report of news about one topic
news(paper) article / news report / news story *Zeitungsartikel, Zeitungsbericht*	a piece of writing about a particular subject that appears in print (in a newspaper or magazine) or digitally (e.g. on a website) News articles can be of any length. In theory, they are meant to be objective and unbiased presentations of the facts, providing answers to the five *wh*-questions, i.e. the questions *who?, what?, when?, where?* and *why?* and often quoting sources or people as support. In practice, however, totally impartial reporting is impossible.

non-fiction / non-fictional text *Sachliteratur, Sachbücher, Sachtexte / nichtfiktionaler Text, Sachtext*
texts that refer to the real world and are classified as *descriptive, *instructive, *argumentative or *expository texts according to their purpose
Examples of non-fictional texts are *news stories, *advertisements, *speeches, *letters, *essays.

novel *Roman*
a long and complex type of *fictional *narrative prose often divided into chapters
The *plot and structure of a novel are normally more complicated than those of shorter fictional works (like *short stories); consequently there may be a greater variety and a more detailed development of *characters and *setting.

omniscient narrator [ɒmˌnɪsiənt] *allwissende/r Erzähler/-in*
a *third-person narrator with an *unlimited point of view
An omniscient narrator can move freely in place and time and can enter the minds of the *characters as he/she wishes.

onomatopoeia [ˌɒnəˌmætəˈpiːə] *Lautmalerei*
the use of a word which imitates the sounds it refers to, e.g. *buzz* or *hum*
In a group of words or a phrase, onomatopoeia may evoke a particular feeling, mood, sound or movement.
Example: Only the s**t**u**tt**e**r**ing **r**ifes’ **r**apid **r**a**tt**le.
From: Wilfred Owen, ‘Anthem for doomed youth’
The repetition of ‘t’s and ‘r’s sounds like the shooting of rifles, which the words describe.

open ending *offenes Ende, offener Schluss*
the ending when a *conflict in a *fictional text is not resolved and the reader is left wondering what might happen next

panoramic presentation *panoramische Darstellung, raffender Bericht*
summarizing in just a few sentences what happens over a longer period of time (e.g. an hour, a week, months) in a story
► scenic presentation

paradox *Paradox(on), Widerspruch in sich*
a statement that seems impossible because it contains two opposing ideas that are both true
Example: In this rich country, there is a lot of poverty.

parallelism / parallel structures [ˈpærəlelɪzəm] *Parallelismus, Übereinstimmung, Parallelität, Ähnlichkeit / Parallelstrukturen*
the deliberate repetition of similar or identical words, phrases, sentence constructions, etc. in the same or neighbouring sentences
Parallelism draws the attention of the reader to certain ideas that the writer may consider important. It may be used to show that the elements are of similar importance, or it may be used in a climactic sequence, with the most important element listed at the end.
Example: Which alters[1] when it alteration finds, Or bends with the remover[2] to remove.
From: William Shakespeare, ‘Sonnet 116’
[1] **alter** change
[2] **remover** person who goes away

parody *Parodie, komisch-satirische Nachahmung*
a *fictional text that copies or imitates someone or something in an amusing way

pars pro toto *Pars pro Toto*
a part or aspect of something representing the whole
Example: under my roof (= in my house)

personification [pəˌsɒnɪfɪˈkeɪʃn] *Personifizierung*	the technique of representing animals or objects as if they were human beings or possessed human qualities **Example:** the wailing wind
persuasive text [pəˈsweɪsɪv] *appellativer Sachtext*	a text in which the writer attempts to appeal to a reader's or listener's emotions Unlike *argumentative texts, persuasive texts do not use solid arguments. The most obvious example of a persuasive text is an *advertisement, but many *speeches are persuasive rather than argumentative texts. ► text type
pitch *Tonhöhe, Stimmlage, Lautstärke*	how high or low a sound is, especially a musical note
play *Schauspiel*	► drama
playwright *Dramatiker/-in, Bühnendichter/-in*	the *author of a *play ► dramatist
plot *Handlung(sgerüst)*	the structure of events in a *fictional text The plot develops in a number of stages: *exposition, *rising action, the *climax, *turning point, *falling action and the *denouement or an *open ending. A plot will have some element of *suspense and *tension.
poem/poetry *Gedicht/Lyrik*	a piece of creative writing structured by *lines, *stanzas and *rhythm A poem can express personal thoughts and feelings (lyrical poem) or it can tell a story (narrative poem). Traditional poets make use of *rhyme whereas modern poets often use *free verse. The *speaker is the voice in which a poem is spoken, especially when the personal pronoun 'I' is used. This speaker is not always identical with the voice of the poet.
point of view *Erzählperspektive*	the perspective from which a story is told The concepts of *narrator and point of view are closely related. There can be a *limited point of view, i.e. the *action, etc. are approached from one angle (possibly the point of view of a *character, including a *first-person narrator), or there can be an *unlimited point of view, i.e. the narrator can examine the action, etc. from the point of view of different characters – in this case the narrator is *omniscient.
prologue [ˈprəʊlɒg] *Prolog, Vorwort*	an introductory speech, etc. at the beginning of a *play, book or film
props *(pl)* *Requisiten*	all kinds of objects used by *actors on stage or in a film
prose *Prosa*	a form of written language that is formed by sentences in a continuous flow and is broken up only by paragraphs
protagonist *Protagonist/-in, zentrale Gestalt*	the principal *character in a *fictional text, sometimes also called the hero His/Her opponent is called the *antagonist.
pun *Wortspiel*	► wordplay

quatrain [ˈkwɒtreɪn] *Vierzeiler*	four *lines with a shared *rhyme scheme
quick write	a short written response to an open-ended question or a prompt to reflect your understanding of a topic
refrain [rɪˈfreɪn] *Refrain*	phrases or *lines repeated at intervals throughout a *poem
register *Sprachstil, der für bestimmte Situationen charakteristisch ist; Register*	the level of language used in a text, e.g. *formal, *informal, *neutral, *slang
reliable narrator *glaubwürdige/r Erzähler/-in*	a trustworthy storyteller The reader may take everything the *narrator tells at face value. <> unreliable narrator
repetition *Wiederholung*	the deliberate use of a word or phrase more than once in a sentence or a text to create a sense of pattern or form, or to emphasize certain elements for the reader or listener
reported thought *erlebte Rede*	thoughts which are presented as *reported speech (i.e. in the past tense)
resolution *Auflösung*	the moment at the end of a *drama, *novel, etc., where all the *conflicts are solved
rhetorical device *rhetorisches (Stil-)mittel*	► stylistic device
rhetorical question [rɪˈtɒrɪkl] *rhetorische Frage (auf die keine Antwort erwartet wird)*	a question to which the answer seems obvious and is therefore not necessary A rhetorical question pushes the reader or listener to a certain conclusion. For this reason, it is popular in political *speeches, etc. when a person is trying to influence others.
rhyme *Reim*	the similarity of sounds between certain words in *poems, usually at the end of *lines ► rhyme scheme
rhyme scheme *Reimschema*	the way a poet arranges his or her *rhymes in a *poem Small letters are used to show that words share a rhyme. If the words 'day', 'make', 'say' and 'lake' appear at the end of four successive *lines, the rhyme scheme is written as **a b a b.** ► alternate rhyme, rhyming couplet
rhyming couplet *Paarreim, Reimpaar*	a *rhyme scheme that is written a a b b
rhythm *Rhythmus*	the arrangement of stressed and unstressed syllables in a *line of a *poem ► metre
rising action *(an-) steigende Handlung*	the second part of the *plot where the *conflict or the *theme of the story in a *fictional text is developed and *suspense created

round character *runde Figur*	a character in a *fictional text who has several character traits and behaves in a lifelike way Usually a round character develops in the course of the story. The main characters are usually round characters. ► flat character
run-on line *Enjambement*	► enjambement
scene *Szene*	a smaller unit of *action in which there is no change of place or break in time In a *drama a scene is a subdivision of an *act.
scenic presentation *szenische Darstellung*	showing an event or describing a scene in detail as it occurs, using *dialogue, *interior monologue and depicting thoughts and emotions ► panoramic presentation
script *Drehbuch*	the written text of a *play or film
scriptwriter *Drehbuchautor/-in*	a person who creates *scripts for films and television
setting *Schauplatz, Handlungsort*	the time and place (and often the *atmosphere as well) in a *fictional text
shape poetry *konkrete Poesie*	► concrete poetry
short story [ˌ-ˈ-] *Kurzgeschichte*	a piece of *fictional *narrative prose, but considerably shorter and less complex than a *novel A short story centres around one or two *characters at a decisive moment in their lives. It is limited in its *theme, *setting and *plot by its length.
showing *szenische Darstellung*	► scenic presentation
simile [ˈsɪməli] *Vergleich, Gleichnis, Simile*	a comparison between two things that are not really like each other. Similes use the word *like* or *as*. **Example:** My love is like a red, red rose. (Robert Burns, 1794)
sitcom (= situation comedy) *Sitcom, Situationskomödie (besonders als Fernsehserie)*	a comic *TV/radio series which usually centres around a *character or group of characters The characters are often stereotypes as they do not evolve over the series. A sitcom may be filmed in front of a live audience or have canned laughter added to make the audience aware of or to reinforce the funny lines.
slang *nachlässige, oft fehlerhafte, saloppe Ausdrucksweise; Slang*	very *informal language, mainly used in *dialogue between people of the same age or from a similar background, etc.
soap (opera) *"Seifenoper", (rührselige) Hörspiel- oder Fernsehspielserie*	a regular TV or radio programme about the everyday lives of a group of people The storyline of a soap (opera), unlike that of a normal *TV/radio series, develops from programme to programme and may often end with a *cliffhanger to encourage the audience to tune in to the next episode.

soliloquy [sə'lɪləkwi] *Monolog, Selbstgespräch*	a *speech delivered by one of the *characters in a *drama, in which he or she reveals his or her thoughts, feelings or motives to the audience ► monologue
solution *(Auf-)Lösung*	the successful ending of a problem, a *conflict or a difficult situation
sonnet ['sɒnɪt] *Sonett*	a special form of a *poem that consists of 14 *lines There are various types of sonnets with different structures and forms. Shakespeare's sonnets comprise three *quatrains (i.e. four lines with a shared *rhyme scheme) and a *couplet (i.e. two successive lines which rhyme).
speaker *lyrisches Ich*	the *fictional person, in theory not identical with the poet, who speaks the text of a *poem
speech *Rede, Ansprache*	a spoken *non-fictional text delivered to an audience The speaker normally wants to convince his/her audience to adopt his/her view on a certain topic. ► argumentative text
spidergram *Wortigel*	a simple diagram for organizing words that belong together because they are of the same type (phrasal verbs, prefixes and suffixes) or they express a key concept
stage directions (pl) *Bühnenanweisungen*	the *dramatist's description of what the stage should look like, and how the *actors should perform the *drama Stage directions may give information about any of the following: the *setting, the objects on stage (the *props), the *characters' appearances, clothes and manner of speaking, as well as their entrances and exits.
stanza *Strophe, Vers*	a group of *lines (*verses) that form a unit in a *poem because they relate to a similar thought or topic
story of initiation [ɪˌnɪʃi'eɪʃn] *Entwicklungsroman, Initiationsgeschichtes*	► coming-of-age story
style *Stil*	the particular way in which a *fictional or *non-fictional text is written Style includes elements such as *register and *tone.
stylistic device *Stilmittel*	a method and technique used to produce a particular effect in a text and on the reader The most common stylistic devices are: *accumulation, *alliteration, *allusion, *anaphora, *assonance, *contrast, *exaggeration, *irony, *juxtaposition, *metaphor, *personification, *rhetorical question, *simile, *symbol, *understatement, *wordplay.
surprise ending *überraschendes Ende, nicht vorhersehbarer Schluss*	an ending in which the reader's expectations regarding the course of the story are not fulfilled, but an unexpected *resolution to the *conflict is presented
suspense *Spannung*	a feeling of worry or excitement that is created when the reader does not know the outcome of the *conflict or *action

suspension of disbelief *willentliche Aussetzung der Ungläubigkeit*	expecting the reader to accept this world or story as existing or true
symbol / symbolic *Symbol / symbolisch*	a thing, word or phrase signifying something concrete that stands not only for itself but also for a certain abstract idea As in the case of a *metaphor or a *simile the meaning of a symbol goes beyond the literal meaning. **Example:** A red rose is often a symbol of love.
synonym *Synonym*	a word that means the same as another word **Example:** Fast and quick are the synonyms of speedy. <> antonym
taboo word *Tabuwort*	a word that is generally considered obscene, vulgar or shocking and is used only if the writer is trying to make a particular point or shock his or her readers
telling *berichtende Darstellung*	► panoramic presentation
tension *(An-)Spannung*	the feeling evoked in the reader when a story/*drama is full of *suspense, i.e. the reader is curious about what will happen
text type *Textsorte, Textart*	the classification of a text according to the *writer's intentions There are different text types: *argumentative texts, *descriptive texts, *expository texts, *instructive texts, *narrative texts, *persuasive texts.
theme *Thema, Gegenstand, Stoff*	the main idea or *motif (e.g. a recurring image or a specific phrase or sentence) that structures and holds together a *literary text
thesis ['θi:sɪs] *These, Behauptung, Postulat*	an idea or a view that an *author of an *argumentative text presents and discusses in a *formal way ► antithesis
third-person narrator *auktoriale/r Erzähler/-in*	a *narrator who refers to all the *characters as he, she, they or by their names A third-person narrator is not a character in the story. This type of narrator can have a *limited point of view (just like a camera) or an *unlimited point of view. In the latter case, the narrator knows everything and is called *omniscient.
tone *Ton, Stimmung*	the way in which a writer treats his or her topic, thereby reflecting his or her emotional attitude towards that topic and also towards the reader The tone can be *formal, intimate, solemn, playful, serious, *ironic, *humorous, angry, etc.
tragedy / tragic *Tragödie, Trauerspiel / tragisch*	a type of *drama in which the main *character (the *protagonist) goes through a series of misfortunes towards his or her downfall Usually this downfall is partly brought about by the protagonist's own faults and weaknesses.
turning point *Wendepunkt*	a sudden or surprising change of the *action in the *plot

tv/radio series ['sɪəri:z] *Fernseh-/ Radioserie*	a regular programme on TV or radio about the lives and problems of a *character or, more usually, a group of characters Each programme is self-contained, i.e. it deals with a particular issue or storyline which is concluded at the end of the programme. The lives of the characters evolve slowly over the course of a series.
understatement *Untertreibung*	a statement in which the true importance of an idea, event or fact is minimized, so that something is deliberately presented as being much less important, valuable, etc. than it really is Understatement is often used for *ironic effect. The opposite is *exaggeration/overstatement.
unlimited point of view *uneingeschränkte Erzählperspektive*	a method of storytelling in which the *narrator can move freely in place and time and enter the minds of the *characters at will
unreliable narrator *unglaubwürdige/r Erzähler/-in*	an untrustworthy storyteller The reader must find out just how much of what the *narrator says can be accepted. *First-person narrators are usually unreliable as they give only one perspective on the *action and the *characters. <> reliable narrator
verse *Vers*	a single *line of a *poem
volta *Volta, Wendung*	the *turning point in a *sonnet, which can be identified by words like *but, yet or* and *yet* The volta might be a *line of the sonnet.
word family *Wortfamilie*	a group of words with a common base to which other words are added **Example:** The words *signal, signature, assign, resign,* etc. belong to the word family of *sign.*
wordplay / play on words / pun *Wortspiel*	the use of a word which may be understood in two different ways or which may be put into a different context to change the meaning

The US System of Government

System of Checks and Balances

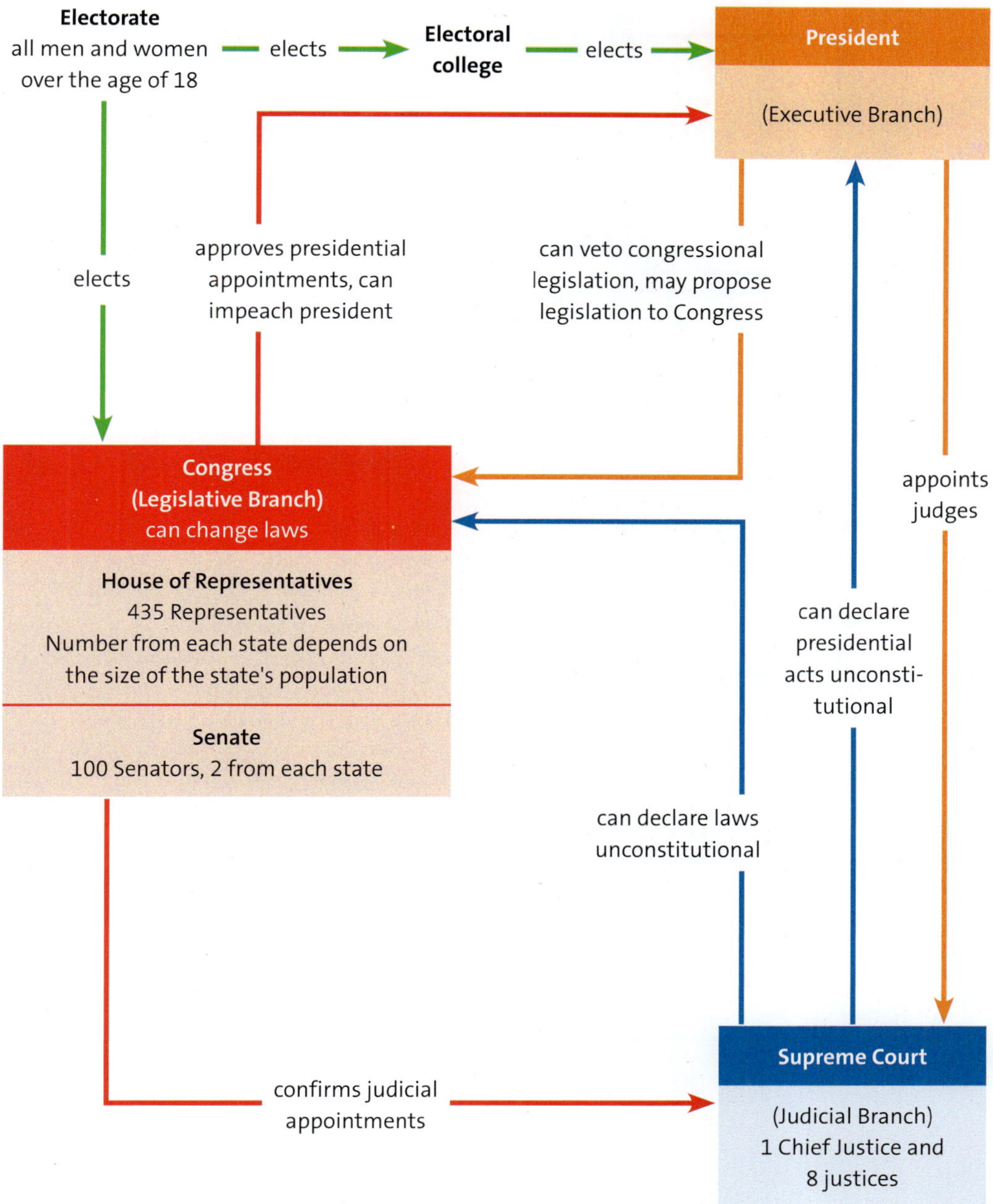

The British System of Government

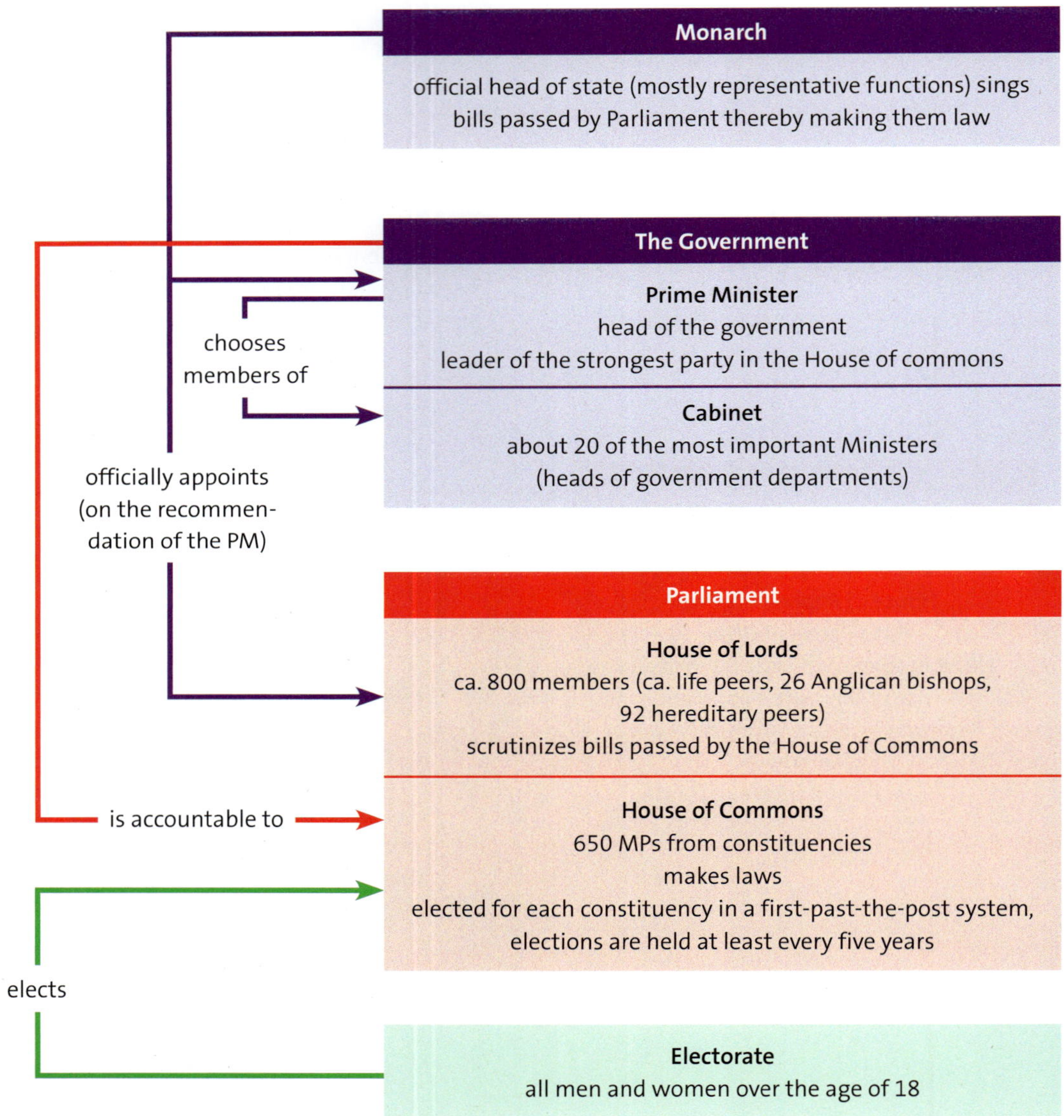

Context uses the same special vocabulary ('Operatoren') for tasks that is used in standard tests, including the 'Abitur'. Be sure you understand what's required of you when you come across one of the verbs below.

'Anforderungsbereich I' COMPREHENSION
refers to text comprehension and definition.

'Anforderungsbereich II' ANALYSIS
focuses on text analysis and comparison, and stylistic devices.

'Anforderungsbereich III' BEYOND THE TEXT
concentrates on discussion, comment, evaluation and text production.

The instructions say	Example	What you are expected to do
analyse *(BE)*, **analyze** *(AE)* [ˈænəlaɪz] *analysieren* ANALYSIS	**Analyse** the narrative perspective in the given excerpt.	Describe and explain certain aspects and/or features of the text in detail.
assess [əˈses] *auswerten, beurteilen, bewerten, einschätzen* BEYOND THE TEXT	**Assess** whether the statement applies to the short story as well.	Give a carefully considered opinion, include all the important aspects of a question.
comment on [ˈkɒment] *kommentieren, Stellung nehmen, darlegen* BEYOND THE TEXT	**Comment** on the future of multicultur-alism in the USA.	Give your opinion, back it up with all the relevant points.
compare *vergleichen, kontrastieren, gegenüberstellen* ANALYSIS	**Compare** X's and Y's views on educa-tion.	Tell how things are alike and/or different, use concrete examples.
describe *beschreiben* COMPREHENSION	**Describe** the living conditions of the family.	Give an account in words, present a picture with words.
discuss *diskutieren, erörtern* BEYOND THE TEXT	**Discuss** advantages and disadvantages of introducing fullbody scanners at airports.	Consider all sides of an issue by providing relevant arguments and concrete examples.
evaluate [ɪˈvæljueɪt] *einschätzen, bewerten* BEYOND THE TEXT	**Evaluate** the chances of the protago-nist's plan to succeed in life.	Form an opinion after carefully considering and presenting advantages and disadvantages.
examine [ɪgˈzæmɪn] *untersuchen* ANALYSIS	**Examine** the author's use of language.	Name and explain the meaning of specific aspects and/or features of the text and their effects on the reader/audience.

The instructions say	Example	What you are expected to do
explain *erklären* ANALYSIS	**Explain** the protagonist's obsession with money.	Make clear and plain; give the reason or cause.
interpret [ɪnˈtɜːprɪt] *interpretieren, deuten, aus-werten* BEYOND THE TEXT	**Interpret** the message the author wants to convey.	Explain the meaning or purpose of something.
illustrate *veranschaulichen* ANALYSIS BEYOND THE TEXT	**Illustrate** the narrator's admiration for the main character. **Illustrate** the way in which school life in Britain differs from that in Germany	Use examples to explain or make sth. clear.
outline *präsentieren, vorstellen, nennen* COMPREHENSION	**Outline** the author's views on love, marriage and divorce	Give the main features, structure or general principles of a topic, omitting minor details.
point out *darstellen* ANALYSIS	**Point out** the author's main ideas on ...	Present the main aspects of sth. briefly and clearly.
summarize (*also:* **sum up** / **write a summary**) *zusammenfassen* COMPREHENSION	**Summarize** the main points of the German newspaper article.	Give a concise account of the mmain points or ideas of a text, issue or topic.
state *darlegen* COMPREHENSION ANALYSIS BEYOND THE TEXT	**State** the author's main arguments ... State the writer's opinion on green energy. State your reasons for applying for an internship.	Present the main aspects of sth. briefly and clearly.
write a characterization of [ˌkærəktəraɪˈzeɪʃn] *charakterisieren, detailliert beschreiben und erklären*	**Write** a characterization of the heroine.	Describe somebody's character and provide suitable examples.